Second Thoughts on Capitalism and the State

Second Thoughts on Capitalism and the State

By

Leslie Sklair

Cambridge
Scholars
Publishing

Second Thoughts on Capitalism and the State

By Leslie Sklair

This book first published 2022

Cambridge Scholars Publishing

Lady Stephenson Library, Newcastle upon Tyne, NE6 2PA, UK

British Library Cataloguing in Publication Data
A catalogue record for this book is available from the British Library

Copyright © 2022 by Leslie Sklair

ISBN (10): 1-5275-8273-6
ISBN (13): 978-1-5275-8273-6

For my beloved family, past, present, future.

CONTENTS

PRAISE FOR THE BOOK

"This profoundly reflective book shows a pathway forward for academics and activists alike who are stymied by the disconnect between deep critical scholarship and emancipatory social change, yet who will still not give up the good fight. As a leading scholar of globalization whose work has been central to the study of transnational capitalist development at multiple scales -- from the urban to the global to the architectural -- Leslie Sklair has produced innovative research for more than four decades. In this marvelous compilation of several key texts, he offers his own best list of paradigm-challenging work while also critically re-examining and interrogating it anew, in dialogue with his readers. This is an epistemological tour-de-force that will invite others to re-assess their own scholarship in similar ways. We are indebted to Sklair for his honesty, but more importantly, for his reluctance to abandon hope that scholarly inquiry can still give life to progressive ideals and alternative social experiments, despite the seemingly intractable collusion linking states to capitalism in ways that now threaten the planet."
—**Diane E. Davis, Charles Dyer Norton Professor of Regional Planning and Urbanism, Harvard University**

"An unusual combination of previously published articles and Sklair's "second thoughts" offers a powerful and often insightful dystopian view of transnational capitalism with its obscenely widening inequality, obsessive consumerism, self-destructive Anthropocene, and iconic architecture in inhumane mega-cities. A must-read tract for the times."
—**Michael Mann, Emeritus Professor of Sociology, University of California Los Angeles.**

"How does social theory grapple with our fast-changing world in an academic context of ideological rivalries? For the most part, authors deploy their chosen intellectual framework with minimal reflection on how their own (changing) subjectivities have determined their choice and deployment of a given framework. Leslie Sklair's book offers us something quite different. As the title suggests, it is as much an explanation of the dynamics of our evolving world as it is a rumination upon the author's attempts to continuously sharpen and re-deploy his theoretical tool-set. Ranging from

the early days of the globalisation of production, to his landmark exposition on the transnational capitalist class, to discussions of the possibilities of building socialism from communities upwards, to his novel approach to interpreting Anthropocene literatures, *Second Thoughts* represents a glittering exposition of how to apply and re-apply critical social theory to the rapidly changing world."
—Ben Selwyn, Professor of International Relations and International Development, University of Sussex.

"During the half century of his illustrious career, Leslie Sklair has marshalled an array of groundbreaking sociological insights into a rapidly changing world. From the sociology of knowledge to development theory, globalization, social movements, architecture and the environment, one can find here in a single volume a critical selection that spans the breadth of his oeuvre. Not to be missed, this is an important collection of essays from one of the most original and unorthodox sociological thinkers of our time."
—William I. Robinson, Distinguished Professor of Sociology, University of California at Santa Barbara

"Leslie Sklair has rightly established a major reputation for his sociological analysis, most notably for his pathbreaking work on the transnational capital class and the social role of contemporary iconic architecture. This new book draws together a series of his published articles, together with his "second thoughts": his subsequent mature reflections on these earlier works. The essays are partly fascinating for illuminating Sklair's theoretical development over his entire intellectual trajectory. But they also distil the main aspects of his theory about the transnational capitalist class and its class fractions, whilst introducing us to his recent innovative assessments, notably, of the Anthropocene period and of alternatives to global capitalism. This is an accessible and enjoyable collection, offering an impressive introduction to the literatures on several wide-ranging fields. Sklair's studies succeed in being both authoritative and significant, whilst overcoming the fragmentation bedeviling our era of hyper-specialization."
—Bridget Fowler, Emeritus Professor of Sociology, University of Glasgow

"*Second Thoughts on Capitalism and the State* brings together a selection of Leslie Sklair's essays originally published over a 40-year period. Each chapter is prefaced by discussions of the intellectual, political and sometimes personal contexts from which the essay arose, along with reflections that variously present a self-critique of the original argument and/or an updating of it. The book concludes with a previously unpublished essay, 'Beleaguered City, Beleaguered Planet', reflecting back on his chapters on the Transnational Capitalist Class, architecture/urban design, human rights, and the Anthropocene and envelops them in a biting critique of our capitalist-dominated planet Earth. Most importantly, the book also includes observations on how we can avoid oblivion. Rejecting the idea that better, social democratic forms of capitalism, can halt the destructive dynamics inherent in the Anthropocene, Sklair argues for a non-capitalist future, built step by step from local to ultimately global networks of socialist producer/consumer cooperatives, gradually breaking the hegemony of the Transnational Capitalist Class and its crucial linkages to the nation state and the interstate system. Viewed in its totality, *Second Thoughts* thus brilliantly demonstrates the indispensability of the famous aphorism popularised by Gramsci: 'pessimism of the intellect, but optimism of the will."

—Jeffrey Henderson, Professor Emeritus of International Development, University of Bristol

"In this curated collection of updated versions of his previous publications, Sklair looks back on a long and distinguished career tackling the biggest and most challenging empirical and moral puzzles of our time. Chapters engage topics ranging from the transformation of global corporate power structures to urban development (il)logics, to the perils and ethics of the Anthropocene, providing a veteran scholar's perspective on large-scale social change. His reflections on how both scholarly dialogue and the passage of time affect individual understandings offer rich material for young scholars seeking to advance scholarship and policy debates with their own unique insights. The humility with which he offers "second thoughts" on his past arguments is refreshing and thought-provoking, and Sklair's prescient insights will help inform new generations of the kind of reflexive and deeply curious scholarship that is much-needed in today's complex and changing world. Few scholars would take time in their twilight years to pull together a collection aimed at updating and contextualizing lessons from their careers for new generations of scholars, students, and global citizens. We should therefore be grateful for the generosity and humility Sklair conveys in this important contribution. Moreover, he challenges us to abolish the notion that scholarship can be neutral and to embrace the urgent ethical challenges posed by the Anthropocene."

—Jackie Smith, Professor of Sociology, University of Pittsburgh

"Leslie Sklair's new book brings together a number of his essays that engage with critical contemporary issues and ground these in sociological theory. Each essay is preceded by a new introductory section and concludes with an extensive section of 'Second Thoughts'. Together with various interpolations in the main text, these reflections give new life to Sklair's influential research. The essays cover an impressive range of topics, including the sociology of science, Chinese economic development, the transnational capitalist class, global social movements and capital flows, the future of socialism, human rights, environmentalism, and urbanisation. Original, insightful, and thought provoking, this new collection highlights and expands the relevance of Sklair's ideas for the twenty-first century."
—**John Scott, Emeritus Professor, University of Plymouth**

"Leslie Sklair is one of the most influential sociologists of the last half century whose work has helped shape our understandings of globalization, capitalism, and the Anthropocene. This volume presents a provocative glimpse into some of his most pioneering work and a vision into how his own insights have developed since they were written. Rather than simply a collection of essays, however, this book represents a framework around which we can understand the development of sociological and theoretical understandings of global capitalism across the last half century. This volume provides not just an historical review, but also the tools necessary to better understand our contemporary globalized capitalist society."
—**J. Michael Ryan, Nazarbayev University, Kazakhstan.**

INTRODUCTION

When Adam Rummens at Cambridge Scholars Publishing invited me to submit a book proposal on a topic of my choice, I was sceptical. I had just declined an invitation from another publisher to write a short book about the climate crisis and the pandemic (this was a time when many publishers seemed to be soliciting such books). After surveying the current literature on these topics I felt that I had little that was genuinely original to say about these two crises. This led me to look back at some of the articles I had published over the years on various aspects of what is usually theorized as crises of capitalism and the state. Reading through these articles I realized that between the late 1960s, when I first started to publish, and the present, that I now had many second thoughts about what I had previously written, though the same themes kept emerging. The idea for this book, selected essays on how sociology and capitalism have changed and how personally I had changed over these 50 years, emerged slowly. My hope is that these essays, all edited, updated, and full of second thoughts will be of interest to sociologists and perhaps also, more generally, to those who wonder about how the social sciences and capitalism have changed over the last fifty years. The chapters are arranged neither thematically nor chronologically, but with an eye on the complexities of the changing nature of capitalism from the relatively halcyon days of the early 1960s to the present. These essays, all but the last one which was adapted especially for this book (the rather personal Preamble to that chapter explains the circumstances) were previously published in a variety of scholarly journals and I thank the publishers who gave permissions for me to re-publish my own writings (gratefully acknowledged alongside the chapter titles). Every essay is introduced with a Preamble explaining the personal context and the intellectual environment in which it was produced. There is some repetition between the chapters in the interests of clarity. The "second thoughts" sections of each chapter combine my auto-critiques of the original chapters with a running commentary on some of the most significant research published after I wrote the essay. To avoid temporal confusion I would advise readers to bear in mind the original date of publication of each essay. Apart from chapter 12 the original versions are currently available via university libraries and other online sites. Every essay has an Abstract, also rewritten in some cases. This book would have been impossible to write without the resources of the magnificent library and librarians at the LSE and elsewhere. The cooperation of scholars all over the world (most of whom I have never met) who provided me with hard-to-find copies of their work and constructive criticism is also much appreciated.

This book was in production when the Russian army invaded Ukraine to almost universal condemnation in February 2022, continuing a war that began with the seizure of Crimea in 2014, though the roots of these wars go back for centuries. The economic and other sanctions imposed on Russia in 2022 highlighted the lucrative business and financial ties between the Putin regime and Western corporations and politicians before and since 2014. Lessons were ignored, not learned.

CHAPTER 1

(1977) IDEOLOGY AND THE SOCIOLOGICAL UTOPIAS.
THE SOCIOLOGICAL REVIEW 25/1: 51-72
[COURTESY OF SAGE]

Preamble

With reports of student activism around the world in 1968 resonating loudly, the 1970s were a period of turmoil in British sociology. It was a time of excited soul-searching for politically engaged sociologists. At the London School of Economics, the institution was in crisis with students (and some junior and senior staff) in open revolt. This led many of us to question the role of sociology in the political arena and, for me, to question the place of Marxism in my sociological practice and, in particular, for the sociology of sociology. This youthful effort (written a few years after my appointment as an assistant lecturer in sociology at the LSE) reads now as a rather over-ambitious attempt to assess the relative merits of some influential publications on the sociology of sociology and the ways in which sociology could be "scientific". However, it may be useful for our understanding of sociology in the new millennium to dig up these historical curiosities, and a timely reminder that the name of Alvin Gouldner (over 150,000 results on Wikipedia in 2021) still resonates.

Abstract

Sociology in the Anglophone world was dominated in the decades after the Second World War by theoretical and polemical debates around the competing discourses of Marxist materialism and the school of functionalism created by Talcott Parsons and Robert Merton in the USA. Critical analysis of the work of some scholars in the re-emerging field of the sociology of sociology strongly suggests that the then-common labels of "Bourgeois" and "Radical" sociologies (capitalized to indicate their status as socio-political movements) conceal as much as they reveal. I suggest that these labels both constitute sociological utopias fulfilling different but complementary ideological functions. However, some of the critiques aimed at "Bourgeois sociology" do expose uncomfortable truths.

Ideological Sources of Sociological Utopias

Like many other innovations, notably television, jet passenger planes, nuclear weapons, and computers, sociology around the 1950s was somewhat esoteric, mostly for the privileged, some cutting-edge academics, and some media people, only rarely penetrating to the wider public. In the decades after World War II, stimulated by much government and private foundation money in the United States and by small sums elsewhere, sociological research blossomed into an industry servicing capitalism and the state. The dominant tendencies, sometimes connected but more often not, were the functionalism of Parsons and then Merton, and the more or less sophisticated empiricism of those driven by a desire to discover how many people thought or were or did something and how this correlated with others who thought or were or did something else. The theoretical enterprise of the American sociologist Talcott Parsons strongly influenced the work of a whole generation of social scientists, for indeed his goal was no less than the development of a general theory of action as the basis of an integrated social science. In this task he was supported by other sociologists, anthropologists, psychologists, economists, and biologists. Large numbers of students, encouraged by the apparent success of this school of thought, carried out many research projects into the functions that various phenomena fulfilled in holding society together. Meanwhile, the technology of empirical research had not been standing still. By the late 1950s techniques of information gathering, recording, storage, and analysis had become relatively cheaply available. So too had large numbers of impecunious students, the reserve army of intellectual labour. It was within the reach of sociologists to construct questionnaires, post them or hire interviewers in person or by phone, and come up with a series of "findings". Thus, like grains of sand and the heap they accumulated, no one grain of sand may be significant but enough of them will eventually make a heap, irrespective of the size, shape, purity, or composition of the individual grains. By the 1960s, computers and their attendant human and mechanical services had spread all around the globe. This was a time when many countries began to augment their censuses to a considerable degree and to permit social scientists, many employed in government agencies and business corporations, to amass huge quantities of data. But who was standing back and reflecting on what sociologists were doing, what their methods and results really meant, or why anyone should be prepared to pay for all this apparently curious, if not trivial information? Doing sociology was one thing, what we are doing when we are doing sociology appeared to be quite another thing, and not a matter for proper, sustained sociological inquiry. But this situation (like so much else) changed rather dramatically in the mid-1960s, particularly in the USA and Western Europe. So, if we can characterize the years between 1945 and 1964 in sociological theory as a time of theoretical and methodological dispute, largely revolving around the rise and (presumed) fall of structural-functionalism, and the increasing use of and disillusionment with multivariate analysis and similar research techniques, then perhaps the years from 1965 may turn out to be marked by the soul-searching of those who were unable to come to terms with functionalism and/or computer-based data collection. 1965-1984 might well be the age of the sociology of sociology.

Sociology of Sociology: Origins

This is not, of course, to suggest that we are in the grip of an entirely new phenomenon, both Durkheim and Weber at the beginning of the twentieth century had turned critical eyes on their discipline. In 1939 Robert Lynd published his justly celebrated book, *Knowledge for What?* Pitirim Sorokin (expelled from the Soviet Union in 1922) published his largely ignored and quite devastating *Fads and Foibles in Modern Sociology* in 1956; and C. Wright Mills had shocked the professionals and delighted the students with *The Sociological Imagination* in 1959. Lurking in the background were many Marxist-influenced works, notably Karl Mannheim's *Ideology and Utopia* which appeared in English in 1936 and Herbert Marcuse's *Reason and Revolution: Hegel and the Rise of Social Theory* (1941). It can even be convincingly argued that the whole process was set in motion by the refusal of Marx and Engels themselves to take the works of some of their contemporaries at face-value, notably in *The German Ideology,* itself an enigmatic text full of "discursive struggles", as Carver (2015) later demonstrated. The theme that runs through all of these works we might now label as a form of reflexive sociology, morphing into the sociology of knowledge and the sociology of sociology in particular. The paradox that has accompanied the writing of the history of the discipline is that sociology can appear to be a profoundly critical and a profoundly conservative activity at the same time. Both its critical and conservative potential inevitably follow from curiosity about how institutions work to produce "consensus" and/or "conflict" in society. Even though many sociologists themselves may not be particularly critical, those whose power rests on their ability successfully to conceal how the controlling institutions they control do work, will quickly adopt conservative postures in response to sociological analyses. The potential of sociologists to sit on the fence can be summed up in two words: "scientific neutrality". The beauty of some of the best sociology appears in its ability to be both critical (debunking, exposing hypocrisy) and conservative ("value-free") simultaneously. A rather confusing paper published many years later by an American sociologist in a British journal (Black 2013) illustrates not only how contentious an issue "value free" sociology still is but, crucially, how naïve some sociologists are about how scientific much so-called "hard" science actually has been and increasingly is. "Science fictions" (see Ritchie 2021) contribute to the dilemma of all scholarly disciplines that encourage us to work out how things operate and can be maintained or changed but forbids us to take a position on whether or how they should be maintained or changed. This injunction naturally favours present arrangements (the status quo or "business as usual") in most cases.

Two books on the sociology of sociology, both published in 1970 (by A.W. Gouldner and R.W. Friedrichs) raise questions around the critical and the conservative roles of sociology. Alvin Gouldner argues paradoxically that the repressive component of sociology and the suppressed liberating potential of sociology together shape the unique contradiction distinctive of sociology. In my opinion what he identifies is neither *unique* nor a *contradiction*. Friedrichs hangs his account on the twin pegs of the Prophetic (engaged) mode and the Priestly (value-free) mode of sociology. This old/new sub-discipline of the sociology of sociology suffers from a two-fold paradox. First, in terms of the general strain of critical and conservative sociology as both look at and attempt to explain the world; second, in terms of critical and conservative postures towards sociology itself. In the argument rekindled in the discipline by Robert Nisbet's influential theoretical history, *The Sociological Tradition* (1967), we can see a neat illustration of the point. In answer to those who hold (or wish to believe) that sociology has its origins and finest aspirations in the critique of political economy and the debilitating effects of capitalism on society Nisbet argues that, on the contrary, sociology arose as a reaction against socialism, industrialism, and the utilitarian culture (as Gouldner himself strongly asserts with respect to what he calls "Academic Sociology"). Nisbet's heroes are not only the traditional Durkheim and Weber, but also Tonnies and de Tocqueville, scholars who spent as much time on the world they were losing as on the world over the horizon. This is not to be confused with a critical position, for however critical in details it might have been, it was part of a general conservative strategy against radical social change. So, the conservative-critical paradox is not simply or only a formal distinction pertaining to method, but a substantive distinction which separates out that practice of sociology which operates to defend the societies we have (with a greater or smaller degree of reactionary or progressive influence on social structures) from that sociology which operates to undermine the social institutions we have and to replace them with something better. Each of these sociologies can clearly be seen to perform an ideological function in the sense that it is used by certain social groups (not only sociologists themselves) to prescribe a set of social values, to produce an unchallengeable picture of society consonant with certain interests, and to provide where necessary a legitimation for the enterprise and its consequences.

Following those who write on the subject (directly or by implication) the conservative position has been labelled "Bourgeois sociology" (with Parsonian functionalism playing a major role) and the position of the critics "Radical sociology" (with the works of Marx and Engels playing a variable role). One further and most important difference should be noted: while "Radical sociology" makes a virtue out of the fact that it takes sides between the status quo and some new order, "Bourgeois sociology" makes a virtue (perhaps its only virtue) out of its claim to "scientific neutrality" (the only place where it is unscientific not to be neutral). My argument in the remainder of this post-mortem on the living body of the sociology of sociology is that both Bourgeois and Radical sociologies are utopias in Mannheim's sense, as interpreted decades later for sociologists (see Kumar 2006, and Neurath (1930/2020) on Mannheim's "Bourgeois Marxism"). The bourgeois "neutrality of science" as well as the radical penchant for socialist humanism have almost obliterated the contentious distinction between ideology and science which Parsons and Marx laboured so hard to achieve through their modes of theory formation.

Marx and Parsons

The theoretical enterprises of both Marx and Parsons were probably neither more scientific nor more successful (or both) than that of their competitors. In the 1950s Parsons, funded by the Carnegie Corporation at Harvard, set out to create a science of social relations, as described by Isaac (2010) almost 20 years after Parsons died. Further, elements of the achievements of others were clearly integrated into or developed out of the works of Marx and Parsons as was the case (briefly) for the French Marxist Louis Althusser whose books were very much in vogue amongst younger radical sociologists at the time. It is still a matter of sometimes bad-tempered dispute whether or not Althusser has provided an accurate account (both textually and in spirit) of what Marx tried to do scientifically, as is Althusser's abounding faith that Marx's scientific achievements matched his intentions (Fuchs 2019). It is I think very striking that, despite their spectacular differences, Parsons and Althusser appear to share some similar somewhat unfashionable views about Freud's scientific achievements. For example, in the distinguished academic journal *Daedalus,* Parsons wrote of "the aspiration of psychoanalysis to scientific status, which in my opinion, in spite of much controversy, has been broadly validated"; and that reading Freud "proved to be one of the few crucial intellectual experiences of my life" (Parsons 1970, 835-837). And in an essay on Freud and Lacan Althusser wrote "Psycho-analytic theory can thus give us what makes each science no pure speculation but a science: the definition of the *formal* essence of its object, the precondition for any practical, technical application of it to its *concrete* objects" (Althusser 1971a, 197-98).

I did not consider when I originally wrote this article that Althusser (or anyone else) was likely to solve fundamental epistemological problems. My views on this have always been pragmatic. While empirical (or substantive as I prefer to say) research is intended to make or break a theory, it is sufficiently distanced from the metatheory that its results need not affect it much. Moreover, it is a common procedural strategy for scientists to respond to the disconfirmation of one theory or hypothesis by replacing it with another that is not disconfirmed by the substantive research ("fits the facts"), where both theories and hypotheses are logically compatible with a common metatheory. This seems to be the case for the metatheory constructed by Marx and his many followers over the years and why I would never claim to be a Marxist (whatever that means these days, see below) but am happy to acknowledge that I am Marx-inspired, gaining insight from his ideas that are developed throughout this book. Prime among Marx's insights in my view are first, the necessity of the abolition of money (the root cause of toxic consumerism) and second the abolition of socially necessary labour time (the root cause of capitalist exploitation of workers) as a means of organizing society. Faced with these goals as the *sine qua non* for ending capitalist exploitation it is no wonder that almost all so-called "alternatives to capitalism" fall short.

Sociology of Sociology: Problems

Three major sets of problems are at the core of the sociology of sociology. First, it should try to explain the origins and growth of sociology; second, it should try to explain how sociology works historically; and third, it should try to explain the functions that sociology fulfils for the various groups within societies, locally and globally? These are not totally discrete problems. Of all the many books on the sociology of sociology published in the second half of the twentieth century Gouldner's *Coming Crisis* is the only one seriously to attempt to tackle all three tasks and, indeed, it is its breadth of scope which gives the work its initially rather overpowering and dogmatic aspect. It is instructive to revisit the debate in which Gouldner has taken the eminent deviance theorist Howard S. Becker to task over the perennial problem of value-free sociology. Becker, in a famous paper provocatively entitled "Whose Side are We On?" (1967) had argued the case for "underdog affiliation" in sociological research (although, let it be noted, he had remained quite ambivalent about the scientific status of sociological research results). Gouldner, in an equally provocatively reply entitled "The Sociologist as Partisan: Sociology and the Welfare State" (1968) condemns Becker's deviance theory thus: "Insofar as this school of theory has a critical edge to it, this is directed at the caretaking institutions who do the mopping up job, rather than at the master institutions that produce the deviant's suffering" (ibid., 107). Without being a great deal more enlightening than Becker about the central question of the scientific status of research results, Gouldner expresses a vision of sociology which takes it beyond those who clearly regulate much of social life, to the social structures they make and the historical processes in which the whole is embedded. *The Coming Crisis of Western Sociology* does not exactly identify these "master institutions" as we might have hoped, although Gouldner does trace the development of social theory through its four great periods, namely Positivism (Saint-Simon and Comte), Marxism (Marx), Classical Sociology (Durkheim and Weber), and Parsonian Structural-Functionalism (Parsons). Somewhat surprisingly, Part II of Gouldner's book (1970) is entirely devoted to "The World of Talcott Parsons". Even more surprising is Gouldner's testimonial for Parsons in this context:

"There is no question, in my mind, that many of the details and many of the fundamental assumptions that Parsons advances in attempting to solve the equilibrium problems are wrong. There is also no question that Parsons has, nonetheless, developed an analysis of this problem that goes well beyond that of his predecessors. He has gone far in setting out elements that need to be considered and in establishing firmer ground for continuing work on it. Anyone concerned with this matter must and can use Parsons as a point of departure and as a grindstone on which to sharpen his own thought" (ibid., 456).

Despite the ups and downs of Parsons' reputation (see Lidz 2021) I don't think that many sociologists anywhere today would agree. The links that Gouldner makes between social theory and its societal origins are often hinted rather than exact, general rather than specific, evasive rather than direct. For all its merits, his book fails to come to any firm conclusion about the scientific status of either his own work, or academic sociology in its various forms, particularly Marxism. In his last book he went on to make the distinction between "critical voluntarist Marxism" and "scientific determinist Marxism" (Gouldner 1980). His argument is that that both are Marxist because Marx's Marxism is itself contradictory. Gouldner's discussions of Marx and Parsons suggest that the scientific nature of their work and their modes of theory formation are not matters that attract his interest to any great extent. The same conclusion holds for Friedrichs (1970) whose *A Sociology of Sociology* unluckily jumped on to the Kuhnian bandwagon just as the points were being switched, not least by Kuhn himself. This gives Friedrichs' not inconsiderable efforts to prod and push the recent history of sociology into a Kuhnian framework of "scientific paradigms" a laboured and unreal appearance (see Bryant 1975). Friedrichs' view of the history and by implication the sociology of sociology revolves around the purported paradigm struggle between Prophetic and Priestly modes referred to above. He argues that the Prophets prefer criticism rather than construction, while the Priests proclaim, under the cloak of neutrality, that in science prophecy has no place: prediction (an eminently constructive activity) must be our guide. Auguste Comte and C. Wright Mills illustrate the span of the prophets. For the priests it is the computer, particularly exemplified at that time by the youthful Department of Social Relations at Johns Hopkins University, USA (and fifty years later Johns Hopkins is still producing socially relevant data. Notably through its major globally recognized site providing information on the Corona pandemic at https://coronavirus.jhu.edu/). The prophets and the priests appear to be split along the conflict/system dichotomy as well, and this dichotomy is considered to be the form in which the paradigm struggle expresses itself, prophets operate with conflict, priests with system. For Friedrichs, all societies are seen to be systemic, but not all are conflictual, the way forward is some sort of "dialectical compromise" between Bourgeois and Radical (mainly Marxist) sociology. This mode of thought has produced some bizarre results, for example in a paper in the journal entitled *Human Studies* Ajzner (2000) suggests that Marxist Axioms may be considered self-contradictory paradoxes of Parsonian statements in sociology! A book that had previously asked the question "what went wrong with sociological theory?" (Mouzelis 1995) went some way to clarifying these confusions and the fact that Mouzelis' book is still very well worth reading more than twenty years after it was published tells us something important about the pitfalls of sociological theory. In the UK the challenges of the sociology of sociology were met rather differently, for example with an article by Alan Dawe on "The Two Sociologies" (Dawe 1970) which also brought utopias into the frame but does not mention Gouldner nor the sociology of sociology, and Dick Atkinson's *Orthodox Consensus and Radical Alternative* (Atkinson 1971) reframes Gouldner's dilemma. Two decades later Stewart Clegg's (1992) brilliantly satirical and theoretically acute analysis of the construction (or should that be "structuration") of "Giddensisation" as a new global brand opens up bold new themes for the sociology of sociology.

Conflicting Sociologies of Knowledge

Another alternative contribution to the sociology of knowledge implicitly portrays the social sciences as an onward march of progress, apparently more characteristic of Bourgeois than Radical sociology. Deutsch, et al. (1971) blithely identify "62 major achievements, or advances, or breakthroughs in Social Science" from 1900 to 1965 (including, strangely, philosophy and mathematics). My intention here is not to expose this article as a crude political confidence trick and/or a major exercise in self-deception, however tempting this prospect might be, but to use it as an illustration of what might be termed "the fallacy of eclectic accumulation". Deutsch and his colleagues put forward a selection which includes something from everywhere, no tendency is left out, no charge of bias can be maintained. In a word, it is apolitical, deliberately avoiding issues of morality and justice. While in no way diminishing the achievements of George Bernard Shaw, Gandhi, Mao Zedong, and V.I. Lenin, all on the list as path-breaking *social scientists* but finding no place for Durkheim, Simmel, Lukacs, Sorokin, Adorno, Herbert Marcuse, and C. Wright Mills seems odd, to say the least. Sociology provides only 7 out of the 62 "contributions", 170 in all, spanning the years between 1900 and 1965. The model of the social sciences which Deutsch and his colleagues present emerges implicitly when they claim: "An inspection of our list shows that many of the later contributions were clearly building on the earlier ones, and that they resulted in clear increases in the powers of social scientists to recognize relationships and to carry out operations . . . Together these advances add up to unmistakable evidence of the cumulative growth of knowledge in the social sciences in the course of this century" (ibid., 455). However, the project did reveal some interesting patterns regarding geographical locations, research communities, and periods of time.

The Contrarians

Two contrarian views (both published before Deutsch's analysis of the smooth progress of the social sciences in the twentieth century) stand out. The first is a speech by a sociology PhD student, Martin Nicolaus, in 1968. This speech at the American Sociological Association Annual meeting was first published in *The American Sociologist*. It is still available on the internet with determined searching. An historic document of the Left all round the world, it is a powerful and moving indictment which challenges sociologists to acknowledge their former hypocrisy, as well as a devastating (however "unscholarly") critique of the discipline that welcomes the Secretary of Disease, Propaganda, and Scabbing (officially known as the U.S. Secretary of Health, Education, and Welfare). A guest speaker by popular acclaim at the ASA while the war in Vietnam was raging, Nicolaus' vivid "eyes down palms up" characterization of many sociologists will be dismissed as bad taste by those who know it to have a grain of truth but destructive of their prospects. This is a truly scholarly article, though not in a sociology journal. Nicolaus brilliantly expands the argument, again but not in the pages of a sociology journal (Nicolaus 1969). A more playful but just as effective critique of establishment sociology in the USA is "The Sunshine Boys; Toward a Sociology of Happiness" by Dusky Lee Smith, first published in *The Activist* (later reprinted in Reynolds & Reynolds eds. 1970). Smith dissects the Sunshine Boys through a critical analysis of the work of three leading members, the Supreme Sunbeam (Seymour Martin Lipset); the Sustaining Sunbeam (Nathan Glazer); and the Subsidiary Sunbeam (Amitai Etzioni); all three of these luminaries are prominently on sociology reading lists in universities all over the world in the 1960s, still cited today. This is a root and branch attack on the American sociological orthodoxy, on those influential sociologists who have explained why America is as it is, why it should stay more or less as it is, and that it is pretty good for most of those involved. This paper could clearly not have appeared in a conventional sociology journal, it is too rude, sarcastic, and accurate in its exposure of the ideological powerhouse from which the pleasant rays of Sunshine Sociology emanate. And Smith (now deceased) could no doubt gain grim satisfaction from the fact that since the essay was first published in 1964 events in America have seriously undermined though probably not shattered the fond illusions of the Sunshine Guild, if not for themselves but possibly for large numbers of sociology students and even some of their teachers. Smith's polemic is reinforced by his sharp historical analysis in the Marxist journal *Science & Society* (Smith 1965), a well-documented and closely argued analysis of the role of sociology in the rise of corporate capitalism in the USA with its bourgeois lumber of pluralism, stable democracy, and naive consensus. This is instructive in two ways. First, as an essay in the history of sociology of sociology itself it deserves serious consideration; second, the relative difficulty experienced by writers of this type of criticism (until very recently) in reaching the sociological masses tells us a great deal about the state of sociology and the nature of its institutional openness to that most cherished of all scientific norms, organized scepticism, an idea that I tried to deconstruct in a book on the sociology of science (Sklair 1972, chapter 4). Dusky Lee Smith's work, like that of Nicolaus, lies outside conventional "Bourgeois" versus "Radical" sociological sparring, and the "healthy controversy of civilized debate". Further evidence had already been provided albeit in a rather more "civilized" form by Baritz (1960) and others.

It is here that the exclusivist aspects of Kuhn's notion of paradigms in hard science begin to make some sense for sociology. There are, indeed, many examples of controversies which do achieve a great deal of exposure in the regular journals, textbooks, and literature of the social sciences. The debates over Parsonian and other varieties of functionalism, in particular the so-called "order versus conflict" debate and the struggles around stratification and inequality in most sociological traditions spring most readily to mind (see for example, Rex 1961, and Sklair 1993, a commentary on Rex). The ways in which many of these controversies, by exhaustion or otherwise, have turned out to be rather less about issues than about words, definitions, and levels of discourse, strongly suggests that there really is only one paradigm within sociology, in which "Bourgeois" and "Radical" co-exist to provide a little interest and variety in a situation which threatens to become dangerously dull. Alternative paradigm candidates, such as might be represented by Smith, Nicolaus, and others are more or less tolerated on the fringes of sociology (as was ethnomethodology for a time) but have no proper enduring place in it. All the apparent critical activity can then be interpreted as follows: modern sociology has nowhere to go because its accumulationist ideal (the promise of steady progress as represented in the work of Deutsch et al.) contradicts its methodological canon of absolute purity of variables in a crippling fashion. Nevertheless, in an attempt to prove that conventional sociology is still alive (even virile), it generates as many pseudo-controversies as possible, whose major function is to establish by assumption (the taken-for-granted-world) the inviolability of the current social order or some reforms of it. The debates centre around the conservation of or adaption to our given social structures (system) and the reform or re-creation of our given social structures (conflict). It is not quite like the Left versus Right. The traffic in sociology is mostly one-way, from Young Radicals to Middle-Aged Sunshine Boys, and a few Sunshine Girls!

Neutralizing Conflict

These discussions, then, take place within one set of categories and it is a major achievement of capitalism friendly (or at least "neutral") social sciences in advanced capitalist society especially in its liberal-democratic form, manifest within the context of sociology, that controversies can actually appear to occur within an arena in which the system itself invites all criticisms and "scientifically and neutrally" rebuffs all its critics, while encouraging them in their work where it is deemed constructive. Friedrichs is totally wrong, I think, to consider that Prophetic and Priestly modes signify genuine differences in sociological practice (as he himself recognizes in his tacit conclusion that we can achieve some state of pluralist cognition in sociology, of which he unblushingly approves). Gouldner seems nearer the mark with his emphasis on "Academic" rather than "Bourgeois" sociology, although he does appear to underestimate the importance of the non-academic, governmental, industrial, and mass media supports of the conventional sociology he describes. It is nothing less than a stunning ideological coup that for so long, and for so many intelligent sociologists, ideas such as the synthesis of Marxism and any other "ism" seem serious and (on the other hand) beliefs that "order versus conflict" orientations on their own really represent overwhelmingly different and opposed ideological postures. To begin to explain how all this has come about in the sociological world, how Bourgeois and Radical sociology have become firm and often mutually indulgent bedfellows, I think it is necessary to look at the ways in which the works of the two main ghosts in the machine in the sociology of the second half of the twentieth century, Karl Marx and Talcott Parsons, are treated. I propose to argue that the answer to my question lies in the theoretical enterprise of Marx and Parsons, their attempts to establish a science of society. As I suggested above, both Bourgeois (conservative) and Radical (critical) sociology constitute sociological utopias fulfilling different but complementary ideological functions. By identifying the social parameters of knowledge, we need not destroy the scientific status of sociological or any other knowledge. But this is not enough. Sociology has been shackled by its ideologies and its utopias, and the time has come for the science of sociology to assert itself in a militant fashion. If claims that Marx and Parsons have laid the foundations for this seem peculiar, it is because we have been too ready to spend our time on these "Radical" and "Bourgeois" sociologies. Utopian and ideological versions of Marxism and Parsonian functionalism (for which Marxists and Parsons respectively are very largely responsible) have deflected attention from what a scientific sociology is actually capable of achieving. And the point is, still, to change the world. This is the inescapable conclusion for the engaged radical scientific sociology for which I have been arguing. Nicolaus expresses this with characteristic verve:

> The trunk of political power has many branches. One of these is the professional organization of sociology, the American Sociological Association. The upper, fatter portion of this branch is grafted seamlessly, with contractual cement, to the civil, economic and military sovereignty which constitutes the trunk. From that source, the organization spreads outward and downward along the institutional scaffolding, carrying the authoritative views on matters of social reality into the universities, junior colleges, and high schools. In addition to the general dissemination of propaganda, professional sociology has the major specific functions of aiding industrial, civil, and military authorities in the solution of manpower control problems of a limited order, and of preparing university candidates for careers in the official bureaucracies. As a source of legitimation for the existing sovereignty, and as a laboratory of refinements in the processes by which a tribute of blood, labor, and taxation is extracted from the subject population, the professional organization of sociology today represents the concrete fulfilment of the charter vision of its founding fathers. (Nicolaus 1969, 375).

Repurposing the famous sentiment at the end of the *Communist Manifesto*, Nicolaus offers us a resounding conclusion: "In the last analysis, the only moves toward liberation within sociology are those which contribute to the process of liberation from sociology. The point is not to reinterpret oppression but to end it" (ibid., 387).

Second Thoughts

My main second thought on this article is that young, relatively inexperienced scholars (I graduated in 1964, received my PhD in 1969, and locate my 1977 self in that category) should be more careful about criticizing those who have already spent a lifetime in the pursuit of knowledge and enlightenment. If I had had the opportunity to read Gouldner's last book (he died in 1980) when I originally wrote this article, I would have evaluated his 1970 book rather differently, focusing more on the internal contradictions of Marxist sociology, while nurturing Marx's genuine insights. My second thoughts about the contrarians, the late Dusky Lee Smith, and Martin Nicolaus (now apparently a self-help guru) are that what they wrote all these years ago serves as a timely reminder of the uses, progressive and/or reactionary (sometimes it is difficult to decide) to which sociology can be put. I had no direct experience of Radical or Marxist sociology in the USA (my first academic visit was in the mid-1980s). I had limited access to left-wing journals in the USA in the 1970s such as *The Insurgent Sociologist* which ran from 1969-1987. It was edited by William Domhoff (the most influential power structure researcher of the era). *The Insurgent Sociologist* was replaced by *Critical Sociology* in 1988. The change of title is suggestive of some of my arguments (see Fitzgerald 1974). Only much later was I made aware of the purge of radical and Marxist sociologists in universities with well-known radical or even Marxist departments active in the "Movement" in the USA, now documented by Oppenheimer (1991, 2020). It is ironic that one of the last articles to be published in *The Insurgent Sociologist* was an attempt to explain "The Marxist Tradition in American Sociology: An Empirical Examination" based on the fluctuating memberships of the American Sociological Association and of its "Marxist Section" and the "Radical Section" of the ASA and of PhD dissertation keywords (Wenger 1986). *The Insurgent Sociologist* seems to have floundered under the weight of an "abstracted empiricism" that even C. Wright Mills (1959) could scarcely have imagined. Another contrarian, Larry Reynolds, updates the contrarian critique with a thorough analysis of "The Sorry State of American Sociology" as the new millennium loomed (see Reynolds 1998, and 2022). This latter item (Reynolds 2022) is an acute appreciation of the work of Dusky Lee Smith and Sydney Willhelm, whose pathbreaking and prescient work on the Negro in the USA deserves to be much better known (Willhelm 1970, 1979, 1983), especially the analysis of the economic writings of Matin Luther King. However, by this time the contrarian focus was on scientism and postmodernism. These days the process is even more complex. This is powerfully exemplified for "critical sociology" and Marxists in an article by two radical Leftist Canadian sociologists:

> Just to set the imagination loose for a minute, the critical perspective might entail the maverick radicalism of a C.W. Mills, the Red Toryism of a George Grant, the patriotic socialism of a James Laxer, the Christian socialism of a T.C. Douglas, the whiggish liberalism of an Edgar Z. Friedenberg, the pro-Soviet standpoint of an Albert Szymanski, the pro-third worldist stance of an Arthur Davis, the detached ironical style of a Thorstein Veblen, the anarchist denunciation of the capitalist state by Kropotkin, Bakunin, or George Woodcock, and one could go on. Of course, even to label something as Marxist does not help that much. Is it Trotskyist, Stalinist, Bukharinist, Marxist-Leninist, Maoist, Titoist, Castroist, Kautskyist, Lukacsian, Goldmannist, Gramscist, Althusserian?" (Nelsen & Nock 1982, 76).

Stimulated by the theoretical complexity exposed by Nelsen and Nock, I began searching to explain to myself why I failed to see the connections between the abstract "Ideology and the Sociological Utopias" and the everyday reality of Genders/Feminisms and Race/Racisms when I wrote the essay in the 1970s. This brought out a new set of second thoughts about what sociologists (myself included) considered to be most important at that time and what we now consider to be the most important issues to address. A good place to start this rethinking is the idea of "Public Sociology" elaborated by the sociologist Michael Burawoy (a Marxist in the Gouldner mould) and the ways in which it has been skewered for its white, male perspectives (Brewer 2005). The next phase of the sociology of sociology is upon us. The impacts of radical feminism and critical race theory on sociology (and on the wider society) which have been growing by leaps and bounds since the 1970s is such that most sociologists (of all varieties of genders and ethnicities) must have been having serious second thoughts about anything they wrote before the 1970s. In his lengthy timeline for the *Concise Encyclopedia of Sociology* J. Michael Ryan (2011) provides a revealing insight into the history of sociology that goes some way to explain why issues of gender and race are almost entirely missing from debates in sociological theory in the 1960s and 1970s in the world of Anglophone sociology, and probably elsewhere. In Ryan's timeline, written in 2010, the term "feminism" first appears indirectly in a reference to *A Vindication of the Rights of Women* by Mary Wolstonecraft (published in 1792), described as "an early feminist classic"; the next is "social reformer and feminist" Jane Addam's Hull House (1910); then in 1963 Betty Frieden's *The Feminine Mystique* "marks the beginning of the second wave of feminism for many" (the first wave of "gender studies" was considered by some to be rather conservative). It was only in the 1970s and thereafter that "feminism" as a distinct sociological field appears to have emerged. Sociologists for Women in Society (SWS), self-described as "an international organization of social scientists—students, faculty, practitioners, and researchers—working together to improve the position of women within sociology and society in general" was founded in 1969 in the USA (socwomen.org). In her presidential address to the organization Patricia Yancey Martin explains: "In 1987, after failing to convince the American Sociological Association to establish a journal on gender, SWS founded a journal—Gender & Society—which, to our delight, is among the more widely cited sociology journals" (Martin 2013, 282). Ryan's timeline cites only seven sociology publications specifically by "feminist" scholars: Nancy Hartsock (1983); Dorothy Smith (1987); Candace West & Don Zimmerman (this reference is to "Doing Gender" 1987); Trin Minh-ha (the first of many to connect

Postcoloniality and Feminism); Donna Haraway (postmodern feminism 1990), and finally Patricia Hill Collins (connecting intersectionality and Black Feminist thought, 1990). What this timeline suggests is that it was radical feminism that took gender studies into the mainstream of sociology.

Race and racism first appear in the timeline with a reference to W.E. du Bois' book *The Souls of Black Folk* (1899) then Oliver Cromwell Cox's *Caste, Class, and Race"* (1948), followed, after a long gap, by Cornell West's *Race Matters* (1994). All this suggests that race and racism took much longer to enter the sociological mainstream than feminism. Ryan's timeline is an impressive scholarly effort that notes many landmarks from many countries (though mostly from the USA and Europe). Some may see it as idiosyncratic but it is certainly a useful rough guide to the development of sociology and, especially, to the reasons why feminism (and gender issues) and race and racism seem to have been somewhat invisibilized in the world of sociological theory before the 1970s. Although Ryan does reference Engels' *The Origin of the Family, Private Property and the State* (1884) it was not until the 1960s that this pivotal text was taken up by radical feminists and began to enter the realms of mainstream sociology. McGregor (2021) highlights its continuing importance, controversial for some radical feminists. Another glaring absence from theorization in the 1970s is discussion of Eurocentrism in both Weberian and Marxist historical sociology as clinically dissected in the work of Gurminder Bhambra, a Professor of Postcolonial and Decolonial Studies. She points out "What these debates all have in common is that they can be carried out in the context of a standard framework of comparative sociology, a framework that I will argue is unable to address the issues raised by the turn to postcolonial studies and global history" (2011, 668, see also Bhambra 2007). One more example of the continuing co-existence of Radical and Bourgeois sociologies. On socialism, unlike when I wrote my article, I now firmly believe that exiting capitalism and the system of hierarchic so-called nation states is even more important now than it was then and that this "system change" entails the abolition of the market, money, and socially necessary labour time, and the creation of smaller scale human settlements, rather than more huge cities and world revolution. These apparently utopian themes are taken up in chapter 11 below (see also, more recently, Bugajska 2021).

References

Ajzner, J. (2000) Marxist Axioms as Self-Contradictory Parsonian Statements in Sociology. *Human Studies* 23/2: 157-178.
Althusser, L. (1971a) Freud and Lacan. In *Lenin and Philosophy and Other Essays* (trans. Ben Brewster). London: NLB, pp. 181-202.
Althusser, L. (1971b) Ideology and Ideological State Apparatuses (Notes towards an Investigation). In *Lenin and Philosophy and Other Essays* (trans. Ben Brewster). London: NLB, pp. 121-173.
Atkinson, D. (1971) *Orthodox Consensus and Radical Alternative: A Study in Sociological Theory*. London: Heinemann Educational.
Baritz, L. (1960) *Servants of Power.* New York: Science Editions.
Becker, H. (1967) Whose Side are we on? *Social Problems* 14/3: 239-47.
Bhambra, G.K. (2007) *Rethinking modernity: postcolonialism and the sociological imagination*: New York: Palgrave.
Bhambra, G.K. (2011) Talking among Themselves? Weberian and Marxist Historical Sociologies as Dialogues without 'Others'. *Millennium: Journal of International Studies* 39/3: 667–681.
Black, D. (2013) On the almost inconceivable misunderstandings concerning the subject of value-free social science. *British Journal of Sociology* 64 1/4: 764-80.
Brewer, R. (2005) Response to Michael Burawoy's Commentary: "The Critical Turn to Public Sociology". *Critical Sociology* 31/3: 353-59.
Bryant, C.G. (1975) Kuhn, Paradigms and Sociology. *The British Journal of Sociology* 26/3: 354- 359.
Bugajska, A. (2021) The Future of Utopia in the Posthuman World. *Academia Letters* (Article 155.) https://doi.org/10.20935/AL155.
Carver, T. (2015) Roughing It: The "German Ideology" Main Manuscript. *History of Political Thought* 36/4: 700-26.
Clegg, S. (1992) Review article: How to become an internationally famous British social theorist. *Sociological Review* 40/3: 576-59.
Dawe, A. (1970) The Two Sociologies. *The British Journal of Sociology* 21/2: 207-218.
Deutsch, K., et al. (1971) Conditions Favoring Major Advances in Social Science: Analysis of 62 advances since 1900 shows that most come from a few centers and have rapid effects. *Science* 171: 450-459.
Fitzgerald, P. et al. (1974) Whither the Insurgent Sociologist: Responses. *The Insurgent Sociologist* 4/3: 72-75.
Friedrichs, R.W. (1970) *A Sociology of Sociology.* New York: Free Press.

Fuchs, C. (2019) Revisiting the Althusser/E.P. Thompson-Controversy: Towards a Marxist theory of communication. *Communication and the Public* 4/1: 3–20.

Gouldner, A.W. (1968) The Sociologist as Partisan: Sociology and the Welfare State. *The American Sociologist* 3/2: 103-116.

Gouldner, A.W. (1970) *The Coming Crisis of Western Sociology.* New York & London: Basic Books.

Gouldner, A.W. (1980) *The two Marxisms: contradictions and anomalies in the development of theory.* London: Macmillan.

Isaac, J. (2010) Theorist at Work: Talcott Parsons and the Carnegie Project on Theory, 1949-1951. *Journal of the History of Ideas* 71/2: 287- 311.

Kumar, K. (2006) Ideology and sociology: Reflections on Karl Mannheim's Ideology and Utopia. *Journal of Political Ideologies* 11/2: 169-181.

Lidz, V. (2021) Politics and the Academic Social Scientist: The Record of Talcott Parsons. *The American Sociologist* 52: 63–87.

Martin, P.Y. (2013) Sociologists for women in society: a feminist bureaucracy? *Gender & Society* 27/3: 281-293.

McGregor, S.M. (2021) Engels on women, the family, class and gender. *Human Geography* 14/2: 186–197.

Mills, C.W. (1959) *The Sociological Imagination.* New York & Oxford: Oxford University Press.

Mouzelis, N. P. (1995) *Sociological theory: what went wrong?: diagnosis and remedies.* London: Routledge.

Nelsen, R.W. & Nock, D. (1982) Science, Ideology, and "Reading, Writing and Riches". *The Journal of Educational Thought* 16/2: 73-88.

Neurath, O. (1930/2020) Bourgeois Marxism. A Review Essay on Karl Mannheim, *Ideologie und Utopie* (original edition 1930, translated from the German by Alan Scott) *Sociologica* 14/1: 235-41.

Nicolaus, M. (1969) The Professional Organization of Sociology: A View from Below. *The Antioch Review* 29/3: 375-387.

Nisbet, R.A. (1967) *The sociological tradition.* London: Heinemann.

Oppenheimer, M. et al. eds. (1991) *Radical sociologists and the movement: experiences, lessons, and legacies.* Philadelphia: Temple University Press.

Oppenheimer, M. (2020) In Memoriam. Dale L. Johnson (1934–2019). *Latin American Perspectives* 47/2: 173–174.

Parsons, T. (1970) On Building Social Systems Theory: A Personal History. *Daedalus* 99/4: 826-881.

Rex, J. (1961) *Key problems of sociological theory.* London: Routledge & Kegan Paul.

Reynolds, L. & Reynolds J., eds. (1970) *The sociology of sociology: analysis and criticism of the thought, research, and ethical folkways of sociology and its practitioners.* New York: McKay.

Reynolds, L. (1998) Two Deadly Diseases and One Nearly Fatal Cure: The Sorry State of American Sociology. *The American Sociologist* 29/1: 20-37.

Reynolds, L.T. (2022) A PAIR TO DRAW TO [sic]: The Forgotten Grassroots Radicalism of Dusky Lee Smith and Sidney M. Willhelm. *Sociological Imagination.* 57/2: 53-78.

Ritchie, S. (2021) *Science Fictions: Exposing Fraud, Bias, Negligence and Hype in Science.* London: Vintage.

Ryan, M.J. (2011) Timeline. In Ritzer, G. & Ryan, J.M., eds, *Concise Encyclopedia of Sociology.* Malden & Oxford: Blackwell.

Sklair, L. (1972) *Organized Knowledge: A sociological view of science and technology.* London: Granada.

Sklair, L. (1993) The siege mentality: The Rex-Parsons debate revisited. In H. Martins, ed. *Knowledge and Passion: Essays in Honour of John Rex.* London & New York: I. B. Tauris, chapter 7.

Smith, D.L. (1964) The Sunshine Boys; Toward a Sociology of Happiness. In Reynolds & Reynolds eds., *op cit.*, pp.371-87.

Smith, D.L. (1965) Sociology and the Rise of Corporate Capitalism. *Science & Society* 29/4: 401-418.

Wenger, M.G. (1986) The Marxist Tradition in American Sociology: An Empirical Examination. *The Insurgent Sociologist* 13/4: 23-38.

Willhelm, S. M. (1970) Who Needs the Negro? Cambridge, MA: Schenkman.

Willhelm, S. M. (1979) Martin Luther King, Jr. and the Black experience in America. *Journal of of Black Studies* 10 (September): 3-19.

Willhelm, S. M. (1983) *Black in a White America.* Cambridge, MA: Schenkman.

CHAPTER 2

(1985) SHENZHEN: A CHINESE "DEVELOPMENT ZONE" IN GLOBAL PERSPECTIVE. *DEVELOPMENT AND CHANGE* 16/4: 571-602. [COURTESY OF SAGE]

Preamble

In 1975, as a member of the Society for Anglo-Chinese Understanding I went on a one-month study tour of China. Since my early teens in Glasgow I had been a member of Habonim (The Builders), a Zionist youth movement where I learned about practical socialism and the kibbutz movement in Israel. I visited Israel twice and got a taste of life on a kibbutz (collective farm). When I began to read about the communes in China my interest in the possibilities of societies being organized along the lines of the kibbutz and the commune intensified. It did not take long for me to be thoroughly disillusioned about Zionism. Most of what we learned in Habonim about Palestine was that the Palestinians all fled voluntarily during the "War of Independence" or the *Nakba* (catastrophe) as the Palestinians called the loss of their homes and land. Some of my Jewish friends who emigrated have been active in the Israeli peace movement. I began as a textile technology student at Leeds University in 1960 and met many students from the Middle East on the course, including some Palestinians with whom I had many conversations about the creation of the State of Israel and how it had impacted their homeland and their families. I changed my course to sociology and philosophy in 1961 and began reading more widely about Zionism and Palestine. After much Holocaust-induced soul-searching I eventually left Habonim and Zionism in 1967. My belief in the prospects for genuine socialism in China lasted a good deal longer. The study tour of China in 1975, especially our visits to communes, made a very deep impression on me. This article and other publications illustrate my optimistic interest in the bold Chinese experiment to attempt to create "socialism with Chinese characteristics" as it was called at the time. Much of this article is based on interviews and discussions that took place during visits to Hong Kong and Shenzhen in the 1980s and later. 1 am greatly indebted to officials of the Hong Kong Chamber of Commerce and local scholars for advice and practical help (especially as I do not speak or read Chinese). My hope is that learning more about Shenzhen in the 1980s may increase our understanding of China in the new millennium.

Abstract

Since 1980 a new socio-economic form has been developing along the China-Hong Kong border, officially known as the Shenzhen Special Economic Zone (SSEZ) and considered by many to be an attempt to implant capitalism into the Communist society. The purpose of this article is to relate what is happening in Shenzhen to the problems of Third World development, and thus begin to evaluate the global significance of this important experiment.

China and Development Zones

This article attempts to throw light on three central problems of development in China and, by implication, the rest of the "Third World" (a concept that is now unfashionable but, in my opinion, still more useful than its alternatives). First, I look at the ways in which the creation of the SEZ in Shenzhen, the largest of four Zones (capitalized to indicate "export processing Zone") in southern China, fits into the widespread economic reforms inaugurated by the Third Plenum of the Eleventh Central Committee of the Chinese Communist Party (CCP) in December 1978. The SEZ economic policy raises the issue of the role of foreign investment (of all kinds) in general, and of the relationships between the People's Republic of China (PRC) and Hong Kong in particular. This is not only because of the overwhelming preponderance of Hong Kong capital in Shenzhen but also for more obvious though less quantifiable reasons. The dialectic between economic forces and political forces has produced an irreversible and continuing dynamic for change in relations between the PRC and Hong Kong. All cases have their unique characteristics, and this one more than most, but the Hong Kong-Shenzhen case is particularly instructive as an example of the intended and the actual role of foreign investment in development.

The people of the Zones and the institutions, both old and new, within which they operate are faced with an historically unique combination of circumstances. This was the first time that a sovereign Communist state so wholeheartedly set out to attract investment from the exponents of capitalist industrial, commercial, and management practices, and never before have such clear and relatively unfettered opportunities for profit-making and profit-taking been provided by a Communist state to capitalist entrepreneurs. While there are many cases of economic cooperation between Communist states and private or state capitalists (Wilczynski 1976), there is no precedent anywhere for what happened in Shenzhen in the first half of the 1980s. As we shall see, the events of the brief history of the SSEZ and the plans for its future go far beyond the sporadic and relatively random connections that have been made between capitalism and Communism in Eastern Europe and elsewhere over the past few decades. When Marx identified the mode of production as the key to the understanding of how any society works and to the explanation of how and why it changes as it does, he insisted that any given mode of production usually had to contend with the presence of other and in some respects competing modes. Mao, in his commentary on Stalin's *Economic Problems of Socialism in the Soviet Union*, implicitly took up this theme in his argument that Stalin had seriously underestimated the difficulty that any socialist society will have in exercising its hegemony within a capitalist world system (Mao 1977). Specifically, the problem arises of the extent to which the socialist mode of production can and does dominate capitalist relations of production in contemporary China. The special problem of the Special Economic Zones is how far the balance between socialism and capitalism has been tipped in favour of capitalism along the Hong Kong border.

I try to connect the experience of Shenzhen systematically with that of other economic Zones in other parts of the world. My argument is that some types of Zones will become increasingly important to the global economy and that they can potentially have quite positive consequences for balanced growth in underdeveloped economies, such as the PRC. This is not, of course, to deny the well documented ill effects that foreign investment has already had in many places (Frobel, et al. 1979), but to argue that there is nothing in principle that renders all types of economic Zones, with elements of capitalism or not, undesirable in practice for the workers in underdeveloped countries. This argument will take us to the fringe of a theory of development based on the shape of the global economy as it is becoming, rather than the shape of a global economy that is slowly receding into the past, while "theory" strives to keep pace with it. I propose that the central concept in this new theory of development must be that of the "development Zone", an idea that I expand upon and operationalize below.

Post-Mao Open Door

The Chinese economic reforms of the late 1970s, generally referred to now as the "post-Mao open door" economic policies, represented a real shift in strategy but not a real shift in goals for the Chinese government (Ma 1983). Except for relatively short periods, notably during the Great Leap Forward and the Cultural Revolution, Chinese economic policy had always been aimed at harnessing the best of foreign technology and methods for the benefit of the Chinese economy. Reluctance to rely on foreign capital and foreign techniques to the same extent as most other Third World countries was a result of the bitter experiences suffered at the hands of the Soviet Union in the late 1950s, and a keen eye for the worst consequences of neo-colonialism elsewhere. The much-vaunted policy of self-reliance meant not "rely on ourselves for everything" but "do not rely on foreigners for anything we can do for ourselves". During the Cultural Revolution, for example, turnkey projects for large chemical fertilizer factories were concluded with foreign companies. It is generally recognized that a major struggle over economic policy, which naturally had profound ideological and political effects, characterized the whole Mao era. The key to this struggle was the centralization-decentralization spectrum. The relevant levels or points on the spectrum have varied over time but they certainly have included the state, the economic regions, the provincial level, the counties, the communes (and constituent parts) and/or townships, enterprises, and households. As Schurmann (1966) and others have argued, it is important to realize that decentralization can mean many things, and in China since 1949 it clearly has. There have been several attempts to stimulate economic growth and social development through shifting the locus of decision making and altering the balance of resource allocation between levels. Even within the framework of a centrally planned economy, therefore, it is quite possible to legislate and practice a certain amount of decentralization. It can be further argued that in a country as large and diverse as China it is absolutely necessary to generate policies that will encourage some measure of decentralization in order that the economy and society will develop at all (see Schurmann 1966, Brugger 1977, and Gray & White 1982). In China, as elsewhere in the Third World and in parts of the First and Second Worlds too, the centralization-decentralization issue largely revolves around urban-rural relations and the relative positions of industry and agriculture. In his seminal speech "On the Ten Great

Relationships" delivered in 1956, Mao Zedong outlined an economic strategy that was to seize upon the faint indications that Marx and Engels had given of what a Communist society might actually look like. Breaking down the contradictions between town and country, between worker and peasant, between intellectual and manual labour, contradictions fostered by the material conditions and ideological constraints of feudalism and by the curious version of capitalism that was replacing it in the Third World was the key task. The speech is notable as much for its theoretical importance as for the fact that Mao devotes a good deal of it to discussing what would nowadays be called "regional policy". The second relationship he considers is between industry in the coastal region and in the interior; the fifth is between central and local authorities (Mao 1977a, 284-307). Mao's regional policy, like his whole economic policy, was thoroughly tempered by strategic military thinking. Throughout the 1950s, the 1960s, and the first half of the 1970s China felt threatened by actual wars conducted by the United States and its allies on its borders, with the declared aim of defeating Communism, and by potential war from a hostile Soviet Union. Regional self-sufficiency in the 1960s was reduced to the village (production team) level with the exhortation that everyone should "store grain, prepare for [the eventuality of] war". The origins of the rural small-scale industrialization policy, possibly the most successful in any large Third World country to date, are similarly related to the geo-politics of Chinese defence strategy. The military rationale of these decentralizing processes declined in the 1970s, stimulated by President Nixon's visit to Beijing in 1972, but the exposure of economic inefficiencies had to wait on the death of Mao in 1976 and the defeat of the Gang of Four and their followers. The campaign to discredit the Dazhai (model commune) experience, the gradual reform of the communes, and the drive to rationalize capital investment, all revealed a qualitatively new phase in the dynamics of centralization-decentralization in China. It would be quite wrong, however, to interpret these changes simply as a shift from decentralization to centralization or to imagine that the reversal of the policy of extreme regional self-reliance automatically meant the drift of power back to the centre. The economic reforms of the late 1970s inaugurated a process of what may be termed "selective decentralization". The key difference with previous decentralizations, however, was that whereas functional decentralization had been tried before (for example, the Soviet-style trusts of the Northeast in the 1950s), by the early 1980s a form of regional decentralization was being encouraged that presaged a radically new theory of development for China, one that owed little to Mao's Ten Great Relationships. It is in this context that the Special

Economic Zones and the general opening-up of the Chinese economy to foreign influence must be placed.

Foreign Investment in China

Given the recent political history of China (remember, this was written in 1985) the question must be asked: why would any sensible capitalist wish to invest in China? In order to understand the variety of forms that foreign direct investment (FDI) may take in China, which is the topic of the next section, we must investigate the several answers to this question. The first answer is the most obvious, namely, that capitalists will invest anywhere as long as they can see a better than average return on their capital in the long term. Though investors often hotly deny it, the main but not the only determinant of FDI is usually the cost of production, of which labour costs tend to be the single most important component. The perennial scandal of "sweatshop labour" is still with us. While China's wage rates are not the lowest in the world, or even in South East Asia, they are sufficiently low to be attractive to many foreign investors. All things being equal, which they rarely are and most certainly are not in China's case, one would expect China to be attracting its fair share of the available FDI, on the criterion of cost. By April 1985 the fourteen open cities that had been established as part of the "open door policy" were said to have attracted US$1.4 billion in foreign investment and technology transfer contracts (*Beijing Review* 15 April 1985, 8-9).). In addition, China has two quite special advantages over most Third World countries, providing the second and third answers to the question "why invest in China?" These advantages are the size of the potential Chinese market and the continuity of the clan system that connects overseas Chinese, even where they are hostile to Communism, with their kin at home. China is the most populous nation on earth, with a population of around one billion people, most of whom are young. One of the most visible effects of the economic reforms of 1979 and since has been the transformation from a low income, low inflation, and low consumption economy to one in which there are substantially increased incomes for numerous groups, moderate inflation, and a veritable consumer boom in the cities and some parts of the countryside. A sign of the times was the announcement in 1984 that peasants were to be subject to personal income tax, where previously a fixed percentage of production had been levied as a tax on the collective. The fact that even a small proportion of Chinese workers and peasants now have money to spend after they have bought the necessities of life, means that there are many millions of extra potential consumers in the global marketplace. Chinese planners are looking very

closely at all imports of consumer goods to try to ensure that domestic
factories rather than foreign manufacturers reap the benefits of these
potential (and in some cases already actual) sales. In the next section I shall
examine the impact that the promise of the "China market" has on FDI in
Shenzhen. Suffice it to say, at this point, that the entry of foreign goods or
goods produced with foreign investors into the domestic market is a factor
in many negotiations over FDI, inside and outside of Shenzhen. The South
of the country has traditionally and up to the present provided the bulk of
Chinese emigration, principally to Southeast Asia but also much farther
afield. Apart from Hong Kong (about 40 per cent of the present population
was actually born in the PRC), there are sizeable and influential Chinese
communities in Malaysia, Singapore, Thailand, and Indonesia. In all of
these countries, the Chinese are over-represented in business with respect to
their numbers, and they have always been wooed by the authorities in the
PRC who have consistently seen these overseas Chinese as economically
and politically worthwhile allies. Services and facilities for them now
constitute a veritable growth industry throughout China. The official interest
parallels and is thoroughly nurtured by the very strong links at the levels of
the clan, village, and kin. As we shall see, many overseas Chinese consider
investment in China as both a patriotic duty and a convenient way to help
their relatives. These three reasons, profitability, future markets, and kinship
therefore help to explain why, in some cases, foreign investors have
overcome their understandable reluctance when faced with the risks and
have committed capital in China. In order to facilitate the utilization of FDI,
the Chinese authorities announced in 1983 their intention to establish (in
addition to the Shenzhen and four SEZs already in existence) eight more
Zones for priority investment. These large areas: Beijing-Tianjin-Bohai
Bay, the nine municipalities and the fifty-seven counties of the Shanghai
Zone, the Wuhan Zone, and the Pearl River Delta Zone (which includes
Shenzhen), already have over 90 per cent of China's foreign investment.
The plan is to concentrate most of the future FDI in these areas where, it is
argued, it can be put to the most effective use most quickly. 222 key cities
have been designated in the eight Zones to transmit development to the
backward areas that surround them. In 1984, fourteen coastal cities were
opened up to relatively unrestricted foreign investment. The rationale for
this policy seems to be the classic neoliberal "trickle-down effect", now
somewhat discredited in the eyes of most radical planners (Friedmann &
Weaver 1979, chapter 5). As I shall argue below, the success of development
Zones depends on organic integration with the local economy, and not
trickles-down from foreign factories to it. While it would be rash to prejudge
the issue, several decades of development planning experience would

suggest that "trickle down" has little to commend it. It is only fair to add, however, that there is no single development strategy with very much to commend it on the available evidence, and that the choice of investment priority areas and open ports seems to be a predictable first step in any process of industrialization. There is a fourth factor, whose salience and complexity are of such dimensions that it merits separate consideration. This is the relationship of Hong Kong on the one side, and Shenzhen (and the rest of Guangdong province) on the other. It is important to realize that there has always been a substantial trading link between Hong Kong and the rest of China (Youngson, ed. 1983). Indeed, Hong Kong could hardly have prospered in the way that it has since the 1950s without the supplies of relatively cheap food, raw materials, and latterly oil from the PRC. While Chinese exports to Hong Kong increased almost twentyfold between 1960 and 1980, Hong Kong exports to China increased over fifty times, in money terms, in the same period, most of the increase being in the 1970s. More and more PRC exports to Hong Kong are being trans-shipped to third countries, indicating both the shortcomings of the Chinese transportation network and the residual resistance that some countries still have to doing business with China directly. The volume of trade and trade-related contacts between the South of China and Hong Kong has obviously increased enormously in the late 1970s and early 1980s. Most of these contacts take place in Guangzhou (Canton), the provincial capital, and in Shenzhen, the SEZ that covers the whole of the PRC side of the Hong Kong border. It is to Shenzhen, the most open door in China, that I now turn.

Origins of Shenzhen Special Economic Zone

Shenzhen SEZ is not so much a single Zone on the familiar Southeast Asian pattern, but more of a region within which a variety of different types of Zones co-exist. The territorial goals of regional planning often vie with the functional goals of economic growth. To this extent, Shenzhen is a microcosm of the Chinese development dilemma. Put simply, in order to have any chance of economic success Shenzhen needs hugely expensive inputs of infrastructure and skilled personnel. Neither the capital nor the other necessary resources nor the time are available to bring the whole of the SEZ up to the standard required for a fully modernized industrial, commercial, and cultural region, and so continual compromises have to be made between the demands of regional integrity, functional specialization, and the needs of investors which tend to arise, from an overall planning point of view, in an arbitrary fashion. This, I think, gives us the clue to the place of Shenzhen in the Chinese effort to achieve economic development.

It is unlike the other three SEZs (Zhuhai, Shantou, and Xiamen) in that it is much larger. The creation of Shenzhen is an attempt to build a modern, industrially based economy on what was, as recently as 1980, a relatively backward and technically primitive rural community. This seems to reflect the Maoist policy of self-reliant development, but this conclusion is more apparent than real. As with the eight Priority Investment Zones and the fourteen coastal cities, Shenzhen has been singled out for special treatment, primarily with respect to resources and the level of autonomy granted to enterprises operating within it. It is in these senses that the label of "selective regional decentralization", within the framework of a strictly and centrally planned economy, must be understood. While each of the Priority Zones has a clear and well established, or at least well intended, comparative advantage (for example, the heavy industry of the Northeast and the general industrial strength of Shanghai), the only obvious advantage of Shenzhen is its contiguity with Hong Kong. Of what, precisely, does Shenzhen's special treatment consist? Shenzhen's appetite for raw materials, capital, labour, and services has been gargantuan, and the level of satisfaction of this appetite has, by Chinese standards, been very high. Great changes have taken place in a very short space of time. The numbers of projects, the foreign capital invested, and the output value produced all rose substantially between 1980 and 1985. Behind the figures, however, there are several points to note. First, most contracts are for small-scale projects. In 1984 Shenzhen signed up only forty projects worth HK$10 million or more, and that was about half as many again as in 1983. Second, though industrial enterprises account for 70 per cent of the total number, in the total output value of the SEZ they accounted for only 16 per cent in 1983 and 23 per cent in 1984. Leaving aside agricultural contracts, the bulk of the investment in the Zone is still in property and tourist developments. Third, the difference between foreign capital promised and capital actually at work in the Zone (often labelled "capital committed"), is very large. It is not possible to produce a set of figures on actual capital from the contradictory data in the Chinese sources, and the figures on capital must be treated with caution. Nevertheless, the commitment of the government in Beijing to the success of the Zone has been evident from the level of material support, well over 3 billion Yuan (about 300 Yuan to the US dollar in the 1980s) have been spent on infrastructure alone to date. We can add to this a high level of political support which has been exemplified in frequent public pronouncements of the leadership, notably Deng Xiaoping (Paramount Leader) and Hu Yaobang (General Secretary of the Communist Party).

The level and forms of autonomy granted to Shenzhen (and the other SEZs) indicate not only the extent of decentralization in practice but also the selectivity necessitated by the existence of China's command economy. In 1983 the State Council fixed upper limits that could be authorized by various local authorities for projects involving foreign investment without reference upwards to the Ministry of Foreign Economic Relations and Trade in Beijing. The municipal authorities in Shanghai could approve investments of up to US$10 million, while those in Beijing and some other places had an upper limit of US$5 million. In Guangdong and Fujian, including all four SEZs, there were even higher upper limits to the FDI that the provincial authorities could approve. However, this autonomy is tempered by the proviso that where investments are relevant to the State Plan and/or involve aviation, railroads, ports, telecommunications, or offshore oil, they must be approved by the Ministry in Beijing. Given that the Sixth Five-Year Plan (1981-5) has over one hundred pages in translation on the "Various Economic Branches" alone (China 1984), one may well wonder exactly how much autonomy is left to the Shenzhen authorities. Initially, in 1979-80, Shenzhen like the other SEZs was controlled fairly tightly from Beijing. By the summer of 1981, however, the central authorities decided to give more autonomy to the SEZs, not directly but through the provincial Management Committees that had been set up to administer the Zones. Whether this was a result of the disappointing record of the SEZs in attracting foreign investment, or because the central authorities were becoming a little less nervous about the whole experiment (or both) is not entirely clear. On 1 January 1982, a new set of laws governing Shenzhen SEZ came into force, updating but not significantly changing the original SEZ laws of 1980. One difference is that while the 1980 version was promulgated from Beijing, the 1982 version was promulgated from Guangzhou. The Guangdong SEZ Management Committee has overall responsibility for all the Zones in the province and it answers directly to, and indeed is an organ of, the Provincial Government. The Management Committee works through Development Companies, whose legal and actual status is far from clear. They appear to be both administrative bodies and commercial actors. Since the Zones were established the administrative structures have changed several times (Wong & Chu 1985).

Organization of the Zone

The Zone authorities may be divided into general and specialized agencies. Of the general agencies the most important are the Shenzhen Development Company (SDC), and the China Merchants Steam Navigation Company (CMSN) located in Hong Kong and in effect the Development Company for Shekou, a relatively self-contained industrial Zone west of Shenzhen city and adjoining the Chiwan oil base, and usually treated separately by the Chinese. SDC has general overall administration and planning responsibility for the whole of Shenzhen SEZ except Shekou. Interviews with cadres from a variety of organizations in Shenzhen strongly suggested that while there was no single, clear administrative hierarchy, or at least none which everyone recognized, SDC was the channel through which most of the key decisions flowed. SDC, for example, was not only responsible for the infrastructure plan for the whole Zone, but it also engaged in its own enterprises with foreigners, in competition with other Shenzhen organizations. It had thirty-seven joint ventures in 1984, mainly in transport, property, livestock, and manufacturing, involving a capital expenditure of about HK$1 billion with another HK$8 billion of foreign investment committed for the future. A noteworthy project under discussion was the construction of a golf club with a well-known Thai partner. Another important agency is the Shenzhen Municipal Industrial Development Service Company (IDSC), whose chief cadre was also Vice Secretary General of the SEZ Management Committee. Whereas SDC had a finger in every pie, IDSC was primarily concerned with industrial investment and the provision of factory space. In fact, IDSC is probably the biggest landlord in Shenzhen, having cornered the market in new factory building in the Zone and also being involved in renting out residential and commercial buildings. The Company has accumulated a good deal of capital from rents and is now branching out into factory building for its own use, and the setting up of joint ventures on its own account. It is, therefore, in direct competition with SDC for the interest of potential foreign investors. In 1984 IDSC was negotiating with a Hong Kong bicycle manufacturer, a tobacco company from the Philippines, and a Japanese machinery manufacturer, amongst others. CMSN, the company responsible for Shekou, is unusual in that it is located in Hong Kong though it is a branch of a state-owned company of the Ministry of Communications in Beijing, and is a long-established entity not created solely for the job of SEZ administration. Indeed, the management of Shekou is only one, albeit increasingly important, of its many activities. To emphasize its difference, Shekou is referred to not as a SEZ but as SKIZ (Shekou Industrial Zone) in the copious glossy promotional literature distributed, though commercial, property, and tourist investment are by no means discouraged. The main emphasis in Shekou is clearly on industrial projects of all sorts, and in a short space of time an impressive industrial base has been established. Conventional wisdom has it that the accessibility and administrative skill of CMSN have played a major part in this success. Another difference between CMSN and the Shenzhen Development Companies is that CMSN permitted to raise loans in Hong Kong in order to finance infrastructural investment in Shekou. Between mid-1979 and mid-1982, thirteen million square feet of land were levelled for factory and house building, a 600-metre wharf was constructed, and roads, water, and power supplies were laid. An advanced telecommunications system installed by Cable & Wireless (UK) promises to give SKIZ the best telephone and telex links anywhere in China. By 1985 Shekou had attracted more than HK$1 billion in direct investment, and over fifty factories with foreign partners were in production. To service this rapid growth, over one million square feet of residential accommodation and nearly one-and-a-half million square feet of industrial and commercial floor space had been built in Shekou. This would have cost CMSN (very approximately) more than 100 billion Yuan. It is not known how much of this was actually borrowed on the Hong Kong money market, but a good deal of it probably was. Given the prevailing high interest rates, it can be safely asserted that much of the revenue CMSN receives from its successful joint ventures in SKIZ finds its way back to Hong Kong in the form of debt servicing. This is, presumably, a burden that weighs much less heavily, if at all, on the Development Companies in Shenzhen. In 2021 *Forbes* magazine valued SKIZ/CMSN at almost US$15 billion It was identified as a construction company employing around 50,000 people.

The specialized agencies in the Zone are numerous. All the major industrial branches have set up companies which fulfil the functions of bureaux of the local authority and, at the same time, separate commercial entities. The Shenzhen Petro-Chemical Industrial Company is a good example. It was established to co-ordinate the exploitation of the offshore oil which is being searched for in the area and has launched an ambitious investment plan for refining the oil and developing oil-based industries. A combined heat and power plant and an ethylene plant (to produce 180,000 tons of PVC per year) are only two of the dozens of projects for which foreign investment is invited. The company is looking for a 4 billion Yuan total investment over the long-term. At present (in the 1980s), the company's activities are restricted to a few rather primitive factories, manufacturing zips, plastic bags, and suchlike, but with the help of the Shenzhen branch of the Hong Kong and Shanghai Bank, they hope to expand quickly. Whereas the Petro-Chemical Company has plans (some would say dreams), the Shenzhen Municipal Electronic Industry General Company has already established a solid base in the Zone, particularly in the Shangbu area which has been designated as an electronics estate. For example, the Electronic Industry Company runs a colour television factory in a joint venture with partners from Guizhou and Hong Kong, which will also be producing printed circuit boards. A third specialized company is the Shenzhen Food and Drink

Development Company, notable for its joint-venture association with Pepsi-Cola in the Happiness Soft Drinks Factory. The Food and Drink Company not only produces and processes food and drink, but it also has several retail outlets in Shenzhen. Recent joint-venture agreements include one with a Belgian mineral water producer and another with a German brewery. There is clearly some duplication of functions between the specialized and the general agencies, in some cases very much like the sort of competition one might routinely find in a capitalist economy, in other cases more like genuine bureaucratic confusion. A regular complaint is that the potential foreign investor is often unable to discover which of the alternative agencies is the correct one to solve any particular problem, to give the required decision or to issue the necessary documentation. Of course, this is not a problem exclusive to Shenzhen or China. The pleas of foreign investors around the world for "one-stop offices" are frequent and well documented by the United Nations Industrial Development Organization (UNIDO 1980). What makes the issue more acute in China than elsewhere is the lack of a body of established and tested commercial or business law. This can have both advantages and disadvantages for firms already doing business in Shenzhen (or China as a whole), but it tends to be a disincentive for firms contemplating direct investment for the first time. The advantage of vague or non-existent laws is, of course, that more or less anything goes and that foreign investors, by virtue of their control of scarce capital and/or technological resources, will tend to have a great deal of informal bargaining power. For example, the American manager of the Happiness-Pepsi-Cola plant was threatened with closure by a municipal official because he had incomplete documentation. Doubting the legality of this threat, the manager simply ignored the threat and, in time, it was removed. The disadvantages inherent in the uncertain legal climate are more obvious. Many investors are unclear as to the exact legal status of the contracts they sign, and a trend to dispute arbitration clauses in contracts is discernible. The HK$70 million investment in the Nanhai Hotel, for example, a joint venture of CMSN, the Bank of China, Hong Kong and Shanghai Bank, and the Miramar Hotel Company (a luxury project advertised as a service for the offshore oil industry) has an external disputes arbitration procedure written into the contract. The Kader Company (of Hong Kong), one of the largest employers in Shekou, has been faced with another type of problem: Kader contracted with CMSN to produce household goods in their factory in SKIZ and to sell an agreed amount on the domestic market, but in 1984 nothing was, in fact, sold in the domestic market due to opposition from the Shenzhen customs authorities. It was not clear who had the legal jurisdiction in this case. The Chinese authorities are obviously concerned about such matters. The issue of investment protection was on the agenda for President Reagan's visit in 1984 and was the subject of serious and continuing discussions in Beijing. Eventually, an Arbitration and Consultancy office for business was set up in Shenzhen in February 1984.

Shenzhen and Hong Kong

Almost all of these issues, of theoretical interest to the rest of us, are of intense personal interest to the people of Hong Kong. No one needs to be reminded that Britain's lease on the New Territories will expire in 1997 and, with it, effective control of Kowloon and Hong Kong. The Chinese government began to press for a speedy resolution of existing problems in 1983, and there is little doubt that new administrative arrangements will be in force by the late 1980s. There is one school of thought that holds the view that Shenzhen, and the other SEZs, were created precisely to demonstrate to the people of Hong Kong, and particularly the business and professional communities, that the PRC was quite capable of running a modern commercial society, albeit in a small enclave, and that the people of Hong Kong need have no fears for the future, summed up in the policy of "one country, two systems". The problem is to reconcile this with the supposed benefits, and the actual effects, of foreign investment in Shenzhen, most of which have come, so far, from Hong Kong. The stated intention of the Chinese authorities in setting up the SEZs was no different from that of most other Third World governments engaged in the same activity. The point of economic Zones is to attract foreign capital in the hope of earning foreign currency and stimulating the local economy.

The question of foreign currency earnings is very much more complex than it at first appears. As I have already suggested, the Chinese are having to spend a great deal of money on infrastructure before substantial amounts of FDI can be attracted into the SEZs. In a pioneering attempt to quantify the issue David Chu of the Chinese University of Hong Kong has estimated that the Chinese will have to spend 3.67 billion Yuan up to the year 2000 in urban and industrial infrastructure alone (Chu 1982, 19). This seems a rather conservative figure. By the end of 1984 the Shenzhen authorities had already spent over 3 billion Yuan on infrastructure. All the signs from Shenzhen are that the pace of urban and industrial development is quickening rather than slowing down, and that a great deal more money will have to be spent on basic infrastructure. A certain amount of this capital investment in Shenzhen might, in the normal course of events, have had to be spent, in any case, to meet the growing needs of the indigenous population, but we are safe in assuming that without its status as a Special Economic Zone, expenditure on infrastructure in the area would have been a very great deal less. While most of the money spent and services utilized in this infrastructure work would have originated in China, and so would have no direct impact on the foreign-currency position, some inputs have certainly been bought in from abroad and so represent a direct drain on China's reserves of foreign currency. For example, the telecommunications system being installed by Cable and Wireless, even though it is in the form of two joint ventures with Chinese partners (the Shenda Telephone Company and the Huaying Oilfield Telecommunications Company), will prove costly to the Chinese. Another area in which infrastructural expenditure will tend to involve large amounts of foreign currency is in oil-related activities, though the Chinese are striking relatively hard bargains with the foreign oil companies in the exploration stage. There is, of course, another side to this coin. Some infrastructure projects themselves have attracted foreign investment. The major example is the highly ambitious multi-billion Hong Kong dollar investment plan for a new town at Futian and a superhighway connecting Guangzhou, Shenzhen, and Zhuhai, activated by Hopewell Holdings Ltd, a major Hong Kong property developer. The New Town Company is a thirty-year joint venture between Shenzhen Development Company (SDC), which is putting up the land, and Hopewell, which is responsible for raising the total capital for the venture, said in the company's promotional brochure to be HK$2,000 million, or about 500 million Yuan. Some of this will, no doubt, end up on the credit side of China's foreign-exchange dealings. It is also the case that wholly owned subsidiaries of foreign firms are formally expected to pay for the infrastructure for their own factories, but this somewhat unworkable requirement seems more honoured in the breach than in the observance. There are, in any case, very few wholly foreign-owned enterprises in Shenzhen. It is not only in the provision of infrastructure, however, that Shenzhen incurs foreign-exchange losses or gains. As the research on economic Zones in other parts of the world indicates (for example, UNIDO 1980), there are several foreign-exchange costs to be set against actual foreign-exchange earnings from ongoing business. First, there is the question of inputs. Where a foreign or joint-venture manufacturer uses only local materials, machinery, services or labour then all of the foreign-exchange earnings (after the normal deductions stipulated in the contract) will be retained in the host country. This, by all accounts and certainly in China, is a very rare state of affairs. In full-blown export processing Zones there may be very little local material input, machinery will be imported, and technical and managerial services will be predominantly sourced from abroad. All these must be paid for in currency or kind. Only the labour (usually young women working at relatively low rates of pay) and the basic utilities will be locally provided. The mechanism of transfer pricing, whereby transnational corporations, large or small, set the prices for intra-firm purchases of machinery, materials, services etc., may seriously undermine the foreign-currency earnings of the host country, while inflating the cash volume of business being transacted. This is a complex question and one on which corporate accountants have exhibited great creativity. This undoubtedly occurs in China.

The second leak in the foreign-currency bucket is the outflow in the form of consumer spending on foreign goods. The classic direct case of this is along the Mexico-USA border, where a high proportion of the wages paid by US firms to Mexican workers in the maquiladoras (duty-free factories) finds its way back into the United States via the supermarkets and other retail outlets on the American side of the border (Martinez 1978, especially chapters 6 and 7, and Sklair 1993). The Hong Kong-Shenzhen border is, of course, not of this type, though the stated intention of the Chinese authorities is to open it up gradually for access from the south and to seal off Shenzhen from the rest of China to the north. Nevertheless, a veritable flood of goods from Hong Kong, largely but not entirely consumer goods, has been filling the shops of Shenzhen in recent years. As I noted earlier, the rate of growth of imports from Hong Kong has been much faster than that of exports to Hong Kong. Guangdong province, and increasingly Shenzhen SEZ, is accounting for more and more of these imports. This, of course, means a drain on foreign currency, though it can be persuasively argued that the Chinese mark-up on foreign goods, particularly those with prestigious associations, more than offsets the import cost to the enterprise involved, at the expense of the local consumers. Economists have laboured hard and long to work out the net effect of all these positive and negative capital flows. My purpose here is merely to indicate the complexity of the issue.

Economic Zones and Local Economy

The second main intention in the establishment of economic Zones is to stimulate the local economy. This is usually interpreted to mean the creation of employment and the upgrading of local and national economic activity, particularly in terms of technological progress (see Dunn 1999 on EPZ issues in the Caribbean). The employment-creating function of economic Zones is, again, quite problematic. Some critics argue that the relevant datum is not the number of jobs created, but the cost per job of the incentives offered to attract the foreign investor. The most thorough discussion of this issue has centered around the case of the Irish Republic (McAleese 1977, National Economic and Social Council 1982, see also Sklair 1988b) and there is evidence that the Chinese had been paying close attention to the Irish experience at that time. We find on the Shannon website on Tuesday 18th June 2019, "The relationship between Shannon and China dates back almost four decades to 1980 when Mr Jiang Zemin, who would later become President of China, led a Chinese Government delegation to study the Shannon Free Zone model, which has since been adopted across China with the development of their hugely successful Special Economic Zones."

In purpose-built Zones like Shenzhen, costs per job can be extremely high, especially if one inserts infrastructure into the equation. Another important consideration in Shenzhen is that the creation of the Zone has drawn many skilled workers, technicians, and managers from other parts of China, where they will be sorely missed. Indeed, there are strong indications that enterprises outside Shenzhen have been, in some cases, so unwilling to lose such labour that they have prevented the transfer of their employees to the Zone. The creation of jobs in foreign-owned or foreign-run enterprises in Shenzhen has thrown up a whole series of novel problems for both Chinese workers and Chinese officials. Workers are recruited by Labour Service Companies, one for Shekou and one for Shenzhen. These are multi-functional organizations, combining the roles of employment agency, administrators of wages and conditions, and the final authority on whether or not an unsatisfactory worker will be fired. As knowledge of the opportunities in the Zone spreads throughout the rest of China, more and more people write directly to the Labour Service Company to enquire about jobs. The Company, when it has suitable employment, will contact the relevant local government department for the potential employee and permission may or may not be forthcoming, encouraged or discouraged by the individual's own work unit. The Labour Service Company also recruits workers directly through public advertisements, requests to provincial authorities and, presumably, through personal contacts of cadres and workers already in employment in the Zone. In these ways, the permanent workforce in manufacturing industry, services, and transportation has grown to over 10,000 between 1979 and 1984. Out of the total SEZ population of about 250,000, including the large numbers of farmers, there are said to be about 100,000 people from outside Guangdong province in the Zone. A large and continually changing proportion of these make up the temporary workforce, mainly engaged in the massive and complex task of building and organizing the infrastructure. Employers generally approach the Labour Company once or twice a year with a list of their labour requirements, though it is not unknown for a foreign employer, particularly one with prior experience of operating in China, to recruit labour directly. In any case, the worker in a Shenzhen foreign-run enterprise differs from his or her counterpart elsewhere in China insofar as conditions of employment and termination are set out in a contract. The "iron rice bowl" whereby a Chinese worker cannot be dismissed without another job being made available has registered a definite hairline fracture in Shenzhen, and this is spreading to the rest of China. In Shekou, the Labour Service Company (an agent of CMSN) also acts as the banker for the workers' wages. The practice in 1984 was that the foreign employer paid the total nominal wage fund (about HK$800 per worker per month) directly to the Labour Service Company in Hong Kong dollars (in the 1980s the US$ was worth about 8 HK$). The Labour Service Company deducted about 20-30 per cent for the welfare fund to pay for pensions and some medical expenses and, via the Bank of China, paid 90 per cent of the remainder as wages in local currency and the other 10 per cent in Foreign Exchange Certificates, thus permitting access to certain categories of restricted consumer goods. The average take-home wage rose from 131Yuan in 1983 to 174 Yuan in 1984 (as reported in *Beijing Review* 7 January 1985, 37). The agreement between CMSN and foreign investors in Shekou appears to involve a profits guarantee scheme under which the employers are entitled to hold back part of the wage fund to offset trading losses. It is not entirely clear how this system is supervised or how, if at all, the workforce is kept informed. Nevertheless, workers in Shekou earn relatively high wages by Chinese standards, and probably enjoy better than average housing, canteen, and other facilities. State-run enterprises, in which most of these workers would have been employed before, have not been uniformly noted for their open accounting methods. Labour Service Company control of the distribution of wages (they claim not to interfere in the setting of wage levels) in Shekou appears to be more stringent than in Shenzhen itself. In Shenzhen city at least one joint-venture enterprise resisted attempts by the local Labour Company to take the wage fund, and a compromise had to be reached. The average wage in 1984 was higher in Shenzhen than in Shekou though wage rises built into Shekou contracts suggest that the position will be reversed over the next few years. In September 1984, a new wage system was introduced in Shenzhen with the clear indication that the prevailing relatively egalitarian structure was to be replaced with a more incentive-based scheme to improve productivity. Cost of living subsidies were to be phased out, and higher wages would compensate for the rising cost of living in the Zone. Such changes do not diminish the control that the Labour Service Companies, and through them ultimately the state, exert on the individual worker. For example, there are indications that the state's one child policy on birth control is being directly enforced through the withholding of women's wages in Shenzhen. In one case that came to light during an interview, a woman worker in a foreign-run factory was forced to leave because the Labour Service Company had refused to hand over her wages for several months. She already had three children and had not agreed to sterilization. Despite the protestations of the foreign manager, unhappy to lose a good and trained employee, she left the factory, presumably to find a less visible and more desirable job. In another case, the arrival of second babies to women in a Hong Kong-owned factory cost the mothers the promotions and wage rises which they would otherwise have had. The signs are that the one-child policy may be more difficult to promote in places like Shenzhen, where the relatively high standards of living minimize the effects of the economic penalties associated with larger families. Most of the women cadres in the Shenzhen Development Company are engaged in birth control work, which is regarded here, as in the rest of China, as an almost entirely female concern. Women constitute something over half of the factory workforce in Shekou and something less than half in Shenzhen as a whole. The sheer variety of industries in the Zone makes it difficult to generalize, but it is safe to say that while craft-based factories (furniture, metal work, engineering, and printing) tend to employ more men than women, assembly-type operations (electronics centered in the Shangbu district west of Shenzhen city, toys, food and drink, garments) tend to employ far more women than men. This is also the case in most export processing Zones, for many years this was also the pattern in the Mexican maquiladora (twin plant) factories (see Sklair 1993, and Tiano 1994). About 70 per cent of the workforce in manufacturing employment in the Shenzhen SEZ is female. If we add to this the work force in transportation (almost entirely male), in services (where the male bureaucrats probably outnumber female service workers), and resident workers engaged in construction, then the total permanent work force will turn out to be about half men and half women. While the sexual division of labour in China, in general, is somewhat less intense than in the rest of the world, it looks very much as if in the Special Economic Zone it is beginning to manifest itself much like that in export-processing Zones all over the world. The depressing litany of "nimble-fingered girls" (Elson & Pearson 1981) and their enforced tolerance of low wages and high labour discipline is being imposed by Chinese cadres and foreign investors alike. It is too early to judge how far these trends will prevail in China. The relations between the foreign investors and their managers in the factories on the one hand, and the local authorities (Labour Service Companies, Development Company etc., and the direct state officials) on the other hand, may or may not be constrained by the relations of each to particular groups of workers. In the absence of independent unions these relations tend to be quite unsystematic, and the general impression is one of trial and error, rather than inflexible rules. There are, however, indications that the recently established Worker's Congress is taking a more militant attitude towards foreign management in Shenzhen, but very few foreign-run companies appear to have unions. By 1983-84 there were about a dozen foreign-invested factories in Shenzhen in a variety of mainly low value-added industries. The official list was as follows: Chi Tai Conti (animal feed); Jing Hua (electronics); Pepsi-Cola (Happiness Soft Drinks); Jiang Hua (marine engineering); Hong Kong and Shanghai (furniture); Far East (biscuits); China International (marine containers); Goodyear (printing); Kader (toys and household goods); Millies (various light industry); Huafa (electronics); Shen Li (plastics); and Peninsular (garments). There is no doubt that since the open-door economic policy was announced in 1979, the Chinese, at all levels of administration, have gradually come to believe that Western (including, of course, Japanese) methods of management and industrial organization must be adopted if the Chinese struggle for modernization is to succeed. During my interviews in Shenzhen in the 1980s (and later) most Chinese cadres and foreign managers constantly introduced the theme that Chinese workers had to be shown how to get used to Western methods. It is in this context that the second goal of the establishment of the Special Economic Zones, the stimulation and upgrading of economic activity, has to be understood and evaluated. The stimulation of economic activity and its relationship to foreign investment raises many of the fundamental issues with which I am concerned in this article. There are two main senses in which the Chinese expect foreign investment to stimulate economic activity. The first, and more obvious, is quantitative: foreign capital will create more factories, services, and facilities. The second is qualitative: foreign capital will bring in new and better techniques, organizational as well as technological. It may not be altogether fanciful to suggest that the Chinese are using Shenzhen to find out if Western (not necessarily capitalist) management styles can, in fact, work properly and efficiently with a PRC labour force, using Shenzhen, perhaps, as a vast Hawthorne experiment. Well into the new millennium an interesting study of the role of privacy as a test of the Hawthorne effect at a huge mobile phone factory in southern China (Bernstein 2012) provides tantalizing information on changing Chinese industrial practices from the shop floor.

Management's right to hire and fire raises both practical and theoretical issues in the Zone, as much for the local authorities as for the traditional opposition of labour and capital. In 1983 the Labour Service Company in Shekou was receiving requests from foreign managers to fire about six workers a month, on average. About five out of these six requests were allowed. Typically, workers would be fired for taking unauthorized or unannounced leave of more than three days, or where the workers proved impossible to train for the job. Such workers would be (in the official jargon) "returned to the Labour Company", where some, at least, might be re-located. Most foreign managers complained of compulsory overstaffing, and of how difficult it was to get rid of surplus and unsatisfactory workers, while the Labour Company argued that foreign investors used temporary labour and/or overtime in preference to employing sufficient numbers of workers. The struggle between "capitalist" methods of coping with the labour requirements resulting from uncertain and fluctuating demand, and the Communist iron rice bowl continues. On the outcome of this and similar struggles hangs the survival of socialism (and perhaps capitalism itself) in China. The theoretical issue raised by management's right to hire and fire, therefore, revolves precisely around the existence of a distinction between capitalist and non-capitalist (for the lack of a better term) organizational techniques. Indeed, it is to the establishment of this distinction, in theory and in practice, that the more thoughtful of the Chinese SEZ planners have publicly dedicated themselves. This comes through clearly, for example, in an interview with the mayor of Shenzhen, Liang Xiang, reported in the *Asian Wall Street Journal* (27 April 1984). The Central Committee of the CCP came to a historic decision on the matter in late 1984 in a manner that left no doubt that it was able to distinguish between its own economic reforms and capitalism. So, in this sense, it can be argued, Shenzhen (and all the other Zones) are not so much a testing ground for capitalism in China but the site of the struggle *between* capitalism and socialism. That the occasion for this struggle should be the introduction of private foreign capital into China is a circumstance that should appeal to the proponents of dialectical contradiction on both sides.

Global significance of Development Zones

On this basis, it is now possible to assess the global significance of the Shenzhen and, with it, to draw some general lessons for other Third World countries that have established or are establishing Zones of varying types. We can and, I think, must distinguish between Zones (typically but not exclusively of the small enclave type, perhaps the true export processing Zone) where multinational foreign investors are simply taking advantage of cheap labour to cut production costs and Zones where balanced socio-economic development is possible. The former tend to be dominated by what have been termed "footloose" industries with low levels of capital investment, utilizing imported materials and components, and involving little if any transfer of technology. The benefits of such enclave industry for the host country are superficial, if they exist at all. Consumer electronics, toys, and garments assembly in Asia, and many of the so-called twin factories along the Mexico-America border, fall into this category. Naturally, there are exceptions to be found even here, when special factors come into play and the presence of a particular factory stimulates a local industry or provides training in skills that can be re-utilized in the local economy. These outcomes are, however, uncommon, and as successive ILO (Edgren 1980) and UNIDO (1980) reports have documented, in some Zones the gradual replacement of the original engineering and textile businesses by electronics and garments signals decreased rather than increased economic possibilities for the host countries. It is important to consider this situation in its historical context. In 1971 UNIDO published an optimistic report, "Industrial Free Zones as Incentives to Promote Export-Oriented Industries" which was nicely in tune with critical trends at that time in the sociology of development, if not development economics (see also Botchie 1984). Briefly, the argument revolved around the best strategy that Third World countries could adopt to break out of the stranglehold of dependency that global capitalism was said to have imposed on its poorer trading "partners". Import Substitution (IS) had been tried but was found wanting, partly because of the tendency of multinationals to take over Third World manufacturing industries and turn IS to their own advantage. Export-led industrialization became the rallying call of the 1970s, and the rapid, and to many totally unexpected, emergence of the newly industrializing countries (NICs) around this time seemed to confirm the thesis. The connection was quickly made between the substantial foreign investment and manufacturing industries in many of the NICs, the existence of "economic Zones" (some NICs like Hong Kong and Singapore seemed to be all economic Zone) and their economic success. Industrial Zones and the packages of incentives to attract foreign firms, at almost any cost became the order of the day. UNIDO (1980) had estimated that there were about fifty genuine export processing Zones in operation in more than thirty countries and regions and perhaps another fifty in development or planned, and Diamond & Diamond (1983) found about 400 free trade and industrial Zones in seventy-eight countries. All of these countries usually offer substantial tax and duty concessions and operating subsidies as investment incentives for foreign firms. In many countries, including Ireland, China, and Egypt, the concessions of the Zones have spilled over into the rest of the country, so that for the foreign investors the idea of the economic Zone has as much a functional as a locational significance. Clearly, when this happens, the use of Zones to bring industry to relatively backward areas may be undermined since all other things being equal most firms will prefer to locate in relatively well-developed areas. This brings me to the second type of Zone, namely those where foreign investment in the form of joint ventures and/or wholly owned subsidiaries is used to upgrade the quantity and quality of manufacturing and service industry, and to pass on some of the benefits to the local population in the form of higher standards of living. I consider these Zones "Development Zones". Whereas most if not all Zones start out with these noble intentions, very few achieve them.

Apart from the commonly accepted social goals of development, there are at least three major dimensions along which the extent to which a Zone is becoming a development Zone may be measured. First, there is the question of linkages, for example, the share of imports (backward) and the share of exports (forward) of the firm's product that comes from and goes to the host economy. A rough guide is that the greater the extent of backward linkages (raw materials, manufactured components, and services) and the greater the extent of forward linkages (sales to intermediate-goods industries) achieved with the host economy, then the more likely is the creation of a Development Zone. Second, the higher the proportion of value added in the host country to the eventual value of the finished products, then the more likely is the creation of a Development Zone. Third, the smaller the proportion of expatriate to indigenous managers, technicians, and skilled personnel, the more likely is the creation of a Development Zone. The Shannon Industrial Zone in the Republic of Ireland is generally recognized to be the most successful Zone in the modern world, in my terms, a mature Development Zone. However, research by outside consultants (The Telesis Report) commissioned by the Irish Government to assess Irish industrial growth specifically drew attention to the poor linkages and low value-added performances of foreign firms in Ireland (see National Economic and Social Council 1982). My own field research confirms this picture for Shannon and the surrounding Midwest region (Sklair 1988b, chapter 5). Of the thirty-six foreign-owned firms interviewed, which included some of the biggest and brightest multinationals in Ireland, not one could claim substantial or even moderate linkages. A few firms, particularly in electronics and other high technology fields, had some local value-added content in their final products but it was unclear whether these purchases were actually manufactured locally or simply foreign products which had been bought locally. Although detailed studies would be necessary to confirm these findings in Zones elsewhere in the Third World, the indications that we have from the research I have already cited suggest that even with all its deficiencies, Shannon can be considered, in my terms, as the best example anywhere in the world of a Development Zone.

That Shenzhen aspires to be a Development Zone is as undeniable as is the fact that the Chinese planners are aware of the disappointing performance of export-processing Zones all over Asia and beyond. Is there, however, any reason at all to expect that Shenzhen (and other Chinese Zones) will escape this fate? I think that, despite the heavy odds stacked against Shenzhen's success, there are at least three credible causes for optimism, each of which provides substantive and analytical support for the thesis that development Zones may provide excellent prospects for Third World development. The first and second factors concern size: the size of the Zone and the size of the country. It seems obvious that the development effects of a single industrial estate of foreign firms will be strictly limited. The all-important backward linkages will only be possible where the economic area, inside or outside the Zone, is sufficiently large for local producers to thrive in sufficient numbers to present themselves as suppliers of the materials, components, and service needs of the multinationals. There are several reasons why foreign firms import rather than buy their supplies locally. Although some countries have local content clauses written into contracts as a condition of start-up grants, tax holidays, or duty-free trade, few investors appear to actively promote the local supply of materials, components, or high-level services. Even where they do, very few are successful. This is what is necessary if the problem of backward linkages is ever to be overcome. On the other side, governments would themselves need to gear their domestic industrialization programmes to take advantage of such opportunities. Roughly the same can be said for forward linkages. None of these policies, even where they are acknowledged as is the case in Ireland, seems to be working. What is quite certain is that if they are to work, it will be in large, multi-functional Zones, not small enclaves. In this respect, and despite their enormous infrastructure costs, both the Midwest of Ireland, as it has radiated from Shannon, and Shenzhen and Shekou give some prospects of success. In the case of Ireland, we can say that the base for such a Development Zone is clearly already established, though not yet achieved. The gamble of trying to turn Shenzhen (quarter of a million people in 327 square kilometres) into a special economic Zone seems less wild when seen in these terms. Information on linkages in Shenzhen is sparse, no doubt reflecting the lack of actual linkages. The Chinese are building a comprehensive industrial base in the Zone, and over the next five to ten years the presence or absence of linkages between the foreign-run and the indigenous economies will be a key measure of the extent to which a Development Zone has been created.

The size of China, and specifically of its domestic market, is the second criterion of the potential success of the Zone. Here we must distinguish the size of the sovereign state; the size of the actual domestic market; and the size of the potential domestic market, comprising actual and realistic potential consumer purchasing power. Obviously, an export-processing strategy makes more sense for Hong Kong, Singapore, and small island states than it would do for China as a whole and, as a corollary, economic unions (common markets, etc.) among small, contiguous states might go some way to creating viable joint domestic markets. Political, ethnic, and military obstacles conspire to make this no more than a pious hope in most parts of the world today. Even in China, the forces of economic provincialism are not entirely defeated by the state plan, though the measure of the central control of agricultural and industrial incomes achieved means that intra-regional inequalities (particularly in consumer purchasing power) tend to outweigh interregional inequalities. China has the advantage of a widely spread, rapidly increasing, and extremely numerous population of consumers already in a money economy, and large groups of these consumers are experiencing a relatively rapid rise in purchasing power. The Chinese authorities, therefore, should be in a good position to ensure that indigenous rather than foreign manufacturers will benefit from this. And this brings me to the third criterion on which some optimism on the outcome of China's attempt to build Development Zones rests: namely the fact that China is a centrally planned economy and society and not a capitalist economy and society. Despite the claims of the convergence school (some less superficial than others) that socialist societies are becoming more capitalist and that capitalist societies are becoming more socialist (for which read free-enterprise and state-run respectively), the essential differences between the Chinese and, say, the American or British or Indian economies and societies far outweigh the similarities. The key to the differences is the State Plan in China, and what it tells us about the way in which social and economic forces are harnessed (or fail to be properly harnessed, as the case may be) in order to achieve definite, and often numerical, targets. This is not the place to argue whether these plans actually work, though my assumption is that they are not necessarily inferior to the so called "invisible" hand of the capitalist market. What seems absolutely clear is that if a country is trying to establish a Development Zone, bearing in mind the necessity to create substantial linkages, high value-added manufactures, and an indigenous cadre of technicians and managers, then the type of control over the economy and the workforce that a central plan when it is working properly can provide is the *sine qua non* for success. For example, the achievements of the Irish industrial effort were registered despite the actions

of many Irish bankers, investors, and successive governments, whose
inability or unwillingness to promote the linkages made possible by the
substantial foreign investment in Ireland was so lambasted in the Telesis
report. It remains to be seen whether the Chinese can build in sufficient
flexibility to their plans. The indications, as of 1985, are mixed. The centre
is certainly preparing to loosen its grip in certain areas of economic action,
such as the system of agricultural procurement and pricing policies. In the
field of foreign trade the influx of Japanese consumer electronic imports and
commercial vehicles shows unsurprisingly that China, in common with
most other countries, is unable to compete for cost and quality in these
products. However, China imports virtually no passenger cars and few of
the other luxury goods that make such dismal reading in the trade statistics
of so many "poor" countries. Over the last few years there have been rising
imports of raw and intermediate materials for the booming Chinese textile
and domestic light industries, chemical inputs for agriculture, and much
small and medium capital equipment. The Sixth Five-Year Plan is very
explicit and clear on this point: "All materials imported directly by local
governments or the various departments should be brought into the unified
plan of the state. We must not indiscriminately import any equipment,
consumer goods in particular, which can be made by China, in order to
protect and promote our national industry" (China 1984, 159). Whether a
statement from the plan actually carries more weight in China than
exhortations from indigenous bourgeoisies and nationalist governments in
other Third World countries is a question that only time, and a continued
close perusal of the trade statistics, will answer. The costs of failure and the
benefits of success in such a policy will weigh very heavily on the scales
when the outcome of the Shenzhen experiment, and others like it in China,
come to be assessed. There is ample evidence to accept that the reasons why
the export-processing and economic Zone strategies of most Third World
countries have had such limited effects are bound up with the failure to
establish backward and forward linkages between foreign-run firms and
indigenous industry. We can add the generally low level of value-added
content accounted for by the host-country economic activity and the
predominance of expatriate as compared to local technicians and managers.
Linkages and value added are connected quite directly insofar as an
economy that is unable to supply needed components and processed
material for the types of industries that multinationals are typically engaged
in, is also unlikely to be able to provide a source of high value in the
processes of production carried out within its borders. There is a contingent
but not uncommon connection between these shortcomings and the lack of
a substantial technical and managerial cadre. The creation of a university in

Shenzhen in 1983 geared to the needs of the SEZ indicates that the Chinese planners are well aware of this. Links between universities, technical training, and export processing are also found (later) in Ireland, the maquilas of Mexico, and elsewhere (see Sklair 2002, 135-38).

It is unrealistic to expect that Third World countries can achieve anything approaching balanced social and economic growth at a national level, a goal for which most if not all First World countries are still striving, without the construction of genuine Development Zones. These must be much larger than the traditional industrial estates: they must be multi-functional; they must be organically integrated into central plans; and they might very profitably involve foreign-run firms and joint ventures. It follows that while there is no guarantee that a socialist society like China could achieve its social and economic goals through the creation of Development Zones, it does stand a better chance of success than societies characterized by private ownership of the means of production, distribution, and exchange. It is not to deny the economic achievements of the NICs to point out that their economic and social goals are not those of China. Even with China's recent policy changes in the areas of the distribution of incomes, goods, and services, and the increasing inequalities that they legitimize, the country is still one of the least inegalitarian societies in the world. Whether this would survive "economic growth" is a contentious issue. The whole point of my use of the concept of Development Zones is that it reflects social as well as economic goals, the precise nature of which is specific to each social system, though all social systems reflect the needs of the human communities that make them up and all human communities share an irreducible minimum of needs. Shenzhen stands as a great social experiment, and its global significance lies in its salience for some of the most crucial divides of our time. In Shenzhen, the underdeveloped world faces the developed world, socialism faces capitalism, indigenous industry faces foreign investment. The outcome of the attempt to create a genuine Development Zone in Shenzhen will count heavily towards the successful modernization of China as a socialist society, and whether or not other Third World countries are encouraged to take the same path.

Second Thoughts

The spectacular transformations of Shenzhen and hundreds of other cities in China since the 1980s dictate many second thoughts on what I wrote in 1985. My naïvely optimistic prediction that "Development Zones" in China and elsewhere would help create a socialism with Chinese characteristics that would spread throughout the Third World and bring prosperity and happiness to the masses did not happen. The history of SEZs in general has been enhanced in recent research by Neveling (2015, 2020) who usefully analyzes the place of special economic Zones from the perspective of the Cold War. Meanwhile, in China, in stark contrast to socialism, a hybrid "capitalism with Chinese characteristics" emerged which led to an increase in inequality all over the country. An expert from the Hinrich Foundation in Hong Kong (motto: "Advancing sustainable [sic] global trade") tells the remarkable story of Shenzhen, reporting that by 2014 the SEZ had 58,000 foreign-invested businesses (many in the service sector) valued at US$15 billion (Olson 2016). As a regular visitor to Shenzhen between 1983 and 2018 I can vouch for Olsen's account. Two short videos on life in Shenzhen, both from 2019, make an interesting contrast. The first is a blatantly urban boosterist account from NBC News in the USA (https://www.youtube.com/watch?v=40EMue19vgo), while the second (https://www.youtube.com/watch?v=ydPqKhgh9Mg) from Bloomberg, has a much more "dystopian" vision.

Little did I think in the 1980s that when about 30 years later I came to write a book on iconic architecture, Shenzhen would be featured in architecture magazines all over the world (Sklair 2017, 183 and *passim*). From the perspective of the 2020s, the 1980s is a completely different world, dominated not so much by various forms of capitalism but by one increasingly globally co-ordinated neoliberal capitalism. As Minor (1994) shows, the expropriation of foreign-owned businesses in most Third World countries has declined dramatically and is now rare. My optimism about the prospects for genuine Development Zones in China and elsewhere failed to anticipate that in recent decades much of the First, Second, and Third World has been transformed into export-processing Zones of various types. What was commonly referred to in the media and in official reports as "multinational corporations" with the emphasis on "multi" (and still is in some quarters) is now transnational corporations, with the emphasis on "trans" and, frequently, "global corporations", some of which come from the Second and Third Worlds (Sklair & Robbins 2002). The potency of the struggle between capitalism and socialism largely dissipated with the dissolution of the USSR on Christmas day 1991 and the not entirely surprising entrance of China into the neo-liberal World Trade Organization (WTO) in December 2001 (see Chorev 2005). As a consequence, my "second thoughts" began to focus on the transformation of the Chinese economy and the concomitant rise of inequalities in China. In the 1980s China was seen as one of the most equalitarian societies in the world, despite being very poor. This has changed dramatically in the years of the Chinese economic miracle, a miracle born of "socialism with Chinese characteristics", and "Globalization with Chinese characteristics" following in its wake (Henderson et al. 2013). In a revealing ethnographic survey of the important SEZ Xiamen, Wank (1999) tells the story of how China is being commodified. A quote from one of his informants gives much food for thought: "Marx said that the market economy is social relations (*guanxi*). We used to read him in political study to understand socialism but I find him an inspiration for doing business" (Boss Short Pants, 1989 interview with the author, ibid). Complementing the observation of Boss Short Pants, in her book on the rural middle classes, Diane Davis (2004) argues that it is the success of the state to control these social groups, thus disciplining both capital and labour, that is the key to successful development. While her case studies focus on Taiwan and Mexico, her argument seems apt for transformations in post-Mao China. One more transformation in Chinese society deserves mention, namely the changing roles and ideological formations of Chinese intellectuals in the post-Mao era (Huang Ping 1991, Mok 1998).

After the turn of the twentieth century we find an interesting set of articles by scholars in India on the SEZs in China (see, for example, Sarma 2007, Tantri 2012, Gebhardt 2013), and Jayanthakumaran (2002) provides a global survey. Under the Data Collection Abroad Programme funded by the Indian Council of Social Science Research, Tantri (2013) carried out field work in Beijing and Shenzhen. This detailed macro-economic study provides an update to my original article, explaining the key role Shenzhen EPZ plays "in China's integration with the world economy". Generally, these scholars compare the situation for Special Economic Zones in India (which date from the 1960s) very unfavourably to that in China, particularly with reference to China's land use policy (one notable exception is the critical assessment of Gopalakrishnan 2007, see also Goodburn & Knoerich 2021a &b).

The ecological implications of the Chinese version of capitalist globalization were barely recognized in the 1980s. In fact, the ecological consequences of industrial factory production and its impact on working class consciousness have both been largely ignored in China as elsewhere, a notable exception being two recent articles by Huber (2017, 2019) on factories in the USA. However, in the context of the potential greenhouse gas emissions from the massive Belt and Road Initiative (BRI) this has become a major issue. There is little serious treatment, so far, of ecological impacts in the semi-official *China Belt and Road Initiative Journal.* However, independent researchers are beginning to provide much evidence of its potential ecological impacts (see, for example, Hilton 2019, Saha

2019, and Griffiths and Hughes 2021). Originally launched in 2013 as "The Silk Road Economic Belt and 21st-Century Maritime Silk Road Development Strategy" it was aimed at bringing development, prosperity and "regional connectivity". The Belt and Road has become a masjor (mainly infrastructure) project incorporated into the Chinese Constitution in 2017 which made internal criticism dangerous. By the 2020s, despite substantial critical lobbying from the USA, around 200 countries appear to have signed up to the project. As BRI works have advanced, critics have begun to accuse China of neo-imperialism and debt-trap diplomacy.

The story of two books by the French economist Thomas Piketty (eminent critic of "bad" capitalism but not capitalism *per se*) sums up issues of heightening inequalities in China succinctly. As reported in the *Guardian* (31 August 2020), the first book (Piketty 2014) was widely praised for its critique of inequality in capitalist societies by the *Wall Street Journal* and most other mainstream media and by Xi Jinping (the President of China for the foreseeable future). The second book turns its focus on inequality in the rest of the world, especially China (Piketty 2020) quoted as follows (also from the *Guardian* as above): "So great was the [Chinese] communist disaster that it overshadowed even the damage done by the ideologies of slavery, colonialism, and racialism and obscured the strong ties between those ideologies and the ideologies of ownership and hypercapitalism, no mean feat". Piketty argues that China's wealth distribution to the top 10% and bottom 50% is "only slightly less inegalitarian than the United States and significantly more so than Europe" To cut a long story short, this second book was never published in China because Piketty refused to make the cuts demanded by the Chinese authorities. Piketty's research is based, he admits, on less than entirely reliable official economic data. For example, there is no inheritance tax in China, and therefore no data on inheritances. From 1978 to 2015 the share of the country's income held by the top 10% of China's population rose from 27% in the late 1970s to 41% by 2015, comparable to the levels of inequality seen in the USA. I did not anticipate in 1985 that what I later conceptualized as "the class polarization thesis" (Sklair 2002, 48-53 and *passim*) which characterizes most capitalist societies (the rich get much richer, the middle class becomes an increasingly economically insecure precariat, and the poor are always with us) would reproduce itself in communist China. Dunford et al. (2020) provide a more benign research-based report on the success and ongoing problems of poverty alleviation in China. In the *Guardian* article quoted above Piketty addresses the widely reported extravagance of wealthy Chinese: "So we find ourselves in the early twenty-first century in a highly paradoxical situation: an Asian billionaire who would like to pass on his fortune without paying any inheritance tax should move to Communist China" (see also, Milanovic 2014). My disillusionment with the prospects for genuine socialism in China is almost complete, leaving aside human rights violations, which we do at our peril. Sometimes China appears to be striving to become the strongest prop for capitalist globalization. Reinforcing this impression, in 2015 Beijing unveiled its "Made in China 2025" export policy (see Sutter 2020). Pioneering research on China's significant and growing investments in European corporations confirms this trend (see de Graaff & Valeeva 2021, and Henderson et al. 2021). An interesting coda to the story of the "struggle between capitalism and socialism as economic systems" is the argument that we cannot fully appreciate the advent of Neoliberalism unless we consider the influence of socialist economic thought on the tradition of neoclassical economics in the West and in Eastern Europe, and *vice versa* (see Bockman 2012, a very long scholarly paper with over 150 notes, but not a single mention of China). Bockman also discusses alternative versions of socialism. Relevant in this connection is the discussion of the place of socialism in Global History, a generally neglected topic (see Mark & Rupprecht 2020). One final second thought on the perils of doing research in a foreign culture and language was triggered by a recollection of a notable paper by one of my former PhD students (Ladino 2002).

References

Bernstein, E.S. (2012) The Transparency Paradox: A Role for Privacy in Organizational Learning and Operational Control. *Administrative Science Quarterly* 57/2: 181-216.

Bockman, J. (2012) The Long Road to 1989. *Radical History Review* 112: 9-42.

Botchie, G. (1984) *Employment and Multinational Enterprises in Export Processing Zones: The Case of Liberia and Ghana.* Geneva: ILO.

Brugger, B. (1977) *Contemporary China.* London: Croom Helm.

China (1984) *The Sixth Five-Year Plan (1981-1985).* Beijing: Foreign Languages Press.

Chorev, N. (2005) The Institutional Project of Neo-Liberal Globalism: The Case of the WTO. *Theory and Society* 34/3: 317-355.

Chu, D. (1982) The Costs of the Four SEZs to China. *Economic Reporter* [Hong Kong] (May): 18-20.

Davis, D.E. (2004) *Discipline and Development: Middle Classes and Prosperity in East Asia and Latin America.* New York & Cambridge: Cambridge University Press.

de Graaff, N. (2020) China Inc. Goes Global: Transnational and National Networks of China's Globalizing Business Elite. *Review of International Political Economy* 27/2: 208–33.

de Graaff, N. & Valeeva, D. (2021) Emerging Sino–European Corporate Elite Networks. *Development & Change.* 52/5: 1147–1173.

Diamond, W. & Diamond, D. (1983) *Tax-Free Trade Zones of the World.* New York: Matthew Bender.

Dunford, M., et al. (2020) Who, where and why? Characterizing China's rural population and residual rural poverty. *Area Development and Policy* 5/1: 89-118.

Dunn, L. (1999) Export Processing Zones: A Caribbean Dilemma. *Development in Practice* 9/5: 601-605.

Edgren, G. (1980) *Spearheads of Industrialization or Sweatshop in the Sun?* Bangkok: ARTEP-ILO.

Elson, D. & Pearson, R. (1981) Nimble Fingers Make Cheap Workers: An Analysis of Women's Employment in Third World Export Manufacturing. *Feminist Review* 7: 87-107.

Friedman, J. & Weaver, C. (1979) *Territory and Function.* London: Edward Arnold.

Frobel, F., et al. (1979) *The New International Division of Labour.* Cambridge: Cambridge University Press.

Gebhardt, C. (2013) Upgrading the Chinese economy by overhauling Special Economic Zones: Innovation model shopping or the emergence of a Chinese innovation model? *Industry & Higher Education* 27/4: 297–312.

Goodburn, C. & & Knoerich, J. (2021a): Importing export zones: processes and impacts of replicating a Chinese model of urbanization in rural south India. *Urban Geography.* https://doi.org/10.1080/02723638.2021.2014669

Goodburn, C. & Knoerich, J. (2021b) Growing Up in (and Out of) Shenzhen: The Longer-Term Impacts of Rural-Urban Migration on Education and Labor Market Entry. *The China Journal* 83/1: 129-147.

Gopalakrishnan, S. (2007) Negative aspects of special economic zones in China. *Economic and Political Weekly* 42/17: 1492–1494.

Gray J. & White, G., eds. (1982) *China's New Development Strategy.* London: Academic Press.

Griffiths, R.T. & Hughes, A.C. (2021) *In the Way of the Road: Infrastructure and its consequences.* Leiden: International Institute for Asian Studies.

Henderson, J., Appelbaum, R.J., & Suet Ying Ho (2013) Globalization with Chinese Characteristics: Externalization, Dynamics and Transformations. *Development and Change* 44/6: 1221-53.

Henderson, J., Feldmann, M., & de Graaf, N. (2021) The Wind from the East: China and European Economic Development. *Development and Change* 52/5: 1047–1065.

Hilton, E. (2019) How China's Big Overseas Initiative Threatens Global Climate Progress. *Yale E360* (January).

Huang Ping (1991) *China's established intellectuals: a sociological study of their participation in political campaigns (1949-1976)*. PhD Dissertation, London School of Economics and Political Science. Department of Sociology.

Huber, M.T. (2017) Hidden Abodes: Industrializing Political Ecology. *Annals of the American Association of Geographers*.
http://dx.doi.org/10.1080/24694452.2016.1219249

Huber, M.K. (2019) Ecological Politics for the Working Class. *Catalyst* 1/3: 7-45.

Jayanthakumaran, K. (2002) *An overview of export processing zones: Selected Asian countries* (Working paper series 2002). University of Wollongong (Australia).

Ladino, C. (2002) "You Make Yourself Sound So Important": Fieldwork Experiences, Identity Construction, and Non- Western Researchers Abroad. *Sociological Research Online* 7/4.
http://www.socresonline.org.uk/7/4/ladino.html

Ma, H. (1983) *New Strategy for China's Economy.* Beijing: New World Press.

Mao Zedong (1977) *A Critique of Soviet Economics.* New York: Monthly Review Press.

Mao Zedong (1977a) *Selected Works of Mao Zedong.* Peking: Foreign Languages Press.

Mark, J. & Rupprecht, R. (2020) The Socialist World in Global History: From Absentee to Victim to Co-Producer. In Middell, M. ed., *The Practice of Global History. European Perspectives.* London: Bloomsbury, chapter 3.

Martinez, O. (1978) *Border Boom Town: Cuidad Juarez Since 1848.* Austin: University of Texas Press.

McAleese, D. (1977) *A Profile of Grant-Aided Industry in Ireland.* Dublin: Industrial Development Authority.

Milanovic, B. (2014) The Return of "Patrimonial Capitalism": A Review of Thomas Piketty's "Capital in the Twenty-First Century". *Journal of Economic Literature* 52/2: 519-534.

Minor, M. (1994) The demise of expropriation as an instrument of LDC policy: 1980-1992. *Journal of International Business Studies* 25: 177-88.

Mok, K-H. (1998) *Intellectuals and the State in Post-Mao China.* New York & Basingstoke: St. Martin's Press & Macmillan.

National Economic and Social Council (1982) *A Review of Industrial Policy.* Dublin (The Telesis Report).

Neveling, P. (2015) Export processing zones, special economic zones and the long march of capitalist development policies during the Cold War. In James, L. & Leake, E. eds., *Negotiating independence: New directions in the histories of the Cold War & decolonisation.* London: Bloomsbury, pp. 63-84.

Neveling, P. (2020) The political economy of special economic zones. Pasts, presents, futures. In Oqubay, A. & Lin, J. eds. *Oxford Handbook of Industrial Hubs and Economic Development.* Oxford: Oxford University Press, pp.190-205.

Olson, S. (2016) *Shenzhen: From fishing village to global metropolis.* Hinrich Foundation, online (16 September).

Piketty, T. (2014) *Capital in the Twenty-First Century.* Cambridge, MA: Harvard University Press.

Piketty, T. (2020) *Capital and Ideology.* Cambridge MA.: Harvard University Press.

Saha, S. (2019) China's Belt and Road Plan is destroying the World. *The National Interest* (18 August).

Sarma, E.A. (2007) Help the rich, hurt the poor: The case of special economic zones. *Economic and Political Weekly* XLII/8: 1900–1902.

Schurmann, F. (1966) *Ideology and Organization in Communist China.* Berkeley: University of California Press.

Sklair, L. (1988) *Foreign Investment, Irish Development, and the International Division of Labour. Progress in Planning* 29: 147-216.

Sklair, L. (1993) *Assembling for Development: The Maquila Industry in Mexico and the United States.* San Diego: Center for US–Mexican Studies.

Sklair, L. (2017) *The Icon Project: Architecture, Cities, and Capitalist Globalization.* New York & Oxford: Oxford University Press.

Sutter, K.M. (2020) "Made in China 2025" Industrial Policies: Issues for Congress. *Congressional Research Service* (11 August).

Tantri, M.L. (2012) China's Policy for Special Economic Zones: Some Critical Issues. *India Quarterly* 68/3: 231–250.

Tantri, M.L. (2013) Trajectories of China's Integration with the World Economy through SEZs: A Study of Shenzhen SEZ. *China Report* 49/2: 227–250.

Tiano, S. (1995) *Patriarchy on the Line: Labor, Gender, and Ideology in the Mexican Maquila Industry*. Philadelphia: Temple University Press.

UNIDO (1980) *Export Processing Zones in Developing Countries*. Vienna: United Nations Industrial Development Organization.

Wank, D. (1999) *Commodifying Communism: Business, Trust, and Politics in a Chinese City*. Cambridge: Cambridge University Press.

Wilczynski, J. (1976) *The Multinationals and East-West Relations*. London: Macmillan.

Wong, K.Y., ed. (1982) *Shenzhen Special Economic Zone*. Hong Kong: Geographical Association.

Wong, K. Y. & Chu, D., eds. (1985) *Modernization in China: The Case of Shenzhen SEZ*. Hong Kong: Oxford University Press.

Youngson, A. ed. (1983) *Hong Kong and China: The Economic Nexus*. Hong Kong: Oxford University Press.

CHAPTER 3

(2009) THE TRANSNATIONAL CAPITALIST
CLASS—THEORY AND EMPIRICAL RESEARCH.
IN F. SATTLER & C. BOYER EDS.
*EUROPEAN ECONOMIC ELITES:
BETWEEN A NEW SPIRIT OF CAPITALISM
AND THE EROSION OF STATE SOCIALISM,*
PP. 497-522.
[COURTESY OF DUNCKER & HUMBLOT,
BERLIN]

Preamble

I first used the term "The transnational capitalist class" (TCC) in my book *Sociology of the Global System* (1991) as a central concept in an attempt to challenge what I and others identified as state-centrism, replacing this mode of analysis with the idea of "transnational practices". I explained this as follows: "The transnational corporation is the major locus of transnational economic practices; what I shall term the transnational capitalist class is the major locus of transnational political practices; and [I argued] the major locus of transnational cultural-ideological practices is the culture-ideology of consumerism (Sklair 1991, 6 and passim). I tried to refine my global system book in the second and third editions published in 1995 and 2002, the latter under the title *Globalization: Capitalism and its Alternatives*, moving on from a conventional critique of capitalism to some ideas about alternatives. *The transnational capitalist class* was published in 2001. Working on these books at the same time forced me to recognize that to begin to understand capitalism in the new millennium it was necessary to study the transnational capitalist class. I was not alone. By this time the new concept of the TCC was beginning to be disseminated all round the world due to the outreach of the research network "Critical Studies on global capitalism". This was established in Prague with the support of the Centre for Global Studies and its energetic director Marek Hrubec at the Czech Academy of Sciences (see Sklair & Timms 2011). Regular conferences in Prague and elsewhere drew in dozens of TCC researchers. I presume that this led to my invitation from some German scholars to contribute to a workshop on "European Economic Elites" in Potsdam. This chapter provides a summary of the development of theory and research on the transnational capitalist class up to the first decade of the twenty first century. There is some overlap between this chapter and other chapters, retained in the interests of clarity.

Abstract

This chapter attempts to rethink the concept of the capitalist class in terms of recent theory and research on capitalist globalization which led me and others to propose the concept of a transnational capitalist class. Building on studies of the capitalist class in specific countries, I try to show how globalization has changed the structure and dynamics of the leading elements of the capitalist class, exploring the question of the extent to which the capitalist class, usually analyzed in terms of national economies, is becoming the ruling transnational class in the global system.

The idea of the transnational capitalist class (TCC)

As in classical Marxist theory the idea of the transnational capitalist class (TCC) conceptualizes class in capitalist society in terms of relations to the means of production, distribution, and exchange; it resists the neo-Weberian attempt to separate class, status, and command. The TCC highlights the central role of the capitalist class globally in the struggle to commodify everything. The argument revolves around three working hypotheses logically deduced from the global system theory that is elaborated below. First, I hypothesize that a transnational capitalist class is emerging and is beginning to act as a global ruling class in some spheres; second, that the key feature of the globalization of the capitalist system in recent decades has been the profit-driven culture-ideology of consumerism organized by this class; and third, that the TCC is working consciously to obfuscate the effects of the central crises of global capitalism. These crises are identified as the simultaneous creation of increasing poverty and increasing wealth within and between countries, conceptualized here as the class polarization crisis; and second, the crisis of ecological unsustainability of the global capitalist system. The global system theory propounded here is based on the concept of transnational practices, practices that cross state boundaries but do not necessarily originate with state agencies or actors. Analytically, transnational practices operate in three spheres, the economic, the political, and the culture-ideology sphere. These are superimposed each on the others rather than separate spheres. The whole is what I mean by the global system. While the global system at the end of the twentieth century is not synonymous with global capitalism, what the theory sets out to demonstrate is that the dominant forces of global capitalism are the dominant forces in the global system. The building blocks of the theory are the transnational corporation, the characteristic institutional form of economic transnational practices, a still-evolving transnational capitalist class in the political sphere, and in the culture-ideology sphere, the culture-ideology of consumerism. The assumption on which my argument is based is that the TCC is the ruling class in the global capitalist system, a fairly obvious proposition. That global capitalism dominates the global system as a whole is less obvious, indeed it is a rather contentious claim. There have been several attempts to theorize what might be seen as a global ruling class, for example concepts such as international bourgeoisie (more or less a staple of dependency theorists), the Atlantic Ruling class (van der Pijl 1984), and the corporate international wing of the managerial bourgeoisie (Becker, et al., 1987). And others have proposed answers to the question: "Who rules the world?" (Goldfrank 1977, Robinson & Harris 2000). Another source of insight into a global ruling class has emerged from the Gramscian turn in International Relations. Robert W. Cox (1987) writes of "an emerging global class structure" and Stephen Gill (1990) identifies a "developing transnational capitalist class fraction". As an attempt to build on this rich literature, the concept of transnational practices and its political form, the TCC, is a step towards consolidating the theoretical link between globalization and the ruling class and providing some evidence that these concepts have genuine empirical referents. This implies, conceptually, that the state is only one, albeit important, level of analysis and empirically that state actors are losing power to global actors in some key areas of economic, political, and culture-ideology decision making.

Four Fractions of the TCC

The transnational capitalist class is conceptualized as the characteristic institutional form of political transnational practices in the global capitalist system. The TCC can be analytically divided into four main fractions:

1. Those who own/control the major transnational corporations (TNCs) and their local affiliates (corporate fraction)
2. Globalizing politicians and bureaucrats (political fraction)
3. Globalizing professionals (technical fraction)
4. Merchants and media (consumerist fraction).

My argument is that together, these groups constitute a global power elite, ruling class or inner circle in the sense that these terms have been used to characterize the class structures of specific countries. The transnational capitalist class is opposed not only by those who reject capitalism as a way of life and/or an economic system but also by those capitalists who reject globalization. Some localized, domestically oriented businesses can share the interests of the global corporations and prosper, but most cannot and perish. Influential business strategists and management theorists commonly argue that to survive, local business must globalize, for example Rosabeth Moss Kanter (1996). Though most national and local state managers fight for the interests of their constituents, as they define these interests, government bureaucrats, politicians and professionals who entirely reject globalization and espouse extreme nationalist ideologies are relatively rare, despite the recent rash of civil wars in economically marginal parts of the world. And while there are anti-consumerist elements in most societies, there are few, if any, cases of a serious anti-consumerist party winning political power anywhere in the world.

The transnational capitalist class is transnational (or global) in the following respects. In the first place the economic interests of its members are increasingly globally linked rather than exclusively local and national in origin. As rentiers their property and shares and as executives, their corporations, are becoming more globalized and as ideologues their intellectual products serve the interests of globalizing rather than localizing capital. This follows directly from the prominence of the shareholder-driven growth imperative over "stakeholder interests" (see Mansell 2013) that lies behind the globalization of the world economy and the increasing difficulty of enhancing shareholder value in purely domestic firms. While for many practical purposes the world is still organized in terms of discrete national (country) economies the TCC increasingly conceptualizes its interests in terms of markets, which may or may not coincide with a specific nation-state, and the global market, which clearly does not. Kees van der Pijl (1993) traces the point when the "national identity [of the corporations] had to be abandoned" to the 1970s, and while few would go this far there is sufficient evidence to show that the global corporation of today is not the same as the multinational corporation of the past.

The TCC seeks to exert economic control in the workplace, political control in domestic and international politics, and culture-ideology control in every-day life through specific forms of global competitive and consumerist rhetoric and practice. The focus of workplace control is the threat that jobs will be lost and, in the extreme, the economy will collapse unless workers are prepared to work longer and for less pay in order to compete with cheap foreign imports. This has been termed "the race to the bottom" by radical critics (for example Ranney 1994 and Brecher & Costello 1994). While this is not new (capitalists have always fought against reductions in the length of the working day and increases in wages) its global scope is unprecedented. This has been regularly reported, from the normally globalizing and capitalism-friendly *Economist* (see "Profits of gloom", 28th September 1996) which asserted that most of the extra profit generated by information technology and globalization was going straight to the owners of capital at the expense of wages, to the *Indian Economic Times* (4th March 1997) which noted that as globalization makes India richer the peasants get poorer. These themes are now common all over the so-called "developing" world. Recent panics in the USA about the dangers of sweatshop-produced toys and other goods imported from China and other relatively low wage economies are only the most recent manifestations of the consequences of the transnational capitalist class in action.

Transnational capitalist class theory suggests that members of the TCC have outward-oriented global rather than inward oriented local perspectives on most economic, political, and culture-ideology issues. The growing corporate and international institutional emphasis on free trade and the shift from import substitution to export promotion strategies in most developing countries since the 1980s have been mostly driven by members of the TCC operating through government agencies, elite opinion organizations, and the media. Some of the credit for this apparent transformation in the way in which Big Business works (capitals to suggest membership of the transnational capitalist class) around the world is attached to the tremendous growth in business education since the 1960s, particularly in the US and Europe, but increasingly at the global scale. Members of the TCC all over the world tend to share similar lifestyles, particularly patterns of higher education (increasingly in business schools) and consumption of luxury goods and services. Integral to this process are exclusive clubs and restaurants, ultra-expensive holiday resorts in all continents, private as opposed to mass forms of travel and entertainment and, ominously, increasing residential segregation of very rich communities. Finally, members of the TCC seek to project images of themselves as citizens of the world as well as of their places of birth. Leading exemplars of this phenomenon have included Jacques Maisonrouge (1924-2012), French-born, who became in the 1960s the chief executive of IBM World Trade; the Swede Percy Barnevik (b.1941) who created Asea Brown Boverei, often portrayed as spending most of his life in his corporate jet; the German Helmut Maucher (1927-2018); formerly CEO of Nestlé's far-flung global empire; David Rockefeller (1915-2017); said to be one of the most powerful men in the United States; the legendary Akio Morita (1951-1999) the founder of Sony; Rupert Murdoch (b.1931); who actually changed his nationality to pursue his global media interests, and Bill Gates (b. 1955), founder of Microsoft and global philanthropist, epitome of the new variant of philanthrocapitalism (see Sklair, J. & Glucksberg 2020). While the personnel naturally change over time (no-one lives forever), Bill Gates and Rupert Murdoch are the only ones of the forementioned whose influence still resonates in the new millennium. However, there is an ever-present pool of potential members of the TCC willing and able to take their places, documented at length by Phillips (2018, 61-300). These men, now joined by a few women, are the subject of numerous biographies and company histories, regularly updated in business magazines and newspapers.

The concept of the transnational capitalist class implies that there is one central inner circle. that makes system-wide decisions, and that it connects in a variety of ways with members of the TCC in each locality, country, and region. The concept of the "inner circle" (developed in Useem 1984) can be fruitfully applied not only to the TCC but also to discrete national, regional, and/or local capitalist classes. Despite all their real geographical and sectoral conflicts, all the component elements of the transnational capitalist class, wherever they are located, share a fundamental interest in the continued accumulation of private profit. What the inner circle of the TCC does is to give a sense of unity to the diverse economic interests, political organizations, and cultural and ideological formations of those who make up the class as a whole. As in any social class, fundamental long-term unity of interests and purpose does not preclude shorter-term and local conflicts of interests and purpose, both within each of the four fractions and between them. The culture-ideology of consumerism is the fundamental value system that keeps the system intact, but it permits a relatively wide variety of choices, for example, what I term "emergent global nationalisms" (see below) as a way of satisfying the needs of the different actors and their constituencies within the global system. The four fractions of the TCC in any geographical and social area, region, country, city, society, and community, perform complementary functions to integrate the essential interests of the whole. The achievement of these goals is facilitated by the activities of local and national agents and organizations which are connected in a complex network of global interlocks, as expertly illustrated some years later in a remarkable series of graphics by Carroll (2010).

A crucial component of this integration of the TCC as a global class is that virtually all senior members of the TCC will occupy a variety of interlocking positions, notably in the interlocking directorates that have been the subject of detailed studies for some time in a variety of countries (see Stokman et al. 1985, Mizruchi & Schwartz 1987, Scott 1990, Alexander 1994). However, just as important are connections outside the direct ambit of the corporate sector, the civil society as it were servicing the state-like structures of the corporations. Leading corporate executives serve on and chair the boards of think tanks, charities, scientific, sports, arts and culture bodies, universities, medical foundations, and similar institutions. It is in this sense that the frequent claims "the business of society is business" and "the business of our society is global business" become legitimated in the global capitalist system. Business, particularly but not only the transnational corporation sector, then begins to monopolize the common symbols of modernity and post-modernity like free enterprise, international competitiveness, and the good life, transforming most if not all social spheres in its own image. While they are all members of a single, global class and share important characteristics, each fraction of the TCC has its own specific characteristics. These can be analyzed terms of their economic base, their political organization, their professional status, and their culture and ideology, what I have conceptualized as the four fractions of the transnational capitalist class.

The Corporate Fraction

The most important fraction of the TCC comprises the leading executives of the world's major corporations (Sklair 2001). These executives wield power to the extent that they control key parts of the global economy. Their actions and decisions have fundamental effects both globally and on the local communities in which their corporations are active, directly or indirectly, in any capacity. This group may also include the leading executives of companies which, while not themselves among the biggest TNCs, are of strategic importance for the global economy. The economic base of these executives is their corporate salaries and their privileged access to shares and other financial rewards in the companies they work for either directly or as privileged members of boards. The executives of the transnational corporations are paid relatively large salaries compared with workers in responsible positions in other economic spheres. It is probably true to say that with the exception of individual sporting and entertainment superstars, senior corporate executives globally have the highest salaries of any employed group. While there is relatively little research on capitalists in the Third World what there is supports the view that capitalism is globalizing to a greater or lesser extent everywhere, not simply in the major economies. This is documented in a study based on the *Fortune Global* 500 companies (Sklair & Robbins 2002). By 2021, the top two countries of domicile for the Global 500 were China and the USA, in that order (see Fortune Global 500 Wikipedia).

The political organizations of the TCC corporate elite are the peak business associations and bodies that connect business with other spheres (governments, global politics, social issues, philanthropy, etc.) operating at various levels. These include the Business Roundtable in the USA, the CBI in Britain, and their equivalents in Europe, Asia, and Japan, and a truly global network of inter-linked Chambers of Commerce (Braendle 2016). The major corporations, not surprisingly, dominate these associations and often are influential in setting the rules for global production and trade, a topic discussed in chapter 6 below. The culture and ideology of TNC executives can be conceptualized as an emerging consumerism, where global brands and tastes are promoted in the effort to turn all cultural products into commercial opportunities. It is important to distinguish here between the preferences and lifestyles of individual members of the TCC, which might vary considerably, and ways in which the class as a class promotes the culture-ideology of consumerism on a global scale. Irrespective of how individual executives live their lives, there is no doubt that global marketing and selling have become the ideological rationale for the global capitalist system as a whole, wherever it penetrates, whatever it is selling. This does not, however, preclude modifying these global formulae to suit local tastes as happens frequently in, for example, the fashion, sports, entertainment, and fast foods sectors. The same can be said for more specific political tastes with respect to the neo-liberal agenda. The idea that capitalist globalization produces an undifferentiated flat world is, at best, a half-truth.

Globalizing politicians and bureaucrats

Compared with corporate executives relatively few ordinary politicians are independently very wealthy, though in most electorally based political systems, to be successful it is important for politicians to be wealthy and/or to have wealthy backers. The ongoing failure of most left-wing politicians to sustain programmes of genuine reform within capitalist hegemony (let alone radical challenges to it) anywhere in the world since the 1970s makes it less difficult to understand why most successful politicians in most countries tend to be globalizing to a greater or lesser extent, even when they hide behind nationalist rhetoric when their local elections come around. Politicians from conservative, liberal, and social democratic parties in most countries commonly come from and return to the corporate or state sector or globalizing bureaucracies in various capacities. In most of the representative democracies elected politicians and officials must respond to the interests of their local constituents, but these interests, more often than not, tend to be defined in terms of the interests of the corporations that provide employment and make profits locally. As one of the most open countries in the world in terms of public access, information on these issues is most advanced in the United States of America. Extensive research on Political Action Committees and other local corporate-politician connections in the USA attests to a phenomenon that is probably even more widespread in countries where there is less public scrutiny of such relationships. Good examples of research on the connections between business and politics in the USA as in Stern (1988) on "The Best Congress Money Can Buy" and Tolchin & Tolchin (1993) on "Buying into America", help us to understand why the public is cynical. Substantive research (for example the analysis offered in chapter 5 below on the tobacco industry) also confirms the important thesis that the corporate sector is well-represented in the higher non-elective offices of state by those who return to the corporations after their periods of what is known as "public service". The related issue of Big Business wielding indirect and sometimes direct political power, as in the prominent cases of Berlusconi in Italy and the Putin-related oligarchs in Russia, suggests further fruitful areas of inquiry. While there have been several impressive contributions to the literature on government-business relations in capitalist countries there has been relatively little research specifically on the relationships between transnational corporation executives and direct political power. William Robinson has argued that it is necessary to distinguish "nation-state" centrism from "state" centrism and that global system theory needs a fourth set of transnational practices, namely transnational state practices (see Robinson 1996, 367). While I appreciate this point, I still maintain that the only way to avoid state-centrism, which I believe is fatal to any genuine theory of globalization, is to conceptualize the political in terms of the transnational capitalist class. Transnational state practices, where they exist, are the business of globalizing state bureaucrats and politicians not the state as such. In an exemplary research project that appears to point in this direction Alejandra Salas Porras demonstrates the critical role of transnational state elites in the construction of the neoliberal project in Mexico (Salas Porras 2021, see especially Table 1). She argues: "Mexican state elites who pushed forward neoliberal reforms transformed the political economy from a state-centered to a market-centered political economy and in the process they became transnational actors increasingly interlocked with global corporate networks, international organizations, think tanks and other policy planning bodies" (ibid, 43). The processes that Salas Porras outlines for Mexico are increasingly becoming the global standard.

The struggle between globalizing and localizing state bureaucrats, becomes a key site in which the hegemony of the transnational capitalist class is mediated. It hardly needs to be said that the TCC interpretation of state power and corporate power is only one of the competing versions of power to be found in the annals of political sociology. This is demonstrated in the works of Michael Mann (see Mann 1984), an article that provides a useful introduction to his ongoing magisterial multivolume theoretical-historical publications on *The Sources of Social Power* (four volumes so far) published by Cambridge University Press.

Capitalist-friendly politicians, and others, notably globalizing bureaucrats, and ordinary people all over the world have been increasingly persuaded that their "national interests" lie in the accelerated growth of the global economy through unfettered competition and free trade and that the only route to national prosperity (ignoring, of the course, the vicissitudes of class) lies in an ever more extreme version of transnational neo-liberalism. In the capitalist global system lower-level political actors are necessarily responsive to the vested interests of a variety of constituencies, so members of these groups rarely adopt a fully-fledged version of the emergent global nationalism of the globalizing bureaucrats. They are characterized more by a rich cosmopolitanism, often also reflecting regional factors, especially within federal systems of government. However, at base, they share to a greater or lesser extent the orthodoxies of a globalizing neo-liberalism against the localizing tendencies of their opponents. The focus on globalizing bureaucrats highlights the struggles that take place within all states between the outward-oriented globalizers and the inward-oriented nationalists. I maintain this, despite the apparent U.S.-Japanese conflict of interest over World Bank policies as analyzed by Robert Wade (1996). While Wade makes many telling points, he neglects to consider sufficiently the argument that it is not the interests of the U.S. and Japanese states that are at issue but the interests of different sectors of big capital as represented by various agents (notably globalizing bureaucrats) in the USA and Japan.

The doyen of Japanese progressive economists in a chapter on "The march of corporate capitalism" sees a definite corporate-driven "globalization trend" in Japan (Tsuru 1993, 192-204). Different state actors, thus, can be powerful forces both for and against capitalist globalization. Struggles between them are expressed in a variety of ways, for example through variations on liberal or restrictive foreign investment regimes and trade policy, official multiculturalism or chauvinism. We could add to this a variety of institutional forms (covering intrusive foreign economic relations agencies, and more or less powerful or effective inter-governmental agencies). While the major international organizations (notably World Bank, IMF, OECD, World Trade Organization) are still mainly driven by representatives of their most powerful members, it is less clear that, for example, the World Bank can be said to be driven by the "national interests" of the USA. For example, in his detailed account of the life and work of the first President of the World Bank, Oliver (1995,187) comments that George Woods was a "New York banker, not a Washington bureaucrat", the implication being that most bankers, unlike bureaucrats, are driven largely by the profit motive. The old Marxist argument that the workers have no nation has to be turned on its head; today globalizing capitalists have no nation and the demands of the global market, not national interests (itself a deeply questionable concept), drive the global capitalist system while the working class and the labour movement that purports to represent it, calls on "its" state, politicians, and employers to protect it against the ravages of globalization. The growth of powerful regional trading blocs like NAFTA, the European Union, and APEC, far from undermining this argument, point to the increasing weakness of nation-states to cope alone with the capitalist globalizing agenda. As I argued above, globalizing bureaucrats fulfil a governance function for the global capitalist system at the local, national, interstate, and eventually transnational levels where individual state officials are often briskly sidelined. Typically, globalizing bureaucrats are to be found dealing with or actually working in national, regional, and local growth coalitions financed by corporate investment; national bureaucracies responsible for external economic relations, for exports, FDI in both directions, market-driven aid agencies, and international organizations. The top ranks of the globalizing bureaucracies combine career bureaucrats with retired corporate executives putting their marketing skills to use "in the public service" as well as upwardly mobile business types *en route* to top jobs

Remuneration in the public sector is considerably less than in the corporate sector, except in cases where corruption permits illegal enrichment, a condition that afflicts most societies (see transparency.org). This is, of course, not restricted to the poorest parts of the world, as cases involving corporations in the USA, Europe, Japan, and South Korea clearly illustrate, then and now. Salaries and perks for most government employees in most countries appear to be relatively modest in comparison with those in the private corporate sector, however there are frequent opportunities for augmenting earnings from directorships, fees, and other sources, if not concurrently then almost certainly later for senior officials. While public service rules sometimes restrict outside earnings, these are rarely lifetime restrictions and they do not cover all the privileges that such positions engender. Since the substantial wave of de-nationalizations and quasi-privatizations of formerly state-owned enterprises from the 1980s to the present all over the world, new categories of corporate executives and officials have been created. These are often the same people who ran the state-owned enterprises, and their links with the TCC will repay further study. Globalizing bureaucrats frequently move to the business sector, working directly for the corporations whose interests they may have been indirectly serving (or impeding) as public employees. The agencies globalizing bureaucrats work for are, in a sense, their political organizations and in many countries local and national government agencies can be identified with, for example, open-door policies that further the interests of the transnational capitalist class (whoever else's interests they may also further or damage). Globalizing bureaucrats also work politically through corporatist agencies that combine representatives of the state, business, and labour. As Grant (2018) argues in his historical survey of the idea of corporatism "there was a failure to agree what was actually being discussed". Perhaps, we might argue, this let both corporations and governments off the hook.

Regulatory agencies provide a more clear-cut case of the influence of Big Business. These agencies are often dominated, usually indirectly, by the major corporations (see, for example, my analysis of Codex Alimentarius in chapter 6 below). The culture and ideology of state and private sector globalizing bureaucrats tend to be more complex than those of TNC executives. Their dominant ideology appears to be in a process of transformation from state interventionism to a form of neo-liberalism which privileges the unrestricted operation of the free market. This is the world view that a country's best interests are to be found in playing a full part in the accelerated growth of the global economy through unfettered competition by destroying old systems of tariff protection and labour regulation and forcing all firms and their workers to become internationally competitive. The neo-liberal dogma that this can only be fully achieved in an entirely market-driven system provides the economic theory for this strategy. It is worth noting the contradiction for globalizing bureaucrats implicit in another dogma of neo-liberalism, that the state should basically never intervene in the economy. This implies that the key role of globalizing bureaucrats in the struggle between capital and labour is invariably to support Big Business, in many if not all countries. The ideology of capitalist globalization is reinforced daily by cultural practices cohering into an emergent global nationalism, a nationalism that seeks to make each country an integral part of the global capitalist system while maintaining its identity by marketing national competitive advantages of various types through its own global brands (American fast foods and entertainment, Japanese cars, Asian electronics, French wines and perfumes, Italian furniture, and the British aristocracy, for example). International tourism, now the most important hard currency earning industry in a rapidly increasing number of local and national economies, plays a key part in this multi-faceted socio-cultural construction.

Globalizing professionals

Top business professionals, notably corporate lawyers and consultants of various types, command substantial salaries in most countries and it is safe to assume that some of these individuals derive other benefits from the companies with which they routinely do business. These professionals, as a group, have attracted a good deal of attention in recent years. This is largely due to the growth of two phenomena which, while not entirely exclusive to the era of globalization, have accelerated rapidly since the 1960s. These are, first, the various business services industries, ranging from information technology to management consulting, financial services, and public relations of various types (Aharoni 1993) and, second, the rise of the think tanks, particularly those associated with the neo-liberal free trade and free enterprise anti-regulation agendas. The dominant elites in these institutions are among the most visible adjuncts of the TCC until, of course, some esoteric ideological dispute upsets the apple cart (see Hull 2006, the standout chapter in one of the first global exposures of "neoliberal hegemony"). Professionals around the world, with notable few exceptions, support the transnational capitalist class through their own professional organizations, in the corporatist organizations noted above, and in think tanks and universities, where they market carefully crafted research-based information and policy to corporations and governments. As these entities tend to be funded indirectly by government departments, and directly by transnational corporations and private capitalists (not always transparently), their independence is often a matter of dispute. The culture and ideology of

these professionals is a complex mix of global nationalism and neo-
liberalism. The global networks of business consultants like Arthur
Anderson (now Accenture after a disastrous Enron-induced collapse in
2001), McKinsey, and Burson-Marsteller (now Burson, Cohn and Wolfe),
contain many individuals who have worked in business services,
government advisory bodies, major corporations, think tanks and sometimes
several at the same time. These organizations are of particular interest
insofar as some of them have been directly identified with the propagation
of the neo-liberal agenda. While the new right thinks tanks are not
excessively well-endowed financially, by targeting elite opinion they have
much more influence than their modest resources would indicate. They
certainly provide a professional forum for both aspiring young and retiring
older members of the TCC which is both culturally and ideologically
hospitable. Capitalist-inspired politicians and professionals are certainly
working on the front line for the corporate elite. Another context in which
globalizing professionals may service the interests of capital is as members
of what Evan (1981) calls International Scientific and Professional
Associations (ISPAs). Peter Haas (1992), rather more conceptually, calls
them epistemic communities. Clearly not all of these are capitalist or
globalizing, perhaps most of the leaders of these Associations or communities
are hostile to global capitalism, but there is enough evidence of the
corroding effects of the corporate sponsorship of research, commercially-
motivated networking, and academic institution building to suggest that
even the most epistemic of communities find themselves from time to time
being persuaded of the correctness or relevance of the corporate case for
other than strictly cognitive reasons. If these professionals, mainly scientists
of various types, can be mobilized in defence of the projects of Big Business
and global capitalism, the impact on public opinion and governments can
be considerable.

Consumerist elites (merchants and media)

Consumerist elites are generally corporate executives, but they are of such
increasing importance for global consumerist capitalism that they require
special treatment. Like other TNC executives their economic base is in
salaries and share capital and their culture and ideology is a cohesive
culture-ideology of consumerism. However, the specificity of the members
of the media elite lies in their political organization, more specifically their
means of political expression through the television and radio networks,
newspapers, magazines, and other mass media they own and control. The
retail sector, particularly the ubiquitous shopping malls that are springing

up all over the world, can in this sense be regarded analytically as part of the mass media. Through the medium of advertising the links between media and merchants and the entire system of marketing (including raw materials, design, production, packaging, financing, transportation, wholesaling, retailing, disposal) become concrete, even if opaque. In the apparently inexorable increase in the global connectedness of the mass media and consumerism we can chart the ways in which the TCC appears gradually to be imposing its hegemony all over the world. Global system theory argues that consumerist elites play a central role in capitalist hegemony. The practical politics of this hegemony is the everyday life of consumer society and the promise that it can be reality for most people in the world. This is certainly the most persistent image projected by television and the mass media in general. In one sense, therefore, shopping can be seen as the most successful social movement in history, few can resist "The Magic of the Mall" (Goss 1993), product advertising in its many forms is the most successful message (Sethi 1977), and consumerism is the most successful ideology of all time. These processes start early, for example, in the schools and colleges (Esland, et al. 1976, Schiller 1999, Cantwell & Kauppinen, eds. 2014). While the USA leads, the rest the world is catching up rapidly as exemplified by a typical article in *Tokyo Business Today* (May 1990, 30-34) on "Corporate Philanthropy" which has an interesting list of many Japanese corporate donations to universities, a theme that Domhoff, Useem, and others discuss for the USA and the UK.

Like capitalism, the process of taking the purchase of the necessities of basic consumption out of domestic production and local marketplaces, redefining this as shopping and relocating it increasingly all over the world into the more controlled environments of supermarkets and malls, did not happen by chance. The transformation of the built environment and of the renegotiation of the meaning of shopping from satisfaction of basic needs for the masses into a form of mass entertainment, for many the major leisure activity, is one of the greatest achievements of corporate capitalism, enhanced by globalization. Advertising agencies have for some time been surveying the global consumer (Englis 1994) and extending the geographical scope of their regular global brand preference rankings. The point of the concept of the culture-ideology of consumerism is precisely that, under capitalism, the masses cannot be relied upon to keep buying, obviously when they have neither spare cash nor access to credit, and less obviously when they do have spare cash and access to credit. The creation of a culture-ideology of consumerism, therefore, is bound up with the self-imposed necessity that capitalism must be ever-expanding on a global scale. This expansion crucially depends on selling more and more goods and services to people whose basic needs (a somewhat ideological concept) have already been comfortably met as well as to those whose basic needs are regularly unmet. Consumerist elites play a part in the regular business groups in most countries and globally, but they also have dedicated organizations for their own purposes. Through their ownership and control of TV channels, radio stations, newspapers, magazine and book publishers, advertising agencies, public relations firms, film and video production and distribution networks, shopping centres and other retail outlets, they broadcast and narrowcast the culture-ideology of consumerism as the normal environment of everyday life for the vast majority of people in the First World, and increasingly over most of the rest of the world. The global project of capitalist consumerism would not be possible without them, which is precisely the reason why the processes of globalization (in my formulation) date from the 1960s onwards, paralleling the technological revolutions that made modern mass media possible. So, in a fundamental sense, the TV channels and mass newspapers and magazines of those who control the media have the same general form as the political organizations of the other fractions of the transnational capitalist class, with the dramatic and power-enhancing difference that there is a massive ready-made and apparently receptive audience for the persistent "buy, buy, buy" messages that they wish to propagate. The subsequent rise of the internet and social media give the TNC unique access to the global community of consumers.

In order to understand how the TCC organizes itself it is necessary to examine the central problem of class rule in capitalist society: how to ensure the continuation of the private accumulation of profit. All ruling classes in all social systems not characterized by pure democracy (however this is defined) have to ensure their power to sustain the normal processes of interaction. So, police forces, courts of law, armies, Gods (religious and/or secular), super-ego, posterity, and other mechanisms of social control play their part to defend the integrity of the existing social system, to permit accommodation to change, and even (on occasion) to ensure the success of unavoidable revolutions in human affairs. While all ruling classes have a siege mentality to a greater or lesser extent, which explains why they have armies and police forces and other agents of physical and social control, there are two specific reasons why the siege mentality of the TCC (or, more accurately, its immediate predecessors) is particularly sensitive. First, the old ideological certainties of the divine rights of kings, emperors, gods, and sacred texts have, of course, seriously diminished in the twentieth century; second, the rise of self-styled democracies of various kinds in recent decades have exposed ruling classes all over the world to much more public scrutiny, though rarely effective democratic control, than ever before (see, for example, Parmar 1995 on Anglo-American "special interest groups", and Richardson 2000, for an European Union insider's account). While it is generally agreed that global capitalism delivers more formal democracy and rule of law than any other large-scale system yet put into practice, the level of cynicism about the performance of actually existing democracies appears to be growing all over the world. In a passionate and meticulously documented analysis of the dramatic decline of local journalism in the USA, Robert McChesney and John Nichols convincingly demonstrate the vital importance of a free press for the flourishing of democracy, linking the erosion of financial support for journalism at the local level with the plummeting reputation of the USA as a leading democracy, citing as evidence The *Economist* in its 2020 Democracy Index: "The United States ranks a woeful 25th, now finding itself in the category of 'flawed democracy' alongside numerous nations never considered especially democratic". McChesney and Nichols recommend the creation of a Local Journalism Institute properly funded out of general taxation and well thought through to attract community support and protect local media from large corporate takeovers, a process that has been identified as being responsible for the destruction of large numbers of genuinely local media all over the USA in recent decades. Radical as it appears, this is a model that seems to work in Norway, Germany, Canada, Denmark, and Sweden, all countries that are regularly considered to be among the most democratic and transparent societies anywhere in the world (see McChesney and Nichols, edited exerpts from https://www.freepress.net/sites/default/files/ 2021-11/to_protect_democracy_recreate_local_news.pdf). In a time of problematic digital media, fake news, and conspiracy theories, it seems obvious that local journalism that can be trusted is a most important element in the defence of democracy.

Enter Gramsci

The theoretical-historical foundations of this argument and line of research originate in Antonio Gramsci's attempt to construct a theory of hegemony and ideological state apparatuses. Much of the voluminous *Prison Notebooks* (Gramsci 1971) written from 1929 to 1935 can be read as a continuous critique of the assumption, not difficult to gather from the Marx-Engels classics, that ruling classes generally rule effortlessly until revolutionary upsurges drive them from power with promises to make everything anew. As many scholars, inspired by, sympathetic with, and hostile to Marxism have pointed out, the general impression of the Marxist classics is often of a rather deterministic sociology, a theory in which "men [sic] make history but not in circumstances of their own choosing", where the emphasis is on the latter rather than the former. It is no accident that Gramsci is associated both with a more cultural and less deterministic interpretation of Marxism and with the concept of hegemony, for they do connect. Gramsci made the connection through the role of the intellectuals in the creation and sustenance of hegemonic forms for the ruling class. He argues: The hegemony of a directive centre over the intellectuals asserts itself by two principal routes: (1) a general conception of life, a philosophy . . . which offers to its adherents an intellectual 'dignity' providing a principle of differentiation from the old ideologies which dominated by coercion, and an element of struggle against them; (2) a scholastic program, an educative principle and original pedagogy which interests that fraction of the intellectuals which is the most homogenous and the most numerous (the teachers, from the primary teachers to the university professors), and gives them an activity of their own in the technical field." (ibid., 103).

While much of this still seems quite valid, it suggests too much of a one-way process, the "directive centre" asserting its hegemony over the intellectuals. Research on intellectuals suggests a more dialectical process where distinct groups of intellectuals, inspired by the promise or actual achievements of global capitalism articulate what they perceive to be its essential purposes and strategies, often with support and encouragement from the corporate elites and their friends in government and other spheres, particularly the media. For example, the historian Richard Cockett (1995) shows how about fifty right wing intellectuals of various types in the UK carried out an anti-Keynesian neo-liberal counter revolution from the 1930s to the eventual triumphs of Thatcher-Reaganism in the 1980s (see also, Harvey 2005). Cockett's book is not simply an idealist account of social change in which the power of ideas eventually turns the tide but, on the contrary, a much more subtle argument in which the bearers of powerful ideas which have few powerful adherents work away until the material forces begin to change in their direction, in this case the crises of capitalism and state power in the 1970s feeding the widespread disillusionment with Keynesian and welfare state solutions to these crises and the legitimation crisis in general. Enter Gramsci, again. "A 'crisis of authority' is spoken of: this is precisely the crisis of hegemony, or general crisis of the state" (Gramsci 1971, 210). Writing in the 1930s from a fascist prison in Italy, he saw the latest crisis of hegemony resulting from the First World War and the Communist advances since then and, if he had lived, would undoubtedly have seen the next crisis of hegemony for international capitalism resulting from the Second World War. Since then, theories of capitalist crisis (fiscal crisis of the state, crisis of welfare, crisis of de-industrialization, and more recently the environmental crisis are just a few of the contenders) have been articulated from all sides. These have generally been seen as crises which need global as well as national and local solutions. The collapse of the Soviet Union and the clamour of capitalist triumphalism since the 1990s, paradoxically, have increased the pressures on the TCC and its allies to solve all the problems of the contemporary world, quickly and globally. My argument is that the global capitalist project is gaining ground as the emerging solution to all these crises and as befits a hegemonic crisis of the first order, the solution is a new conception of global hegemony. But while Gramsci was thinking of a new socialist order, for the new millennium this raises the real prospect as the 21st century approaches of both an "emerging supranational corporate agenda" (Ranney 1994) and a "transnational neo-liberalism" (Overbeek 1993, the latter a product of the Amsterdam School of critical political economy). The devastation of the 1970s oil shocks, the subsequent debt crises, corporate restructuring and downsizing, and the apparent inability of politicians to deal with these problems in any way other than short-term palliatives, suggests that the local effects of globalization increase the pressures on the emerging transnational capitalist class to deliver what the culture-ideology of consumerism promises, more private possessions leading to better and happier lives for all. However, the pressure is usually refracted through the political system and the attempts of governments to get to grips with the problems of unemployment, inflation, stagflation, deskilling, job insecurity, international competitiveness, law and order, immigration and migration, and multiculturalism, to name but a few of the current crises.

The politics of the culture-ideology of consumerism

The culture-ideology of consumerism raises expectations that can be satisfied in at least two ways. The first is redistribution of resources, the social-democratic localizing solution. The second is increasing the size of the cake to be distributed (the neo-liberal globalizing solution of never-ending growth). An unwelcome result of the Thatcher-Reagan neo-liberal experiments in the UK and US and copied widely throughout the world, has been the absolute enrichment of the "lucky" few combined with the relative impoverishment of the many, and the economic stagnation of many more middling groups in rich and poor countries alike. Robert C. Feenstra (1996) argued in the *American Economic Review* that the real wages of less-skilled workers in the USA have fallen dramatically since the late 1970s. This was true for many other countries then, and still is in many cases. The widening gap between the much better off and the rest has produced an arrogant over-confidence in the over-privileged and a sometimes violent, sometimes fatalist reaction from the under-privileged. At the same time, the corporate elite has commonly and with good reason felt insecure, particularly in the foreign countries where they do business. Though both phenomena appear to have declined in the past decades (replaced, in most cases by "the war on terror", especially since 9/11), it is not very surprising that TNCs have routinely taken pre-emptive action to put their case before the public and the authorities with whom they have to deal. For reasons which cannot be dealt with here, Big Business tends to be unpopular and its claims tend to be treated with a high degree of cynicism, so it often resorts to indirect ways of creating support for its causes and influencing public policy on behalf of its sectional interests. One of the most important ideological tasks of Big Business is to persuade the population at large that the business of society is business and to create a climate of opinion in which moderately radical trade unions and other oppositions (especially new consumer and environmental movements) are considered to be sectional interests while business groups are not. This is, of course, a large part of the creation and maintenance of global capitalist (I would add, consumerist) hegemony. There is a good deal of agreement among scholars that as communist parties used to do in countries where they were illegal or circumscribed, Big Business often creates front organizations to propagate its messages. Many apparently straightforward civic organizations are largely run by and funded by the corporate elite. Most of the research on these phenomena has been carried out on business groups in the USA and most focuses on the ways in which Big Business, both domestic and foreign, influences the US government and its various state apparatuses to legislate in the interests of capital. The research of Domhoff over several decades (1967, 1980, 1996, 2007) provides the most influential gateway into the study of power in the USA along with radical publications like *Multinational Monitor* (it ceased publication in 2009) and others associated with the name of Ralph Nader. Ryan, et al. (1987) provides evidence from *Fortune 500* corporations and Rowell (1996) demonstrates this globally for the environmental field. Ironically, in Australia Poole (1989) had used similar evidence to argue that "Big Business Bankrolls the Left".

In Latin America the case of the Chicago boys in Chile (and elsewhere) is well-known, and one study of this comes to the measured conclusion: "available data reveal that policymakers have mainly interacted with the leadership of a few carefully selected conglomerates" (Silva 1996, 316). Research on South Korea (Jung 1988, Kim 2008) and on Asia in general (MacIntyre 1994) comes to a similar conclusion. Findings from research on the USA have been replicated to some extent by research from other countries. All this evidence-based information reveals great power combined with fragility at the core of capitalism. The problem of Big Business is best illustrated in the heartland of capitalist hegemony, the USA. In the 1970s, corporations in the USA deliberately sought "to reverse a dramatic decline in public confidence in Big Business which they blame on the media" (Dreier 1982, 111). To do this, Dreier explains, business mobilized through think tanks, university business journalism courses, awards and prizes to encourage more favourable reporting, detente between business and media, advocacy advertising, and increased TV sponsorship of culture. An important addition to Dreier's list is the development of "Business Ethics" both as an area of academic research and as a set of responses for Big Business under threat. Tsalikis & Fritzsche (1989) identify over 300 sources on the topic. These strategies are elegantly exposed in, appropriately enough, an article in the now defunct *Propaganda Review* by Luigi Graziano (1989). Anti-Big Business sentiment has existed in the USA and elsewhere since at least the 19th century, nourishing an impressive scholarly literature. Galambos (1975) and Piott (1985) provide early histories, and Lipset & Schneider (1983) locate it in a general lack of confidence in institutions. Right-wing ideologues rush to defend Big Business as "America's Persecuted Minority" (Rand 1967) and Ludwig von Mises, the doyen of so-called "free market" capitalism (von Mises 1956) offers an envy-based polemic.

The reason for all this activity is that the capitalist class always faces the threat of challenge from below. No doubt at some periods, in the USA and elsewhere, Big Business is more popular and at other periods less popular, but the point is that capitalist hegemony needs constant support, attention, and originality to sustain itself. This is no less true for capitalism in the global compared with the national or local context. The parallel developments of cheap global mass media and substantial increases in various forms of global business relations (FDI, strategic alliances, global brands, executive and professional cross-border flows) are simultaneous indicators of the unprecedented global reach of contemporary capitalism as well as the global exposure of its promises and performance. If the preceding analysis has provided evidence that a transnational capitalist class is emerging and is beginning to act as a global ruling class in some spheres, it remains necessary to show concretely how this class is related to the crises of global capitalism. The next three chapters attempt to do this.

Second Thoughts

While I remain generally committed to the concept of the transnational capitalist class some research that emerged in the new millennium has forced me to reconsider the available evidence. In 2010 I was asked by the publisher of Zed Books to evaluate a manuscript by the Canadian sociologist, William Carroll on the making of the transnational capitalist class. I was already familiar with his publications on corporate networks but, as I see now, I had failed to fully appreciate their significance or the significance of the work of his colleagues in what came to be called the Amsterdam School of interlocking directorates. I endorsed Bill Carroll's book enthusiastically as "The most significant recent contribution on the transnational capitalist class" (see Carroll 2010, front cover). I accepted the value of his criticism of my own book's failure to "map the social organization of the transnational capitalist class" (ibid, 2). He and his Amsterdam colleagues provide dozens of remarkable maps, tables, and diagrams that illustrate the uneven architecture of corporate social organization. Complementing this, a more recent book on alternative policy groups (Carroll 2016) gives us further insight into what he has labelled as "a qualified version" of the transnational capitalist class thesis, stimulating more research by scholars all round the world as corporate capitalism continues to evolve globally. Robinson & Sprague (2018) provide a balanced history of these early years of TCC research. Writing the original article in the first decade of the 21st century as someone who paid little attention to social media I have only recently registered that my critique of the power of ideological communication, especially in terms of the culture-ideology of consumerism, was too mild. In retrospect, I cannot explain why the progressive voices of the Left have been drowned out by the reactionary voices of the Right. The transnational capitalist class is certainly in crisis, but not exactly the crisis I anticipated.

References

Aharoni, Y., ed. (1997) *Changing Roles of State Intervention in Services in an Era of Open International Markets*. Albany: State University of New York Press.

Alexander, M., Murray, G., & Houghton, J. (1994) Business power in Australia: the concentration of company directorship holding among the top 250 corporates. *Australian Journal of Political Science* 29: 40-61.

Becker, D.G., et al., eds. (1987) *Postimperialism*. Boulder CO: Lynne Reinner.

Braendle, U., Rahdari, A.H., & Dehkordi, H.F. (2016) Promoting Responsible Business Practices: A Case of Chambers of Commerce. *Revista Internacional de Organizaciones* 16: 41–58.

Brecher, J. & Costello, T. (1994) *Global Village or Global Pillage Economic Reconstruction from the Bottom Up*. Boston: South End Press.

Burch, P. (1981) The Business Roundtable: Its Make-up and External Ties. *Research in Political Economy* 4:101-27.

Cantwell, B. & Kauppinen, I., eds. (2014) *Academic capitalism in the age of globalization.* Baltimore: Johns Hopkins University Press.

Carroll, W.K. (2010) *The Making of a transnational capitalist class: Corporate Power in the 21st Century*. New York & London: Zed.

Carroll, W.K. (2016) *Expose, Oppose, Propose: Alternative Policy Groups and the Struggle for Global Justice*. London & Halifax, Nova Scotia: Zed Books & Fernwood Publishing.

Cockett, R. (1995) *Thinking the Unthinkable: Think-Tanks and the Economic Counter-Revolution, 1931-1983*. London: Harper Collins.

Cox, R.W. (1987) *Production, Power, and World Order: Social Forces in the Making of History*. New York: Columbia University Press.

Dinan, W. & Miller, D., eds. (2007) *Thinker, Faker, Spinner, Spy: Corporate PR and the Assault on Democracy*. London: Pluto Press.

Domhoff, W.H. (1967) *Who Rules America?* Englewood Cliffs: Prentice Hall.

Domhoff, W.H. (1981) Provincial in Paris: Finding the French Council on Foreign Relations. *Social Policy* (March-April): 5-13.

Domhoff, W.H. (1996) *State Autonomy or Class Dominance? Case Studies on Policy Making in America.* Hawthorne NY: Aldine de Gruyter.

Domhoff, W.H. (2007) C. Wright Mills, Floyd Hunter, and 50 Years of Power Structure Research. *Michigan Sociological Review* 21:1-54.

Domhoff, W.H. ed. (1980) *Power Structure Research*. London: Sage.

Dreier, P. (1982) Capitalists vs. the Media: An Analysis of an Ideological Mobilization among Business Leaders. *Media, Culture and Society* 4/2: 111-132.

Englis, B.G., ed. (1994) *Global and Multinational Advertising*. Hillsdale NJ: Lawrence Erlbaum.

Esland, G., et al. eds. (1976) *Schooling and capitalism: a sociological reader.* London: Routledge & Kegan Paul for the Open University Press.

Evan, W.M., ed. (1981) *Knowledge and Power in a Global Society* Beverly Hills: Sage.

Feenstra, R.C. (1996) Globalization, Outsourcing, and Wage Inequality. *American Economic Review* 86/2: 240-245.

Galambos, L. (1975) *The Public Image of Big Business in America, 1880-1940: A Quantitative Study in Social Change*. Baltimore: Johns Hopkins University Press.

Gill, S. (1990) *American Hegemony and the Trilateral Commission*. Cambridge: Cambridge University Press.

Goldfrank, W.L. (1977) Who Rules the World? Class Formation at the International Level. *Quarterly Journal of Ideology* 1/2: 32-37.

Goss, J. (1993) The "Magic of the Mall": An Analysis of Form, Function, and Meaning in the Contemporary Retail Built Environment. *Annals of the Association of American Geographers* 83/1: 18-47.

Gramsci, A. (1971) *Selections from the Prison Notebooks*. London: Lawrence & Wishart.

Grant, W. (2018) Corporatism. In Brown, G.W., et al. eds., *A Concise Oxford Dictionary of Politics and International Relations*. Oxford: Oxford University Press (4th edition).

Graziano, L. (1989) How Business Ethics became "Issues Management". *Propaganda Review* (Summer): 29-31.

Haas, P.M. (1992) Introduction: epistemic communities and international policy coordination. *International Organization* 46/1: 1-35.

Harvey, D. (2005) *A Brief History of Neoliberalism*. Oxford: Oxford University Press.

Hull, R. (2006) The Great Lie: Markets, Freedom, and Knowledge. In Plehwe, D., et al. eds., *Neoliberal Hegemony: A Global Critique*. London & New York: Routledge, chapter 7.

Jung, K.-H. (1988) Business-Government Relations in the Growth of Korean Business Groups. *Korean Social Science Journal* 14/1: 67-82.

Kanter, R.M. (1996) *World Class: Thriving Locally in the Global Economy*. New York: Simon & Schuster.

Kim Yun Tae (2008) *Bureaucrats and Entrepreneurs: The State and the Chaebol in Korea*. Seoul & Edison NJ: Jimoondang.

Lipset, S.M. & Schneider, W. (1983) *The Confidence Gap: Business, Labor, and Government in the Public Mind*. New York: Free Press.

MacIntyre, A.J., ed. (1994) *Business and Government in Industrialising Asia*. Ithaca: Cornell University Press.

Mann, M. (1984) The autonomous power of the state: its origins, mechanisms and results. *European Journal of Sociology* 25: 185-213.

Mansell, S.F. (2013) *Capitalism, Corporations and the Social Contract: A Critique of Stakeholder Theory*. Cambridge: Cambridge University Press.

Mizruchi, M. & Schwartz, M., eds. (1987) *Intercorporate Relations: The Structural Analysis of Business.* Cambridge: Cambridge University Press.

Oliver, R. (1995) *George Woods and the World Bank.* Boulder, CO: Lynne Reinner.

Overbeek, H. ed. (1993) *Restructuring Hegemony in the Global Political Economy: The Rise of Transnational Neo-liberalism in the 1980s.* London & New York: Routledge.

Parmar, I. (1995) Special Interests: The State and the Anglo-American Alliance, 1939-1945. London: Frank Cass.

Phillips, P. (2018) *GIANTS: The Global Power Elite.* New York: Seven Stories Press.

Piott, S. L. (1985) *The Anti-Monopoly Persuasion. Popular Resistance to the Rise of Big Business in the Midwest.* Westport, CT: Greenwood Press.

Poole, W.T. (1989) How Big Business Bankrolls the Left. *National Review* [Australia] (10th March): 34-39.

Rand, A. (1967) America's Persecuted Minority: Big Business. In Ayn Rand, ed., *Capitalism: The Unknown Ideal.* New York: New American Library, pp. 44-62.

Ranney, D.C. (1994) Labor and an Emerging Supranational Corporate Agenda. *Economic Development Quarterly* 8/1: 83-91.

Richardson, K. (2000) *Big Business and the European Agenda. Reflections on the activities of the European Round Table of Industrialists, 1988-98.* Brighton: Sussex European Institute, Working Paper No. 35.

Robinson, W.R. (1996) *Promoting Polyarchy.* Cambridge: Cambridge University Press.

Robinson, W.R. & Harris, J. (2000) "Towards a Global Ruling Class?": Globalization and the transnational capitalist class. *Science & Society* 64/1: 11-54.

Robinson, W.R. & Sprague, J. (2018) The transnational capitalist class. In Juergensmeyer, M., et al. eds. *The Oxford Handbook of Global Studies.* Oxford: Oxford University Press.

Rowell, A. (1996) *Green Backlash: Global Subversion of the Environmental Movement.* London: Routledge.

Ryan, M.H., Swanson, C.L., et al. (1987) *Corporate Strategy, Public Policy and the Fortune 500: How America's major corporations influence government.* Oxford: Oxford University Press.

Salas Porras, A. (2021) Transnational State Elites and the Neoliberal Project in Mexico. *New Global Studies* 15/1: 23-46.

Schiller, D. (1999) *Digital Capitalism: Networking the Global Market System.* Cambridge, Mass.: MIT Press.

Scott, J. ed. (1990) *The Sociology of Elites.* Aldershot: Edward Elgar, Volume 3, Interlocking Directorships and Corporate Networks.

Scott, J. (1996) *Stratification and Power: Structures of Class, Status and Command.* Cambridge: Cambridge University Press.

Sethi, S.P. (1977) *Advocacy Advertising and Large Corporations.* Lexington: D.C. Heath.

Shoup, L.H. & Minter, M. (1977) *Imperial Brain Trust: The Council on Foreign Relations and United States Foreign Policy.* New York: Monthly Review Press.

Silva, E. (1996) From Dictatorship to Democracy: The Business-State Nexus in Chile's Economic Transformation, 1975-1994. *Comparative Politics* 28/3: 299-320.

Sklair, J. & Glucksberg, L. (2020) Philanthrocapitalism as wealth management strategy: Philanthropy, inheritance and succession planning among the global elite. *The Sociological Review* 69/2: 1-16.

Sklair, L. (1991) *Sociology of the Global System.* Hemel Hemstead: Harvester Wheatsheaf.

Sklair, L. (2001) *The transnational capitalist class.* Malden & Oxford: Blackwell.

Sklair, L. (2002) *Globalization. Capitalism and its Alternatives.* Oxford: Oxford University Press.

Sklair, L. & Robbins, P. (2002) global capitalism and Major Corporations from the Third World. *Third World Quarterly* 23/1: 81-100.

Sklair, L. & Timms, J. (2012) Report on Prague conference on global capitalism. *International Critical Thought* 2/1: 125-126.

Sklar, H., ed. (1980) *Trilateralism: The Trilateral Commission and Elite Planning for World Management.* Boston: South End Press.

Smith, J. (2008) *Social Movements for Global Democracy.* Baltimore: Johns Hopkins University Press.

Stern, P.M. (1988) *The Best Congress Money Can Buy.* New York: Random House.

Stokman, F.N. et al., eds. (1985) *Networks of Corporate Power: A Comparative Analysis of Ten Countries.* Cambridge: Cambridge University Press.

Stout, P.A. et al. (1989) Trends in Magazine Advertorial Use. *Journalism Quarterly* 66/4: 960-964.

Tolchin, M. & Tolchin, S. (1993) *Buying into America.* Washington: Farragut.

Tsalikis, J. & Fritzsche, D.J. (1989) Business Ethics: A Literature Review with a Focus on Marketing Ethics. *Journal of Business Ethics* 8/9: 695-743.

Tsuru, S. (1993) *Japan's Capitalism: Creative Defeat and Beyond.* Cambridge: Cambridge University Press.

Useem, M. (1980) Which Business Leaders Help Govern? *Critical sociology* 9/2-3: 107-120.

von Mises, L. (1956) *The Anti-Capitalistic Mentality*, Princeton: Van Nostrand.

van der Pijl, K. (1984) *The Making of an Atlantic Ruling Class*. London & New York: Verso.

van der Pijl, K. (1993) The Sovereignty of Capital Impaired: Social Forces and Codes of Conduct for Multinational Corporations. In Overbeek, H. ed., *op cit.*, chapter 2.

Wade, R. (1996) Japan, the World Bank, and the Art of Paradigm Maintenance: The East Asian Miracle in Political Perspective. *New Left Review* 217 (May-June): 3-36.

CHAPTER 4

(1997) SOCIAL MOVEMENTS FOR GLOBAL CAPITALISM: THE TRANSNATIONAL CAPITALIST CLASS IN ACTION. *REVIEW OF INTERNATIONAL POLITICAL ECONOMY*: 4/3): 514-538. [COURTESY OF TAYLOR & FRANCIS]

Preamble

In the 25 years before I retired from teaching (roughly 1980 to 2004) I was fortunate to have a group of PhD students who enthusiastically shared my interest in the workings of global capitalism and its allies in all spheres of life. During this period the sociology of social movements was flourishing, in particular the emergence of a transnational anti-capitalist, anti-globalization movement had started to capture headlines all over the world. The struggle of the Zapatistas in Mexico in the 1990s and the "Battle of Seattle" in 1999 were the main events but pockets of resistance were being researched in all five continents. Most of this research focused on anti-capitalist social movements. Then I came across an article by Boies and Pichardo (1993-4) which introduced me to the concept of "elite social movement organizations" (hereafter ESMOs) and a book by the historian Richard Cockett (1995) which convinced me that social movements *for* capitalism were just as important as social movements *against* capitalism.

Abstract

The thesis that "Capitalism does not just happen" is argued with reference to Gramsci's analysis of hegemony and how it can be mobilized in the critique of state centrism. This involves problematizing the assumption that ruling classes rule effortlessly, and raises the issue: does globalization increase the pressures on ruling classes to deliver? My version of global system theory is outlined in terms of transnational practices in the economic, political, and culture and ideology spheres, and the characteristic institutional forms of these, namely the transnational corporation, transnational capitalist class, and the culture-ideology of consumerism. The transnational capitalist class is organized in four over-lapping fractions: TNC executives, globalizing bureaucrats, politicians and professionals, and consumerist elites (merchants and media). Social movements for global capitalism and elite social movement organizations (ESMOs) are analyzed. Each of the four fractions of the TCC has its own distinctive organizations, some of which take on social movement-like characteristics.

Global capitalism and social movements

The focus of social movement research, old and new, has always and quite properly been on anti-establishment, progressive and reactionary, deviant, left and right wing revolutionary movements of various types. The aim of this article is to help redress the balance and to show how global capitalism, which I take to be the single most important (though not, of course, the only) global force, is in many respects vulnerable. It is a social system that struggles to create and reproduce its hegemonic order globally, and to do this large numbers of local, national, international, and transnational organizations have been established, some of which engage in practices that clearly parallel the organizational forms and actions of what are conventionally called new social movements. My argument is that the global capitalist project is gaining ground as the emerging solution to all these crises and as befits a hegemonic crisis of the first order, the solution is a new conception of global hegemony, "in other words, the possibility and necessity of creating a new culture" (Gramsci 1971, 276; written in 1930). But while Gramsci was thinking of a new socialist order in the 1930s, for the 1990s this raises the prospect of what Ranney (1994) terms an "emerging supranational corporate agenda". The devastation of the 1970s oil shocks, the subsequent debt crises, corporate restructuring and downsizing (the race to the bottom) and the apparent inability of politicians to deal with these problems in any other way than by short-term palliatives, suggest that the local effects of globalization increase the pressures on capitalist corporations, state apparatuses, politicians and professionals, and cultural-ideological elites, what I shall go on to define as the transnational capitalist class, to deliver. If this is true, and I shall argue that it has been increasingly the case since the relatively prosperous 1950s and 1960s, then what I conceptualize as the "siege mentality of global capitalism" is not such a surprising outcome.

The siege mentality of capitalist ruling classes

All ruling classes in all social systems not characterized by "pure democracy" (however defined) have to ensure their power to sustain the "normal processes of interaction". So, police forces, courts of law, armies, gods (religious and/or secular), superego, posterity, and other mechanisms of social control play their part to defend the integrity of the social system, to permit accommodation to change, and even (on occasion) to ensure the success of inevitable revolutions in human affairs. The functionalist theory of social control, notwithstanding the imputed normalcy of the processes involved, demonstrates most completely the existence and salience of the siege mentality of capitalism (Sklair 1993). The siege mentality entails the view that social systems are always potentially vulnerable to attack, no less from inside than from outside. Approval, and reward for behaviour which sustains it, must be maintained to ensure the persistence of the system; adaptation and change of system properties must be possible where the defiance proves to be too strong for the system to resist; accommodation where neither the system nor the deviance is clearly more powerful. The siege of Troy is reputed to have lasted ten years. But sieges imply stable territory to be defended and identifiable enemies to take aggressive action. What is the stable territory of capitalism in the era of globalization? In the classical literature of structural-functionalism, Merton, by stipulating that the opposition between cultural goals and institutional means might provoke deviant responses in people unable to live up to either or both, is not speaking of any old goals or means. As has often been pointed out, Merton is really speaking about how a dominant system (in this case, middle-class, white America) defines its goals and means not only for itself but for the whole society, all the other systems and sub-systems. The development of "subcultural theory" was a recognition of the fact that Merton was often rather ambiguous about the system in question, sometimes suggesting that it was in fact the whole society he was referring to, at other times suggesting that it was the less inclusive system of middle-class, white America. If the former, then it was patently not the case that the goals and means he identified held for every system and sub-system in the total society; if the latter, the theory can cover only those who were part of the system in the first place, you cannot deviate from goals and means pertaining to a social system within which you have no part, on the functionalist definition. Parsons' avowed aim to create a general theory of action for the social sciences meant that he was always on the look-out for general features of social action and interaction. The most important of these is that: "All social action is normatively oriented, and the value-orientations embodied in these norms must to a degree be common to the actors in an institutionally integrated interactive system" (Parsons 1951, 251). This is not all. Parsons goes on to say: "Probably a stable interactive relationship without common value-patterns is not empirically possible" (1951, 261). This is consensus theory (the functionalist theory of hegemony) with a vengeance. All systems are, as it were, crucially tied in with the big system which makes society possible. Thus: "Without deliberate planning on anyone's part there have developed in our type of social system, and correspondingly in others, mechanisms which, within limits, are capable of forestalling and reversing the deep-lying tendencies for deviance to get into the vicious circle phase which puts it beyond the control of ordinary approval-disapproval and reward-punishment sanctions ..... there are, in fact, important unplanned mechanisms in the social system which in a sense 'match' the inherent tendencies to socially structured deviance" (ibid., 319-20) What is lacking in the functionalist theory of hegemony, and what renders it quite inferior to Marxist theories of hegemony, is a concept of interests, particularly class interests. In a system genuinely based on consensus, conformity to basic system goals would clearly be un-objectionable and probably very simple to implement. But when privileged minorities try to impose their definitions of goals, means, and needs on majorities, conformity becomes objectionable on moral grounds, and complicated rationales must be constructed to justify its imposition. Parsons asks the same questions as Hobbes "how do we solve the problem of order?" and reaches a not dissimilar conclusion: people make (or act as if they had made) a social contract, without looking at the small print of the contract, and they are encouraged to speculate continually on the dire consequences of violating its precepts or, worse, giving it up altogether. But both had the siege mentality, both could not help but see that social order was a real problem only for those with privileges to defend, and both feared the consequences when the masses started to challenge these privileges. The functionalist approach to hegemony is a special case of this general position. The siege mentality, therefore, is only politic, for any social conformity not based on consensus will always tend to break down, challenges to hegemony will always be imminent. The power to create conformity and to reward it rests with some social groups rather than others, and with some strategically located individuals rather than others. A clear illustration of the correctness of this interpretation of the fragility at the core of capitalism is the "problem of business" in the heartland of capitalist hegemony, the USA. In a path-breaking article Dreier (1982) shows that

since the 1970s, Big Business in the USA has been mobilized "to reverse a
dramatic decline in public confidence in Big Business which they blame on
the media" (ibid., 111). To counteract this, Big Business mobilized a five-
prong campaign, establishing think tanks to provide expert comment
(notably the American Enterprise Institute, Ethics and Public Policy Center,
and institutions like the Hoover, Heritage, and Hudson, all revitalized with
corporate money); university business journalism courses (the National
Association of Manufacturers Foundation for Economic Freedom textbook
and workshops, journalism schools funded by corporations (GM, ITT, etc.);
awards and prizes to encourage more favourable reporting (UCLA's Loeb
Awards, Champion at Dartmouth focused on "Recruiting excellence from
classroom to boardroom" (2021 slogan); detente between business and
media through conferences (the Ford seminars, for example); advocacy
advertising and increased TV sponsorship of culture (notably the Mobil Oil
TV series; the Advertising Council's campaign on the American System;
corporate adverts in *Columbia Journalism Review*; Friedman's "Free to
Choose" TV series; US Chamber of Commerce's "What's the Issue"; pre-
recorded interviews for broadcast; canned editorials; columns and cartoons
for newspapers; PR consultants as experts etc., etc.. An important addition
to Dreier's list is the development of "business ethics", both as an area of
academic research, in their survey article Tsalikis and Fritzsche (1989)
identify over 300 sources. All these activities illustrate a siege mentality for
a capitalist system that is losing its hegemony, elegantly exposed in,
appropriately enough, an article in *Propaganda Review* by Graziano (1989).
Dreier concludes, correctly in my view, that the reason for all this activity
is that the "capitalist class always faces the threat of challenge from below"
(ibid., 130). Where the USA leads others follow, sooner or later. No doubt
at some periods, in the USA and elsewhere, Big Business is more popular
than at others, but the point is that capitalist hegemony needs constant
support, attention and originality to sustain its hegemony. The question now
needs to be raised: "Is this more or less true for capitalism in the global as
compared with the national context in the USA?"

Global System Theory

Since the 1980s a great deal of attention has been paid to globalization by
scholars (see Lechner & Boli 2000, its sixth edition was published in 2020)
and practitioners, notably in the business press and the annual reports of
most of the largest corporations. It is important at the outset to distinguish
between national-international and transnational or global approaches to
globalization. This distinction between national-international and transnational

or global signals the difference between state-centrist approaches based on the pre-existing even if constantly changing system of nation-states and global approaches based on transnational forces and institutions where the state is one among several key actors and, in genuine theories of globalization, no longer the most important actor (Ohmae 1995, Sklair 1995 and 2002). Not all writers are clear about this distinction, with resultant confusions. The global system theory propounded here is based on the concept of transnational practices, practices that cross state boundaries but do not necessarily originate with state agencies or actors. Analytically, they operate in three spheres: the economic, the political and the cultural-ideological. The whole is what I mean by the global system. While the global system, at the end of the twentieth century, is not synonymous with global capitalism, what the theory sets out to demonstrate is that the dominant forces of global capitalism are the dominant forces in the global system. The building blocks of the theory are the transnational corporation, the characteristic institutional form of economic transnational practices, a still-evolving transnational capitalist class (TCC) in the political sphere, and the culture-ideology of consumerism in the culture-ideology sphere. The capitalist class is defined here quite conventionally as those who own and/or control the major means of production, distribution, and exchange. As I argued above, class hegemony does not simply happen as if by magic. The capitalist class expends much time, energy, and resources to make it happen and to ensure that it keeps on happening. Like other classes and collectivities of various types one of the ways in which the TCC achieves its aims is through social movements. The TCC is not necessarily the ruling class. The assumption on which my argument is based is that the TCC is the ruling class in the global capitalist system, while the working hypothesis, as it were, is that the global capitalist system is the dominant system that regulates the global system as a whole (a rather contentious claim when this essay was originally published but less so in in the twenty first century). Logically, if the capitalist system is the dominant global system, then the TCC is the global ruling class.

The Composition of the transnational capitalist class

The transnational capitalist class is the characteristic institutional form of political transnational practices in the global capitalist system. It can be analytically divided into four main fractions: TNC executives; globalizing bureaucrats; globalizing politicians and professionals; consumerist elites (merchants and media). While each of the fractions performs distinct functions for the TCC, personnel are often interchangeable between the fractions. Key individuals can belong to more than one fraction at the same time, and the transition from membership of one to another group is more or less routinized in many societies.

The TCC is transnational in at least three senses. First, its members tend to have outward-oriented global rather than inward-oriented national perspectives on a variety of issues. The growing TNC and World Bank emphasis on what is euphemistically called "free trade" and the shift from import-substitution to export-promotion strategies of most developing countries over the last decade or two have been driven by members of the TCC. Some of the credit for this apparent transformation in the way in which Big Business works around the world is attached to the tremendous growth in business degrees, particularly in the USA and Europe, but increasingly all over the world. In 1990 the North American International Business organization surveyed 184 business schools in the USA offering graduate degrees in international business. Arizona's American Graduate School of International Management (Thunderbird) came top of the list, graduating 920 master of international management students in 1989. The second-placed Wharton School (University of Pennsylvania) graduated 743 international MBAs. A spokesman for Wharton commented: "We wanted to be a school of management of the world that just happens to be headquartered in Philadelphia" (Carey 1990: 36). Between 26 per cent and 40 per cent of all Wharton students on graduate business programmes were then from outside the USA. Research on INSEAD in Paris suggests that business schools are beginning to have a significant impact on the behaviour and ideology of European executives as well (Marceau 1989). Salas Porras (1998) discusses a related development, the spread of the "global entrepreneurial movement" as Mexican firms develop strategies to become "global players". There is now a huge literature in the popular and academic business press on the making of the global manager and the globalization of business and management (see, for example, Warner 2005 on The Routledge Global HRM Series, one of many such scholarly business publications all over the world), confirming that this is a real phenomenon and not simply the creation of a few "globaloney" myth makers. Second, members of the TCC tend to be people from many countries, more and more of whom begin to consider themselves citizens of the world as well as of their places of family origins. Some of these high profile "captains of business" at the time when this paper was originally published are listed in chapter 3 above.

Third, as noted previously, members of the TCC tend to share similar lifestyles, particularly patterns of higher education enabled by family wealth (increasingly in business schools) and consumption of luxury goods and services. Integral to this process are exclusive clubs and restaurants, ultra-expensive resorts in all continents, the right places to see and be seen, private as opposed to mass forms of travel and entertainment and, ominously, increasing residential segregation. Each fraction of the TCC sees its mission as organizing the conditions under which its interests and the interests of the system as a whole (which usually but not always coincide) can be furthered in the global, national, and local context. The concept of the transnational capitalist class implies that there is one central class that makes system-wide decisions, and that it connects formally or informally in a variety of ways with the TCC in each locality, region, and country. Despite real geographical comparative advantages and disadvantages and conflicts between different business sectors the whole of the transnational capitalist class shares a fundamental interest in the continued accumulation of private profit. The guiding hypothesis of this research programme is that in the struggles within ruling class structures at all levels the balance of power is swinging decisively from the localizers (inner-oriented economic nationalists) to the globalizers (outward-oriented neoliberals). What the TCC does as a class is to give a unity to the diverse economic interests, political organizations, and cultural and ideological formations of a very disparate group of people. As in any social class, fundamental unity of interests and purpose does not preclude shorter-term conflicts of interests and purpose, both within each of the four fractions and between them. The culture-ideology of global capitalist consumerism is the fundamental value system that keeps the system intact, but it permits a relatively wide variety of choices, for example what I have termed forms of "emergent global nationalisms" (see also Gherardi 2009, on the new mobile spirit of capitalism). The four fractions of the TCC in any geographical and social area, region, country, society, community, perform complementary functions to integrate the whole. The achievement of these goals is facilitated by the activities of local and national social movements which are connected in a complex network of global interlocks. A crucial component of this integration of the TCC as a global class is that virtually all senior members and many less senior members of the TCC will occupy a variety of interlocking positions, not only the interlocking directorates that have been the subject of detailed studies for some time in a variety of countries but also connections outside the direct ambit of the corporate sector, the civil society as it were servicing the state-like structures of the corporations. Corporate executives also regularly serve on and often chair the boards of thinktanks, charities, scientific, sports, arts, and culture bodies, universities, medical foundations and similar institutions (Domhoff, 1967; Useem, 1984; Scott 1990). It is in this sense that the claim "the business of society is business" becomes legitimated in the global capitalist system. Business, particularly the transnational corporation sector, then begins to monopolize symbols of modernity and post-modernity like free enterprise, international competitiveness, and the good life, and to transform most, if not all, social spheres in its own image. Having specified the structure of the TCC in general, before we can move on to the variety of social movements it creates (globally, internationally, and in regions, countries, cities, communities) it is important to note that these particular places where this class operates in the unfolding era of globalization, while broadly similar in fundamentals in so far as they are all parts of the global capitalist system, all have their peculiarities. So, the homogenizing effects of globalization, one defining characteristic of the phenomenon, and the peculiarities and uniqueness of history and culture, are always in tension. This tension creates a globalizing dialectic in which the thesis is the historical local (communities, real and imagined of all types, the relatively recent invention of the nation-state being the most prominent in the modern phase); the antithesis is the emerging global, of which the global capitalist system driven by the transnational capitalist class is the dominant, though not the only force. The synthesis is as yet to be formulated.

Social movements for global capitalism

Most of the literature on social movements deals with mass-based social movements against established authorities, often capitalists and those directly or indirectly in the service of capitalism. There is little theory or research on social movements for capitalism. In a convincing argument for the importance of "elite social movement organizations" (ESMOs) Boies and Pichardo (1993-4) show how the theory of resource mobilization, which dominates the study of social movements, at least in the USA, inhibits the study of ESMOs. This is more or less what I mean by social movements *for* global capitalism, as elites appear to have ready access to resources. Theories of the state (Marxist, structuralist, instrumentalist, and class-dialectical) fare little better for none of them seems able to cope with the phenomenon of ESMOs. The majority view appears to be that though elite cultural, political, and economic organizations do exist in most parts of the world elites have no need of social movements to secure social changes in their own interests as these tend to happen anyway. Boies and Pichardo see this as a profoundly mistaken view and while I cannot put words into their mouths, I presume that they would generally accept the siege mentality argument developed above. Indeed, their analysis of the Committee on the Present Danger, an elite social movement organization in the USA founded in 1976, provides excellent evidence both for their conception of ESMOs and for what I am calling the siege mentality of corporate capitalism. Boies and Pichardo make a very telling point about the differences between elite and non-elite social movement organizations, namely that the high social status of ESMO members makes it likely that these organizations will rely on finance and expertise rather than personnel and mass-based activities (ibid., 64). This certainly distinguishes ESMOs from most social movements like environmental, labour, peace, and human rights movements of various types. Combining this ESMOs framework with my analysis of the four fractions of the transnational capitalist class, I shall now argue that each fraction of the TCC has thrown up its own social movements for global capitalism locally and that these are slowly being transformed into global movements.

TNC executives (the corporate fraction)

As noted in the previous chapter, the most important fraction of the TCC in the global capitalist system is composed of the leading executives of the major transnational corporations (TNC). Those who own and/or control the most important corporations (there are several lists, the *Fortune Global 500*, ranked by revenues, now in its 67th year is probably the most referenced). These major corporations are supported by their local affiliates operating either directly as wholly owned subsidiaries or indirectly as related entities of various types, in any part of the world. The executives of these corporations wield power to the extent that they control parts of the global economy and their actions and decisions can have fundamental effects on the local communities in which their corporations are active in any capacity. The TCC also includes the leading executives of companies which, while not themselves among the biggest TNCs, play a strategic role in the global economy (for example, advertising and public relations agencies). The economic base of these executives is their corporate salaries and their often-privileged access to shares and other financial privileges in the companies they work for either directly or as nominated members of boards. Their ESMOS are the peak business associations and organizations that connect business with other spheres (governments, global politics, social issues, etc.) operating at various levels (see, for example, Burch 1981; Grant and Marsh 1977; Lynn and McKeown 1988). The culture and ideology of TNC executives is an emerging cohesive culture-ideology of global capitalist consumerism, where global brands and tastes are promoted in the effort to turn all cultural products and human emotions into commercial opportunities. It is important to distinguish here between the individual preferences and lifestyles of executives, which might vary considerably, and the culture-ideology of the class as a whole. Irrespective of how individual executives live their lives, there is no doubt that global marketing and selling have become the ideological rationale for the system as a whole. This does not, however, preclude modifying these global formulas to suit local tastes, as happens frequently in, for example, the fashion and fast foods sectors. The same can be said for more specific political tastes with respect to the neoliberal agenda. I tend to agree with Useem (1984) and Gill (1990) and others, that top business elites tend to be more progressive on social and sometimes even labour issues than, for example, some of the think tanks and other institutions that their corporations help to finance (see Alpert and Markusen 1980, Cockett 1995). More systematic research is clearly needed on this question.

Transnational corporations and their executives have commonly and with good reason felt insecure, particularly in the foreign countries where they run factories and provide services, whether from physical assault (Gladwin and Walter 1980) or expropriation (Minor 1994). Though both appear to have declined in the past decades, it is not very surprising that TNCs have routinely taken pre-emptive action to put their case before the public and the local authorities with whom they have to deal. For reasons which cannot be dealt with here, Big Business tends to be unpopular and its claims tend to be treated with a high degree of cynicism and so it often resorts to indirect ways of creating support for its causes and influencing public policy in the direction of its sectional interests. As noted above, some have argued that one of the most important ideological tasks of Big Business is to persuade the population at large that "the business of society is business" and to create a climate of opinion in which trade unions and radical oppositions (especially consumer and environmental movements) are considered to be sectional interests while business groups are presented as representing the common, public interest. This is, of course, a large part of the contemporary analysis of capitalist (I would add, consumerist) hegemony. There is a good deal of agreement among scholars that Big Business (like the Communist Party in countries where it was illegal or circumscribed) often creates front organizations to propagate its messages. Many apparently straightforward civic organizations which also have some of the characteristics of social movements are largely funded by and sometimes managed by corporate personnel. Most of the research on these phenomena has been carried out in and on the USA and most focuses on the ways in which Big Business, domestic (Domhoff 1990) and foreign (Tolchin & Tolchin 1988), exert influence on the US government and its various state apparatuses to legislate and rule in the interests of global capital at home and abroad. In their contribution to a book on socialism in Chile, David Eisenhower (apparently a distant relation of the former president Dwight) and Dale Johnson (1973, 51-3) provide a useful checklist for studying such organizations and their activities: "Official conspiracies are those institutionalized ways in which corporate interests shape and guide policies of the U.S. government ..... The main apparatus of official conspiracies consists of organizations controlled by members of the corporate elite class that sponsor research, commission studies, publish influential journals, issue reports, engage in formal and informal dialogues with government officials, formulate policy guidelines, see that their men [and, increasingly, women] are appointed to key government posts, etc." They also provide a useful guide to corporate influence on issues of foreign policy citing corporate-controlled research-planning advising and report-issuing public affairs groups; businessmen's organizations; executively commissioned task forces, committees and missions; citizen (read business) advisory councils and committees; United States representatives to U.N.-sponsored panels; research institutes; and foundations (ibid). Since the 1970s there have been many excellent studies documenting and analyzing these phenomena in the USA, notably Shoup and Minter (1977) on the Council on Foreign Relations, Burch (1981) on the Business Roundtable, Useem (1980) on business leaders in government, Sklar (1980) on the Trilateral Commission, while Domhoff (1990) makes a strong case for a pervasive corporate ruling class whose organizations steer the state in various policy directions. These findings from research on the USA have been replicated to some extent by research from other countries (Scott 1990: passim). In the section on consumerist elites below I will document how this fraction of the TCC works assiduously to inculcate consumerist values and practices in all spheres of social life.

Globalizing bureaucrats fulfil a governance function for the global capitalist system at the local, national, inter-state and eventually global levels where individual states are not directly involved. Typically, these people are to be found dealing with or actually working in local urban and regional growth coalitions fueled by foreign investment; national bureaucracies responsible for external economic relations (exports, FDI in both directions, market-driven aid agencies); international organizations, notably the World Bank, IMF, OECD, WTO, regional development banks and some agencies of the UN; and, in my sense, global or transnational organizations like the Bilderberg Group (see Thompson, in Sklar, ed., 1980), The Trilateral Commission (Sklar, 1980; Gill, 1990) and the International Industrial Conference, organized every four years by the Conference Board and Stanford Research Institute (Townley, 1990). The senior personnel in the major philanthropic foundations (notably Ford and Rockefeller) also fall

96

Chapter 4

into this category. Their economic base is state or foundation salaries, which tend to lag substantially behind the private corporate sector but their opportunities for augmenting these salaries are considerable. They frequently move to the private sector, working directly for the corporations whose interests they may have been indirectly serving (or impeding) as public employees. The agencies they work for are, in a sense, their political organizations and in many countries particular local and national state agencies can be identified with, for example, open-door policies, that further the interests of the global capitalist class (whoever else's interests they may also further). Globalizing bureaucrats also work politically through corporatist agencies that combine representatives of the state, business, and labour. The culture and ideology of globalizing bureaucrats tend to be more complex than those of TNC executives. Their dominant ideology appears to be in a process of transformation from state interventionism to neoliberalism which privileges the unfettered operation of their mantra, the free market. This ideology is reinforced daily by cultural practices cohering into what can be termed an emergent global nationalism, characterized as the view that the best interests of the country (almost all countries) lie in rapid integration with the global capitalist system while maintaining a corporate (and often cleverly manufactured national identity by marketing national competitive advantages of various types through global brands and tourism (now the most important hard-currency-earning industry in an increasing number of local and national economies). Despite some notable exceptions, it is difficult to see the top ranks of the globalizing bureaucracies in any other light than retired corporate executives putting their marketing skills to use in the public service or the upwardly mobile *en route* to top TNC jobs.

Globalizing politicians and professionals are a diverse group of people who perform a variety of personal and technical services for the TCC. Politicians from both conservative and social democratic parties commonly come from and return to the corporate sector and ESMOs (particularly bodies like the Council on Foreign Relations and the Trilateral Commission) in various capacities. In most representative democracies elected politicians and officials must respond to the interests of their local constituents, but these interests are more often than not defined in terms of the interests of the corporations that provide employment and make profits locally. Research on these issues is most advanced in the USA. It is often claimed that the USA is one of the most democratic countries in the world in terms of public access. The works of Useem (1984) on Political Action Committees, and many others on local corporate-politician connections (Domhoff, 1990; Tolchin, 1988), attest to a phenomenon that is probably even more widespread in countries where there is less public scrutiny of such relationships. Research on the USA also confirms the important thesis that the corporate sector is well represented in the higher non-elective offices of state by those who return to the corporations after their periods of public service (Scott 1990: Vol. I, passim, esp. Freitag). Globalizing professionals, as a group, have attracted a good deal of attention in recent years. This is largely due to the growth of two phenomena which, while not exclusive to the era of globalization, have accelerated rapidly since the 1960s. These are, first, the business services industries, ranging from information technology to consulting and public relations of various types; and, second, the rise of the thinktanks, particularly those associated with neoliberal free trade and free enterprise agendas (Alpert & Markusen 1980; Cockett 1995; Marchak 1991). The dominant elites in these institutions are among the most publicly visible members of the TCC. They are organized politically in their own professional organizations, in the corporatist organizations noted above and in thinktanks and universities, where they market more or less research-based information and policy to corporations and governments. As they are largely funded by governments, transnational corporations and private capitalists, their independence is often a matter of dispute. As with globalizing bureaucrats, the culture and ideology of these politicians and professionals is a complex mix of global nationalism and neoliberalism. The global network of business consultants like McKinsey and Burson-Marsteller (now Burson Cohn & Wolfe) contains many individuals who have worked in business services, government advisory bodies, major corporations, ESMOs, and sometimes several at the same time. In a notable study of the Trilateral Commission Gill (1990) illustrates how this elite social movement organization has played host to a galaxy of ruling-class stars of particular significance for a globalizing agenda. Gill tries to develop a Gramscian analysis connecting the hegemonic needs of modern capitalism, the creation of what he labels a "transnational capitalist class fraction" and what he identifies as the "internationally oriented" Trilateralist Commission. Gill argues that, in the context of the networks and linkages suggested by the research of Domhoff (1967), Useem (1984), and Scott (1990), the vanguard elements represented in organizations such as the Conference Board (which represents blue-chip American and increasingly transnational corporate capital) and the Trilateral Commission are able to develop a general class consciousness and cohesion. The process involves rotation of corporate leaders into and out of the American executive branch. What is suggested here is that it is possible to denote a relationship between the transnational class fractions discussed earlier and steering patterns in American capitalism. (Gill 1990, 165) While many might doubt that the ESMOs commonly identified in the USA really do have the power and influence that those who write about them claim and, more specifically, that the Trilateral Commission can bear the theoretical weight of Gill's analysis, it is still nevertheless a strong argument that the corporate elite in the USA is very active in a very wide range of organizations and activities that are not directly concerned with the balance sheets of their corporations. What I have termed capitalist-inspired politicians and professionals are certainly working on the front line for them.

While **consumerist elites (merchants and media)** are a part of the TNC executive fraction of the TCC, their role in the day to day functioning of the system of global consumerist capitalism is so important that they require special treatment. Like other TNC executives, their economic base is in salaries and share capital and their culture and ideology is a cohesive culture-ideology of consumerism. However, the specificity of the members of the media elite lies in their political organization, more specifically their means of political expression through the TV networks, newspapers, magazines, and other mass media they own and control. The retail sector, particularly the ubiquitous shopping malls that are springing up all over the world, can in this sense be regarded analytically as part of the mass media. Through the medium of advertising the links between media and merchants and the entire marketing system (raw materials, design, production, packaging, financing, transportation, wholesaling, retailing, disposal) become concrete. In the apparently inexorable increase in the global connectedness of the mass media and consumerism we can chart the ways in which the TCC appears gradually to be imposing its hegemony all over the world. Global system theory argues that consumerist elites play a central role in global capitalist hegemony. As I noted above, the practical politics of this hegemony is the everyday life of consumer society and the promise that it is a global reality for most of the world's peoples. This is certainly the most persistent image projected by television and the mass media in general. In one sense, therefore, shopping is the most successful social movement, product advertising in its many forms the most successful message, consumerism the most successful ideology of all time. In his absorbing paper on "The magic of the mall" Goss (1993) points out that shopping is the second most important leisure-time activity in the USA (after watching TV, and much of TV promotes shopping anyway). "Shopping has become the dominant mode of contemporary public life" (ibid., 18). While this is true at present only for the First World and perhaps some privileged elites elsewhere, the rest of the world appears to be following rapidly (Findley et al., 1990), at a time when malls are being critically re-evaluated in the USA (Robertson 1990). Goss argues that the idea of the mall signals a third, public, space after home and work/school, to see and be seen in. Malls, it seems, are not just places to buy and sell but are increasingly taking on other functions (for example, education, culture, and child care), very much oriented, however, to the middle classes. Malls aim to provide safe, secure environments for "normal consumers", but are more reluctant to provide genuine public services like drinking fountains, public toilets, telephones, etc. where deviants or non-shoppers (often defined as deviants) can congregate. Goss reports that the average length of time spent in shopping centre trips in the USA has increased from twenty minutes in 1960 to nearly three hours in the 1990s, no doubt facilitated by the omnipresent grazing opportunities in the fast food outlets. Art and museums are now being brought into the mall directly: the first US National Endowment for the Arts grant to a private corporation went for art projects in malls. This gradual process of replacing the purchase of many of the necessities of consumption from local shops and marketplaces, redefining this as shopping and relocating it increasingly all over the world into the more controlled environments of department stores and malls is at the core of capitalist globalization. Shopping has been transformed from the relatively simple satisfaction of basic needs for most people into a form of mass entertainment, a major leisure activity, one of the greatest achievements of global capitalism. This transformation has been achieved in an amazing variety of ways, from advocacy advertising where large corporations take out series of very expensive adverts to persuade people of the virtues of free enterprise (Sethi, 1977) to commercialized classroom and colleges (Esland 1976), from advertorials where sponsors pay for insertions that look like editorial content in the mass media (Stout et al. 1989) to the ultimate capital investment, strategic philanthropy (Kyle, 1990).

This article has attempted to articulate a set of ideas about a transnational capitalist class and set out a method to study it in action. This method assumes that those who own and control the most substantial economic resources (principally the TNCs) will be in a position to further their interests to an extent and in ways not available to most other groups in society. However, those who run the transnational corporations cannot achieve their ends alone. They require help from sub-groups, notably consumerist elites, globalizing bureaucrats and politicians and professionals, to carry out their work effectively. This help is often organized through elite social movement organizations, social movements for capitalism. Global system theory provides some underlying arguments to support this way of analyzing the class structure of global capitalism and to study the extent to which these movements cross local, national, and international boundaries to become truly global manifestations of the TCC in action.

Communication between the four fractions of the transnational capitalist class is facilitated in a variety of ways, notably interlocking directorates, cross-memberships of groups in different spheres (business, government, politics, professions, media, etc.) and leadership roles of business notables in non-business activities, thinktanks, charities, universities, medical, arts and sports foundations and the like. In these ways the idea that the business of society is business is promulgated through all spheres of society with the consequence that non-business activities become more and more commercialized, as can be clearly demonstrated for social services, the arts, sports, science, education, and most other spheres of social life. The membership of the TCC illustrates the extent of these interlocks and cross-connections. What has been attempted here is the analysis of how the TCC acts as a class, moving somewhat beyond the general truth that capitalists seek to maximize their profits in any way that they can, including improving the business climate (putting pressure on governments to act in the interests of business), improving their knowledge base (employing consultants) and improving their image (doing good works). The widely accepted argument that most foreign and domestic TNCs all over the world have globalized in significant ways was linked to evidence of the globalizing project of the globalizing bureaucrats (in local and national government and international agencies) and politicians and professionals (leaders of the major parties, establishment academics, scientists, thinktanks, business consultants). A series of detailed case studies on resource allocation, material rewards, key decisions, institutional changes, and agenda building would be necessary to establish beyond reasonable doubt that the TCC, globally, really has acted as a class since the early 1980s. My contention is that the theory and method outlined in this article would be of value in such an endeavour, as I argue for the case of the TCC in Australia (Sklair 1996) and more generally (Sklair 2017). While capitalism increasingly organizes globally, the resistances to global capitalism can only be effective where they can disrupt its smooth running (accumulation of private profits) locally and can find ways of globalizing these disruptions. No social movement appears even remotely likely to overthrow the three fundamental institutional supports of global consumerist capitalism that have been identified, namely the TNCs, the transnational capitalist class and the culture-ideology of consumerism. Nevertheless, in each of these spheres there are resistances expressed by social movements. The TNCs, if we are to believe their own propaganda, are beset by opposition, boycott, legal challenge and moral outrage from the consumers of their products and by disruptions from their workers. The transnational capitalist class often finds itself opposed by vocal coalitions when it tries to impose its will in the old and the new ways. The problem for global capitalism is that each of its own social movements, in the form of elite social movement organizations, throws up alternative mass movements in many forms to challenge its hegemony.

Second Thoughts

My second thoughts on this essay, written almost twenty-five years ago, are that I may have seriously underestimated the complexity and durability of elite social movements for global capitalism and, more alarmingly, the baleful impact that the transnational capitalist class would have on democratic processes all over the world. In 2019 a fourth version of the Committee on the Present Danger was convened in the USA but this time with the tacit support of the Trump regime. It is ironic that in 2019 The Committee was mainly warning about the danger of China, by now (like Russia and India) more or less authoritarian capitalist states. The EU, for many on the Left in previous decades a bastion of democracy, now harbours several similarly authoritarian capitalist states. In the 2020s all over the world levels of trust in governments and progressive politicians are in decline. Is it ridiculous to argue that the only thing that keeps the global system together in a time of coronavirus pandemic, precarious economies, and the Anthropocene is the TCC-sponsored culture-ideology of consumerism? The tremendous growth of so-called "Public Affairs consultants in recent decades, chronicled by Walker (2014) for the USA but now operating globally, lobbyists claiming to represent the "grassroots", is yet one more layer in the complex structure of elite social movements for global capitalism. Another significant second thought was triggered by my encounter (rather late in the day) with the innovative concept of "degrowth". I reviewed the book *Degrowth: A Vocabulary for a New Era* (D'Alisa et al. 2014) in the *British Journal of Sociology*. This was the first book on degrowth in English. While my review was not uncritical I came to the following conclusion: "this book should be compulsory reading for all students in universities and sixth form colleges everywhere. The authorities would be well advised to ban it. Perhaps, as in 'Fahrenheit 451', in the transition to degrowth global societies idealists will memorize some of these short and inspiring prose poems showing that another world is possible. But if the corporate capture of sustainable development [the topic of chapter 10 below] teaches us anything, banning may not be necessary, as the ideological entrepreneurs of the transnational capitalist class seem to be taking an unhealthy interest in degrowth already."

La Décroissance (Degrowth) is the name of a popular French monthly magazine, first published 2004, apparently now printing a regular section on "the nonsense of sustainable development". The social movement now known as *Décroissance* emerged institutionally at a conference in Paris in 2008, followed by conferences in other European cities. It is now an international research and activist network, a social movement with anti-capitalist tendencies. Degrowthers argue that degrowth is: "largely ignored, if it is not a taboo" (ibid., xxiv). There are many reasons why degrowth is a marginal concept in the marketplace of ideas. It emerged largely in the non-Anglophone world. The term *décroissance* was used first by the social theorist André Gorz in 1972 (in a public debate in Paris) asking if it is compatible with capitalism. This issue remains unresolved in the 2020s, "There is no agreement among degrowth theorists concerning the inevitability of capitalist expansion" (ibid., 61). In my view, capitalism could not survive degrowth, and human survival on planet Earth depends on degrowth. The central sociological correlates of degrowth (regrettably ignored by most sociologists) are commonly identified as sharing, simplicity, conviviality, care, and the commons. My speculations around the idea of producer-consumer cooperatives (P-CCs), as elaborated in Chapter 11, were at least partially inspired by the debates that the concept of degrowth have stimulated, most recently by Kallis, et al. 2020).

References

Alexander, M., Murray, G., & Houghton, J. (1994) Business power in Australia: the concentration of company directorship holding among the top 250 corporates. *Australian Journal of Political Science* 29: 40-61.

Alpert, I. & Markusen, A. (1980) Think tanks and capitalist policy. In G. W. Domhoff, ed. *Power Structure Research*. Beverly Hills, CA: Sage, chapter 7.

Ashworth, G. & Voogd, H. (1990*) Selling the City: Marketing Approaches in Public Sector Urban Planning*. London: Belhaven Press.

Boies, J. & Pichardo, N. (1993-4) The Committee on the Present Danger: a case for the importance of elite social movement organizations to theories of social movements and the state. *Berkeley Journal of Sociology* 38: 57-87.

Browning, B. (1990) *The Network: A Guide to Anti-Business Pressure Groups*. Victoria: Canonbury Press.

Burch, P. (1981) The business roundtable: its make-up and external ties. *Research in Political Economy* 4: 101-27.

Carey, P. (1990) The making of a global manager. *North American International Business* (June): 36-41.

Carroll, W. & Lewis, S. (1991) Restructuring finance capital: changes in the Canadian corporate network 1976-1986. *Sociology* 25: 491-510.

Cockett, R. (1995) *Thinking the Unthinkable: Think-Tanks and the Economic Counter-Revolution, 1931-1983.* London: Harper Collins.

Connell, R. W. (1977) *Ruling Class, Ruling Culture.* Cambridge: Cambridge University Press.

Cox, R. W. (1987) *Production, Power, and World Order: Social Forces in the Making of History.* New York: Columbia University Press.

D'Alisa, G., et al. eds. (2014) *Degrowth: A Vocabulary for a New Era.* New York & London: Routledge.

Domhoff, G. W. (1967) *Who Rules America?* Englewood Cliffs: Prentice-Hall.

Domhoff, G.W. (1990) *The Power Elite and the State: How policy is made in America.* New York: Aldine de Gruyter.

Dreier, P. (1982) Capitalists vs. the media: an analysis of an ideological mobilization among business leaders. *Media, Culture and Society* 4: 111-32.

Eisenhower, D. & Johnson, D. (1973) The low profile swings a big stick. In D. Johnson, ed. *The Chilean Road to Socialism.* New York: Anchor Books, chapter 2.

Esland, G., et al. eds. (1976) *Schooling and capitalism : a sociological reader.* London: Routledge and Kegan Paul for the Open University Press.

Evan, W. (1981) *Knowledge and Power in a Global Society.* London: Sage.

Fennema, M. (1982) *International Networks of Banks and Industry.* The Hague: Martinus Nijhoff.

Findley, A. et al., eds. (1990) *Retailing Environment in Developing Countries.* Andover: Routledge.

Gherardi, L. (2009) *La mobilité ambiguë: Espace, temps et pouvoir aux sommets de la société contemporaine.* Sarrebruck: Éditions universitaires européennes.

Gill, S. (1990) *American Hegemony and the Trilateral Commission.* Cambridge: Cambridge University Press.

Gladwin, T. & Walter, I. (1980) *Multinationals under Fire.* New York: Wiley.

Goldfrank, W. (1977) Who rules the world? Class formation at the international level. *Quarterly Journal of Ideology* 1/2: 32-7.

Goss, J. (1993) The "magic of the mall": an analysis of form, function, and meaning in the contemporary retail built environment. *Annals of the Association of American Geographers* 83/1: 18-47.

Gramsci, A. (1971) *Selections from the Prison Notebooks* (edited and translated by Q. Hoare & G. N. Smith). London: Lawrence & Wishart.

Grant, I. & Marsh, D. (1977) *The CBI*. London: Hodder & Stoughton.

Graziano, L. (1989) How business ethics became "Issues Management". *Propaganda Review* (Summer): 29-31.

Haas, P. (1992) Introduction: epistemic communities and international policy coordination. *International Organization* 46: 1-35.

Jarley, P. & Maranto, C. (1990) Union corporate campaigns: an assessment. *Industrial and Labor Relations Review* 43: 505-24.

Kyle, A. (1990) The ultimate capital investment. *California Business* (1 July): 36-41.

Lechner, F. & Boli, J. eds. (2000) *The globalization reader.* Malden & Oxford: Blackwell.

Lynn, L. & McKeown, T. (1988) *Organizing Business: Trade Associations in America and Japan*. Washington, DC: American Enterprise Institute.

Marceau, J. (1989) *A Family Business? The Making of an International Business Elite*. Cambridge: Cambridge University Press.

Marchak, M. P. (1991) *The Integrated Circus: The New Right and the Restructuring of Global Markets*. Montreal & Kingston: McGill-Queens University Press.

McGraw, T. (1992) A global society. In S. Hall, et al. eds., *Modernity and its Futures*. Cambridge: Polity and Open University.

Minor, M. (1994) The demise of expropriation as an instrument of LDC policy: 1980-1992. *Journal of International Business Studies* 25: 177-88.

Mizruchi, M. & Schwartz, M., eds. (1987) *Intercorporate Relations: The Structural Analysis of Business*. Cambridge: Cambridge University Press.

Ohmae, K. (1995) *The End of the Nation State.* New York: The Free Press.

Parsons, T. (1951) *The Social System*. Glencoe: The Free Press.

Poole, W. (1989) How Big Business bankrolls the Left. *National Review* (10 March), pp. 34-9.

Rand, A. (1967) America's persecuted minority: Big Business. In Rand ed. *Capitalism: The Unknown Ideal*. New York: New American Library, pp. 44-62.

Ranney, D. (1994) Labor and an emerging supranational corporate agenda. *Economic Development Quarterly* (February): 83-91.

Richardson, K. (2000) *Big Business and the European Agenda. Reflections on the activities of the European Round Table of Industrialists, 1988-98.* Brighton: Sussex European Institute, Working Paper No. 35.

Robertson, K. (1990) The status of the pedestrian mall in American downtowns. *Urban Affairs Quarterly* 26: 250-73.

Ross, R. & Trachte, K. (1990) *global capitalism: The New Leviathan.* Albany: SUNY Press.

Salas-Porras, A. (1998) The strategies pursued by Mexican firms in their efforts to become global players. *CEPAL Review* 65: 133-153.

Scott, J. ed. (1990) *The Sociology of Elites*, 3 vols, Aldershot: Edward Elgar.

Sethi, S. P. (1977) *Advocacy Advertising and Large Corporations.* Lexington, Ky.: D. C. Heath.

Shoup, L. & Minter, W. (1977) *Imperial Brain Trust: The Council on Foreign Relations and United States Foreign Policy.* New York & London: Monthly Review Press.

Silver, J. (1990) *Global scan. A survey of the global consumer.* Advertising Research Foundation, 36th Annual Conference, New York.

Sklair, L. (1993) The siege mentality: The Rex-Parsons debate revisited. In H. Martins, ed. *Knowledge and Passion: Essays in Honour of John Rex.* London & New York: I. B. Tauris, chapter 7.

Sklair, L. (1995) *Sociology of the Global System*, 2nd edition, revised and updated. London & Baltimore: Prentice Hall/Harvester Wheatsheaf and Johns Hopkins University Press.

Sklair, L. (1996) Conceptualizing and researching the transnational capitalist class in Australia. *Australia and New Zealand Journal of Sociology* 32 (August): 1-18

Sklair, L. (2017) *The Icon Project: Architecture, Cities, and Capitalist Globalization.* New York & Oxford: Oxford University Press.

Sklar, H., ed. (1980) *Trilateralism: The Trilateral Commission and Elite Planning for World Management.* Boston: South End Press.

Stauffer, R. (1979) *Transnational corporations and host nations: attitudes, ideologies and behaviours.* University of Sydney, Transnational Corporations Research Project.

Stokman, F. et al., eds. (1985) *Networks of Corporate Power: A Comparative Analysis of Ten Countries.* Cambridge: Polity Press.

Stout, P., et al. (1989) Trends in magazine advertorial use. *Journalism Quarterly* 66/4: 960-4.

Tolchin, M. & S. (1988) *Buying into America.* New York: Berkley Books.

Townley, P. (1990) Global business in the next decade. *Across the Board* (January/February): 13-19.

Tsalikis, J. & Fritzsche, D. (1989) Business ethics: a literature review with a focus on marketing ethics. *Journal of Business Ethics* 8: 695-743.

Useem, M. (1980) Which Business Leaders Help Govern? *Critical sociology* 9/2-3: 107-120.

Useem, M. (1984) *The Inner Circle: Large Corporations and the Rise of Business Political Activity in the U.S. and UK.* New York: Oxford University Press.

van der Pijl, K. (1984) *The Making of an Atlantic Ruling Class.* London: Verso.

Walker, E.T. (2014) *Grassroots for Hire: Public Affairs Consultants in American Democracy.* Cambridge: Cambridge University Press.

Wallis, B. (1991) Selling nations. *Art in America* (September): 85-91.

Warner, M. (2005) Whither international human resource management? *The International Journal of Human Resource Management* 16/5: 870-874.

CHAPTER 5

(1998) THE TRANSNATIONAL CAPITALIST CLASS AND GLOBAL CAPITALISM: THE CASE OF THE TOBACCO INDUSTRY. *POLITICAL POWER AND SOCIAL THEORY* 12, PP.3-43. [COURTESY OF EMERALD]

Preamble

I gave up my habit of weekend smoking in my late twenties as a result of witnessing the slow painful death from lung cancer of the chain-smoking mother of a close friend. A few decades later I began to study the transnational corporations and their role in a variety of social evils (some corporations, of course, are less evil than others and some are almost admirable). The global tobacco industry was a natural choice for a research project. This coincided with my growing interest in capitalist globalization, changing patterns of consumption, and advertising, all over the world, theorized as the culture-ideology of consumerism. The project also gave me the opportunity to address an issue I felt strongly about in a scientifically objective way in a manner that was clearly not value free. How, I asked myself, can the study of an industry that knowingly contributes to ill-health and often death and cynically targets children to encourage addiction to tobacco be value free?

Abstract

The tobacco industry presents challenges, at both the theoretical level and the empirical level, to the thesis presented in this paper. Theoretically, the concept of even a relatively unified transnational capitalist class is threatened by legal restrictions on the advertising, sale, and use of tobacco products. Real curbs on the freedom of tobacco companies to advertise their wares wherever and whenever they wish, and a growing move to ban smoking in public places in many countries, restrictions that apply to very few legal products, suggest that the unity implied by the concept of the TCC, and thus the concept itself, are flawed. The empirical evidence presented in this case study, however, demonstrates that, far from challenging the concept of the TCC, analysis of those who own and control the tobacco industry provides telling evidence for the existence of a transnational capitalist class and shows that its members continue to play an important role in serving the interests of global capitalism through building the economic power of their corporations, the political power of their industry and the culture-ideology of consumerism.

Big Tobacco

> "I'll tell you why I like the cigarette business. It costs a penny to make. Sell it for a dollar. It's addictive. And there's fantastic brand loyalty." (Warren Buffett, former major stockholder in RJR (quoted in Hewat 1991, 12).

The global tobacco industry

According to *Fortune* magazine (5 August 1996, F26), the global tobacco industry in 1996 was dominated by three firms. Largest by a long way was Philip Morris Companies Inc, number, 31 in the *Global 500* rankings, with revenues in excess of $53 billion; second was BAT Industries Plc (British American Tobacco), ranked 122 with more than $24 billion in revenues; and third was Japan Tobacco, ranked 158 with revenues of $20.5 billion. RJR Nabisco, ranked 234 with revenues of $16 billion, is also a major player in the global tobacco industry though it is often classified as a food company. American Brands (acquired by BAT in 1995), Rothmans International, the German firm Reemstma (Imperial Brands), and several state monopolies make up the strong second tier. The tobacco sector was, along with food services (Pepsico and McDonald's) and pharmaceuticals, the most profitable of *Fortune* magazine's 45 business sectors (profits as a percentage of revenues) in 1996. Despite the gathering pace of the anti-smoking movement onslaught on the industry and its continuing legislative successes in many places in the 1990s (see below), there are no definitive signs that these corporations are collapsing. Evidence on the continuing profitability of the cigarette companies is often presented as surprising, for example "Still smokin: Improbably, tobacco companies are far from finished" *The Economist* (11 March 1995) and, more recently, in the ongoing series of Tobacco Industry reports by the Salomon Brothers team in New York (Salomon Brothers 1994).

The world market for tobacco has experienced several transitions (Finger ed. 1981; Nath 1986, chapter 5; Goodman 1993). By the 1960s the tremendous growth in sales that had seen the cigarette replace all other forms of tobacco consumption had begun to slow down. The tobacco TNCs were still relatively small, with national monopolies in most of the large countries of the world inhibiting their growth overseas. Added to this, health alarms from prestigious sources (the Royal College of Surgeons in the UK, and the Surgeon General in the USA) began to implicate tobacco smoking in cancers, heart diseases and other serious medical problems, implications that the industry denied while, apparently, being aware of at least some of the health risks of smoking. The anonymous donation in 1994 of 4,000 pages of documents belonging to Brown and Williamson (the American subsidiary of BAT) to Dr Stanton Glantz, a long-time anti-smoking campaigner, revealed that the company and very probably the industry as a whole were aware of the health risks and addictiveness of tobacco. The documents were summarized in a series of articles in *Journal of the American Medical Association* and now have their own website, http://www.library.ucsf.edu.tobacco (Glantz et al. 1996). In March 1997, in exchange for an end to litigation by 22 states in the USA, Liggett (makers of Chesterfield), the smallest of the US tobacco majors, admitted that the industry had lied about its knowledge of the link between smoking and disease and that it had deliberately targeted under-age smokers. The company also agreed to pay the states $25 million and 25% of annual pre-tax profits for 25 years as part-payment of Medicare bills incurred by the states to treat sick smokers. However, this will not affect the hundreds of private lawsuits pending against the industry. Though the other cigarette companies immediately responded by blocking Liggett's release of documents in the courts, by June 1997 the tobacco industry in the USA had agreed to pay $14.8 billion annually over the next 25 years to State health authorities, probably funded from increased cigarette prices. Further curbs on advertising and promotion and industry-funded programs to help people stop smoking were also part of the settlement. There is no reason to believe that this is anything more than yet another twist in the continuing story of "America's Hundred-Year Cigarette War" (Kluger 1996). These and other widely publicized events of the summer of 1997 have led some to believe that the tobacco industry in the US and, perhaps, the rest of the world, is on its last legs. My analysis predicts that the industry, supported crucially by state agencies, despite attacks from other parts of the state apparatus, and the promotional culture of cigarettes (see below), will continue to sell cigarettes and make good profits while the TCC retains its powers within global capitalism.

Paralleling these developments in the social and medical environments of the industry there occurred what Shepherd (1985, 86) describes as the "virtual disappearance of the private, nationally-owned tobacco company and its replacement by a transnational corporation subsidiary" (see also, Goodman 1993; McGowan 1995, chapter 7). While this judgement may have been a little premature it is not entirely without foundation. PM, BAT, RJR, and Reemtsma have more or less bought up the industry in eastern Europe and the former USSR. Japan Tobacco, previously a state monopoly, responded to the lifting of restrictions on imported cigarettes, which had captured over 20 per cent of the Japanese market by 1996, by aggressively marketing its own brands, notably Mild Seven, abroad. While China National Tobacco Corporation has joint ventures with foreign TNCs, the national monopoly looks secure for the time being. The Chinese government at this time raised 12 per cent of its annual revenues from cigarette taxes. Where country legislation substantially prohibits foreign brands, smuggling has become a multi-billion dollar and often violent business (Shepherd 1985). Of the estimated 80 billion foreign cigarettes sold in China in 1994, according to the *International Herald Tribune* (5 March 1997), not a single one had been imported legally. The issue has been raised in the Philippines parliament where La Suerte Cigar and Cigarette Factory was exposed for selling Philip Morris brands for 15 pesos per pack while the official tax alone on these cigarettes was 66 pesos per pack (*Business Daily* 5 March 1997).

Cigarette sales in most First World countries declined in the 1990s, though the price wars have given way to a more stable market since mid-decade. In addition, there does seem to be some evidence that the premium price brands, notably Marlboro, are increasing their market share all over the world, thus making up for some of the lost revenue in volume. The situation in the Third World and the New Second World of Eastern Europe and the former USSR is more complex. Philip Morris and RJR bartered 34 billion cigarettes with Russia in 1990 to prevent civil unrest caused by a shortage of local brands. The *Washington Post* journalists James Rupert and Glenn Frankel (1996) tell us, "Foreign cigarette brands became the leading advertisers on Russian television and radio. Tobacco ad revenues maintained municipal transport systems from St. Petersburg to Sofia, Bulgaria. In Bucharest, Reynolds provided a year's supply of bulbs for traffic lights in exchange for permission to add the Camel logo to each yellow light". These and other similar facts exposed in the *Washington Post*'s four-part series "Big Tobacco's Global Reach" (see below) make the idea of the cigarette TNCs as capitalist liberators of Eastern Europe less fanciful. Industry sources (Annual Reports) and critics (Nath 1986, Shenon

1994) alike have documented the targeting of Third World (and increasingly New Second World) consumers as a deliberate strategy to compensate for the serious decline in revenues anticipated in the First World. PM, RJR, and BAT brands in 1995 had over two thirds (often more than 90%) of the market in Barbados, Ghana, Honduras, Hong Kong, Kenya, Morocco, Nicaragua, Sri Lanka, and Turkey; and over one third in Pakistan, Slovak Republic, and Zaire (*Tobacco Reporter* October 1996). Marlboro is the top selling imported brand all over the world. Whereas in 1985 the global tobacco companies had legal access to only 40 per cent of the potential world market for cigarettes, by 1994 this had risen to 90 per cent (Shenon 1994). The main reasons for this dramatic increase were the trend to deregulation of foreign investment and trade in general, strategic alliances between local and global cigarette companies, and the dilution of government monopolies all over the world. Social factors are also cited, for example, increasing prosperity of the new middle classes and the drive to upgrade their consumption patterns, which often means preference for expensive imported over cheaper local cigarettes (Goodman 1993), the so-called liberation of women to indulge in previously male-dominated pastimes like drinking alcohol and smoking cigarettes (Greaves 1996), and massive advertising. Philip Morris and RJR bartered 34 billion cigarettes with Russia in 1990 to prevent civil unrest caused by a shortage of local brands. A prominent financial magazine reports: "Tobacco companies have poured billions into a frenzied burst of cross-border acquisitions ..... profit margins will rise as the cigarette makers persuade increasingly affluent smokers to change from local brands to higher-margin international names" (*Institutional Investor*, 31 May 1996, 37).

There is no doubt that the tobacco transnationals are increasingly targeting the Third World (Frey 1997). In a special Report on the tobacco industry for the *Washington Post* (four damning articles from the 17th to the 20th of November 1996) Frankel and his colleagues document how globalizing bureaucrats, particularly from the USA, have helped the TNCs to penetrate Third World markets. The case of Thailand, however, demonstrates that a determined anti-smoking opposition can at least delay the process, though not prevent the rise in smoking, especially among the young.

The most comprehensive international data source on smoking reports that the distribution of manufactured cigarette consumption in the 1980s was clearly skewed in terms of the First World/Third World divide (Nicolaides-Bouman et al. 1993). Of the countries represented in the data where average daily consumption was six cigarettes or more per adult (data from 1982-83) only one was in Africa; the four in the Americas included Canada and the

USA; nine were in Asia, including Japan, Israel, Hong Kong, Macau, Taiwan, and South Korea; Australia, New Zealand and the Philippines; and 17 European countries. Of those countries where fewer than six cigarettes per adult were smoked 26 were in Africa, 26 in Latin America and the Caribbean, 22 in Asia, 12 in Europe, and Fiji (ibid., Table iv). This pattern is changing.

Tobacco and Health

The World Health Organization estimated that in 1995 the average number of cigarettes smoked per day was around 22 in industrialized countries and 14 in developing countries, mirroring a decline in the habit of 1.4 per cent per annum in the former but an increase of 1.7 per cent in the latter. However, it appears that while there are fewer smokers in the First World, they may be smoking more expensive brands, so tobacco company profits continue to rise. The Annual Report of the Worldwatch Institute for 1996 estimated that cigarette production worldwide had reached an all-time peak of more than 5.5 trillion, an increase of 50 billion over 1994, though due to population increase the number of cigarettes produced per person fell from 1,029 in 1994 to 996 in 1995. WHO has documented the rise in cigarette smoking per person per year in key Third World markets from the 1970s to the 1990s. In many countries (China, Indonesia, South Korea, Bangladesh, India, and Thailand) per capita consumption has increased as has the country's rank order in cigarettes smoked per capita on the WHO database of 111 countries. Smoking declined between the 1980s and the 1990s in the Philippines, Singapore, and Malaysia. The latter two are too small to make much difference to cigarette company profits, but highly significant in that both introduced strict controls on advertising and sale to minors in the 1970s and have enforced these rigorously (Kallat 1990), but even here teenage smoking appears to be on the increase again.

Gender, class, age, ethnic and religious variables would undoubtedly give a sharper picture, but the brute fact remains: the potential for cigarette industry growth lies not in the First World where fewer and fewer people are smoking, even if these smokers can be persuaded to smoke more and more expensive cigarettes, but in the Third World, where groups that previously were outside the market for manufactured and particularly globally-branded cigarettes, are rapidly being brought into its orbit. Given the health risks of cigarette smoking which are widely known and the increasing levels of local campaigning to expose these risks (Slama 1995), for the industry to be surviving, let alone thriving, suggests that it has managed to assemble a powerful coalition of support over a wide range of social groups and institutions.

Alongside geographical globalization, the tobacco majors have also been pursuing a business strategy of product diversification. McGowan explains this in terms of the increasing salience of passive smoking as a serious medical risk, which dates from the 1980s. He reports that between 1988 and 1994 passive smoking was the cover story on *Time* or *Newsweek* eight times and was discussed in major newspapers in the USA more than 500 times (McGowan 1995, chapter 2). The Roper Organization, in a study for the Tobacco Institute, admitted that environmental tobacco smoke and passive smoking was "the most dangerous development yet to the viability of the tobacco industry" (quoted in Gantz 1996, 392). Not surprisingly, the companies looked round for other products to spread their risks, even though cigarettes continued to be highly profitable. While this may have accelerated in the 1980s, the process has been going on for some time. Wagner (1971, 233) cites full pages adverts from 1970: "Liggett and Myers, the tobacco company, has become L&M, the pet food, liquor, wine, cereal, popcorn, watch band, and tobacco company." American Tobacco became American Brands and RJR dropped "Tobacco" from its name as the 1971 television ban on cigarette advertising in the USA was imposed. BAT has also been diversifying since the 1960s (Nath 1986, chapter 5; Taylor 1985, chapter 2). Tobacco company diversification is convincingly illustrated by the images that adorn Annual Reports, a source that deserves more attention by academic researchers (see Sklair 2001, Table 8.1). This lacuna is surprising as corporate Annual Reports represent the means of communication with the financial community and the general public over which the corporations have the most control. The covers of the 1995 Annual Reports of the three largest tobacco TNCs are very similar in appearance, all being composed of brand labels, all mixtures of cigarette and other products. In the Philip Morris Annual Report the major cigarette brands, Marlboro and L&M, nestle comfortably in a display of cheese, coffee, chocolate, breakfast cereal, beer, and other relatively harmless delicacies. BAT lines up its major global cigarette brands, 555, Kent and Lucky Strike, with insurance and financial products. RJR Nabisco, rather more deliberately, stacks Salem, Winston, Camel, and other less-well known cigarette brands (the RJR side of the business) alongside the snack foods that comprise the Nabisco side. It is no accident that these similarities exist; all the successful global tobacco companies, while proclaiming their belief in their products and waging well-organized and well-funded campaigns to protect their own rights to market and the smoker's right to smoke, have nevertheless been very active in acquiring and developing businesses in other areas. This is not simply part of the growth mania that characterized the 1980s. On the contrary, management gurus in the 1990s have been largely recommending a return to core competencies and warning against the excesses of conglomeration. Philip Morris acquired Kraft Foods in 1988, and General Foods (combined in 1995) plus more than two dozen beers. In the 1996 Annual Report the back cover has a tear-off card listing Philip Morris brands in these categories. Shareholders are invited to detach the guide and refer to it when they shop. Philip Morris is now one of the biggest food processors in the world and also has substantial financial services and real estate holdings. The BAT mix of cigarettes and financial services and the RJR Nabisco mix of cigarettes and snack and other food products can all be seen as sensible precautions against the day when world-wide legislation seriously inhibits the ability of these companies to sell cigarettes as they are able to do now. This day, of course, may never come, but it would be reckless not to have a fallback position.

Tobacco and politics: the unfolding debate

The debate over tobacco and politics consists, generally, of six inter-related sets of arguments. The following summary is derived from the Tobacco Institute in Washington D.C. with Tollison (1986) and Tollison & Wagner (1992) representing the industry position; and Taylor (1985), Glantz et al. (1996), and Slama ed. (1995) representing the anti-smoking movement.

The tobacco industry arguments are:

(i) Tobacco is a valuable cash crop and export commodity, and cigarette manufacturing is a valuable and relatively labour intensive industry; therefore, the economic effects of restricting the sale and use of tobacco products would be serious for many economies and catastrophic for some.

(ii) Cigarettes are the most highly taxed products in most countries and represent a significant proportion of tax revenues in many; therefore, they have an economic value far greater than their employment effect alone.

(iii) There is no definite proof that smoking causes lung cancer or heart disease or anything else; so more scientific research is needed.

(iv) Even if smoking is harmful to health, attempts to ban or seriously restrict it are an infringement of citizen's rights in a democratic society; thus, the anti-smoking movement is the thin edge of a totalitarian wedge.

(v) Smoking gives real pleasure to millions of people and many are able to give it up; therefore, it has positive social and psychological functions and cannot be addictive.

(vi) Cigarette advertising and promotion are directed to existing smokers to encourage brand-switching and do not persuade children or anyone else to start smoking.

The parallel anti-smoking movement's arguments are:

(i)The economic costs of smoking in terms of ill-health, working days lost, fire hazard and environmental pollution far outweigh the economic contribution of the industry; therefore, phasing out the industry would be, at worst, cost neutral.

(ii) The money spent on cigarettes would be spent on other products and tax revenue losses would not be too serious.

(iii) The standards of scientific proof demanded by the tobacco lobby are entirely unrealistic; therefore, the attempt of the industry to maintain that the link between smoking and disease continues to be "controversial" is a political and not a scientific statement.

(iv) Cigarette smoke in public places infringes the rights and damages the health of non-smokers (passive smoking) and in the home, those of family members, especially children; therefore, a total ban is necessary to protect the majority of the population.

(v) The majority of adult smokers appear to want to abandon the habit and while some do, most cannot; therefore, smoking is addictive and its pleasures often have a terrible cost.

(vi) Some cigarette advertising and promotion deliberately target children and young people and is critical to the survival of the industry.

It is not my intention here to adjudicate between these arguments, my own opinion for what it is worth as a long-term ex-smoker, is that while the industry's arguments over advertising, health, and scientific proof are entirely nebulous, the arguments over economic costs are more difficult to resolve. As far as freedom is concerned, the argument that adults should be allowed to smoke where they do not endanger the health of others is very strong. Without the promotional efforts of the industry, as with so many luxury and harmful products, the habit would probably die out as its habitués do so. The substitution of alcohol or other addictive drugs for cigarettes in the argument raises some additional questions. It is necessary to outline them in order to understand the politics of the tobacco lobby and the anti-smoking movement. What we find, in summary, is that the tobacco industry is synergistic with many other industries fundamental to what I have termed the culture-ideology of consumerism (Sklair 2002, chapter 7). McGowan (1995, chapter 1) lists the friends of the tobacco industry in the USA, these are: congressmen from the six tobacco-growing states, the Department of Agriculture, the lobbying network led by the Tobacco Institute (funded by the industry), retailers, restaurant associations, the Advertising Council (against all restrictions on advertising), the American Civil Liberties Union (protecting the rights of all groups, including smokers), and all the supplier and related industries. Read (1996) provides a similar analysis for the UK, as do Currie & Ray (1984) for Kenya). In a widely cited and well-argued book Taylor (1985) calls this the "smoke ring". One small indication of how the "smoke ring" works and how ubiquitous it is emerges from the campaign to defeat the "anti-smoking" Proposition 5 in California in 1977, kick-started by a rumour at a meeting of the California Association of Tobacco and Candy Dealers at Las Vegas, six months before the vote (ibid, 198). Experts from both sides of the argument appear to confirm the point that the tobacco industry is highly politicized; compare, for one example, the health policy researcher and anti-smoking campaigner Stanton Glantz (1996, chapter 9) and the former Philip Morris public relations expert Edward Grefe (1981). It was reported in 1994 that the Tobacco Institute had suffered severe cutbacks and was experiencing "internal squabbles" (Stone 1994). It may be the case that the companies themselves and the public relations agencies representing them (notably Burson Marstellar) are lobbying more directly, probably supporting the "Committee of Counsel" (made up of the top attorneys from the tobacco majors, "The Secret Six") which has met regularly since 1958 to discuss industry policy. Central governments and local authorities are generally very ambivalent on the issue and are liable to become even more so as unemployment and tax revenues remain problematic. There are, however, some exceptions. For example, 22 states in the USA, notably Florida led by a campaigning anti-smoking governor, have sued the tobacco companies for recovery of Medicare expenditures on sufferers from tobacco-related diseases. In England, the City Council in Birmingham in alliance with the Regional Health Authority has created a "Smoke Free Birmingham" project; in 1997, New Dehli became the first city in India to ban smoking in public places see Slama (1995). At time of writing, many anti-tobacco cases are grinding their way through the courts in several countries.

The tobacco industry and global system theory

The global system theory outlined in the previous chapter and its central concept of the transnational capitalist class suggests how we might fruitfully analyze the promotional culture of cigarettes and the social forces that support it. TNC executives, globalizing bureaucrats, politicians, professionals, and consumerist elites all play their parts individually and in concert to bring this promotional culture of cigarettes and smoking into as many institutional sectors of all societies as they can and to create a dependency on both the addictive drug (nicotine) and the money (financial dependency, philanthropy of many types) that the tobacco industry brings with it. To understand this, we must start with the people who own and control the money that funds it, the tobacco corporate elite.

The corporate elite in the tobacco industry

The corporate elite in the tobacco industry consists of the leading actors in the major tobacco TNCs. As Useem (1984) and others have argued, an effective way to identify this elite is by studying boards of directors of major corporations. In the tobacco industry these are Philip Morris (PM), RJR Nabisco (RJR) and BAT. While there were no direct board links between the companies, there were many indirect links in that pairs of directors from different companies met on the boards of third companies or organizations and/or serve on yet other boards where their direct contacts met. The Annual Reports of the companies for 1995 provide several examples; S. Wolf sits on the board of PM and J. Medlin on the board of RJR, and both were directors of USAIR. J. Reed (PM) and R. Ridgway (RJR) were both on the board of CitiCorp. Links between BAT and the corporate elite in the USA were established through L. Denlea, of the BAT subsidiary Farmers Group in the USA who also sat on the board of the *Fortune* 1000 marine services company Alexander & Baldwin, and directly through C. Yuetter, on the board of Conagra with C. Harper, Chairman of RJR Nabisco Holdings. A former US Secretary of Agriculture and US Trade Representative, active in the campaign to liberalize the global cigarette market, Yuetter also linked with Reed of CitiCorp, through Reed's membership of the policy advisory committee to the US Trade Representative. The purpose of bringing non-executive directors on to the boards of major corporations is said to be two-fold. It improves the lines of communications between companies, useful for spreading information about the system and explaining difficult decisions; and it improves the image of corporations insofar as they are seen to be entrusting important decisions, notably remuneration and replacing the

CEO, to prestigious outsiders. The intercorporate links of the tobacco majors are impressive. Outside directors on the Philip Morris board included R. Murdoch of News International and R. Parsons of Time Warner, key consumerist elites as we shall see below, and Reed of Citibank, one of the world's most powerful financial institutions. An interesting aside to John Reed's involvement with Philip Morris is that, as CEO, he recruited William Campbell, a former PM executive, as an executive vice president "in charge of building the worldwide brand" (*Fortune* April 29, 1997, 53). While the text in *Fortune* explains that Campbell is one of the seven tobacco executives being investigated by the Department of Justice for perjury over their sworn testimony that nicotine is nonaddictive and does not cause disease, the picture that adorns the story is of a smiling Campbell, cigarette in hand, in Marlboro regalia advertising Marlboro Adventure Team products (dubbed "The most sinister cigarette promotion of all time"). I would certainly include this article as an important instance of the cigarette promotional culture. The RJR Nabisco board included Clendenin of BellSouth and Medlin of the Wachovia banking corporation. On the BellSouth board we also find P. Ridgway who sat on several major boards (3M, Union Carbide, Bell Atlantic, and CitiCorp). On the BAT board, Lord Armstrong had been on the boards of NM Rothschild, RTZ, and Shell. Yuetter was on the boards of Caterpillar, ConAgra, Texas Instruments, and FMC Corporation. Altogether, the board members of these three tobacco companies connected with over fifty major corporations. This small but high-level network can be enlarged in various ways, for example by studying further secondary and tertiary contacts, strategic alliances between corporations rather than direct interlocks on boards, memberships of industrial and business groups, and extra-corporate linkages through social clubs, schools, charities, universities, think tanks, and the like.

It is evident that members of the tobacco industry corporate elite connect with the other fractions of the transnational capitalist class through these boards of directors. The route to government agencies is through the globalizing bureaucrats. RJR had two such directors, John Chain, a former Commander in Chief of the Strategic Air Command of the US Air Force, and Rozanne Ridgway, a former Assistant Secretary of State. BAT had three important linkers in Lord Armstrong, former Secretary of the Cabinet and Head of the Home Civil Service in the UK; Rupert Pennant-Rea, former Deputy Governor of the Bank of England; and Clayton Yuetter, former Secretary of Agriculture and US Trade Representative. Yuetter has been accused of being "hand-in-glove" with Philip Morris and RJR when he was undermining foreign tobacco monopolies as President Reagan's Trade Representative (Barnet & Cavanagh 1994, chapter 2). This, obviously, did not disqualify him for the seat on the BAT board, on the contrary it opened up a line of communication between the three companies. It is inconceivable that these individuals cut off all their previous connections and expertise in government when they sit on the boards of the tobacco companies. Indeed, announcements of such appointments frequently make direct reference to this expertise as the rationale for the appointment. The same can be said in many cases for globalizing politicians and professionals. Margaret (Baroness) Thatcher, though not a board member, is an excellent case in point. The former British Prime Minister was employed by Philip Morris for an undisclosed sum (the *Washington Post* put it at two million dollars) to advise on market entry strategy in China and Eastern Europe, where she is said to be held in high regard among influential groups. The PM board had a strong contingent of business and not-for-profit sector professionals ready to lend their good names and, by implication, the good names of their institutions, to the company's products. These included Dr Elizabeth Bailey of College Retirement Equity Fund, part of the *Fortune Global 500* insurance company TIAA-CREF) of which Dr Bailey is a trustee. It planned to divest its $1.5 billion stock in Philip Morris in 1997. On the RJR board sat Julius Chambers, Chancellor of North Carolina Central University (funded with Reynolds money as was its more illustrious neighbour, Duke University) and, again, Rozanne Ridgway, Co-Chair of the Atlantic Council of the United States. On the BAT board sat Rosalind Gilmore, Director of the Securities and Investments Board (the UK equivalent of the SEC), a former Director of Lloyds and Chair of the Building Societies Commission (the UK Savings and Loan industry watchdog). The consumerist elites, of course, play a direct and indispensable role in the propagation of the culture-ideology of consumerism in general, and the promotional culture of cigarettes, in particular. The presence of Rupert Murdoch (News International) and Richard Parsons (Time Warner) and, to a lesser extent, Jane Evans (SmartTV, Burbank, CA) on the board of PM clearly illustrates this point. While the media are its public face, the banking and, increasingly the credit card industry are the foundations on which the culture-ideology of consumerism rests. The CEO of Citicorp John Reed (who is a big linker in network theory language), as has been noted, sat on the PM board, as did the RJR board member, Rozanne Ridgway. Other bankers included W. Donaldson on the PM board, R. Groves and J. Medlin (RJR), and R. Pennant-Rea, former Deputy Governor of the Bank of England on the board of BAT). This list of the network of board members in these three tobacco corporations cannot be said to be definitive, though it is suggestive. What it suggests is that the tobacco industry appears to be supported by a corporate elite, drawn from a wide spectrum of men and women from prestigious institutions, interlinking the corporate and the non-corporate worlds. Each of these three corporations (and several others in the industry) has a network of connections from the corporate centre through joint ventures, strategic alliances, and other business links to local and national government agencies and the people who run them, to the advertising and media industries, to the retail and entertainment sectors and many other social spheres (particularly those who come to rely on their largesse for sponsorship money) wherever they do business in the world, effectively all the inhabited parts of the planet.

Globalizing bureaucrats, politicians, and professionals have long been friendly to the tobacco industry, very few have taken the real risk of expressing public and militant opposition to it. The reasons are obvious, the tobacco lobby is rich, well-organized, and well-connected in most countries, and not just in the First World. For example, in the 1980s President Moi of Kenya appointed the BAT (Kenya) chairman to one of the 11 seats in parliament in his gift. 40 per cent of the company was held by government ministers in a private capacity (Currie & Ray 1986). This was almost 40 years ago. In 2021 the London-based *Private Eye* (#1548, 10 June, p.7) reported that "Research that found smokers were protected from Covid-19 was recently retracted after Big Tobacco funding was uncovered." The money came from the Foundation for a Smoke-Free World, a typical tobacco lobby group financed by the major tobacco company Philip Morris International, who also funded "Project Whitecoat", which reportedly recruited scientists to confuse the public about the health risks of nicotine. This, according to *Private Eye* is only "the tip of an iceberg" (ibid.) concealing tobacco industry efforts to overturn legislation.

There are many more smokers than active anti-smokers, and those who stand for public office or who depend on the state or the business community for their prosperity generally avoid antagonizing such interests. The major exceptions to this rule in the case of the tobacco industry are those public health officials and medical researchers who have campaigned against the health risks since the 1960s (the major medical associations have mostly come off the fence on the issue), those anti-smoking politicians whose secure electoral bases have saved them from the revenge of the industry (for example, President Clinton in 1996, though some tobacco money did go to the Democrats), and those lawyers who have taken on the task of suing the tobacco corporations for destroying the health of their clients (often on a no win-no fee basis). This certainly appears to be a formidable coalition, but in the context of the majority of local and national politicians who stay neutral and the other massed professionals working directly and indirectly for the smoking interests, lawyers, advertisers, business consultants, industry funded medical researchers (see Glantz 1996), the sides look less evenly matched. It is also important to balance out the picture of smokers under continual social pressures to give up or to indulge their habit in private rather than public spaces, with the continuing actual and iconic presence of the cigarette in most societies. Actually, there are very few countries where non-smoking regulations are strictly enforced, for every case of a Frenchman who refuses to stop smoking and is arrested when the plane reaches the USA (*Associated Press*, 1 January 1997), there are many more of lack of enforcement of the rules. In the 1990s in the USA where the anti-smoking movement has gone furthest, especially in the legal system, although there are widespread advertising bans in the print media, characters still smoke in films, plays, photographs, and other representational forms, and this may be increasing as part of a new hedonistic culture. For example, in the *Washington Post* (7 January 1997) we find articles on "Is There a Backlash Against Healthy Living?" and "While US cracks down, Europe mostly ignores smoking rules". Consumer goods manufacturers frequently pay for their products to be placed in films and other media vehicles, for example in 1980 Marlboro (Lois Lane's brand) bought 22 placements of the logo in "Superman II" for $42,000; Sylvester Stallone and Sean Connery, among others, have accepted "placement" payments from cigarette companies. The sight of small groups of smokers, huddled together outside buildings, is now common in many countries, no doubt for some people adding to rather than detracting from the attraction of the habit. The key issue is the extent to which anti-smoking bureaucrats, politicians and professionals have been able to stop cigarettes being marketed, sold, and smoked. Laws and the enforcement of laws on the advertising, sales, and consumption of cigarettes vary from country to country (Frey 1997, Table 4) and sometimes from city to city. However, available evidence suggests that while advertising restrictions and, to a lesser extent, restrictions on where people can smoke, have gradually been introduced all over the world, the production of cigarettes is still increasing and, more significantly, the sales of the major global brands have been increasing faster than other brands. As detailed above, most of this increase has been in Asia, Africa, and Latin America. How, then, has the tobacco industry managed to achieve these results?

The promotional culture of cigarettes versus the anti-smoking movement

Each fraction of the transnational capitalist class has very substantial interests in promoting the smoking culture. The reasons are simple and blatantly commercial. Cigarettes are relatively small, low volume, low weight, products with a long shelf life and a devoted band of adherents in all societies. The industry employs many millions of people directly and indirectly in growing and processing the leaf, getting it to market, manufacturing, promoting, and selling cigarettes, and all the ancillary products and services involved. TNC executives clearly have a direct interest in selling as many cigarettes to as many people as possible. Globalizing bureaucrats, politicians, and professionals, similarly, have direct and indirect interests in the sale of tobacco products for the revenues they raise and for the business and funding the tobacco industry provides. However, it is the consumerist elites (merchants and media) who are most intimately involved in the actual promotional culture for cigarettes. The literature on this is voluminous (for example, Klein 1993, McGowan, 1995, Glantz 1996, Read 1996.) The *British Medical Journal* (18 January 1997) reported that US tobacco companies spend around $US6 billion per year on promotional activities compared with only $750 million on direct advertising. Though direct advertising of cigarettes is gradually being banned in the First World, it is still a powerful force in many Third World countries. Data from the late 1980s show that one or more of PM, RJR and BAT occupied a top ten position in advertising revenues in South Africa, Hong Kong, Malaysia, Philippines, Argentina, Chile, Bahrein, Kuwait, Oman, Qatar, Saudi Arabia, and the United Arab Emirates, while only in Belgium/Luxembourg, New Zealand, and North America in the First World, was this the case (*Advertising Age*, 4 December 1989).

Tobacco Sponsorship

Tobacco sponsorship of various types has been growing at the expense of direct advertising all over the world for some time, providing money for sports, the arts, medical research, and a host of other good causes. Philip Morris disbursed $45 million in 1994 in cash ($55 million in both 1993 and 1992) and $16.5 million in nonmonetary support (in both 1991 and 1992). The company gave $405,000 to 29 arts organizations and $70,000 to the National Board for Professional Teaching Standards (USA) in 1994. RJR Nabisco Foundation donated US$37 million in 1994 ($45 million in 1992, $35 million in 1991) and nonmonetary support was $4 million (in 1989). Its largest grants were for medical research ($900,000 to a North Carolina School of Medicine), general educational purposes (for example, $780,000 for a Maths and Science Initiative in New Jersey), $343,000 for conservancy in New York, plus some home-base support (North Carolina Tobacco Foundation and RJR Success Academy [sic] in Winston-Salem). It is clear that the largesse of both companies impacts substantial numbers of people and organizations. The BAT Annual Report of 1995 cites a figure of £8 million (about $12 million) as "Payments for charitable purposes" during the year, £3 million of which was paid in the UK. The company has been widely criticized for some of these activities, for example, for donating money to the Medical Research Council of the UK without the full knowledge of council members, and for various donations to high schools in England. When the chairman of BAT, Sir Patrick Sheehy, retired he endowed a professorship in International Relations at Cambridge University in his name, a proposal that the university's senior staff approved by a vote of two to one. This prompted criticisms from the Imperial Cancer Research Fund and the Cancer Research Campaign in the UK and doubts as to whether they could continue to work with the university. The new chairman, Lord Cairns, also came under fire. The *Observer* newspaper in London (25 August 1996), under the title "Cigarette giant in aid ploy", charged BAT and Cairns (a former merchant banker) with trying to subvert British aid policy in the interests of the cigarette trade. Cairns, through his positions as chair of both the Commonwealth Development Corporation which had distributed over two billion $US worth of investment to developing countries, and the Overseas Development Institute, was also accused of orchestrating political support for the industry through the All-Party Group on Overseas Development, which funds Conservative and Labour members of parliament. The most visible public expression of the cigarette promotional culture is the long-standing and relentless sponsorship of youth-oriented sporting and entertainment events all over the world where glamour, athletic prowess, and sexual success are identified with brands of cigarettes. This assertion is confirmed by a multitude of examples over recent decades. For example, the Miss Ghana and Miss Gitanes beauty contests in Africa; cricket in Pakistan; Marlboro and Chinese soccer (football), and BAT 555 Nightman Disco in Beijing. Newsletters of the anti-smoking movement in Asia, AGHAST (Action Groups to Halt Advertising and Sponsorship by Tobacco, a campaign of the International Organization of Consumer Unions, based in Malaysia) and in the USA, the Boston-based INFACT, provide contemporary examples. Notwithstanding this massive financial support over a wide range of social institutions, many argue that the most fundamental weapon in the armoury of the cigarette industry is the social and sexual allure of the cigarette since its introduction as a mass consumer product, commonly dated from its manufacture by the French state tobacco monopoly in 1845 (Goodman 1993, 97ff.). A young barber from Sichuan province in China expresses the 1990s version of this sentiment: "I know that smoking is not a good habit, that it's harmful to your health. But I have no choice. To carry on social relationships and to do business, I have to smoke" (as quoted in "The Biggest Habit in the World, the Greatest Risk" *International Herald Tribune,* 22 March 1996).

Cigarettes Are Sublime

In satirical cultural studies mode while struggling to give up smoking Richard Klein wrote his splendid book *Cigarettes Are Sublime* (1993) illustrating the thesis through the tropes of smoking and smokers in opera, movies, novels, photography, the military, and the pleasures of everyday life. "On the day when some triumphant antitabagist crushes under his heel the last cigarette manufactured on the face of the earth, will the world have any reason to grieve, perhaps to mourn the loss of a cultural institution, a social instrument of beauty, a wand of dreams" (ibid., 49). This echoes the most potent defence of the tobacco industry today against its critics, that of its protection of individual liberties against repressive statist forces, identifying eco-fascism and communist totalitarianism. A Philip Morris advocacy advertising campaign in 1989 commemorated the 200th anniversary of the Bill of Rights, with the implication that restrictions on smoking and advertising tobacco products threatens civil rights. Between 1987 and 1992 the tobacco industry gave about half a million dollars to the American Civil Liberties Union, which has testified in Congress against bans on cigarette advertising; the Supreme Court in Canada criticized a proposed ban on cigarette advertising and corporate sponsorship on free speech grounds. Klein's analysis of the social power of the cigarette is confirmed by many researchers who are hostile to the tobacco industry. Chapman's study of advertising and the tobacco industry (despite its silly title) demonstrates this with reference to the campaigns for Marlboro and for Winfield, the most successful brand in Australian history (Chapman 1986). From a feminist perspective, Greaves (1996) elaborates the meanings and uses of cigarettes for vulnerable women, allowing a variety of women to speak for themselves about their smoking. This, again, suggests that making it more difficult for smokers and pre-smokers to have access to cigarettes is unlikely to undermine the habit. The precisely directed support of the tobacco industry for the women's movement and minority group causes in the USA, notably through magazine advertising and sports sponsorships, helps to explain why these groups have been ambivalent on the issue. The ways that the cigarette companies have attempted to target children through their advertising and promotional culture, however, have raised much more controversy. For example, Glantz (1996, chapter 6) describe how a campaign to show cigarette adverts for Kool backfired when the ad was run directly before a screening of "Snow White" in Massachusetts and sparked off a massive public outcry. Green (1990) documents how RJR used its "Smooth Character" Joe Camel (complete with a *Rolling Stone* magazine poster and a tear-off health warning) to entice children to smoke. Widespread criticism of these and other cigarette company practices led to the announcement in late 1990 by the Tobacco Institute that the industry would voluntarily end youth-oriented cigarette sampling, movie placements, and other marketing practices (reported in *Advertising Age*, 17 December 1990). There is a veritable flood of evidence to demonstrate that this pledge and others by the Tobacco Institute were rapidly flagrantly dishonoured in the USA and in most other countries (for example, https://www.tobaccofreekids.org/us-resources). Under the title "Poll Shows Camel Ads are Effective with Kids" (see Wong 1996, especially note 18), the Camel campaign was criticized by the Surgeon General and the AMA and the advert "I'd Toddle a Mile for a Camel" (a cynical play on the slogan "I'd walk a mile for a Camel") was roundly condemned. On 13 November 1996, the *Washington Post* reported: "A group of advertising executives today is joining anti-smoking advocates to launch a national campaign in New York in an attempt to shame the US advertising industry into eliminating cigarette ads that are attracting teenagers." Research is cited to the effect that while in 1991, 27.5 per cent of high school students reported having smoked in the previous ten days, by 1995 this had risen to 34.8 per cent. In the UK, cigarette companies have admitted breaking voluntary agreements on billboard advertising near schools, to widespread condemnation (*Times Education Supplement* 14 June 1996). Similar stories came from Singapore (Nath 1986, chapter 5, and Kallat 1990).

Tobacco and Human rights

The industry is supported, often covertly, by an army of lobbyists, publicists, and ideologues all over the world. Among its most effective techniques are the continual defence of the smokers right to smoke and its attempts to label the smoking and disease connection as controversial. Most prominent in this connection is Burson-Marsteller, Philip Morris's PR firm, which has created front organizations, notably the National Smokers Alliance in the USA in the guise of citizens groups to undermine anti-smoking information. Though most active in the USA, the cigarette lobby has a global reach. For example, as an Environmental Protection Agency report on the dangers of passive smoking winged its way around the world, an article in *Business Daily* published in the Philippines (10 January 1997) reported that "independent" journalists from the USA and Britain had rushed to attack the anti-smoking lobby. The anti-smoking movement, while it does not have anything like the massive funding worldwide of the tobacco industry is, nevertheless, also well-organized and clearly prepared for a very long-term campaign. It works through national voluntary associations, most prominently Action on Smoking and Health (ASH) in the UK, USA and Australia, and many smaller, more focused groups (against underage smoking, smoking in specific public places, cigarette advertising, etc.). The global centre of the movement is the regular World Conference on Tobacco and Health (WCTH) which, since its first meeting in New York in 1968 has provided a forum for anti-smoking activists, scientists, and practitioners to publicize their activities and to network. A watershed was reached at the Tokyo conference in 1988 when it was decided to ban industry representatives from the next meeting, in Perth in 1990, and the mood of the WCTH appears to have hardened towards the tobacco corporations (compare Ramstrom 1980, on the Stockholm conference and Slama 1995, on the meeting in Paris). Hewat (1991) labels his chapter on the anti-smoking movement: "Davids versus Goliaths" and the core of the movement, Daube's Dozen, after Mike Daube, formerly director of ASH in London and assistant commissioner for public health in Western Australia, who organized the WCTH in Perth. The other 11 were a mixture of writers, medical researchers and public health activists from Australia, the UK, the US, Japan, and Hong Kong. A comparable list today would undoubtedly include more of the same from the Third World. WHO has also been actively supporting the anti-smoking movement in a variety of ways, publishing statistics on smoking-related diseases and death rates, which are publicized in the mass media, and working with health professionals in most countries. On a less organized level, the anti-smoking movement worldwide has had many noteworthy successes. In the USA, an ever-increasing number of smoking notables, ranging from the man who modelled as the Marlboro cowboy to the grandson of the founder of R.J. Reynolds Tobacco Company, from sports bodies, artists and scientists formerly in receipt of tobacco money to many professional associations, have denounced the habit and the methods the industry uses to promote it. In China, the Supreme Leader Deng famously vowed to stop smoking in a highly publicized gesture at a meeting of the National People's Congress. Globalizing bureaucrats who promote the interests of the tobacco industry are opposed by those, mostly in the health and education spheres, who are part of the anti-smoking movement. Indeed, the struggle between pro-tobacco government agents and agencies in revenue and industrial departments and anti-smoking activists in health and education, appears to be an increasingly global phenomenon. The cases of the USA and the UK are now well-documented (McGowan 1995, Read

1996) and evidence from other places is also building up (see Nath 1986, on the Third World in general; Currie & Ray 1984 on Kenya; Kallat 1990 on Singapore; Frankel 1996 on Thailand. The London *Sunday Times*, published a report "Africa- Ashtray of the World" on 13 May 1990). Disagreements at the local and country-wide levels between groups for and those against the tobacco industry have been paralleled internationally through the United Nations system by conflicts between the Food and Agriculture Organization, supporting the interests of tobacco growers, and the World Health Organization, in the interests of disease reduction, on the role of tobacco in development (Huebner 1981; Taylor 1985, chapter 14; Nath 1986; Nyoni 1994). The dilemma this poses for development professionals is well expressed in the confused and contradictory "World Bank policy on tobacco" in the 1993 *World Development Report* issue on health (World Bank 1993, 89). Nevertheless, despite all this practical and ideological mobilization by the anti-smoking movement over at least the last three decades, more cigarettes are being sold globally than ever before, the tobacco corporations make larger and larger profits, most of their shareholders seem content to take their dividends, and the promotional culture of cigarettes shows no sign at all of abating. The tobacco industry links directly both with the economic crisis of increasing wealth and increasing poverty, and with the ecological crisis of planetary and individual well-being. The culture-ideology of consumerism promises that global capitalism will deliver prosperity for all and that this prosperity will be sustainable. The tobacco industry, through its marketing of cigarettes actually does promise both, but in perverse and, ultimately, dishonest forms. Most people, however poor, can "afford" to smoke cigarettes. The promotional culture of cigarettes connects the consumer, however episodically, with the glamorous world of the adverts and smoking icons. Together with other "affordable" fashionable consumer goods (access to sports and entertainment through television, global branded soft drinks, fast foods, popular music, counterfeit clothes and accessories) cigarettes help to mask the increasing gap between richer and poorer all over the world. Billions of small acts of consumption help dissolve the economic crisis of global capitalism for individuals while intensifying it for the mass of the world's population.

The Tobacco Industry and the Ecological Crisis

The promotional culture of cigarettes impacts the ecological crisis in many ways. It encourages farmers and governments to grow tobacco on land that could be producing nutritious food crops with less environmental stress.

Tobacco prices make it one of the most valuable crops in the global marketplace. Second, smoking tobacco is widely acknowledged to be the most significant cause of death on the planet, and a smoking-disease epidemic is predicted for the coming millennium, for example by the World Bank. The promotional culture of cigarettes, by enriching those who control tobacco production and glamourizing smoking, helps mask the ecological crisis of global capitalism. The tobacco transnational capitalist class orchestrates the response of the industry to these crises and, for the moment, appears to be doing it very effectively. We can, therefore, conclude:

(i) the tobacco industry is organized globally in the promotion of a cigarette culture;

(ii) the personnel and organizations involved provide evidence for the existence of a transnational capitalist class in the industry strongly connected with the TCC in general;

(iii) despite heavy legislative blows and widespread restrictions on its abilities to carry on its business without proper regulation by local, city, and central governments all over the world, the industry is making more, not less, money and exerting more, not less, power than in previous decades. In these ways, it plays its part in mystifying and intensifying the general economic, health, and ecological crises of global capitalism.

The continuing ability of the tobacco industry to market its life-threatening products profitably is a key test case for the hegemony of the global capitalist project. In the words of one expert: "Now the U.S. government is leading negotiations among eleven countries on a Trans-Pacific Partnership Agreement (TPPA), 'a true 21st century trade agreement that will reflect U.S. priorities and values'. The open question is whether a priority is to *support* tobacco trade as it contributes to 6 million deaths per year—one billion deaths in a twenty-first century epidemic. The TPPA has six chapters that might provide material support to the tobacco industry" (Stumberg 2013, 384). We meet Professor Stumberg of the Georgetown University Law Center in Washington D.C. again in the next chapter.

Second thoughts

I have few second thoughts about this essay. Despite setbacks, notably in the law courts of the USA, the tobacco industry continues to thrive, and innovate. The *Financial Times* (17-18 July 2021) reported, presumably in sorrow and anger: "Big Tobacco struggles with kicking the habit: Cigarette makers look to diversify away from their core business but health campaigners and investors remain sceptical", supplemented with WHO data indicating that smoking, including second-hand, kills about 8 million people annually. This article also commented on the widely reported story that Philip Morris had bid for the health products company Vectura (which makes inhalers), a move described by the business and human rights adviser of the Dutch bank ABN AMRO as "the most cynical form of vertical integration I could imagine" (ibid). The takeover bid was successful prompting widespread condemnation. "Vectura has sold out millions of people with lung disease, and instead prioritised short-term financial gain over the long-term viability of Vectura as a business," said Sarah Woolnough, chief executive of Asthma UK and the British Lung Foundation who spoke for many vulnerable people: "There's now a very real risk that Vectura's deal with Big Tobacco will lead to the cigarette industry wielding undue influence on UK health policy" (*Financial Times* 16 September 2021*)*. Some of this coverage in the UK had mentioned the US-based charity "Tobacco Free Kids" which had previously reported in the online news site *Insider*: "US tobacco giant Reynolds American just spent $16 million in political donations as Biden seeks to ban menthol cigarettes …. The deluge of money from a Big Tobacco company shows how difficult it might be for Biden to restrict cigarettes". In the UK the criticism comes from the campaigning group "Action on smoking and Health" https://ash.org.uk/fact-sheets/. From the EU we learn: "Tobacco consumption is the single largest avoidable health risk, and the most significant cause of premature death in the EU, responsible for nearly 700,000 deaths every year. Around 50% of smokers die prematurely (on average 14 years earlier). Despite considerable progress made in recent years, the number of smokers in the EU is still high – 26% of the overall population and 29% of young Europeans aged 15-24 smoke" (Overview | Public Health (europa.eu). Globally, "The EU is also working with its international partners to reduce global tobacco consumption. EU countries, together with the European Commission, are active partners in the WHO Framework Convention on Tobacco Control (FCTC), a legally binding international treaty that aims to reduce the health and economic impact of tobacco consumption. Conferences of the Parties of the Convention are held every second year where they take decisions, adopt protocols, and issue guidelines" (ibid). Yet still, this other vicious global pandemic persists, with new also dangerous products (notably vaping, the practice of inhaling and exhaling vapour containing nicotine and flavouring produced by a device designed for this purpose), keeping shareholders and the market happy. In 2021 the government of New Zealand announced plans to raise the legal smoking age each succeeding year, meaning that smoking tobacco will be illegal for people born after 2008. However, so far there is no ban on vaping in New Zealand and little evidence that other countries are following the lead of New Zealand.

References

Barnet, R. & Cavanagh, J. (1994) *Global Dreams: Imperial Corporations and the New World Order*. New York: Simon & Schuster.

Chapman, S. (1986) *Great Expectorations: Advertising and the Tobacco Industry*. London: Comedia.

Currie, K. & Ray, L. (1984) Going up in smoke: The case of British American Tobacco in Kenya. *Social Science and Medicine* 19/11: 1131-39.

Finger, W.R., ed. (1981) *The Tobacco Industry in Transition*. North Carolina: Center for Public Policy Research.

Frankel, G. (1996) Big Tobacco's Global Reach: Thailand Resists US Brand Assault. *Washington Post* (18 November).

Frey, R.S. (1997) The international traffic in tobacco. *Third World Quarterly* 18: 303-19.

Glantz, S., Slade, J. et al. (1996) *The Cigarette Papers*. Berkeley and Los Angeles: University of California Press.

Goodman, J. (1993) *Tobacco in History: The Cultures of Dependence*. London: Routledge.

Greaves, L. (1996) *Smoke Screen: Women's Smoking and Social Control*. London: Scarlet Press.

Green, M. (1990) An open letter to RJR Nabisco: Luring kids to light up. *Business and Society Review* 73: 22-26.

Grefe, E. (1981) *Fighting to Win: Business Political Power*. New York: Harcourt, Brace Jovanovich.

Hewat, T. (1991) *Modern Merchants of Death*. Victoria [Australia]: Wright books.

Huebner, A. (1981) Making the Third World Marlboro Country. In Finger, ed. *op cit.*, chapter 14.

Kallat, P. (1990) Smoke Out. *The Mirror* [Singapore] (15 June): 1-3.

Klein, R. (1993) *Cigarettes are Sublime*. Durham: Duke University Press.

Kluger, R. (1996) *Ashes to Ashes: America's Hundred-Year Cigarette War, the Public Health, and the Unabashed Triumph of Philip Morris*. New York: Knopf.

McGowan, R. (1995) *Business, Politics, and Cigarettes: Multiple Levels, Multiple Agendas*. Westport, CT: Quorum Books.

Nath, U. R. (1986) *Smoking: Third World Alert.* Oxford: Oxford University Press.

Nicolaides-Bouman, A., Wald, N., et al. (1993) *International Smoking Statistics.* Oxford: Oxford University Press.

Nyoni, N. (1994) Kicking the Habit: Dependence on tobacco crop poses Third World dilemma. *Ceres* 26/3: 15-16.

Ramstrom, L., ed. (1980) *The Smoking Epidemic: a matter of worldwide concern.* Stockholm: Almqvist & Wiksell.

Read, M. (1996) *The Politics of Tobacco: Policy networks and the cigarette industry.* Aldershot: Avebury.

Rupert, J. & Frankel, G. (1996) In Ex-Soviet Markets, US Brands Took on Role of Capitalist Liberator. *Washington Post* (19 November).

Salomon Brothers (1994) *International Cigarette Markets-Globalization, Privatization & Smuggling.* New York, (October 13).

Shenon, P. (1994) Asia's having one huge nicotine fit. *New York Times* (15 May) Sections 4, 1, &16.

Shepherd, P. (1985) Transnational Corporations and the International Cigarette Industry. In R. Newfarmer, ed. *Profits, progress and poverty.* Notre Dame: University of Notre Dame Press, chapter 3.

Sklair, L. (2001) *The transnational capitalist class.* Oxford: Blackwell.

Sklair, L. (2002) *Globalization: Capitalism and its Alternatives.* Oxford: Oxford University Press.

Slama, K. (1995) *Tobacco and Health.* New York: Plenum.

Stone, P. (1994) Tobacco's road. *National Journal* [USA] 26 (1 January): 19-23.

Stumberg, R. (2013) Safeguards for Tobacco Control: Options for the TPPA. *American Journal of Law & Medicine* 39: 382-441.

Taylor, P. (1985) *The Smoke Ring: Tobacco, Money and Multinational Politics.* London: Sphere.

Tollison, R., ed. (1986) *Smoking and Society: Toward a More Balanced Assessment.* Lexington, MA: D.C. Heath.

Tollison, R. & Wagner, R. (1992) *The Economics of Smoking.* Boston: Kluwer.

Useem, M. (1984) *The Inner Circle: Large Corporations and the Rise of Business Political Activity in the U.S. and UK.* New York: Oxford University Press.

Wagner, S. (1971) *Cigarette Country: Tobacco in American History and Politics.* New York: Praeger.

Wong, K.L. (1996) Tobacco Advertising and Children: The Limits of First Amendment Protection. *Journal of Business Ethics* 15/10: 1051- 1064.

World Bank (1993) *World Development Report: Investing in Health.* New
    York: Oxford University Press.

CHAPTER 6

(2002) THE TRANSNATIONAL CAPITALIST CLASS AND GLOBAL POLITICS: DECONSTRUCTING THE CORPORATE-STATE CONNECTION. *INTERNATIONAL POLITICAL SCIENCE REVIEW* 23/2: 159-174. [COURTESY OF SAGE]

Preamble

This article was written in 2002, long before Brexit, which many major corporations opposed. The corporate lobbying groups identified then all seem to be thriving in the 2020s. While the concept of the transnational capitalist class (TCC) as elaborated in my book of the same name published in 2001 and the idea of capitalist globalization have by no means been universally accepted, increasing volumes of research on corporate-state connections make it difficult to deny that capitalism has been changing. The original article contained case studies of Codex (the UN-sponsored food standards agency) and the struggle over the Multilateral Agreement on Investment (by a lucky chance I was working in the USA at the time and was able to arrange interviews with local officials and activists). The original article also contained a brief case study of the tobacco industry, but this has been replaced by a more substantial analysis of this toxic business in the previous chapter.

Abstract

Transnational corporations (TNCS) engage in a variety of political activities that take place at all levels of the political sphere, from community and urban through national to global politics, and involve many different groups of actors. This article addresses two sets of questions: (1) What forms do these activities take? (2) To what extent do they enhance or undermine democracy? The specific organization of politics for global capitalism is conceptualized in terms of the systemic influence of the transnational capitalist class (TCC). The role of this class is analyzed through two case studies: Codex Alimentarius and the Multilateral Agreement on Investment.

Deconstructing the Corporate-State Connection

The events of 11 September 2001 and the upscaling of the "war on terror" have understandably dominated the media and politics in many parts of the world. However, the period from 1995 to the first decade of the 21st century may also be seen as a turning point for capitalist globalization and perhaps as a turning point for humanity. In 1995 the World Trade Organization opened its doors for business and the OECD began, with very little publicity, to plan for a Multilateral Agreement on Investment (MAI). Both of these institutional movements signaled the wide-ranging intent of those who promote capitalist globalization, those who own and control the transnational corporations and their allies in state, international and transnational politics, and bureaucracies, the professions, and consumerist elites. These initiatives of what I have termed the transnational capitalist class stimulated renewed efforts of counter-movements, the origins of which are traced back to protectionism, new social movements, and green movements. While none of these counter-movements mounted a coherent challenge to capitalist globalization, they all contributed to what is now a variety of anti-globalization movements with the emerging potential to offer a serious alternative to global capitalism. The struggle to resist globalization from above through globalization from below has begun. The focus of most contemporary social movements has been on polarization issues (primarily class, ethnic, and gender polarization) or ecological issues, but the greatest challenge remains to make viable connections between them. Many of the successes of the anti-globalization movement, in the short time since its emergence, have been due to its capacity to make these connections. Transnational corporations clearly engage in political activities of various types, but the exact forms of these engagements and the roles of the various actors in them have not been subject to a great deal of systematic research. These political activities take place at all levels of the political sphere, from community and urban, through national to global politics and involve many different groups of actors. These emanate from government, from political parties, and from what we might call the "service industries" of politics in capitalist societies, notably the media, think tanks, and what Louis Althusser conceptualized as the "Ideological State Apparatuses" (Althusser 1971b). Wolff (2006) provides the key link to consumerism. In this article I focus on global politics, and attempt to address two sets of questions: (1) What forms do these activities take? and (2) Do they enhance or undermine democracy? It is common on the Left to argue that in the age of capitalist globalization, in most countries political parties rarely make any significant difference because no political party that seriously challenges capitalist globalization stands much chance of being elected, or if elected, much chance of hanging onto office, or if hanging onto office actually seriously threatening the power and interests of capital. If we accept this argument, then the focus turns to the global political system as a whole rather than the parts of the system described by national politics. While TNCs have always been political actors, the demands of economic globalization require them to be political at the global level in a more systematic sense than previously. The political action of TNCs at the global level, like almost all political actions, is a mixture of the haphazard and opportunistic on the one hand, and well-organized and systemic behaviour on the other. One way to capture this theoretically is to conceptualize the systemic organization of politics for global capitalism in terms of a transnational capitalist class (TCC). The material base of this class is in the corporations they own and/or control. In my formulation (see chapters 3 and 4 above) the TCC is composed of four main, interlocking groups: Corporate executives and their local affiliates (the corporate fraction); globalizing bureaucrats and politicians (the state fraction); globalizing professionals (the technical fraction); and merchants and media (the consumerist fraction). While each of these groups performs distinct functions, personnel are often interchangeable between them. Key individuals can belong to more than one fraction at the same time, and transitions from membership of one to another group are more or less routinized in many societies, as in the "corporate-state connection" of my title.

Economic Power and Political Power

Historically, the relationship between the economic power and the political power of major global corporations has been very controversial as exemplified in the crudely militaristic forms of empire-building in previous centuries and state-sponsored intervention supported by Big Business (all the way from South Asia and the Middle East at the peak of British imperialism to the notorious "Yankee imperialism" in South America and elsewhere more recently). Research on organizations influential in regional and global politics suggests that major corporations are currently developing more subtle methods to achieve political objectives that will serve their economic interests. This development is monitored by the radical activist group, Corporate Europe Observatory (see CEO [sic], 1997). The European

Roundtable of Industrialists (ERT) is a typical example of how this process operates, and how the corporate interest can shift the emphasis of policy making even in a rich and powerful coalition of states like the European Union, with substantial implications for global politics. ERT was founded in 1983 by a group of visionary captains of industry, notably Agnelli of Fiat, Dekker of Philips, and Gyllenhammer of Volvo. It performs an agenda-setting role in European institutions for global free trade and competitiveness. A report on ERT, written by a former Head of Group Public Affairs for British American Tobacco Industries in London provides an interesting insight into the mentality of the organization (see Richardson 2000). ERT is comprised of the leaders of around 45 TNCs, prominent among which in the 1990s were BP, Daimler-Benz, Fiat, Shell, and Siemens, all globalizing corporations. The European Centre for Infrastructure Studies (ECIS), an offshoot of ERT, is said to have been instrumental in persuading the European Commission to establish the massive Trans-European Networks (a programme of 150 environmentally sensitive infrastructure projects), by-passing the European Parliament and bringing together regional and national governments, municipalities, EU institutions, research institutes, banks, and corporations. In a very familiar pattern for globalizing elites, former European Commissioner V-P Henning Christopherson joined the Board of ECIS when he left the Commission. So, it is not too far-fetched to argue that corporate interests are, at least, highly influential in the making of EU transport policy. One central consequence of the political efficacy of the coordinated power of TNCs is the failure of governments everywhere to shift the balance from private cars and lorries to public transport and rail freight, despite almost universal rhetoric on the need to do this. CEO (1997) gives two telling examples: (1) German milk is freighted to Greece to be made into feta cheese (which could easily be made in Germany) and then sent back to Germany for sale, similar patterns are found for many other products; and (2) in the 1960s, Unilever had soap factories in most European countries, now there is just one huge factory in England to supply all of Europe. So, dairy and other products companies in Germany and Unilever in Britain contribute to the enormous increase in long distance transport of goods through Europe because lean production and Just-in-Time deliveries (key concepts in economic globalization) make production much more "efficient" for producers, and in a sense also for consumers if the real price of products actually falls with no decline in quality, but "inefficient" for essential road users and all those who lose jobs; and in the long term, for our relationships with the environment. Such practices are, of course, not confined to Europe. In 1995, the EU and the United States government in consultation with over 1200 corporations active in the USA and the EU, established a corporate Transatlantic Business Dialogue (TABD) to pursue globalization-friendly policies. According to its Business Coordinator in the USA: "TABD is a private-sector force designed to respond to the new reality of trade; namely that companies are functioning globally and their involvement in the making of international trade policy is a natural outgrowth of such globalization" (cited in CEO 1997: 28). This is, of course, one small organization among thousands of others, but its leading personnel included one European Commissioner (Sir Leon Brittan from the UK), senior executives from major European and American corporations, high officials from the Treasury and State Departments in the USA, and the former GATT Secretary-General, Peter Sutherland. Organizations such as these can be found in many parts of the world, for example, within the networks of the International Chambers of Commerce and the many overseas branches of national chambers of commerce (the USA alone has branches in over 100 countries), the World Economic Forum and, also, now within the UN system (Karliner 1999). Two case studies of how the economic and political powers of TNCs are related in different spheres of global politics further illustrate these processes. My first case study examines the Codex Alimentarius Commission, where corporate power is exercised in the global politics of food. Second, I attempt to explain the temporary defeat for corporate interests in the campaign for a Multilateral Agreement on Investment, an instructive lesson for the global politics of foreign investment.

Codex Alimentarius

Codex Alimentarius was established under the auspices of the United Nations in 1963 with the express purpose of facilitating world trade in food and drinks through the establishment of mandatory international standards. Clearly, under some circumstances, this could result in food standards (for hygiene, nutrition, safety and so on) being raised all over the world to those of the strictest regulatory authorities or, conversely, they could be reduced to some set of lowest common denominators (*Public Citizen* 1997, 38-42). One of the key issues that has exercised Codex over the years is the fact that countries that impose the highest standards of food safety and quality and those with the lowest standards are both accused of unfair trade practices (see Rosman 1993, an article on pesticide regulation that contains 160 references to CODEX and criticizes the lack of public representation in CODEX processes). In December 2021 CODEX concluded a series of sessions on food safety and a participant sent me this assessment of proceedings: "you have the chair from the country that is hosting the committee, a country that often has trade interests in the matters discussed and the secretariat of CODEX hosted by FAO that should guide the discussions by referring to and explaining procedural matters. They are leading and organizing the discussions and deciding who will have the floor and organizing negotiations for compromises".

Potential conflicts between the safety and quality regulatory tasks of Codex, on the one hand, and the facilitation of global trade talks on the other, are endemic to the organization. Thus, it is important to know who, exactly, makes the policies that governments and intergovernmental organizations generally take as their benchmarks for food. Codex is an intergovernmental body run by the FAO and the WHO, taking turns to host biennial Commission meetings in Rome and Geneva. According to the official guide to Codex history and practices, representation at sessions is on a country basis. National delegations are led by senior officials appointed by their governments. Delegations may, and often do, include representatives of industry, consumers organizations, and academic institutes. A number of international governmental organizations and international NGOS also attend in an observer capacity. Although they are "observers", the tradition of the Codex Alimentarius Commission allows such organizations to put forward their points of view at every stage except in the final decision, which is the exclusive prerogative of Member Governments (FAO/WHO 1999, 13). Much is made of the openness of Codex procedures (notably country Codex Contact Points and National Codex Committees) and the overall impression is of commendable transparency, joined-up intergovernmental thinking, and genuine representation in this most vital area of public policy. However, when we probe beneath the surface a rather different picture emerges. A first clue that the system is not as even-handed as it appears comes from Codex USA (located in the Department of Agriculture, a case, some might argue, of poacher turned gamekeeper). While observer status is important, membership of the official government delegations is the key to understanding the decision- making process. Guidelines issued by the Codex office in the USA explain the process of the selection of delegates to Codex meetings in more detail. United States delegates to Codex are government officials from the lead agencies involved (USDA, FDA, EPA, and Commerce) who develop official USA positions on issues to be considered. All interested parties are invited to provide information and comments on these issues. As the delegates prepare for the meetings of their committees, they form delegations comprising individuals whose support they think necessary at the meetings. These individuals participate as members of the official USA delegations at their own expense. The maximum for each delegation is 25 persons per committee and the criteria that govern selection of non-governmental members to delegations are (1) obtaining informed views; (2) whether opportunities to provide written comments would be an adequate alternative; and (3) provision of balanced representations of all interested parties. Individuals and representatives wishing to become members of the United States delegation are invited to contact the US delegate or Codex manager, who may seek volunteers and may identify and solicit for membership from labor groups, the academic community, trade associations, specific business firms, public interest groups, and from other sources, including the public at large. Non-government members of the delegation are expected to attend all Codex committee sessions and be available to assist and attend meetings called by the USA delegate. Thus, being a non-government member will be an expensive and time-consuming responsibility (see Rosman 1993, especially note 82).

Avery and her co-researchers have documented the affiliations of the 2578 people who participated in the 1989-91 session of Codex (Avery, et al. 1993, 162). In the 12 specialist committees in which the work of this session was conducted, 105 governments and 140 food and agrochemical companies were represented. In addition to those representing national governments, there were 660 industry representatives compared with a mere 26 from public interest groups. One of the largest and most controversial corporations in the world, Nestlé, had 38 representatives, more than most countries. At the two meetings on food additives and contaminants 41 percent of those present were from TNCS and industry federations; and at the meetings on pesticide residue levels, 127 (33 percent) were from TNCS compared with 80 from all the developing countries. In the 1989-91 session the United States policy for selection of delegates produced a total of 243 delegates, of whom only two came from NGOs, ten were consultants, 112 were from government, and 119 (49 percent of the total) were from industry. Overall, industry supplied 35 percent of the membership of the ten largest national delegations and 22 percent of all delegates. Only eight NGOs provided members of delegations, four in the Canadian delegation and two each in the USA and Netherlands delegations. Industry supplied 61 percent of the delegation from Switzerland, 44 percent of the Japanese, 40 percent of the French, 34 percent of the German, 31 percent of the British, 23 percent of the Canadian, 22 percent of the Italian, and 21 percent of the Dutch delegations, reflecting the global importance of food industry corporations domiciled in these countries. Most of the major food TNCs (led by Nestlé, and including Philip Morris/Kraft, Unilever, Pepsico, Coca-Cola, Heinz, and CPC International) and agrochemical TNCs (including Ciba-Geigy, ICI, Rhone Poulenc, Bayer, Dupont, Dow, Monsanto, Hoechst,

Shell, and Sumitomo) were represented on Codex committees, some of
them as official delegates (Avery, et al. 1993, Tables 5.1.1; 5.3.1; 5.4.1;
5.5.1; and Appendix Tables 5, 6, and 7). Rather disingenuously, the official
Codex Guide informs us that "a feature of the committee system is that, with
few exceptions, each committee is hosted by a member country, which is
chiefly responsible for the cost of the committee's maintenance and
administration and for providing its chairperson" (FAO/WHO, 1999, 15).
This system generally results in most of the meetings being held in and
financed by groups in First World countries in which the major food
industry TNCs are domiciled. Examples of this are clearly to be seen in the
1999-2000 meetings of the commodity committees. The Fish and Fishery
Products committee was hosted by Norway; Milk and Milk Products, and
Meat Hygiene by New Zealand; Cocoa and Chocolate, and Natural Mineral
Waters by Switzerland; Processed Meat and Poultry Products by Denmark;
Fats and Oils, and Sugars by Britain; and Processed Fruits and Vegetables,
and Cereals by the United States. The only exception was Mexico, which
hosted Fresh Fruit and Vegetables, of which it is a major exporter to the
United States. While Codex gives some prominence to the role of
consumers and their organizations in formulating policy on food, it is very
wary of encouraging this role at the global or local level. The Guide
specifically states: "The Commission has continued to involve consumer
interests in its work while recognizing that it is at the national level that
consumers can make their most valuable and effective input" (FAO/WHO
1999, 22). The Codex strategy is one of ensuring that consumer input is
safely channeled through national governments. The last point to be made
about the Codex process as an exemplar of how members of the
transnational capitalist class operate in global politics concerns the role of
the globalizing professionals, the food scientists and technologists on whom
the whole activity is said to rest. The official position unsurprisingly states:
"From the very beginning, the Codex Alimentarius has been a science-based
activity" (FAO/WHO 1999, 27). This is, of course, not quite as simple as it
sounds. The history of the links between science, Big Business and public
policy and, in particular, the "cheap food" policy (see Appleby, et al. 2003)
on which most capitalist industrialized societies are based, suggests that
science-based corporations are sometimes reluctant to err on the side of
caution (the precautionary principle) at the expense of their short-term
profits. Governments always have to balance out the interests of consumers
in the safety and quality of what they consume, the interests of food industry
workers, and the interests of who own and control the food companies. The
scientists (the technical fraction of the TCC in this case) provide the
technical basis for decisions but when the scientists differ (as, for example,

was for many years the case in the debate over the health risks of smoking) governments, industry, and consumers in the main tend to accept the least costly and most reassuring conclusions (at least until it is too late). Preliminary evidence from the 1999-2001 round of Codex deliberations suggests that, despite some very well-publicized and costly failures in the global food system (in terms of both human and animal health and industry profits), nothing much has changed in the last decade. The Food Labelling Committee that met in Ottawa in May 2000, for example, consisted of more than 200 official participants attached to member country delegations and over 60 observers, five from international governmental organizations and about 50 from NGOS (including industry groups). Of the official country participants, 48 were from TNCs and/or industry associations, while only four were from NGOs (mostly consumer protection organizations). Of the NGOs, 13 were from citizens or consumer groups of various types while at least 35 were industry associations. Codex produced a list of Observer Organizations participating in its activities in June 2000 that shows a similar distribution. In addition to intergovernmental organizations, including UNCTAD, OECD, and the World Trade Organization (WTO). Veggeland & Borgen (2005) provide a detailed analysis of the relationship between the WTO and Codex. Their conclusion is not surprising: "the WTO mattered as a set of constraints and opportunities that changed the incentives of member states .... The overall conclusion is that after 1995, Codex members have changed their behavior because of the increased uncertainty with respect to how decisions in Codex may be binding for them under the WTO Agreements" (ibid., 703). Codex produced a list of Observer Organizations participating in its activities in June 2000 that shows a similar distribution. In addition to intergovernmental organizations (including UNCTAD, OECD, and the WTO) almost 150 international NGOs were listed. Of these over 80 were clearly industry associations, there were perhaps ten consumer groups, and the rest were technical organizations of various types, some of which may be controlled by corporate interests. Precisely the types of disasters (BSE, food poisoning, and contamination) and ongoing problems (pesticide residues, inadequate and misleading food labelling) that Codex was established to prevent, are still with us (*Public Citizen* 1997). The next big battle will be over genetically modified organisms (GMOs) and while Monsanto and other major biotechnology corporations suffered setbacks to their plans in the late 1990s GMOs are still very much on the agenda and still controversial (Dryzek et al. 2009, Rosenow 2018). Despite campaigns by consumer groups and professionals independent of the TNCs for reforms to the Codex process, there are few signs that WTO procedures will diminish the ability of food and agrochemical TNCs to cut corners with nutritional quality and food safety in order to increase profitability.

Research published in the 2010s has thrown new light on Codex. Halabi writes: "studies and analyses of Codex decision-making frequently accuse it of subordinating its agenda to industry interests. For the most part, these criticisms are proven indirectly by, for example, counting industry representatives at Codex meetings or as part of national delegations. But the real threats to the integrity of Codex's processes have emerged not through routine industry participation on national delegations or as observers, but through hidden efforts to influence scientists supplying Codex's committees and subcommittees with purportedly objective information (Halabi 2015, 407). This is fair comment, but representation is still important, "Codex has done little to diminish the appearance of imbalance toward trade or industry influence. Codex's structure has always leaned in favor of not only trade promotion but giving countries with substantial interests in a given food or subject area privileged status within the standard setting process" (quoted from Halabi & Lin (2015, 16). A follow-up article by Halabi & Lin (2017) compares regulation in the public Codex system with the private, corporate global food system. They argue: "In light of the regulatory lacunae in public regulatory space, private actors, such as Global G.A.P. [Good Agricultural Practice] (or other multinational food companies, supermarket chains and non- governmental organizations), are increasingly filling the gaps by employing private standards, certification protocols, third-party auditing, and transnational contracting practices. The emergence of private governance in the food safety arena has been alongside the gradual decline of states traditional command-and-control regulation, which is increasingly being replaced by more flexible, market-oriented mechanisms. Although private standards such as those of Global G.A.P. are, in theory, not mandatory for suppliers, many have a de facto mandatory status, as a large part of buyers in global agri-food markets now require their suppliers to meet such private requirements, which are usually stricter than their public counterparts" (ibid. 2017, 19). However, this might seem a rather contradictory conclusion to an article that reveals the unwillingness of a corporate-dominated global food industry to accept responsibility for unhealthy infant feeding and other products and their consequences, one of the causes of the global obesity pandemic.

The last words in this complex story, for the moment, belong to Maryse Arendt, an infant feeding professional (Arendt 2018) and her correspondent, who address many of the issues raised above, suggesting that Codex is becoming even more embedded in the system of global corporate capitalism.

She shares the frustration of a lawyer: "I used to attend the meetings of the Codex Alimentarius Commission and the Committee on General Principles, as the lawyer from the WHO. I can tell you that it was always difficult, for there is a lot of pressure from vested interests in those meetings" (S. Shubber, personal communication, November 26, 2015) as quoted in Arendt (2018, 707), see also Arendt (2021).

The Multilateral Agreement on Investment (MAI)

The OECD had been discussing ways of freeing the TNCS from restrictive legislation for decades, but negotiations to establish the MAI were not opened until 1995 (by which time many would argue that there were in fact very few effective restrictive regulations left). Similar proposals that had been mooted in the fledgling WTO ran into opposition led by representatives from India and Malaysia. In any case, it was considered by proponents that the First World dominated OECD was perhaps a more suitable venue for these matters. Generally, OECD member states, irrespective of which political party was in government, had been content to rely on toothless voluntary agreements on the conduct of what the organization chose to call multinational enterprises (perhaps considered to be a less threatening term than transnational corporations). Business input to OECD negotiations had been institutionalized in 1962 with the creation of the Business and Industry Advisory Committee (BIAC), through which the interests of business, dominated, unsurprisingly, by Big Business were channeled. As with Codex, there is a peculiar relationship between official governmental participation (like Codex, the OECD is an intergovernmental organization) and what can be labelled "official adjunct" personnel and organizations. In the United States the body responsible for input to the BIAC on behalf of the United States government is the private interest group, the US Council for International Business (USCIB). The Confederation of British Industries (CBI), the private interest group that speaks for Big Business, is responsible for BIAC input on behalf of the British government, and the powerful employer's organization Keidanren, runs BIAC Japan. There are similar arrangements in other member countries. Formal discussions on the MAI began at the OECD in May 1995. The existence of the MAI proposals was known to few people outside the narrow confines of the specialist trade and investment communities until an NGO posted a leaked report on MAI on the Internet in 1997. Many other environmental, consumer, labour rights, and development groups rapidly began to alert the wider public to the possible dire consequences of the MAI, notably expanding corporate rights to sue local authorities for any presumed constraints on trade. In response, some details of the negotiations were posted on the OECD Internet site and the OECD published a Policy Brief on it (Number 2, 1997) and wider consultations began. As a result of the NGO/OECD Consultation, a "joint NGO Statement", extremely hostile to the MAI, was released in Paris on 27 October 1997, and re-released in an updated form on 11 February 1998. Two days later a full-page advertisement making the case against the MAI, supported by 600 organizations in 67 countries, appeared in the *New York Times*, the *International Herald Tribune*, and other opinion-forming newspapers. The central theme of the advertisement was the role of the major corporations in promoting and influencing the MAI. The headline of the advertisement: "Top Secret: New MAI Treaty. Should Corporations Rule the World" (*New York Times*, 13 February 1998) alerted a mass audience that something important was afoot. While it is true that the United States and Canada between them provided over 200 of these organizations, substantial support also came from many other countries. There were 15 organizations from Australia, 15 from Austria, 10 from Brazil, 10 from Germany, 16 from Italy, 12 from Japan, 18 from the Netherlands, 10 from Russia, 13 from the UK, and 65 from Mexico (many had also been involved in the struggle against NAFTA, see Sklair 1993, chapter 11). The most prominent actors involved in this anti-MAI initiative were international environmental organizations, notably Friends of the Earth (active in over 70 countries), and the US-based *Public Citizen* and the Sierra Club. The campaign against the MAI in the United States is an object lesson on how global corporations can be challenged through local action and by mobilizing the parliamentary system in democracies. The Boston Area MAI Action Groups, for example, created a website (available through the MAI portal) that successfully connected national conferences on MAI with local action. In the USA we find the message: "So please, call your representative and senators. (Call the Capitol switchboard at 202-225-3121.) Talk with the aide who deals with "international trade and investment. .... Ask for your representative's position on 'full debate,' and how he [sic] intends to deal with a fast-track proposal when it does come up. Then ask for his mailing address and write a letter to confirm the conversation. See our sample letters." (underlined in original, to access sample letters).

Crucial in this campaign was the work of Robert Stumberg, a law professor at Georgetown University. His research was instrumental in mobilizing local and state officials all over the United States against the MAI on the (very real) grounds that the Agreement would seriously limit the already limited autonomy of municipal and state authorities in the realms of economic, environmental, and social affairs, Stumberg had also been active in the tobacco control campaign, as documented in the previous chapter. It is likely that pressure from these officials on the Federal government, already embroiled in various trade and investment disputes with the EU and other international bodies, heightened its awareness of the political risks involved in the MAI. The British government was also ambivalent on the issue, as was made clear in the debate on MAI reported in Hansard (23 February 1998, 147-154). It is an interesting comment on New Labour to note that the debate was led by Dr Nick Palmer, who was both a consultant for the major pharmaceutical TNC Novartis (his former employer) and a member of the World Development Movement, that spearheaded the campaign against the MAI in Britain. Dr Palmer (who noted that the Conservative benches were entirely empty) was extremely hostile to the MAI, but the Labour government gave it a guarded welcome, while noting that there was a growing public hostility to some of the provisions in the proposed agreement. As in the United States, campaigners in Britain also had some success in connecting the local, the national, and the global. For example, according to the MAI Coalition, in mid-1998 around twenty local authorities in England (including Birmingham City Council, Oxfordshire County Council, and Bournemouth Borough Council) had passed resolutions expressing concern about the local impacts of any MAI. Links had also been forged with the churches, trade unions, academic researchers, and political parties (MAI Coalition Newsletter, July 1998). The rapid growth of local, national, and global campaigns against the MAI was not good news for those working quietly behind the scenes to prepare public opinion in the United States, Europe, and elsewhere for what they hoped would be more or less a *fait accompli,* MAI by stealth. The official United States government nominated representative on the BIAC was, as noted above, the United States Council for International Business (USCIB), a membership-based organization comprising more than 300 corporations and interested parties. In fact, USCIB has had the official role of representing USA business on international issues since 1947, it is also the official USA representative on the ILO and other international bodies. While nominally representing the interests of the government of the United States, the focus of the work of the USCIB since the 1980s has been on open markets and level playing fields for trade and investment in the interests of major North American corporations. To this end, USCIB participated in the BIAC informal working groups of experts who met with official OECD negotiators regularly in Paris. USCIB also advised the us Trade Representative and the State Department and met with them regularly on MAI and other matters. At the crucial January 1998 consultation between BIAC and OECD negotiators where, presumably, the growing campaign against the MAI was high on the agenda, the Executive Director of USCIB and counterparts from

Canada, Britain, France, Germany, and other member countries met with senior OECD personnel. Also included in this meeting were executives from ten individual corporations, seven of whom ranked in the top 100 investors in the world (Shell, Volkswagen, GE, Nestlé, Unilever, Texaco, and Kobe Steel). The problem for USCIB (and its partners in BIAC) was that no senior politicians had backed the MAI publicly. It appears that many globalizing politicians and professionals realized the potential for political damage inherent in the MAI and, though they wanted it, they wanted it without too much fuss. In the United States, for example, the problems of the IMF and other more specific trade and investment issues had higher priority than the MAI in the latter part of the 1990s. The pro-MAI coalition in and around the OECD had planned to complete the Agreement for signing at the OECD ministerial meeting in April 1998, but this was postponed, and more consultations took place. However, it was becoming clear that the MAI was insupportable. In September 1998 a report by Catherine Lalumiere, a European deputy from France, suggested that the negotiations should be moved to the WTO. The French government took this as its cue to withdraw from the increasingly unpopular MAI process and, finally, in December 1998 the OECD officially abandoned the attempt to establish the MAI (see Henderson 1999). Some governments (Japan, for example) welcomed the suggestion that the matter should be taken back to the WTO, probably under a new name. Given the coalition against the WTO which arose in the late 1990s (and which shows no sign of abating in the early years of the new century), this seems an unlikely prospect in the near future. A "Statement" against the WTO and the deregulation of the global economy organized by Friends of the Earth, published on 4 August 1999 brought together almost 800 organizations from over 75 countries in anticipation of the Seattle meetings. However, it should also be noted that there are many more countries in the WTO system than there are in the OECD, and that in the long term most major TNCS are probably just as interested in investing in developing countries as in the rich and to some extent investment-saturated economies of the OECD. This is certainly the case for the tobacco TNCS, as we saw in the previous chapter (for the influence of Philip Morris and RJR in the MAI campaign see INFACT 1998). The level of public debate that was generated over the MAI (and subsequently the issues raised by the WTO), mainly in elite circles but also in the public domain, suggests that these relatively obscure trade and investment debates have been successfully politicized by those who are unhappy with some or all of the consequences of global capitalism and the role of the globalizing corporations within it. Even though the early negotiations were largely unnoticed, they were never "secret" as some of their critics have claimed, though the OECD did not exactly mount a public awareness campaign.

MAI was clearly of great significance as the first truly global attempt to establish binding norms for foreign investment. However, it was not an attempt to regulate foreign investors but an attempt to regulate those who might try to interfere with foreign investment, namely community, municipal, and national governments. That was its fatal flaw. Therefore, the failure to establish the MAI is a valuable comment on the spheres in which corporations are replacing states as the dominant forces in the governance of the global economy and the spheres in which they are not. The BIAC Chairman's message in the 1998 Annual Report attributed the failure to push through the MAI to the financial crisis that swept through Asia and other emerging markets in 1997, which had "fanned the flames of opposition to globalization and amplified the chorus of criticism of liberalized trade and investment rules." But this seems to miss the point. It was not the "flames of opposition to globalization" that destroyed the MAI, it was the fact that the party politicians and other officials in the governments of OECD member countries saw the MAI as a vote-loser and, in some cases, as a threat to their autonomy vis-a-vis global capital. If my explanation is correct, and the coalition of globalizing bureaucrats and corporate executives inside and outside the OECD was defeated by a coalition of national and local politicians (not necessarily all of the same political persuasion) and a wide variety of global and local campaigning groups, then we can learn important lessons about strategies and tactics of global corporate politics from this case. Tactically, while many intellectuals are sceptical if not cynical about elections and popular sentiments, if national and local politicians can be persuaded that policy decisions such as the implementation of MAI could seriously damage them in electoral terms, then this "democratic tactic" could be powerful in such cases. However, strategically, it remains true that even left-leaning governments (to stretch the term unbearably) like New Labour under Blair and the Democrats under Clinton began by supporting the MAI in the OECD and were only persuaded to abandon it by the apparent groundswell of popular and legislative opinion against it. It is very probable that a new form of the MAI will be reintroduced when conditions are ripe, for example if and when rising inflation and rising unemployment undermine the opposition to foreign investment and the jobs that major corporations usually offer. Relying solely on governments of whatever political party to defend the popular classes (to use an old-fashioned but apt term) is not a viable long-term strategy while the hegemony of global capital continues to be exercised through the transnational capitalist class.

Corporate Power and Genuine Democracy

Much of the research on corporate-state connection can be found only in the form of obscure reports from and about obscure lobby groups (Pedlar & Schendelen eds. 1994). This perfectly illustrates my thesis that the TNCs do work, quite deliberately and sometimes rather covertly, as political actors, and often have direct access to those at the highest levels of formal political and administrative power with considerable success. The research of Corporate Europe Observatory (CEO) and INFACT could, I am sure, be replicated for most countries, and many cities, all round the world. Everywhere, we find corporate executives, globalizing politicians and professionals, and consumer elites (merchants, marketers, advertisers) telling us in public and doing their best to ensure in private that the globalizing agenda of contemporary capitalism driven by the TNCS and their allies is inevitable and, eventually, in the best interests of us all. They would see the corporate lobbies working effectively within the European Union and the OECD, within Codex, and for the tobacco industry globally, as doing a fine job in paving the way to universal prosperity. I have argued that the TNCS and their allies are political actors and that they do achieve significant success in getting across their message that there is no alternative to global capitalism. The route to prosperity for all, the corporations argue, is through international competitiveness decided by the "free" market and "free" trade, institutions and processes that they largely control themselves or through their friends and allies in local and national governments and international organizations. Does this present a problem for democracy? In one sense it does not. TNCs are legal bodies with every right to act legally to further their interests. They are formally owned by millions of individual shareholders whose main interest is in seeing the value of their investments increase, although effective control is usually vested in small groups of owner-executives and institutional shareholders. The other side of the matter is that all major trade and investment treaties are profoundly undemocratic in structure and process. In 1994, just before the United States Congress was due to vote on the Uruguay Round of GATT, the Washington-based organization *Public Citizen* offered to donate $10,000 to the charity of choice of any member of Congress who had read the 500-page agreement and who could answer ten questions about it. Only one member, a "free-trader", eventually accepted the challenge, and as a result he changed his vote from "for" to "against" the agreement (after having voted for NAFTA which, presumably, he had not read). Congress approved GATT in December 1994, the inference being that most legislators in the USA voted for an agreement that would fundamentally change the global economy without knowing what was in it in any detail. Neither do most legislators in the member countries of the European Union appear, on the whole, to be better informed than those in the United States on such matters. So, apart from the very big issues about whether to join or accede to treaties, which are very occasionally put to the vote in a referendum, our elected representatives appear to nod through on a regular basis legislation that effects our daily lives in many different ways (see Judge 2021). As the evidence from Codex, MAI, and the tobacco industry suggests, the interests of global capital are generally better represented because the TNCS have the resources and the commercial motivation to ensure that their interests are fully represented. Even such a relatively well-endowed organization as Greenpeace Germany had only one Brussels-based lobbyist in 1997: "In comparison with the swarms of industry lobbyists to be found in Brussels corridors, environmentalists are an endangered species" (CEO 1997, 57).

The political activities of the TNCs and their allies, therefore, raise serious doubts about how well our democracies are working with respect to everyday economic issues, global trade and investment, environment, health and safety of workers and citizens in general. Attempts by bodies, like the ILO and the now-dismantled UN Centre on Transnational Corporations, to develop universal codes of conduct to encourage the best practices of TNCs and to outlaw their much-documented bad practices all over the world have come to very little. As we have seen, the MAI promised to give more freedoms to the TNCs without imposing any compensating responsibilities, and such initiatives are likely to be resumed. This is all in the name of globalization, free trade, and international competitiveness. In her research on opposition in Europe to the Transatlantic Trade and Investment Partnership (TTIP, aborted in 2019) Julia Rone (2021) provides an important case study of the complexities of protest against austerity and free trade, an interesting counterpoint to the campaign against the MAI decades earlier.

Second thoughts

In 2021 it is too early to tell what the Trans-Pacific Partnership or, for that matter, Brexit will mean for the corporate-state connection. The political economist John Ravenhill has argued that rather than thinking about the global economy it would be more fruitful to think in terms of regional blocks, and "Factory Asia", "Factory North America" and "Factory Europe" (Ravenhill 2017). Whatever the outcome of current and future negotiations it seems unlikely that the control of the global economy by the transnational capitalist class and its allies will weaken, wherever their "factories" are located. Dyreng et al. (2016), in a long and very technical paper in an accounting journal, analyze research carried out by the nonprofit activist group ActionAid International, on a sample of UK firms with subsidiaries in tax havens. To non-specialists like myself this appears to show that public pressure does increase the likelihood of some firms paying up, but it also suggests that it may be cheaper to pay penalties than to pay taxes. In 2021 a new fiscal regime to establish a minimum global corporate tax rate of 15% was agreed by 136 governments all round the world, apparently ending the scandal of corporate tax havens. However, the enthusiasm with which these proposals were greeted by some major corporations in Silicon Valley suggests that, as usual, this might be a boost to the creative accounting industry as much as to cash-strapped national and local authorities struggling to fund public services, especially in poorer regions and countries. Cassee (2019) provides a comprehensive survey of the implications of global corporate tax rates for social justice.

Equally complex is the little-known issue of "investor-state dispute settlement" (ISDS), through which investor corporations use corporate courts to sue governments and local authorities. The origins of this classic system of undemocratic corporate-state connection date from the 1950s when the Iranian government attempted to nationalize the Anglo-Persian Oil Company (now BP) and end 50 years of British control of the oil industry in Persia. This provoked a military coup (Operation Ajax) organized by the British and the US which unseated the President, Mosaddeqh (who was jailed) and replaced him with less troublesome locals. From the 1990s the use of corporate courts expanded gradually, and in recent decades with the advent of increased attempts to introduce environmental legislation "investor-state dispute settlement" (ISDS) all over the world. In the words of one of the leading critics of ISDS: "States' ability to pass measures for the public interest is undermined from above, from global standards and institutions, as well as from a transactional model that protects investors' reliance. Under investment treaties and ISDS, the relationship between foreign investors and states is interpreted through a regulatory model unless the investor has a legitimate expectation, but this legal regime always plugs foreign investor rights and states' right to regulate into global institutions, and it does so by excluding public domestic imperatives" (Perrone 2021, 201). Perrone introduces the powerful concept of "norm entrepreneurs", a well-organized and well- connected group of business leaders, lawyers (as a newly created category of investor-state dispute arbitrators) and bureaucrats with a globalizing agenda to protect and enhance corporate foreign investors rights. We could label this the international legal wing of the transnational capitalist class, thereby "embedding foreign investor rights into their world- making project of free enterprise and a global economy .... an audacious move, but one for which international arbitration would prove to be a fertile terrain. Some of the norm entrepreneurs, moreover, would become arbitrators themselves" (Perrone 2021, 80). These arbitrators, who are not exactly judges, have themselves provoked controversy (Franck 2007, 2017, Gallacher & Shrethsa 2011) as has the process itself (Paulsson 2010, Reddie 2017, Chao Wang et al 2021). A final piece in the jigsaw of investor-protection for corporations is ICSID (the International Centre for Settlements of Investment Disputes, World Bank Group), established in 1966, its publication *ICSID Review*, and its most useful *Annual Reports*, freely available on its website. By the end of 2021 the ICID Convention had 164 signatories, 155 of them contracting states. Though many ISDS cases concern environmental issues (see Perrone 2021, chapter 4 "ISDS in Action" and Chao Wang, et al. 2021 on environmental disputes affecting indigenous communities), there appears to be no reference at all to "environment" in the 2021 *Annual Report*. As a last word on the role of the legal system in environmental issues it is interesting to read about the impact of Specialized Environmental Courts on corporate risk-taking in China (Huayun Zhai, et al. 2020, and see also Sklair ed. 2021, p. 114 note 3).

About a decade after I wrote this article I became aware of the Sackler family, owners of the company Purdue Pharma, another example of how we might deconstruct the corporate-state connection in the era of capitalist globalization. Patrick Keefe, an acute investigative journalist at the *New Yorker*, provides a detailed account of the role of the Sackler family in the opiod crisis in the USA, and also abroad. Keefe quotes Allen Frances of the Duke University School of Medicine: "Their name has been pushed forward as the epitome of good works and of the fruits of the capitalist system, But when it comes down to it, they've earned a fortune at the expense of millions of people who are addicted, It's shocking how they have gotten away with it" (Keefe 2017, 36). As Keefe demonstrates, and a series of Youtube documentaries televised in the USA confirm (for example, https://www. youtube.com/watch?v=zGcKURD_osM), they got away with it by false advertising, corrupting sections of the medical profession, and taking advantage of corporate-friendly regulation and regulators. The pill they marketed was the highly addictive OxyContin, often referred to as a "common drug of abuse". In December 2021, after hundreds of thousands of deaths and millions of lives wrecked, Purdue Pharma and the Sackler family were brought to some semblance of justice as the company was driven into bankruptcy, facings thousands of lawsuits. The evidence presented in the previous chapter suggests there are many similarities between the tobacco industry and the story of Purdue Pharma, not least the role that philanthropy plays in deflecting criticism away from large corporations and their owners. Keefe cites Sackler philanthropy at the Metropolitan Museum in New York, the National Gallery in Washington, at Harvard, at the Guggenheim New York, at the Louvre, at Columbia, Oxford, and other universities. Corporate philanthropy is a valuable tool in the arsenal of the transnational capitalist class. Finally, I need to acknowledge that my focus on capitalists tends to distract me from spending more time on the workers and recalling what I learned about corporate social responsibility from another PhD student (see Timms forthcoming 2022).

References

Althusser, L. (1971b) Ideology and Ideological State Apparatuses (Notes towards an Investigation). In *Lenin and Philosophy and Other Essays* (trans. Ben Brewster). London: NLB, pp. 121-173.

Appleby, M., Cutler, N. et al. (2003) What Price Cheap Food? *Journal of Agricultural and Environmental Ethics* 16: 395–408.

Arendt, M. (2018) Codex Alimentarius: What has it to do with Me? *Journal of Human Lactation* 34/4: 704–710.

Arendt, M. (2021) Advocacy at Work During Codex Committee on Food Labelling Meeting. *Journal of Human Lactation* (December): 1-3.

Avery, N., et al. (1993) *Cracking the Codex: An Analysis of Who Sets World Food Standards.* London: National Food Alliance.

Cassee, A. (2019) International tax competition and justice: The case for global minimum tax rates. *Politics, philosophy & economics* 18/3: 242-263.

CEO (1997) *Europe Inc.: Dangerous Liaisons Between EU Institutions and Industry.* Amsterdam: Corporate Europe Observatory.

Chao Wang, Jing Ning, & Xiaohan Zhang (2021) International Investment and Indigenous Peoples' Environment: A Survey of ISDS Cases from 2000 to 2020. *International journal of environmental research and public health.* https://doi.org/10.3390/ijerph18157798

Dryzek, J.S. & Goodin, R.E., et al. (2009) Promethean Elites Encounter Precautionary Publics: The Case of GM Foods. *Science, Technology, & Human Values* 34/3: 263-288.

Dyreng, S.D., et al. (2016) Public Pressure and Corporate Tax Behavior. *Journal of Accounting Research* 54/1: 147-186.

FAO/WHO (1999) *Understanding the Codex Alimentarius.* Rome & Geneva: FAO/WHO.

Franck, S.D. (2007) Empirically Evaluating Claims about Investment Treaty Arbitration. http://scholarship.law.unc.edu/nclr/vol86/iss1/2

Franck, S.D. (2017) Inside the Arbitrator's Mind. *Emory Law Journal* 66/5: 1115-1703.

Frey, R.S. (1997) The International Traffic in Tobacco. *Third World Quarterly* 18: 303-319.

Gierzynski, A. (2000) *Money Rules: financing elections in America.* Boulder: Westview.

Gallacher, K. & Shrethsa, E. (2011) Investment Treaty Arbitration and Developing Countries: A Re-Appraisal. *The Journal of World Investment & Trade 12*/6: 919-928.

Huayun Zhai, et al. (2020) The Impact of Specialized Environmental Courts on Corporate Risk-Taking: Evidence from a Natural Experiment in China. *Asia-Pacific Journal of Financial Studies* 49: 99–118.

Halabi, S.F. (2015) The Codex Alimentarius Commission, Corporate Influence, and International Trade: A Perspective on FDA's Global Role. *American Journal of Law & Medicine* 41: 406-421.

Halabi, S. F., & Lin, C. F. (2017). Assessing the relative influence and efficacy of public and private food safety regulation regimes: Comparing Codex and Global G.A.P. standards. *Food and Drug Law Journal* 72/2: 262-294.

Henderson, D. (1999) *The MAI Affair: a story and its lessons.* London: Royal Institute of International Affairs.

INFACT (1998) *Global Aggression: The Case for World Standards and Bold Action*: *Challenging Philip Morris and RJR Nabisco.* New York: Apex Press.

Jacobs, D. (1999) *Business lobbies and the power structure in America.* Westport, CT: Quorum.

Judge, D (2021) Walking the Dark Side: Evading Parliamentary Scrutiny. *The Political Quarterly* 92/2: 283-92.

Karliner, J. (1999) Co-opting the UN. *The Ecologist* 29: 318-21.

Keefe, P.R. (2017) Empire of Pain: The Sackler Family's ruthless promotion of opiods generated billions of dollars—and millions of addicts. *New Yorker* (30 October).

Paulsson, J. (2010) The Power of States to Make Meaningful Promises to Foreigners. *Journal of International Dispute Settlement* 1/2: 341– 52.

Pedlar, R.H. & Schendelen, M.V., eds. (1994) *Lobbying the European Union: Trade Associations and Issue Groups.* London: Frank Cass.

Perrone, N.M. (2021) *Investment treaties and the legal imagination : how foreign investors play by their own rules.* Oxford: Oxford University Press.

Public Citizen (1997) *Nafta's Broken Promises: Fast Track to Unsafe Food.* Washington DC: Global Trade Watch.

Ravenhill, J. (2017) The political economy of the Trans-Pacific Partnership: a "21st Century" trade agreement? *New Political Economy* 22/5: 573-594).

Reddie, A. (2017) Power in international trade politics: is ISDS a solution in search of a problem? *Business and Politics* 19/4: 738–757.

Richardson, K. (2000) *Big Business and the European Agenda. Reflections on the activities of the European Round Table of Industrialists, 1988-98.* Brighton: Sussex European Institute, Working Paper No. 35.

Rone, J. (2021) *Contesting Austerity and Free Trade in the EU: Protest Diffusion in Complex Media and Political Arenas.* New York & London: Routledge.

Rosenow, D. (2018) *Un-making environmental activism: beyond modern/colonial binaries in the GMO controversy.* London: Routledge.

Rosman, L. (1993) Public Participation in International Pesticide Regulation: When the Codex Commission Decides, Who Will Listen? *Virginia Environmental Law Journal* 12: 329-65.

Singer, T.O. & Stumberg, R. (1999) A Multilateral Agreement on Investment: Would It Undermine Subnational Environmental Protection? *The Journal of Environment & Development* 8/1: 5-23.

Sklair, L. (1993) *Assembling for Development: The maquila industry in Mexico and the United States.* San Diego: Center for US-Mexican Studies.

Timms, J. (forthcoming 2022) *Questioning corporate social responsibility: Campaigns for the rights of workers in global production networks.* Abingdon: Routledge.

Weggeland, F. & Borgen, S.O. (2005) Negotiating International Food Standards: The World Trade Organization's Impact on the Codex Alimentarius Commission. *Governance: An International Journal of Policy, Administration, and Institutions* 18/4: 675–708.

Wang, C., Ning, J. & Zhang, X. (2021) International Investment and Indigenous Peoples' Environment: A Survey of ISDS Cases from 2000 to 2020. *Int. J. Environ. Res. Public Health.* https://doi.org/10.3390/ijerph18157798

Wolff, R.D. (2006) Ideological State Apparatuses, Consumerism, and U.S. Capitalism: Lessons for the Left. *Rethinking Marxism* 17/2: 223-235. https://doi.org/10.1080/08935690500046785

World Bank (1993) *World Development Report.* New York: Oxford University Press.

CHAPTER 7

(2011) THE TRANSITION FROM CAPITALIST GLOBALIZATION TO SOCIALIST GLOBALIZATION. *THE JOURNAL OF DEMOCRATIC SOCIALISM* 1/1:1-14. [COURTESY OF JDS]

Preamble

As the new millennium started to roll the aphorism "it is easier to imagine the end of the world than the end of capitalism" became increasingly believable. Usually attributed to the Marxist cultural theorist, Fredric Jameson, it was not clear if the reference was to the planet as a viable home for the human species, or the planet *per se*. Science fiction supplied plenty of ways to imagine both of these scenarios, but few genuine ways to imagine the end of capitalism. This essay represents one of several attempts to set off on the long and very much incomplete journey to grapple with the possibility of the "transition" from capitalist globalization to socialist globalization, in my rather idealistic sense. In addition, I now realize that the pathbreaking research of the late John Friedmann on "Agropolitan development" in the 1970s (see Friedmann 1979), planted the seed of my attempt to develop the idea of producer-consumer cooperatives almost forty years later.

Abstract

Historically, there have been many ways to effect transitions from one form of society to another. I begin this discussion with the assumption that the only way of making a successful transition from capitalist globalization to socialist globalization will be through a democratic process in which capitalist forms of democracy are themselves transformed into socialist forms of democracy. The article concludes with an attempt to sketch the main principles of a post-capitalist alternative form of democratic socialist globalization, based on networks of sustainable consumer-producer cooperatives operating at all appropriate social, economic, and geographical scales.

Three Modes of Globalization

The debate around globalization is entering a new and more mature phase reflected in the fact that it is now generally accepted that we live in an era of globalization. Here I attempt to deconstruct it by distinguishing three modes of globalization in theory and practice, namely: generic, capitalist, and alternative globalizations. My argument is that globalization in a generic sense is too often confused with its dominant actually existing type, capitalist globalization. I define generic globalization in terms of (a) the electronic revolution; (b) postcolonialisms; (c) the subsequent creation of transnational social spaces; and (d) qualitatively new forms of cosmopolitanism. Capitalist globalization undermines the emancipatory potential of these four elements of generic globalization, resulting in what are conceptualized here as new types of class polarization crises along with multiple crises of ecological unsustainability (Sklair 2002). Dealing with these crises will entail changing the parliamentary systems that have proved so successful in raising standards of living and improving human rights for billions of people over the last century or so all round the world but, at the same time, have proved so dysfunctional in creating more accountable and less easily corruptible forms of democracy and the protection of human rights (discussed in the next chapter). This state of affairs presents many opportunities for the transnational capitalist class that controls capitalist globalization all over the world. The vast majority of electorates appears to want more accountability and an end to corruption, but the present systems tend to be dominated by those who have little genuine interest in accountability and ending corruption, whether of the cruder or more subtle varieties. However, there are enough political activists and progressive social movements in the world to make these changes possible, even if this is quite unlikely at present. The current context for any discussion on improving democratic processes is, I argue, the fact of capitalist globalization, and the context for a progressive alternative to capitalist globalization is some form of democratic socialist globalization.

Globalization and Socialism

To talk of socialism these days invites scorn, pity, and bemusement in varying measure. Certainly, the historical experience of actually existing (mostly so-called) socialisms and communisms has been mixed, to say the least. The emergence of what I have labelled generic globalization and its concrete manifestation in capitalist globalization since the middle of the twentieth century have undoubtedly forced us to rethink the tenets of all the variants of classical socialism and communism. We can identify some fundamental differences between capitalist globalization and socialist globalization in the economic, political, and culture-ideology spheres. In the economic sphere, while capitalist globalization (through the transnational corporations) prioritizes the accumulation of private profit, socialist globalization would prioritize the creation of employment that is worthwhile both for individuals and for the community as a whole. In the political sphere, while capitalist globalization, directed by the transnational capitalist class, organizes society through parliamentary democracy based largely on states and national societies, in socialist globalization society would be organized through participatory forms of democracy, locally and globally. And in the culture-ideology sphere, while the value system of capitalist globalization revolves round the culture-ideology of consumerism, the value system of socialist globalization would revolve around human rights and responsibilities. These differences are structurally inter-connected. The potential for the gradual elimination of the culture-ideology of consumerism and its replacement with a culture-ideology of human rights and responsibilities means, briefly, that instead of possessions being the main focus of our cultures and the basis of our values, our lives should be lived with regard to a universally agreed system of human rights and the responsibilities to others that these rights entail. This does not imply that we should stop consuming. What it implies is that we should evaluate our consumption in terms of our rights and responsibilities and that this should become a series of interlocking and mutually supportive transnational practices. By genuinely expanding the culture-ideology of human rights from the civil and political spheres, in which capitalist globalization has often had a relatively positive influence, to the economic and social spheres, which represents a profound challenge to capitalist globalization, we can begin seriously to tackle the ongoing crises of class polarization and ecological unsustainability. In contrast to capitalist globalization, socialist globalization would prioritize the creation of employment that is worthwhile both for individuals and for the community as a fundamental human right. In the long term, a global economy dominated by the interests of those who own and control transnational corporations and their local affiliates may work less well for the vast majority of people than a global economy organized around the interests of direct producers and consumers of essential goods and services. My own suggestion, again for the long term, is that it is worth beginning to think about the idea of producer-consumer cooperatives (P-CCs) made up of those who produce and consume those essential goods and services. At present this sounds like just another call for fairer distribution, another war on poverty to make the daily lives of the world's poorest a little better. However, if current predictions about shrinking supply and ever-expanding demand for resources essential for a decent standard of living prove correct, more and more of us, within and outside what used to be called the Third World, are liable to be affected. Most of the discussions of localization are worthy up to a point, and that point is the issue of how the local connects with supralocal levels of organization. There is no reason, in principle, why neighbouring P-CCs could not make mutually beneficial non-exploitative connections with each other and with others further distant (the electronic revolution makes this possible in an historically unprecedented fashion) and eventually global networks of P-CCs may emerge. This constitutes the first stage of what I mean by socialist globalization. At present, these theoretical arguments can be fortified in two ways. First, the experiences of successful and failed P-CCs can be examined to discover what made the successes succeed and what made the failures fail. Second, some obviously dysfunctional elements of the global economy, for example the global corporate food system that has produced a worldwide crisis of obesity alongside malnutrition, and the private automobile culture that has contributed to a worldwide crisis of greenhouse gas emissions and respiratory health diseases. All of these are also to a significant extent responsible for the ecological catastrophe we look likely to be facing.

The Transnational Cooperative Movement

It is not widely known that the cooperative movement around the world is already enormous and steadily, in some places spectacularly, growing. The International Cooperative Alliance (ICA) headquartered in Geneva, was founded in 1895; by 2010 it had 248 member organizations from 92 countries active in all sectors of the economy. Together these cooperatives represent nearly one billion individuals worldwide committed, on paper if not always in practice, to the ICA principles of voluntary and open membership, democratic control, economic participation, autonomy and independence, education and training, co-operation among cooperatives,

and concern for community (https://www.ica.coop/en). Although definitions
of cooperative economic activity vary to some extent, and it would be wrong
to characterize the ICA as an anti-capitalist movement, there is no doubt
that it is already a viable socioeconomic model for many millions of people.
This, of course, is not always clear evidence of embryonic socialist
globalization, but it does point in the direction of alternative globalizations,
away from at least the worst excesses of capitalist globalization. The
International Labour Organization (ILO), a Geneva-based agency of the UN,
now has a dedicated section on its website (see https://www.ilo.org/global/
topics/cooperatives/news/WCMS_791694/lang--en/index.htm) providing
details of cooperative movements around the globe. In a series on "Spotlight
Interviews with Co-operators" dated 13 May 2021, notably an interview the
inspirational Misako Shinozaki, Chairperson of Seikatsu Club Consumers'
Cooperative Kanagawa, Japan, presents a vivid picture of genuine
cooperative life and values. However, these admirable initiatives are firmly
located within the capitalist marketplace of cooperative banks (Women
Citizens Community Bank) and billion yen investments in various mutual-
aid businesses, focused on improving social and cultural life for members
of Seikatsu and to some extent the wider society but, inevitably, to some
extent in competition with the capitalist mode of production. This does
present a dilemma for my argument about the necessity to create a global
society of producer-consumer cooperatives. Organizations like Seikatsu and
leaders like Misako Shinozaki represent the best short term opportunity in
specific local contexts to reform capitalism but, I would argue, the historical
record suggests that in the long term all attempts to reform capitalism
fundamentally to ensure global social, environmental, and economic justice
are bound to fail, especially when humanity is faced with the potential
existential crisis revealed by the Anthropocene and now, possibly
Coronavirus and its variants (see chapters 10-12).

Research in the USA on cooperatives (see Trimarco & Bamburg 2009, and
Kelly & Massena 2009) provides some interesting evidence of the
flourishing of cooperatives in recent years. Published in *Yes Magazine* (an
independent non-profit founded in 1996 whose slogan is "building a just
and sustainable world") these articles are posted on various cooperative
movement websites. Trimarco & Bamburg (2009) argue: "Difficult times
call for creative strategies. Time and again during periods of economic
hardship and market failure, cooperatively owned businesses have emerged
as a democratic, grassroots, and DIY response. It happened during the
economic upheavals of the 19th century and again during the Great
Depression. Today, as the current economic crisis deepens, co-ops are again
coming to the fore as producers and consumers seek stable sources of

employment, goods, and services. There are no easy numbers to quantify this growth, but signs of a new upsurge are becoming clearer". They go on to document the success of many co-ops in the USA, notably farmer-owned agricultural cooperatives, especially those established by recently laid-off employees assisted by the US Federation of Worker Owned Cooperatives. This organization has been working internationally since 1953 and has a useful website (see *International Community Development Projects |NCBA CLUSA* for its Global Program based on "sustainable Development goals). The co-op internet suffix "co-op domain", which can only be used by active cooperatives, has also grown in recent years, enrolling 5,800 addresses since its inception in 2000. Trimarco & Bamburg usefully distinguish four types of co-ops in the USA. The first, nearest to the P-CCs in my formulation, are the worker-owned and managed cooperatives, like ReBuilders Source in New York. The other three types, producer, purchasing, and consumer cooperatives, generally operate by pooling their buying power to get lower prices. Most co-ops in the USA are of the latter type, all the way from very small neighbourhood ventures to huge credit unions, utilities, retailers, and financial service companies. While the latter three types have more in common with capitalist businesses than socialist workers democracies or the P-CCs that I would advocate as the best long-term prospect for building a viable socialist globalization, any exposure to cooperative economic activity and living has the potential to raise consciousness in the direction of socialist democracy. As Chomsky somewhere observes, we should never under-estimate the subversive power of the good example. It is significant that the cooperative movement has experienced very rapid growth in Argentina since that country's devastating economic crisis around the turn of the new millennium. As of 30 June 2008, there were 12,670 cooperatives with over 9.3 million members in the country (approximately 23.5% of the population). These were said to employ over 87,000 people active in many sectors, mostly in agriculture and livestock, savings and credit unions, utilities such as water, telephone, and electricity, and health, education, housing, and tourism (Valente 2010). The cooperative model clearly helped to stabilize an economy and society in deep trouble, the Argentina experience is only one of many.

Mondragon

The best-known cooperative in radical circles is the Mondragon *Corporación Corporativa* (MCC). While it would not consider itself to be a socialist enterprise, and its original motivation comes from Catholic social justice thinking, it provides some useful pointers to the transition from capitalism to socialism in a globalizing world. MCC was founded in 1956 as an employee-owned cooperative manufacturing paraffin stoves in the Basque Country. Since then it has expanded both at home and, from the mid-1990s, abroad, encompassing more than 250 separate businesses, employing around 80,000 people, with a turnover in excess of 10 billion euros. Of particular interest in this context is its attitude to and strategy for employment creation as a key component of its globalization. Decisions to expand abroad are made on the basis of reducing production costs and maintaining or preferably increasing domestic employment while creating jobs abroad and not, as in the ubiquitous race to the bottom of capitalist globalization, destroying jobs at home to take advantage of lower wages and other business costs abroad (see Luzarraga, et al., 2007). The successful experience of the Mondragon family of cooperatives and their affiliated companies demonstrates that there really could be alternatives to capitalist globalization and that the emancipatory potential of generic globalization is, in this as in other cases, beginning to fill in some of the spaces between capitalism and socialism (Sklair 2009). It is important to note, however, that for all progressive ventures struggling to prosper as islands within a sea of capitalist globalization, compromises are often made. In the case of Mondragon, many of the enterprises outside Spain are not themselves cooperatives, and their workers have no options to become cooperative members. Some of the original cooperative principles have been watered down, for example the ratio of the wages of highest to lowest paid employees has risen over the years. As the experience of organic food producers has suggested, increasing scale tends to dilute socialist or quasi-socialist principles and facilitate capitalist structures and values. Two rather different though equally enthusiastic views of the Mondragon phenomenon illustrate clearly the rather contradictory conclusions that it is possible to draw from it. Both originate from the USA and both can be located on the Mondragon website. The first, "*The Mondragón Cooperative Corporation (MCC): An Introduction*" by Fred Freundlich of Ownership Associates, Inc., Bilbao, was a paper presented at a conference sponsored by the National Bureau of Economic Research in the USA on "Shared Capitalism: Mapping the Research Agenda" in Washington D.C. in May 1998. Freundlich describes how economic difficulties in the 1980s led to a legal-structural unification of the company in 1991. While the MCC now appears at first glance to be much more like a conventional conglomerate, key Mondragón principles are still in place. Each individual cooperative firm remains, legally and, to a large degree, functionally, an autonomous unit controlled ultimately by its General Assembly of worker-members. Each firm joined (or, in a few cases, rejected joining) the MCC by a vote of its

General Assembly, and can vote to leave at any time. Still, the new arrangements have generated controversy within the group over issues such as the centralization of authority, the bureaucratic distancing of senior management from the membership, and others. MCC enterprises also have a Social Council which meets monthly to facilitate communication between management and the frontline and to represent frontline workers perspectives in discussions with senior management, reminiscent of the workers councils in Germany and elsewhere. Freundlich's account of MCC, therefore, is clearly much closer to the caring capitalism, perhaps even caring capitalist globalization, model than to Mondragon as an exemplar of a revolutionary socialist globalization. The second analysis, "Mondragón Worker Cooperatives Decide How to Ride Out a Downturn" by Georgia Kelly and Shaula Massena (*Yes! Magazine* in June 2009) focuses on how MCC has developed a different way of doing business, putting workers, not shareholders, first. In their words: "Here's how it played out when one of the Mondragón cooperatives fell on hard times. The worker/owners and the managers met to review their options. After three days of meetings, the worker/owners agreed that 20 percent of the workforce would leave their jobs for a year, during which they would continue to receive 80 percent of their pay and, if they wished, free training for other work. This group would be chosen by lottery, and if the company was still in trouble a year later, the first group would return to work and a second would take a year off. The result? The solution worked and the company thrives to this day." Kelly and Massena emphasize that there have been no job losses due to the global financial crisis in any MCC firms. Typically, in times of difficulty, employees move to other jobs within the companies, or hours are cut without cutting pay with wages for unworked hours repaid through extra hours worked when business picks up. In MCC cooperatives, each worker has one vote, and pay scales are much more egalitarian than in the non-co-op sector, for example top management is rarely paid more than six times the lowest-paid worker and profits and losses are distributed among all the members equitably. There is undoubtedly a long-running debate within and beyond the Mondragon family of cooperatives between these two emphases: MCC as a more humane way of operating within the container of capitalist globalization contrasted with MCC as a challenge to transnational capitalist relations of production in a free market of capital and labour. Mondragon is one small though, in my view, significant example of an expanding global trend to find viable alternatives to capitalist globalization that would challenge the crisis of class polarization (in the attitude to the creation of worthwhile and sustainable employment through the globalization process). While there is at present not a great deal of evidence that the other global crisis of ecological unsustainability is being seriously addressed throughout the Mondragon system, there is a rapidly growing movement around the ideas of ethical and sustainable investment. This is a lucrative niche for most of the major capitalist financial institutions that may be beginning to sow some potentially subversive seeds in the world of capitalist globalization, and it is addressed in an interview with the CEO of Mondragon Josu Ugarte in 2015), available online at Worker Cooperatives in a Globalizing World.

Cooperative Socialist Globalization

For socialist globalization, as proposed here, to be viable it has to be genuinely democratic and, I would argue, non-hierarchical. Parliamentary democracy, famously described by Winston Churchill as the "worst form of Government except all those other forms that have been tried from time to time" (in the House of Commons on 11 November 1947 as Leader of the Opposition) is typically cynical. The types of democracy that we find in capitalist societies tend to be deeply flawed (though usually better for human rights than none at all). The form of democracy appropriate for socialist globalization would be participatory rather than representative, with delegates subject to recall when they break their electoral promises rather than at the end of parliamentary cycles when the damage has been done. These arguments can also be fortified in two ways. First, as noted above, the experiences of successful and failed small-scale democratic projects can be examined to discover what made the successes succeed and what made the failures fail. Second, some obviously dysfunctional elements of the global polity (for example, the frequent resort to violence by states and/or terrorists not sponsored by the state, the relative failures of electoral politics in systems where money can buy votes in a variety of ways, notably lobbying and advertising). These dysfunctional aspects of democracy can be deconstructed in order to show how these systems would work more efficiently and more fairly if they were run in the interests of democratic networks of Producer Consumer Cooperatives rather than those of the transnational capitalist class and the corporations that provide the wealth on which its power rests.

The question is: How do we get from here to there? The present system of states and international society is clearly not adequate for the task. We must acknowledge that here is not one place but many places and that these analytic places are themselves dynamic complexes of material realities and political opportunities. There are also going to be many places. However, and this is the main and strong lesson that this argument hopes to deliver for the so-called anti-globalization movement: the contradictions of capitalist globalization can only be resolved in the interests of the vast majority by grasping the dynamics and opportunities of generic globalization and mobilizing them to create the conditions for successful socialist globalization. In my view this will involve a gradual withering away of the state, not the privatization of state functions that the TCC driving neo-liberal capitalist globalization is currently engaged in but a multitude of networks of producer-consumer cooperatives, from the small and localized to the larger and transnational. This will entail a transformation from the international system of capitalist globalization dominated by the transnational capitalist class that we have now (led by corporate elites and globalizing politicians and bureaucrats) to something more democratic and sustainable. One model of how this transformation is already occurring comes, appropriately, from the response to the perils of global climate change known around the world as the Transition Communities movement. This was established around 2005 by Rob Hopkins, a young British ecological design teacher (Hopkins 2008).

Transition Towns and Communities

The central idea of Transition Towns is that it is imperative to plan ahead at the local level for when the oil runs out, and to build in resiliency and self-sufficiency (see, for example, some country studies in Aiken 2012, Kenis & Mathijs 2014, Polk 2015, Biddau 2016, Cretney 2016). Hopkins (2012) argues that whole communities must design what he calls an "elegant descent" from the lifestyles that characterized the era of peak oil. Life lived at low and sustainable levels of energy use could be a more satisfying and pleasurable life than what we experience in societies obsessed with what I have termed the culture-ideology of consumerism. The website of the movement urges us to "buy stuff", offering books and films (Transition Network Shop | Purchase Books & Film). While the global Transition Town movement has no direct link to the cooperative movement it seems to be to one more small step away from the capitalist market system, so worth considering here. After some success with these ideas in Kinsale, a small community in Ireland, Hopkins moved to Totnes in Devon where a series of local Transition activities were set in train by Transition Town Totnes (TTT). This can best be illustrated in terms of the Totnes Energy Descent Action Plan (EDAP), inaugurated in 2008. This involved local residents forming groups to work out plans and timelines (15-20 years) for the key aspects of their lives. Energy, food, building, transport, health, heart & soul, economics, and livelihoods are the most commonly discussed issues involved in creating a comprehensive plan for a zero carbon Totnes (see Hopkins in Chamberlin 2009, esp. Part Three). The Transition Network has some of the characteristics of a social movement; it claims almost 100 similar initiatives in England (a few larger, as in Bristol), most are smaller (as in Camden in London, where I live). According to the website of the movement more than 150 official Transition Towns (defined as communities with an active group of citizens committed to propagating Transition principles), have been established. The first Transition Town in the USA was in Boulder County, Colorado, by 2021 there were 287 (see https://transitioninitiative.org/hub/united-states/). However, it is often unclear exactly how much is plans and how much is action, and how much actual economic and political support Transition has in each case. Already, different strategies are emerging within the movement; for example, the view that the real value of the Transition Towns approach isn't the emphasis on energy descent (which may be neither sufficient nor even ultimately valuable for resilience), but rather its concisely crafted methodology for catalyzing community participation via a messy open source organizational process which allows people to deviate from the energy descent approach if they wish. The politics of the Transition movement globally are as yet rather vague, the general impression being the traditionally apolitical quest to include everyone in a common big tent. Nevertheless, the following excerpt from a report in the *New York Times* by Jon Mooallem (2009) of a conversation with Councilman John T. Reuter, of Sandpoint, Idaho (a Transition Towns site) seems to make a valid point about its political potential in a way that is relevant to this discussion of democracy and socialist globalization. "What Reuter said he felt was wonderful about the Sandpoint Transition Initiative was how quickly it was rejuvenating people's faith that the changes they craved were worth working for ... To say the group has only created a community garden so far really isn't sufficient [he told me] It's something really more substantive: they're bringing people to the process." Mooallem suggests that it was easy to argue that at the initiative's core, in place of any clearly defined philosophy or strategy, was only a puff of enthusiasm. But Reuter seemed to argue that enthusiasm is an actual asset, a resource our society is already suffering a scarcity of. Mooallem concludes: "There's just something happening here that's reviving people's civic sense of possibility ... Politics is the art of the possible, right? ... I think what the Transition Initiative is doing is expanding what's possible in people's minds. It is expanding people's ability to dream bold. And that's what we need to do: dream bold. Because people have been limited by their own imaginations." It will not be lost on readers that this comment was made in the USA in the early days of the

Obama administration and that the initial enthusiasm for that apparent transition in American politics appears to have declined substantially since then. But what I am arguing is a long-term perspective on how to go beyond capitalist globalization. Transition ideas are clearly useful as one among other first steps. In the long-term, the creation of socialist globalization will produce new forms of transnational practices. Transnational economic units will tend to be on a smaller and more sustainable scale than the major TNCs of today; transnational political practices will be driven by democratic coalitions of self-governing and cooperative communities, not the unaccountable, unelected and individualistic transnational capitalist class working through globalizing politicians and bureaucrats in national political parties. And cultures and ideologies will reflect the finer qualities of human life not the desperate variety of the culture-ideology of consumerism. These sentiments might appear utopian, indeed they are, and other alternatives are also possible, but in the long term, muddling through with capitalist globalization is not a viable option if Planet Earth and all those who live here are to survive.

Second Thoughts

Re-reading this article now I see that I allowed "optimism of the will" to overwhelm "pessimism of the intellect". Specifically, my argument on the possibilities of conventional progressive politics and politicians to facilitate the transformation of capitalism into socialism seems increasingly naïve. However much we resist the conclusion that conventional politics all over the world is, with very few exceptions, a compromising and often corrupting business, the evidence that it is continues to pile up from all over the political spectrum. It is becoming ever more difficult for the relatively few good people in political parties to act effectively to achieve democratic socialist globalization. Those who want this will have to take responsibility for building such communities themselves. To achieve this will take plenty of "optimism of the will" and even more "realism of the intellect". However, my views on the importance of scale in human settlements were reinforced by the evidence of cooperative initiatives all over the world, summarized in this chapter. This led me to focus more research time and thought on the embryonic idea of self-sufficient producer-consumer cooperatives. If I had read Kasmir (1996, 2016, 2017), and Bretos et al., 2019) before I had written the article I would have (sadly) been rather more critical of the transformative potential of Mondragon. Once again, the question of small scale looms large. Peter Marcuse (2015) raises many important points on cooperatives but, again, the problem is planning for a radical exit from the capitalist market and the capitalist system as a whole. Jossa (2014) and Lenin (1923) provide some surprising insights into classical Marxist debates on the significance of cooperatives. In addition, I now realize that the pathbreaking research of the late John Friedmann on "Agropolitan development" in the 1970s (Friedmann 1979), planted the seed which led to my development of the idea of producer-consumer cooperatives almost forty years later. Many theorists of cooperatives do connect producers and consumers, for example Ajates (2017, 2018, 2020); her meticulous case-study based research on multi-stakeholder cooperatives in food and farming is an important contribution to the literature, but always in the context of capitalism, not as an alternative to it (see also Goodman et al. 2011, Carolan, 2013, Schneiberg 2013). More recently, Koretskaya & Feola (2020) do address the issue of agri-food systems "beyond capitalism", illuminating the possibilities of change and diversity through a series of illuminating practical vignettes and poststructuralist theory in which cooperatives (even producer-consumer cooperatives) are mentioned in passing. They conclude that the application of this imaginative theoretical framework to cases of community supported agriculture shows how the coexistence of capitalist, alternative-capitalist or non-capitalist elements in Community Supported Agriculture might improve existing agri-food systems. This may be true but it leaves unanswered (and unasked) the question of whether or not the population of the world could be adequately fed in a world dominated by global capitalism and the transnational capitalist class. I continually ask myself if producer-consumer cooperatives could feed the world. We already know that man-made famines condemn thousands to early deaths. Important issues such as food self-sufficiency (see Clapp 2017) and global versus local food systems (see Norberg-Hodge et al. 2002) have been debated for decades without much consensus as has the theoretical-historical concept of "food regimes" (see Bernstein 2016).

The producer-consumer nexus remains problematic. More than twenty years ago David Goodman wrote in his introduction to a special issue on agro-food studies in the journal *Sociologia Ruralis*: "Yet, for all its contemporary prominence, consumption is still very much a theoretical 'black box' in agro-food studies" (Goodman 2002). A few years later some path-breaking theory and research on "distant consumers" (Friedmann & McNair 2008) added even more layers of complexity onto the continuously globalizing capitalist food system. Though it is not specifically a cooperative venture, as a coda to this chapter it is appropriate to reference an initiative of the Global Tapestry of Alternatives movement "Resilience in the face of COVID-19: Weaving Solidarity and Hope in the Times of Crises". This is the first volume in a beautifully illustrated series aimed at giving a voice to scholars and activists in the Global South, Colombia, Costa Rica, India, Philippines, Kenya, Bangladesh, and India feature in this volume with much more to come, see https://globaltapestryof alternatives.org/reports:pandemic:01

References

Aiken, G. (2012) Community Transitions to Low Carbon Futures in the Transition Towns Network (TTN): Community as seen by Transition Towns. *Geography compass* 6/2: 89-99.

Ajates, R. (2017) Going back to go forwards? From multi-stakeholder cooperatives to Open Cooperatives in food and farming. *Journal of rural studies* 53: 278-290.

Ajates, R. (2018) *Farmers' Cooperatives and Sustainable Food Systems in Europe.* Abingdon: Routledge.

Ajates, R. (2020) Agricultural cooperatives remaining competitive in a globalised food system: At what cost to members, the cooperative movement and food sustainability? *Organization* 27/2: 337-355.

Bernstein, H. (2016) Agrarian political economy and modern world capitalism: the contributions of food regime analysis, *The Journal of Peasant Studies* 43/3: 611-647.

Biddau, F. et al. (2016) Socio-psychological aspects of grassroots participation in the Transition Movement: An Italian case study. *Journal of social and political psychology* 4/1: 142-165.

Bretos, I., et al. (2019) Multinational Expansion of Worker Cooperatives and Their Employment Practices: Markets, Institutions, and Politics in Mondragon. *Industrial & Labour Relations Review* 72/3: 580-605.

Carolan, M. S. (2013) The Wild Side of Agro-food Studies: On Co-experimentation, Politics, Change, and Hope. *Sociologia Ruralis* 53/4: 413-31.

Chamberlin, S. (2009) *The Transition Timeline: For a Local, Resilient Future.* Totness: Green Books & Transition Network.

Clapp, J. (2017) Food self-sufficiency: Making sense of it, and when it makes sense. *Food Policy* 66: 88-96.

Cretney, R.M., et al. (2016). Maintaining grassroots activism: Transition Towns in Aotearoa New Zealand. *New Zealand geographer* 72/2: 81-91.

Friedmann, J. (1979) Basic Needs, Agropolitan Development, and Planning from Below. *World Development* 7: 607-613.

Friedmann, H. & McNair, A. (2008) Whose Rules Rule? Contested Projects to Certify 'Local Production for Distant Consumers'. *Journal of Agrarian Change* 8/2 & 3 (April and July): 408–434.

Gerhardt, S. (2004) *Why Love Matters: How Affection Shapes a Baby's Brain.* Hove: Brunner-Routledge.

Goodman, D. (2002) Rethinking Food Production-Consumption: Integrative Perspectives. *Sociologia Ruralis* 42/4: 271-7.

Goodman, D., DuPuis, E.M., & Goodman, M.K. (2011) *Alternative food networks: Knowledge, practice, and* politics. Abingdon: Routledge.

Hopkins, R. (2008) *The Transition Handbook: From Oil Dependency to Local Resilience.* Totness: Green Books.

Hopkins, R. (2012) Peak Oil and Transition Towns. *Architectural Design* 82/4: 72-77.

Jossa, B. (2014) Marx, Lenin and the Cooperative Movement. *Review of Political Economy* 26/2: 282–302.

Kasmir, S. (1996) *The Myth of Mondragón: Cooperatives, Politics and Working-Class Life in a Basque Town.* New York: SUNY Press.

Kasmir, S. (2016) The Mondragon Cooperatives and global capitalism. *New Labor Forum* 25/1: 52-59.

Kasmir, S. (2017) Cooperative Democracy or Cooperative Competitiveness: Rethinking Mondragon. In Panitch, L. & Albo, G. eds. *Socialist Register: Rethinking Democracy.* London & New York: The Merlin Press & Monthly Review Press.

Kelly, G. & Massena, S. (2009) When Worker Owners Decide How to Ride Out a Downturn. *Yes Magazine* (5 June).

Kenis, A. & Mathijs, E. (2014) (De)politicising the local: The case of the Transition Towns movement in Flanders (Belgium). *Journal of rural studies* 34:172-183.

Koretskaya, O. & Feola, G. (2020) A framework for recognizing diversity beyond capitalism in agri-food systems. *Journal of Rural Studies* 80: 302-13.

Lenin, V.I. (1923) On Cooperation. In *Selected Works*, volume 9. London: Lawrence & Wishart, pp. 402-409.

Luzarraga M., Telleria, D.A, & Irizar, I. (2007) *Understanding the Mondragon Globalization Process: Local Job Creation Through Multi-Localization.* https://www.researchgate.net/publication/237604098

Marcuse, P. (2015) Cooperatives on the Path to Socialism? *Monthly Review online* 66/9.

Mooallem, J. (2009) The End is Near! [Yay!] *New York Times* (16 April).

Norberg-Hodge, H., Merrifield, T. & Gorelick, S. (2002) *Bringing the Food Economy Home: Local Alternatives to Global Agribusiness.* London: Zed Books

Polk, E., (2015) *Communicating global to local resiliency: a case study of the transition movement.* New York & London: Lexington Books.

Schneiberg, M. (2013) Movements as Political Conditions for Diffusion: Anti-corporate Movements and the Spread of Cooperative Forms in American Capitalism. *Organization Studies* 34/5–6: 653–82.

Sklair, L. (2009b) The emancipatory potential of generic globalization. *Globalizations* 6/4: 525-39.

Trimarco, J. & Bamburg, J. (2009) Worker Co-ops. *Yes magazine* (5 June).

Valente, M. (2010) Big Growth of Worker Co-ops in Argentina *Grassroots Economic Organizing* (geo.coop).

CHAPTER 8

(2011) THE GLOBALIZATION OF HUMAN RIGHTS.
JOURNAL OF GLOBAL ETHICS 5/2: 81-96.
[COURTESY OF ROUTLEDGE]

Preamble

Once you start researching globalization there is a great temptation to see it in everything, everywhere. Many social scientists seem to have rejected the concept of globalization for little better reason than its popularity in the media and general everyday discourse. This, of course, is absurd. My interest in the globalization of human rights was stimulated by debates around moral relativism and the Holocaust that I encountered as an undergraduate, and in my first book *The Sociology of Progress* where I recklessly tried to construct an argument for "moral progress". An article I wrote (Sklair 1969) concluded with the assertion: "The future of ethics, therefore, lies not with moral philosophy, but with the study of man [sic] in society" and it was some time before I fully realized that "the study of *man*" was part of the problem rather than the solution, an example of my own "everyday sexism" (Bates 2014). Rather counter-intuitively I began to wonder if theorizing about the nature of human rights might prove counter-productive for a sociological understanding of what they actually are. This led me to study how laws pertaining to human rights were formulated and how the global institutions established to protect human rights operated. Researching this article further convinced me that the sentiment that Gramsci borrowed from the novelist Romain Roland "pessimism of the intellect, optimism of the will" was an important support for the Left. I am grateful to my friend and colleague Jackie Smith whose scholarly research and grass roots activism and organizing have inspired many of the second thoughts of my new conclusion.

Abstract

The argument of this article is that what I term generic globalization has created unprecedented opportunities for advances in human rights universally, but that the dominant actually existing historical form of globalization, capitalist globalization, undermines these opportunities. Substantively, I argue that taking the globalization of human rights seriously means eliminating the ideological distinction that exists between civil and political rights on the one hand, and economic and social rights on the other. Doing this systematically undermines the three central claims of capitalist globalization – namely, that globalizing corporations are the most efficient and equitable form of production, distribution, and exchange; that the transnational capitalist class organizes communities and the global order in the best interests of everyone; and that the culture-ideology of consumerism will satisfy our real needs.

Generic globalization and human rights

Generic globalization may be defined in terms of four phenomena, moments both in the temporal sense and in terms of social forces, of increasing significance since the middle of the twentieth century. The first moment, the electronic revolution, notably transformations in the technological base and global scope of the electronic mass media and to most of the material infrastructure of the world today (the electronic moment); the second I identify as post-colonialisms (the post-colonial moment); the third (reflecting my increasing interest in the sociology of architecture and cities) I theorized as the creation of transnational social spaces (the spatial moment); and the fourth, qualitatively new forms of cosmopolitanism (the cosmopolitan moment). These four phenomena are the defining characteristics of my version of globalization in a generic sense. Each offers tremendous potential for the expansion of human rights, both quantitatively in terms of increasing the numbers of people whose lives can be improved by access to human rights, and qualitatively, in terms of the quality of human rights access. While the electronic, the post-colonial moments, and new forms of cosmopolitanism have been the subject of an enormous amount of theory and research in recent decades, the idea of transnational social spaces, is of relatively recent origin and opens up some new lines of theory and research.

The electronic revolution and human rights

The electronic revolution has brought knowledge of human rights entitlements to the notice of millions, possibly billions, of people who have been denied them and also to those who are in a position to deny human rights to others. The rapid spread and relative cheapening of the mass media of communication, all the way from radio and television, to the Internet and mobile phones, makes it much more difficult to conceal human rights abuses than ever before in human history. While this does not necessarily result in the reduction of abuses, the more publicity and transparency there is the more likely it is that organized pressure can be brought to bear on those who abuse human rights. Further, the electronic revolution has made mobilization against human rights abuses and denial of human rights much easier to organize, locally, nationally and globally. On the other hand, human rights abuses on the internet via social media sites of various types create a whole new set of problems that governments and media corporations (now amongst the most highly valued entities on stock markets all over the world) seem unable and/or unwilling to address effectively.

The post-colonial revolution and human rights

The post-colonial revolution that started in Latin America in the nineteenth century and gathered unstoppable momentum in the second half of the twentieth century incorporates many different kinds of post-colonialisms. Their relationship to the idea of generic globalization pursued here is highly complex, encompassing processes such as multi-causal cross-border migration, the increasing ability of "others" to find their own voices on the world stage and for these voices to be heard, and so-called multiculturalism (Krishnaswamy & Hawley 2008, esp. chapters 18 & 19). Thus, the paradigm shift that Edward Said began with his critique of Orientalism (Said, 1978) continues to reverberate as post-colonialisms meet globalization in the terrain of human rights. This is one part of the general problem of Orientalism and post-colonialism (how First and Third World elites structure ideas of and in the Third World). The thorough analysis of the Israel/Palestine struggle by Cypel (2006) continues to throw much light on these issues. Media interest on migrants (increasingly climate migrants) and asylum seekers, is intense and often unsympathetic and alarmist; scholarly interest is at a high level as Uhde (2021) demonstrates in her analysis of competing theories.

Transnational social spaces and human rights

The creation of transnational social spaces can take place from above and from below. From above, the applications of international law and the work of United Nations agencies and human rights NGOs can create relatively safe transnational social spaces for vulnerable groups (as illustrated in the case studies contained in Risse, et al. eds. 1999), but all too often this has been in response to human rights catastrophes rather than preventing them in the first place. Rajagopal (2003) argues persuasively that in general, state-centrist international law has failed and that the struggle to create what I am calling here transnational social spaces in which human rights are protected, especially in the Third World, is now the responsibility of transnational social movements working with communities, as well as of states. This more localist view is supported by the plethora of evidence that Rajagopal presents (see also Bandy & Smith 2005).

New forms of cosmopolitanism and human rights

The final aspect of generic globalization, new forms of cosmopolitanism, differs from the others in that the idea of cosmopolitanism is quite ancient. It had its most important modernist reincarnation in the proposal of Kant at the end of the eighteenth century for the achievement of perpetual peace through the construction of a cosmopolitan order. However, this left many questions unanswered about the relations between democracy, capitalism, and human rights, and these have to be urgently asked in this transformed world of the twenty-first century. While there are many different forms of cosmopolitanism (Vertovic & Cohen 2002), the thread that runs through all of them is the problem of a multitude of different cultural, ethnic, linguistic, and religious groups jostling to live on this one planet, sharing its resources, landscapes, atmosphere, cities, streets, soil, oceans, and diasporas. For some groups this thread is perceived as a life-threatening weapon. This is the challenge of new forms of cosmopolitanism for the globalization of human rights.

Capitalist globalization and human rights

In the absence of global catastrophe, generic globalization is irreversible in the long run because the vast majority of the people in the world see that it could serve their own best interests, even if, in a system dominated by capitalist globalization, it is not necessarily serving their best interests at present. There is a veritable torrent of theory and research on how capitalist globalization works, and who wins and who loses as it conquers the globe and transforms our lives. My textbook (Sklair 2002), one of many on the topic, has 34 pages of references. Nevertheless, there is relatively little theory and research on globalization as a generic phenomenon, thought about and even on occasion practiced outside its historical container of globalizing capitalism. Capitalist globalization can be fruitfully analyzed and researched in terms of transnational practices, practices that cross state borders but do not necessarily originate with state agents, agencies or institutions. Analytically, transnational practices operate in three spheres, the economic, the political, and the culture-ideology sphere, by which I mean the ways in which the institutional structures of consumption are relentlessly reinforced by the values inherent in consumerism (Sklair 2002, chapter 7 and *passim*.) Two crises, both with dire consequences for human rights, beset capitalist globalization, namely class polarization and ecological unsustainability. The inability of the capitalist system to resolve these crises makes it imperative that we begin to think seriously about long-term alternatives to capitalist globalization. Here I shall explore one path out of capitalism through the disjuncture between capitalist globalization (where we are) and alternative forms of globalization (where many of us want to be). Such a transformation could be achieved by the gradual elimination of what I take to be the driving force of capitalist globalization, namely, the culture-ideology of consumerism, and its replacement with a culture-ideology of human rights. This means, briefly, that instead of our possessions being the main focus of our cultures and the basis of our values, our lives should be lived with regard to a universally agreed system of human rights and the responsibilities to others that these rights entail. This does not imply that we should stop consuming. What it implies is that we should evaluate our consumption in terms of our rights and responsibilities, notably our responsibilities in the context of the looming ecological crisis. The main thrust of this argument is that by genuinely expanding the culture-ideology of human rights from the civil and political spheres, in which capitalist globalization has had a relatively positive influence, to the economic and social spheres, which represent a profound challenge to capitalist globalization, we can begin realistically to tackle the crises of class polarization and ecological unsustainability. But political realism dictates that this change cannot be accomplished directly; it must proceed via a series of transitional stages.

Most progressive democratic alternatives to capitalist globalization sound very utopian. Many would agree with their desirability but most would question their practicality. In most societies, at varying levels of prosperity and poverty, there are constant reminders of the class polarization crisis, as the very rich seem to get ever richer, the very poor seem to be trapped in cycles of deprivation, and the groups in the middle experience unprecedented levels of insecurity. This has been labelled the precariat, a concept popularized by Standing (2011), though I would recommend the more politically astute Foti (2017) for very different ideas about this tricky concept. Likewise, the ecological crisis affects everyone, in various ways, consciousness of which has led to much discussion of the idea of "environmental justice" (see Grear & Kotze, eds. 2015 and Coolsaet, ed. 2020). How could such a society begin the movement from capitalist to alternative, non-capitalist forms of globalization, and why would its members want to move in these directions? The rise of anti-capitalist and anti-globalization movements and networks since the mid-1990s suggest that there is a great deal of dissatisfaction about the way we live revolving around the emotional and spiritual crises of the rich, and the material and social deprivations of the poor (see, for example, Bandy & Smith 2005). While they propose alternatives to capitalist globalization, most of these movements tend to focus either on issues of class or regional polarization (for example First World against Third World) or on ecological unsustainability (the environmental justice movement), rarely connecting both crises. This is why many consider that there is no adequate focal point for these movements and networks. This is precisely the reason why it is necessary to engage with the discourse and organization of universal human rights. Fine (2010) published an acute contribution to this debate focusing on the dehumanization process in international human rights law, demonstrating how it affected the treatment of both perpetrators of crimes against humanity and their victims. He illustrates this with reference to the Eichmann trial in Jerusalem in 1962, and especially Hannah Arendt's "banality of evil" thesis, another level of legal and moral complexity. The globalization of human rights provides a logical and substantive link between genuine democracy and alternative post-capitalist globalization. If we can demonstrate that the achievement of a global system of human rights is not possible under the conditions of capitalist globalization (capitalism can only justify itself in the long run by its alleged superiority in providing better lives for all), then it follows that some other form of globalization will be required if human rights are to be realized for all peoples.

The inter-state system of human rights

Turning now to the inter-state system of human rights, the period immediately following 1945 was a watershed for the emerging human rights movement. Though the Nuremberg Trials were not the first occasion in history when the victors passed moral judgements on the vanquished, the enormity of Nazi crimes appeared to justify moral as well as legal penalties. It is not to deny other previous and subsequent holocausts to argue that what happened in Europe in the 1940s made many people in all walks of life rethink the seductive appeal of cultural relativism (Marrus 1987, esp. chapter 2). United Nations-sponsored tribunals on former Yugoslavia and Rwanda further reinforced the idea of crimes against humanity as crimes for which the international community would not excuse the perpetrators. The Pinochet case (Steiner & Alston 2000, 1198-1216) opened up spaces for bringing those with ultimate responsibility for gross violations of human rights to the bar of international justice. The first conviction for genocide was handed down by the War Crimes Tribunal in The Hague in the summer of 2001, a 46-year prison sentence for the Bosnian Serb general Krstic. And while the death of Slobodan Milosevic in detention in 2007, six years after he had been indicted, spared him from a likely lengthy sentence, the international tribunal at The Hague sentenced another Bosnian Serb general, Dragomir Milosevic, to 33 years in prison for his war crimes during the siege of Sarajevo. Nevertheless, it is true to say that many of those directly responsible for war crimes and crimes against humanity continue to evade punishment or even being brought to court.

Truth commissions had been established in formerly authoritarian states in Latin America, Asia, Africa, and Europe (UNDP 2000, Table A3.1 lists fourteen). In particular, the Truth and Reconciliation Commission in South Africa started a long, incomplete, and painful process of bringing abusers and abused face to face to establish "truth" and seek reconciliation (see Moon 2008). It also condemned some acts against the oppressors. These processes have both challenged and promoted the legal order surrounding human rights. Outside the sphere of "official" international law the Russell Tribunal on Vietnam set up in 1967 (Zunino 2016), while it did not stop the war it highlighted the importance of "transitional justice" inspiring the World Tribunal on Iraq which deliberated from 2003 to 2005 in 20 cities around the world (Çubukçu 2018, and more generally on "transitional justice and unofficial tribunals" (Stan & Nedelsky, eds. 2013).

Two categories of human rights

Scholars and activists generally distinguish between two categories of rights. The first is civil and political rights, like freedom from torture, equal protection before the law, and the right to free speech and political association. The second category is economic and social rights, for example, rights to decent jobs, food, health care, education, and shelter (Chaney 2021). The legal basis of all these rights is the United Nations Charter and associated regional agreements, the European Convention on Human Rights, the American Convention on Human Rights, and the African Charter on Human and People's Rights. The Universal Declaration of Human Rights was proclaimed in 1948 and after decades of political wrangling, two treaties, the International Covenant on Civil and Political Rights (hereafter ICC) and the International Covenant on Economic, Social and Cultural Rights (hereafter ICE), were passed into international law. Most states have signed these legal codes, though many have reserved their positions on one or more items. One further pillar in the UN system of human rights is the Convention on the Elimination of all forms of Discrimination Against Women (CEDAW).

Parallel with the UN Charter, the Universal Declaration of Human Rights, the ICC, and the ICE, a series of specific human rights treaties has emerged, but their acceptance in full by member states is far from universal. The most important of these treaties are the 1951 Convention on Genocide (140 ratifications, accessions, and successions by 2007), the 1969 Convention on Racial Discrimination (85), the 1981 CEDAW (98), the 1987 Convention on Torture (74), and the 1990 Convention on Rights of the Child (140). However, it can be argued that there are in place growing numbers of legal instruments to protect human rights and that most states in the world have committed themselves to uphold them, at least in part and in principle. Nevertheless, many states, including some of the richest, for example, the USA and the UK, as well as some of the poorest, for example, China and Myanmar (Burma) have at one time or another been investigated and/or named and shamed for human rights violations at the UN and continue to be named and shamed (see Smith & Cooper 2010 on the establishment of the UN Universal Periodic Review process in 2003). The UN Commission on Human Rights was the body responsible for carrying out such investigations and passing judgements. The Commission operated through two mechanisms. Items under the first, the 1503 procedure (examination of complaints), rose from 25,000 per annum in the mid-1980s to 300,000 in 1993 (much of this was organized letter-writing), and stabilized at around 50,000 in 2000. From 1972 to 2005, eighty-four states had been investigated. However, the process of investigation under 1503 was secret, leading Amnesty International and other human rights organizations to charge that it is as much an instrument for concealing as for exposing violations (Steiner & Alston, eds. 2000, 618). The 1235 procedure gave governments and/or non-governmental organizations a public opportunity to name and shame violators at Commission meetings, and eighty-five member states were investigated between 1989 and 2005. As of January 2007, thirteen countries were under investigation. Usually governments defend themselves vigorously (Iran, China, and others have done so). Why do they take the trouble? The answer suggests that for governments, even the most repressive, the human rights movement is significant all over the world, particularly when it draws in transnational economic practices like trade and investment. In March 2006 the UN Commission on Human Rights was replaced by a Human Rights Council, consisting of 47 members on staggered three-year terms (the United States refused to join). The human rights records of all 192 members of the UN will be reviewed by the Council. The difficulties of this process are highlighted by the lack of progress in the apparently unambiguous question of forcible female circumcision (ibid. chapter 6, A). In 2012, the United Nations General Assembly unanimously adopted the first-ever resolution against the practice, proclaiming 6 February the "International Day of Zero Tolerance for Female Genital Mutilation" and in 2021 a target to eliminate it by 2030 was set.

With few exceptions, all these UN conventions, treaties, and targets establish positive rights for individuals and positive duties for states to protect these rights. However, all these conventions and treaties have limitation clauses that qualify the rights of individuals and dilute the duties of states which may declare themselves to be under exceptional circumstances, notably states of emergency. As a result, these conventions and treaties have rarely been allowed to challenge the autonomy of governments to do exactly as they please or simply fail to act. State sovereignty remains the general principle on which the inter-state legal system rests (with the notable exception of transnational trade treaties). Connected with this issue is the debate contrasting indivisibility (all human rights are equal in importance) with hierarchy (some rights are more important than others). Though there is a good deal of controversy, most writers and practitioners do accept that there is a hierarchy of rights, with civil and political rights at the top and economic and social rights some way behind or, in some theories, not proper rights at all. For example, since CEDAW was created in 1981 there has been much debate over women's rights. Some complain that women's rights are being prioritized unfairly above all others, while others argue that women's rights are ghettoized within CEDAW. More states have entered reservations to the ratification of CEDAW than to any other human rights treaty (Renzulli 2017).

Economic and social rights (hereafter ESR), usually defined as the duty of the state "primarily to provide material resources to the rights-bearer, like decent jobs, housing or food or health care" (Steiner & Alston eds. 2000,

183) are at the centre of the argument between supporters and opponents of capitalist globalization. While capitalists, imbued with neoliberal values and the culture-ideology of consumerism, tend to accept that civil and political rights (or, more rhetorically, freedom from state interference) need to be protected to guarantee a minimum of social order, economic and social rights are more problematic for them. Neoliberals argue that the sanctity of private property, paradoxically the core economic right, is the only basic human right essential to a market-driven society, while goods such as jobs, housing, food, education, and health care are not human rights at all, but commodities allocated like all other commodities by the market. This view is enshrined in the rhetoric of neoliberalism in homilies of the type: "no one owes you a living" (interestingly close to the old Soviet principle of "those who do not work do not eat"), and the now largely discredited Thatcherite slogan "there is no such thing as society" (individuals have to take responsibility for themselves and their families). Opponents (socialist or not) of capitalist globalization argue that everyone, irrespective of circumstances, has the right to a basic level of economic and social well-being (as enshrined in Articles 23 and 25 of the Universal Declaration of Human Rights). Some radical legal scholars problematize private property, even suggesting that it might be incompatible with the concept of human rights (Dine & Fagan, eds. 2006).

The origins of the Economic and Social Rights system are to be found in the International Labour Organization (ILO), created in 1919 as an associate agency of the League of Nations to serve as a bulwark against the appeal of Bolshevism to workers all over the world. The ILO articulated the principles that people everywhere were entitled to a decent standard of living and that workers were entitled to some basic rights. From the 1940s on these principles gradually evolved into a vague and general right to development as decolonization loomed (see Ishay 2008). The paternalistic impulse of this movement can be gleaned from the fact that what we now know as development appears in chapter IX, International Economic and Social Co-operation, Article 55(a) of the UN Charter, where the UN committed itself to promote higher standards of living, full employment, and conditions of economic and social progress and development for all the peoples of the world. Struggles over the establishment of a single human rights covenant foundered on cultural differences of various types (related to gender, religion, ethnicity, and so on), so two separate conventions, the International Covenant on Economic, Social and Cultural Rights and the International Covenant on Civil and Political Rights (as noted above), resulted. This outcome sent the message to the international community that entitlement to economic and social rights generally was seen as subject to available resources, and the obligations of states to achieve them was, thus, not absolute but something that might be accomplished sometime in the future. My argument is that capitalist globalization (locked into crises of class polarization and ecological unsustainability) will never achieve the various social and economic targets set by the World Bank, UN agencies, and similar organizations. While some progress has been made for some communities, now that we have the Anthropocene (climate crisis) and the Coronavirus to deal with, achieving all the targets seems increasingly unlikely.

Who is responsible for protecting human rights?

The issue of who exactly is responsible for ensuring that rights were established and protected remains unresolved. Intuitively, we might think that the state is responsible, but the historical record seems to contradict this assumption (see Cohen 1993, 1995, and Schwendinger & Schwendinger 2014 on "crimes of the state"). Dominant groups in some countries, for example the USA, have tended to pay less attention to providing for economic and social rights, while those in others, for example China, have tended to pay less attention to civil and political rights. A central principle of what I mean by socialist globalization is that neither of these sets of rights can be fully realized without the other. Having the right to vote in freely contested elections has a very different meaning for well-fed people compared with starving people, just as having a satisfying job that supports a decent standard of living has a very different meaning for someone under threat of arbitrary arrest all the time compared with someone who can generally rely on the rule of equitable law. The role of the state should be central to this analysis in the sense that states that actually do guarantee civil and political rights might also be expected to guarantee economic and social rights. However, under the neoliberal discipline of capitalist globalization, civil and political rights have gradually been disconnected from economic and social rights. This is the socio-legal aspect of class polarization under capitalist globalization. Steiner & Alston eds. (2000, 300) express this rather diplomatically: "Pressures to reduce the size of the public sector, to privatize various functions previously performed by governments, and to stimulate growth by reducing taxes, all render governments less able to accept responsibility for economic and social rights". Governments, of course, normally do have choices in these matters, but those under the disciplines of the World Bank, the World Trade Organization, and the transnational corporations for the most part choose not to prioritize economic and social rights.

What the Indian Constitution of 1950 called "directive principles of state policies" illustrates this clearly. Baxi (in Steiner & Alston eds. 2000, 283-4) shows how these principles have been put into practice in terms of social action litigation, when ordinary people write to the courts about violations of the human rights of impoverished groups in India. This means, in Baxi's view, that: "The law of standing, that is persons who can bring complaints of rights-violation, has been thus revolutionized; and access to constitutional justice has been fully democratized". The courts commission and fund researchers to establish the facts, in Baxi's striking phrase, to "provide the material for doing justice", and compensation and detailed measures of rehabilitation for victims are accorded the status of a constitutional right (Steiner & Alston eds. 2000, 285). Examples abound. The Supreme Court of India monitors the treatment of the blinded of Bhagalpur, and relief and medical treatment for the victims of Bhopal, one of the world's worst chemical disasters (see Hanna 2005 and 2017). The Supreme Court is also responsible for the administration of the Agra Protective Home for Women, and prison administration in the State of Bihar. No doubt there are very many more examples of violations of rights that go unresolved and remain invisible in India (the unsatisfactory treatment of complainants in the cases of Enron and the Narmada dam and the corruption scandal of the Enron energy project in Maharashtra in the 1990s (see Mehta 2000). More generally social action litigation shows what is possible, if difficult. So, while quite realistic about the limited impact of social action litigation in India and the ongoing struggle between the judiciary and the executive, and about specific courts and specific institutions in violation of people's rights, Baxi does show how a large and relatively poor state could nurture a legal system that turns abstract rights into economic and social realities. This puts to shame the feeble protestations of capitalist globalizers that the rich states of the First World cannot afford to protect economic and social rights for all. However, to put this in context, genuine justice is generally slow in most countries. In India when Baxi was writing, there were 23 cases pending per 1000 persons, over 2000 per judge, and Bangladesh had more than twice as many, according to a report cited by UNDP (2000, 101). And the victims of the Bhopal disaster in 1984 at the Union Carbide plant in India continue to suffer and die as their cases drag through the courts, as the Bhopal Medical Appeal charity makes clear in the appeal for more funds I received in the summer of 2021. In 2017 it had been widely reported that a proposed merger between Dow Chemical (the owners of Union Carbide) and DuPont might result in the victims of Bhopal being denied proper compensation and justice.

Despite the onward march of capitalist globalization, states (or more to the point politicians and governments) could restructure their priorities in the direction of satisfying the economic and social rights of the large majority of their people while at the same time enhancing their civil and political rights. At the beginning of the twenty-first century, in the richest countries the resources were already available to provide adequate diet, housing, education, health care, and environmental security for everyone. This, however, would necessitate higher taxes and reduced consumption of luxury goods and services by the relatively rich. There is no reason in principle why a political party could not campaign on such a programme and win. However, under the conditions of capitalist globalization, driven by the culture-ideology of consumerism, this seems unlikely to occur in the short term. Realistically, such a programme is more likely to be forced on rich countries by a combination of the effects of the twin crises of ecological unsustainability and class polarization. This could happen gradually or catastrophically, depending on various factors, including mass mobilization and political leadership. In poor countries the issues are similar in principle but differ in practice. Democratic political systems, even in poor countries with weak states, do not exclude the election of governments that genuinely set out to redistribute societal resources to benefit their poorer citizens and give them the tools to improve their own conditions. It is important here to distinguish clearly between what I am conceptualizing as the culture-ideology of consumerism and rights to adequate consumption. The human right to adequate consumption (we can define this as the basic minimum level that even averagely well-off people would settle for), properly conceived, entails the social responsibility of those who are democratically elected to make such decisions to ensure that this is available to all. The crisis of ecological unsustainability dictates that this will entail reductions in consumption for those who consume the most all over the world. These are the responsibilities involved in the globalization of human rights, responsibilities that people in a society based on the principles of socialist globalization will gladly teach their children and perhaps in the short term, more reluctantly, practice themselves.

Human rights and social responsibilities

The discourse and organization of human rights provokes a series of fundamental questions on how we think about justice in the global system (for a range of views see for example Hrubec 2010, and Mills & Karp 2015). Why does the language of rights rather than responsibilities (or duties) tend to dominate treaties, constitutions, and political debate? In what ways, if any, is it superior to the language of responsibilities? Would the values and goals of a movement for human responsibilities be different to those of the human rights movement? The question that is most often posed, particularly by those who wish to highlight the importance of cultural difference rather than universality, is whether, and to what extent, the language of rights entails what are considered to be rights. This is an indirect expression of the thesis that the language and the substance of the western liberal tradition appear to dominate both the discourse and the organization of the human rights movement.

In the Western liberal tradition human rights tend to be conceptualized individualistically, but the civic duties and responsibilities of individuals tend to be marginalized or excluded entirely from consideration. As discussed above, the fact that the international human rights movement originated within and through the inter-state system and the efforts of those who were representatives of it means that the discourse and the movement have always carried the tensions inherent in trying to reconcile individual rights and state sovereignty. Despite what is written down in treaties and conventions and the laws of individual countries, even when they are generally upheld, rights are never absolute even in the most democratic societies. This is partly because parliamentary democracies are so imperfect, and partly because the agencies of the state, even in parliamentary democracies, almost always place their own security and interests above the rights of citizens (and even more in the case of refugees and asylum seekers). Under the conditions of capitalist globalization, what state functionaries consider vital to the national interest is much more likely to be driven by the interests of those who own and control Big Business (as interpreted and implemented by their allies in the bureaucracy and government at all levels) than by those of ordinary people or the principles of ecological sustainability. Thus, capitalist globalization encourages states to reduce their duties and responsibilities to their citizens, and to restrict them to the protection of those rights compatible with or not hostile to the interests of Big Business. A good example of this process is the way in which many states have restricted the right to protest against capitalist globalization (for example in Davos when the World Economic Forum is meeting there, and around Parliament in London and elsewhere, at WTO, G8, and other official events). And since these words were written in 2011 it is arguable that in most societies rights to peaceful protest have been curtailed even further, often cynically using the pandemic as an excuse.

Different cultures predispose their members to see the world differently and the idea that individuals have duties and responsibilities to each other is far more common in some cultures than in others. For example, according to Jomo Kenyatta, the Gikuyu people in Kenya live on the basis that "collective activities make heavy tasks easier" (quoted in Steiner & Alston, eds. 2000, 346). Principles such as this logically and emotionally lead to a greater belief in the virtues of communities based on the duties and responsibilities of people to each other as well as their rights. The Confucian value system in China and elsewhere is also frequently cited in this context. Heather Widdows (2007) provides a penetrating analysis of an emerging "moral neocolonialism" around bioethics, which has become increasingly important. Cameron (2014), writing on UNESCO's "Universal Declaration on Bioethics and Human Rights", sees it as eminently worthy, though, as usual, non-binding.

Significantly, the first human rights treaty to highlight duties as well as rights was the African Charter on Human and People's Rights of 1986, though in practice human rights are no better (in most cases much less) protected for the poor and under-privileged in Africa than elsewhere. By 2000, fifty-three states in Africa had signed up to the Charter but, as with all other human rights treaties, the signatories included many parties that appeared to routinely violate the very rights they were obliged to protect. Nevertheless, it is important to seek a balance between utter cynicism and utter naivety in this as in other fields. The world would not necessarily be a better place if there were no international human rights legislation and is not necessarily a worse place because of it. One of the reasons why political parties which adopt the main tenets of neoliberal capitalist globalization have been so successful in countries with parliamentary democracies all over the world is precisely because of the appeal of responsibility over rights rhetoric for so many of those who bother to vote. In relatively rich societies poor people whose rights are violated often lack public sympathy or face real, often racist, hostility, typically orchestrated by the right-wing mass media, because they are perceived as making little positive contribution to society (the unemployed) at best, or as being a drain on society (so-called welfare scroungers and bogus asylum seekers) at worst. These popular idioms are consistently used to justify reductions in welfare services or to exclude some services as rights altogether. In many countries the welfare state seems only minimally constructed with human rights as a priority. On the contrary, as Deacon et al. (1997) demonstrate, the ideological basis of attacks on systems of social security in the context of capitalist globalization is embedded in the capitalist state. The right to suitable employment, enshrined in many international treaties and national constitutions, is a good case in point. Work-share programmes that have been introduced in the USA, Canada, and the UK appear to recognize that the state has some obligation to ensure adequate employment or provide unemployment benefits for adults, but while these programmes rarely produce many good jobs they do depress welfare claims. Usually, the unemployed must accept the responsibility of taking any job deemed appropriate by the authorities that is offered to them. There is no easy solution to this problem. It appears intuitively obvious that small communities organized through something like producer-consumer cooperatives are better suited to solving it than very large societies centrally organized on the basis of individuals and their households and the "global marketplace".

Responsibilities and rights are two sides of the same coin: each human right implies at least one type of responsibility and each responsibility implies a right. It would be entirely illogical to assert the right for everyone to have a satisfying job without asserting the responsibility for someone or some institution to ensure that such jobs exist in sufficient numbers. But this is exactly what most international human rights treaties and conventions, and national laws, do. Generally, they assert these rights without specifying who or what has the responsibility for delivering them. The state, of course, is usually intended to be the institution responsible for enforcing rights, but even where the state has the resources to do this there is always a let out (exceptional circumstances, usually defined by the state or the courts). This line of argument leads radical critics of the discourse and organization of human rights to argue that the human rights system acts as much to protect the violators as to protect the violated. Certainly, the UN Commission on Human Rights has been criticized on the grounds that states vie to place their representatives on the Commission not to pursue abuses but to ensure that their own abuses and those of friendly states are spared embarrassing exposure. It remains to be seen whether or not the new UN Human Rights Council does any better. The official human rights establishment, further, is increasingly under challenge from those who seek compensation for historical breaches of human rights, the reparations movement. Biondi (2003, 9) argues in the context of African American history: "Reparations changes the discursive image of African Americans from victims to creditors and revises the dominant narrative of American social, political, and economic history". This analysis can be convincingly extended to most other cases of human rights abuse. As more and more evidence of direct corporate involvement in such abuses is uncovered, Biondi highlights the importance of the discovery of documents demonstrating the complicity of, for example, Aetna Insurance and railroad and other companies with slavery in the USA. It is clear that the reparations movement could have major consequences for some of the leading corporations sustaining capitalist globalization. This would create major problems for the state-based official human rights establishment. And this is not exclusively a historical issue. As Holzer (2007), for example, shows in his analysis of Shell Oil in Nigeria, framing TNCs as moral as well as economic actors has critical implications for the evaluation of the human rights records of corporations today, in terms of political and civil rights as well as economic and social rights. Product liability suits brought against tobacco (and other) companies in most countries do occur, but top-ranking individuals are rarely held responsible and their companies usually survive and prosper or re-invent themselves. Corporate executives are much more likely to go to jail for financial crimes than for causing death and disease.

At the official level, globally, UN agencies have to balance universal human rights with the principle of non-interference in the internal affairs of member states. Kofi Annan has stressed that the UN Charter was issued in the name of the peoples not the governments of the United Nations, but this obviously conflicts with Article 2(7) of the UN Charter: "Nothing contained in the present Charter shall authorize the United Nations to intervene in matters which are essentially within the domestic jurisdiction of any State . . ., but this principle shall not prejudice the application of enforcement measures under Chapter VII [threats and aggression]" (quoted in Steiner & Alston, eds. 2000, 588). The problem is that it is never those people whose rights are being violated who get to decide which matters are "essentially within the domestic jurisdiction of any State". The fundamental flaw in the UN-oriented human rights approach is that most individuals are not in a position to dictate, or even have a say, in what their rights should be. Responsibilities and rights have a different logical and practical status. Logically, most people are in a position to decide what their own responsibilities to specified others are and should be, and to act on these decisions. Practically, only in very extreme cases (for example the responsibilities of parents to look after their children), is the full weight of the law used to punish people for evading their responsibilities. The responsibility of corporate executives, politicians, and officials for ensuring that private and public goods and services are safe is rarely enforced in court. If capitalist societies were societies fully committed to justice (I would argue) employers should be responsible for ensuring that their workers and their families have a decent standard of living, and that no one goes hungry, unsheltered, uneducated, or sick for want of resources. Increasingly, under the conditions of capitalist globalization, it is NGOs rather than governments or businesses that are most active in pursuing, extending, and protecting economic and social rights.

Human rights, NGOs, and civil society

Non-governmental organizations in the field of human rights are part of a broad range of organizations and movements, variously referred to as transnational advocacy networks, transnational social movements, and even (by optimistic liberals) a nascent transnational civil society. Between 2005 and 2010, 787 separate International NGOs (INGOS) were identified, mostly in rich, well-educated, democratic countries with large populations, leading to "unequal distribution of human rights TNGOs across countries" (Min Zhou 2015, 577). INGOS generally exclude official governmental bodies (including the UN and other inter-state networks) and those attached to the private economic sector. At the UN Beijing World Conference on Women in 1995, for example, 40,000 people representing thousands of these groups attended the NGO forum. The mainstream view of global civil society is that it is what is left over when we subtract all the organizations of the state and private business. As there has been phenomenal growth in NGOs all over the world it is said that global civil society has grown with them. Global civil society defined in this way is a flawed concept. The power and influence of the TNCs and their local affiliates in economic life, of the transnational capitalist class in political life, and of consumerism in culture-ideology ensure that the spaces for global civil society to exist free from the influences of capitalist globalization (including globalizers in the state) are strictly limited. Thus, excluding groups attached to private economic interests from civil society seems to me a serious error as there is a mass of evidence to suggest that those who have private economic interests wield increasing influence in what are often misleadingly termed public interest groups (Dinan & Miller 2007). This does imply the strong thesis that for there to be a genuine global civil society, its institutions and actors must oppose capitalist globalization, and for them to be effective, they have to have something convincing to put in its place. As argued above, it is time to start to think the unthinkable and to work out how the capitalist inter-state system can be replaced while we are monitoring it to prevent and/or make restitution for abuses. No doubt there are many theoretical possibilities, and a society based on the culture-ideology of human rights I propose here is one of them.

The polarization effect of capitalist globalization expresses itself to some extent in the way that the global human rights establishment operates. Wichterich (2000) probes the fact that it is acceptable for experts to jet around the world building networks but it is usually considered a waste of time and resources for slum dwellers to do the same. What she has labelled as the "New International Women's Politics" is largely based on global networks of women's groups dominated by organizations based in First World countries, often pursuing a single issue and missing the bigger picture. She identifies the US-based WEDO (Women's Environment and Development Organization) as a paradigm case of the conference-centred political process, modelled on the structures of male-dominated international politics and NGO practice. Early formal successes in establishing organizations and gaining entry to the corridors of power proved to be an illusion, as evidence mounted that nothing much has changed in the lives of many of the women on whose behalf the organizations were set up in the first place. Wichterich's analysis challenges both the mainstream neoliberal and liberal but less convincing view that the position of most women (and everyone else) has dramatically improved under capitalist globalization. To reiterate: the class polarization thesis maintains that the rich are getting richer, the poor are getting poorer, and the middle groups are becoming increasingly insecure. Fundamentally, Wichterich casts doubts on the effectiveness of the monitoring method used to measure the progress of women in development because women's NGOs in general followed structures and procedures that the World Bank, UN, and other powerful organizations laid down for them. She argues: "This professionalization has brought to the fore a new transnational and transcultural class of lobbyists, who appear really on top of their subject and tools, competent and eloquent, who tour the world with a high salary, a high expense account, and an equally high appraisal of themselves" (Wichterich 2000, 157), leading to a hierarchical differentiation among women's NGOs. Such phenomena are not restricted to the women's development organizations. In his quite positive discussion of the role of international NGOs in the successful campaign to ban the use of landmines (the Ottawa Convention), Anderson (in Steiner & Alston, eds. 2000, 950–3) comments that most of the organizations involved were fundamentally elite organizations. While they obviously did essential work, they talked mainly to each other and did little to reduce the democratic deficit. Anderson's conclusion is that this form of civil society is not really part of democracy; rather, it is a substitute for democracy. The ability to be a pressure group, not democratic legitimacy, is the hallmark of INGOs. Similar organizations working with similar agendas on other issues have also had some real successes. For example, the equally elitist campaign that led to the creation of the 1998 Rome Statute on the International Criminal Court resulted in some important war crimes trials. Some argue that the coalition of NGOS that disrupted the 1999 Seattle WTO meeting and subsequent events in the capitalist globalization calendar would have had an even more dramatic effect in raising consciousness if they had been more elitist and less libertarian. Steiner & Alston, as legal

insiders, are more optimistic about the benefits that NGOs can deliver than
Wichterich, a radical feminist journalist. We find some support for
Wichterich's view from the African legal scholar, C.A. Odinkalu (in Steiner
& Alston, eds. 2000, 946–7), who argues: "The current human rights
movement in Africa – with the possible exception of the women's rights
movement and faith-based social justice initiatives – appears almost by
design to exclude the participation of those people whose welfare it purports
to advance. ... Instead of being the currency of a social justice or
conscience-driven movement, 'human rights' has increasingly become the
specialized language of a select professional cadre with its own rites of
passage and methods of certification".

The Kenyan-American scholar Makau Mutua locates the problem in what
he terms the conventional doctrinalist nature of Western human rights
groups that tend to focus on human rights abuses in repressive foreign
countries, leaving local civil rights groups to focus on domestic issues.
"Until recently, and to a large extent even today, none of these American
INGOs focused on human rights issues in the United States, except to seek
the reform of U.S. foreign policy and American compliance with aspects of
refugee law" (Mutua in Welch 2001, 152). He argues that the careers of the
founders and current luminaries (even the non-white non-Westerners) of all
the major western INGOs illustrate the dominance of the conventional
doctrinalists. Apart from Amnesty International, they all take funds from
foundations and corporations; and their fund-raising "gimmicks" (annual
awards dinners where rich supporters buy a table for their associates)
reinforce their image with the great and the good. Conventional doctrinalists
stress a narrow range of civil and political rights, and Mutua argues that: "in
a reflection of this ideological bias, INGOs mirrored the position of the
industrial democracies and generally assumed an unsympathetic and, at
times, hostile posture towards calls for the expansion of their mandates to
include economic and social rights" (in Welch 2001, 155). Recent rhetoric
on the indivisibility of rights, he claims, has not been matched by action,
though this may be changing. Mutua focuses on human rights in Africa in a
later book (Mutua 2002), exposing the damage that Eurocentrism inflicts on
the struggle for human rights in the continent. Under the conditions of
capitalist globalization and the system of hierarchical states the ever-closer
connections with officialdom are a mixed blessing for NGOs, and the
evidence on such collaborations suggests that it is the neoliberal agenda of
globalizing business and governments, often mutually reinforcing, that
drives the process.

It is likely that most prominent human rights organizations face the problem of representation, a central issue of democratic politics. Who, speaks for whom, and with what right? Among the thousands of campaigns and movements working for human rights locally and/or globally, two stand out. The biggest is Amnesty International (AI), founded in 1961. By the beginning of the twenty-first century, AI had around one million members in more than 160 countries, and national sections in around 50 countries. Its budget of $25 million was raised from individual subscriptions and funding from private foundations. As noted above, it does not accept money from governments. The other is Human Rights Watch, founded in 1988. It began its existence as Helsinki Watch, established to monitor the human rights commitments of the superpower agreement of 1975 (the Helsinki Accords). In contrast to AI, Human Rights Watch is a non-membership organization with regional divisions and a budget of around $16 million. It has prime access to the mass media, particularly in the USA, and its regular reports of abuses of human rights all over the world are highly visible and, like AI, often controversial. Both AI and Human Rights Watch have influential websites that are heavily used, and both have been subject to a good deal of academic research, some of it rather critical (see, for example, Welch 2001, Part 1; and Carmody 2021 on Amnesty International and Keys 2016 on Human Rights Watch). Despite the powerful work they do, in some respects these are both elitist organizations that have ambiguous positions with respect to capitalist globalization. Perhaps the point is that in order to achieve much within the confines of capitalist societies, in the short term it is easier and sometimes more effective to be an elitist movement.

The record of states on the protection of human rights

Despite the enormous amount of international, regional, national, and local legislation and political agitation on their behalf, most people in the world suffer violations of one or more of their economic, social, civil, or political rights on a regular basis. Therefore, we must pose the question: how far have states, individually or as part of the UN system, acted as effective protectors and enforcers of human rights over the last few decades? There are two dimensions to this question. First, radical political change can transform a society from one in which most human rights are routinely violated to one in which most human rights are generally protected, or vice versa. South Africa in the 1990s was widely regarded as a notable success story of radical political change for protecting human rights. State policy deliberately sought to bring about a transition from a society based on racist denial of human rights for the majority of the people to one in which the protection of human rights for all was forced onto the political agenda. A good example of the opposite process was the military coup against the democratically elected government of the Chilean President Allende in 1973, followed by the military dictatorship of General Pinochet characterized by gross violations of human rights. However, the subsequent arrest and detention of Pinochet on a visit to the UK and his indictment in Chile (he died during the legal process) may one day be seen as a watershed in the struggle between state-sanctioned human rights violators and human rights law enforcers.

Second, states can for a variety of reasons change their attitudes towards human rights violations in other states and begin to exert pressure for change in these other states. Again, this can work both ways. Governments can decide to stop tolerating or to start tolerating human rights abuses in other countries. The US government and the European Union are the most visible, simply because they usually have the most clout internationally. The Carter presidency (1976–1980), when US foreign policy was used aggressively to target states that abused human rights, stands out in this respect. Even here, while eight abusing states (all in Latin America) had their security assistance (arms supplies) terminated, many other gross violators, for example, Indonesia, Iran, South Korea, the Philippines, and Zaire, did not suffer this penalty (Cohen, in Steiner & Alston, eds. 2000, 1096-99). Indeed, it may be nearer the mark to argue that despite the high level of rhetoric from successive US and other First World governments on the sanctity of international human rights, they have more often found excuses for gross violators (like national interest, employment in the domestic armaments industry, constructive engagement) than actually punished them in any way. It is difficult to escape the conclusion that this is inherent in the structure of the inter-state system with its inbuilt rhetoric of international competitiveness. This manifests itself in relatively harmless ways (in sport and other forms of cultural practice, for example), through its more serious forms (trade), to its most destructive (wars and proxy-wars). Given the infrequency with which states in the capitalist global system act decisively against even the most blatant violations of human rights (for example, freedom from torture), let alone what are usually seen as more contentious rights (for example, the right to a decent standard of living and a healthy environment), it is likely that there are forms of post-capitalist democratic globalization that will do better. Not for the first time, it is the nature of the state itself in capitalist globalization that comes under scrutiny.

This is an invitation to think the unthinkable, to think of a world that has gone beyond the separate states of the inter-state system in which most of us live. It is necessary to phrase the issue in this way to highlight two important facts. First, there are many millions of stateless people today (for example, refugees and asylum seekers); and second, there are many more millions who live within the borders of so-called nation-states but find this problematic (for example, indigenous peoples, progressive minded people who are repelled by nationalism, and people with transnational loyalties and identities). The existing state system encouraged by capitalist globalization has proved itself incapable of dealing with the rights of minorities on too many occasions to inspire much confidence that it is a satisfactory political form. A more radical solution is to question the assumption that the state and the current inter-state system, based on more or less exclusive nationalisms, are the best available forms of political life, and to think through alternatives to them. This is the political project of the democratic socialist globalization that I espouse and it is a long-term project. We still have to work out how to get from here (and here is many places) to there (and that might be many places too). An admirably clear expression of the connections between human rights and human development on record served as the introduction to the UNDP *Human Development Report* for the year 2000:

> Human rights and human development share a common vision and a common purpose – to secure the freedom, well-being and dignity of all people everywhere. To secure:
>
> Freedom from discrimination – by gender, race, ethnicity, national origin or religion.
>
> Freedom from want – to enjoy a decent standard of living.
>
> Freedom to develop and realize one's human potential.
>
> Freedom from fear – of threats to personal security, from torture, arbitrary arrest and other violent acts.
>
> Freedom from injustice and violations of the rule of law.
>
> Freedom of thought and speech and to participate in decision-making and form associations.
>
> Freedom for decent work – without exploitation. (UNDP 2000).

There is widespread agreement on what changes are desirable to improve the lives of the majority of the people around the world. In this age of apparently relentless capitalist globalization, change is clearly in the air.

Despite rising aspirations, development and freedoms are not happening quickly enough for most people. Global systems like capitalism are not born and do not die in the course of a few generations, but they do change. New generations face new challenges and meet them or fail to meet them and this changes the conditions for how the next set of challenges will be met by subsequent generations. Of course, how the future will turn out is a matter of conviction and cannot be predicted with any scientific precision. Political will, while not the only factor, cannot be discounted in the creation of a better future, just as lack of political will or political will of an evil sort can be a factor in the creation of a worse future. Socialist globalization or any other alternative to capitalist globalization will have to be created by people working together. What I have been arguing here is: (i) that capitalist globalization cannot resolve the crises of class polarization and ecological unsustainability; (ii) that the gradual elimination of privately owned Big Business and its replacement by some form of democratic socialist globalization is more likely to resolve these crises than muddling through with capitalist globalization; and (iii) that the globalization of human rights can play a powerful part in this transformation. There are many radical initiatives, more or less well organized, more or less transnational, that are continuously feeding into an emerging anti-capitalist globalization movement. As this movement inspires ever larger numbers of people to become active in the pursuit of human rights and the social responsibilities that are an integral part of them, we can begin to work out alternatives to capitalist globalization. Socialist globalization, by which I do not mean the entirely discredited socialism of world communist revolution, provides many alternative paths. For the one I recommend, see chapter 11 below, socialism "community by community".

Second Thoughts

I have had many second thoughts and some third thoughts about this essay, written more than ten years ago. These thoughts swirl around the complex dialectic that troubles those of us who try to balance pessimism of the intellect with optimism of the will. Although I was dimly aware of it at the time I regret that I did not fully appreciate the significance of the research project on forensic anthropology for the study of human rights being developed by Claire Moon, my colleague at LSE (Moon 2012). Also important is the troubling issue of "denial and stigmatization" elaborating on Stanley Cohen's analysis of "bystander passivity" (Cohen 2001, and Moon & Treviño-Rangel 2020). A short evocative film explains Moon's research project (based at the LSE in London) on the poignant and challenging idea of the "human rights of the dead", see https://www.you tube.com/watch?v=9tKCVIKGHeQ.

Post-9/11, amid genuine and bogus attempts to fight the "war on terror" (like the "war on drugs" it often seems self-defeating), the argument continues between those who believe in constructive engagement and those who believe in aggressive sanctions as the best way to change regimes that grossly violate human rights. The defeat of apartheid in South Africa suggests that selective sanctions that damage those in power and those who most benefit from the regime (often difficult to target accurately) rather than blanket sanctions that emiserate the masses (as in successive US policies towards Cuba and Iraq) are most effective in the long run. The value of encouraging and materially supporting local human rights organizations within all countries cannot be overstated. A good example of this can be found in a case study of community led conflict resolution in D.R. Congo supported by the British charity Peace Direct (see, Poole 2014, with its extensive bibliography). It is no exaggeration to say that many governments in liberal democracies and all governments in authoritarian states treat human rights organizations with suspicion. It is almost impossible to argue that the human rights situation globally has improved in the new millennium, now in its second decade. Almost, but not entirely impossible according to Kathryn Sikkink in her optimistic book promising "Evidence for Hope" (2017), a classic case of glass half full or glass half empty. Along the same lines Jackie Smith and Joshua Cooper (2020), both human rights scholar/activists, enthusiastically endorse moves towards localizing human rights, digging deeper into the grassroots to make human rights violations (all the way from making life more difficult for welfare claimants to genocidal atrocities) more visible, a process facilitated by the digital turn in communications. Perversely, this also makes it easier to target journalists and others brave enough to publicize abuses. Human rights journalism and advocacy are increasingly dangerous professions.

The creation by the United Nations of a Universal Periodic Review process at the beginning of the new millennium certainly upgraded the urgency in the UN and other international institutions of the need to deal with human rights abuses. The idea of the "boomerang effect" in human rights advocacy and practice (Rodríguez-Garavito 2015; taken further in Tsutsui & Smith 2018), highlights the importance of challenging abuses at the local, city, and regional scales as well as at the level of the state. These are clearly steps forward in raising consciousness, but the question still remains: to what extent do these organizational changes prevent abuses? A summing up of the impact of the Universal Periodic Review process of the UN in its first decade takes us back to the rather pessimistic conclusions I reached in 2011: "while the UPR has thus far proven to be a cooperative mechanism, its Achilles heel lies in the will of the states to participate in the mechanism and to implement the recommendations" (UN/UPR, 2014, 75). In his meticulous analysis of the UPR process in the four parts of the UK Chaney (2021) exposes the hypocrisy of a government that claims global leadership. Some would argue that almost all governments around the world are guilty of hypocrisy to some degree on human rights. On the other side of the Atlantic in May 2020 a group of human rights scholars and activists in the USA released research on human rights issues in the USA, under the auspices of the U.S. Human Rights Cities Alliance & Cities UPR Working Group-US Human Rights Network (USHRN). This report was submitted to the United Nations Universal Periodic Review of the United States of America Third Cycle-36th Session of the UPR Human Rights Council as "The Growth of Corporate Influence in Sub-National Political & Legal Institutions Undermines U.S. Compliance with International Human Rights Obligations." This remarkable document summarizes 59 human rights issues around which corporations, reactionary legislators in local, state, and the Federal government undermine the laws of the USA and international laws on human rights. This is not a case of "American exceptionalism", most countries around the world breach their own laws on a daily basis, for example on levels of atmospheric pollution in the UK. Is access to clean air a human right? Are human universal rights achievable within the capitalist system? Without a reliable and universally accepted consensus on how to define and measure human rights such questions are impossible to answer. On the 8th of October 2021 the U.N. Human Rights Council passed a clean environment resolution, 43-0 with China, India, Japan, and Russia abstaining. The resolution proclaims: "The human right to a safe, clean, healthy and sustainable environment". The USA, reported to be against the resolution, did not have a vote due to the withdrawal of the Trump Administration from the U.N. Human Rights Council in 2018. The resolution is couched in typical UN diplomatic jargon, with many clauses explaining why the resolution is so important. The final clauses of the resolution are instructive and appear to confirm my rather pessimistic analysis; they read:

> [the Council commits] "(d) To continue to take into account human rights obligations and commitments relating to the enjoyment of a safe, clean, healthy and sustainable environment in the implementation of and follow-up to the Sustainable Development Goals, bearing in mind the integrated and multisectoral nature of the latter;
> 4. Invites the General Assembly to consider the matter;
> 5. Decides to remain seized of the matter."

What, I wonder, would the vast majority of people around the world make of this?

One final second thought on human rights was stimulated by a re-reading of the classic study of urban social movements, citizens, and cities by Manuel Castells. In his chapter on the rent strike in Glasgow in 1915 he writes: "Parliament [in the UK] passed a Housing and Town Planning Act in 1919, mandating local governments to build housing for the workers and providing the necessary funds. For the first time in history, housing was considered a right for the people, and the state was held responsible for it. Public housing was born" (Castells 1983, 27). This apparently optimistic assessment of the impact of social movements on the future of public housing is somewhat brought down to earth by a review article of a later book by Castells and colleagues on public housing in Hong Kong and Singapore (see Cuthbert 1992). In their global survey of public housing Chen, et al. (2014) provide a great deal of evidence that while many states seem to have accepted responsibility for decent housing for all, in practice the provision of public housing was and is very uneven. Just as Castells has come in for radical criticism another controversial classic, *Planet of Slums* by Mike Davis (2006), has been problematized in terms of the contentious label of "slum" (see Angotti 2006). Housing crises of the poor seem always to be with us, almost everywhere. And what are we to draw from the fact that "public housing" does not seem to appear in the voluminous literature that grows day by day of the UN Sustainable Development Goals enterprise?

References

Angotti, T. (2006) Apocalyptic anti-urbanism: Mike Davis and his planet of slums. *International journal of urban and regional research*. 30/4: 961-967.

Bandy, J. & Smith, J. eds. (2005) *Coalitions across borders: Transnational protest and the neoliberal order*. Lanham MD: Rowman & Littlefield.

Bates, L. (2014) *Everyday Sexism*. London: Simon & Schuster.

Biondi, M. (2003) The rise of the reparations movement. *Radical History Review* 87 (Fall): 5–18.

Cameron, N.M. (2014) Humans, Rights, and Twenty-first Century Technologies: The Making of the Universal Declaration on Bioethics and Human Rights. *Journal of Legal Medicine* 35/2: 235-272.

Carmody, M. (2021) Making Human Rights International? Amnesty International, Organizational Development, and the Third World, 1970–1985. *Human Rights Quarterly* 43/3: 586-606.

Castells, M. (1983) The Industrial City and the Working-Class: The Glasgow Rent Strike of 1915. In Castells, *The City and the Grassroots*. Berkeley & Los Angeles: University of California Press, pp. 27-37.

Chaney. P. (2021) Human rights and social welfare pathologies: civil society perspectives on contemporary practice across UK jurisdictions – critical analysis of third cycle UPR data. *The International Journal of Human Rights* 25/4: 639-674.

Chen, J., Stephens, M., & Man, Y., eds. (2014). *The future of public housing: Ongoing trends in the east and the west*. Berlin & Heidelberg: Springer.

Cohen, S. (1993). Human rights and crimes of the state: The culture of denial. *Australian and New Zealand Journal of Criminology* 26/2: 97–115.

Cohen, S. (1995) State Crimes of Previous Regimes: Knowledge, Accountability, and the Policing of the Past. *Law & Social Inquiry* 20/1: 7-50.

Cohen, S. (2001). *States of denial: Knowing about atrocities and suffering*. Cambridge: Polity Press.

Cook, R.J. (1994) *Human Rights of Women: National and International Perspectives*. Philadelphia: University of Pennsylvania Press.

Coolsaet, B. ed. (2020) *Environmental Justice: Key Issues*. Abingdon: Routledge.

Çubukçu, A. (2018) *For the Love of Humanity: The World Tribunal on Iraq*. Philadelphia: University of Pennsylvania Press.

Cuthbert, A.R. (1992) In search of the miraculous (Review article). *International journal of urban and regional research* 16/2: 25.

Cypel, S. (2006) *Walled: Israeli society at an impasse*. New York: Other Press.

Davis, M. (2006) *Planet of Slums*. London: Verso.

Deacon, B., Hulse, M., & Stubbs, P. (1997) *Global social policy: International welfare organizations and the future of the welfare state*. London: Sage.

Dinan, W. & Miller, D. eds. (2007) *Thinker, faker, spinner, spy: Corporate PR and the assault on democracy*. London & Ann Arbor, Michigan: Pluto Press.

Dine, J. & Fagan, A., eds. (2006) *Human Rights and Capitalism*. Northampton, MA: Edward Elgar Publishing.

Fine, R. (2010) Dehumanising the dehumanisers: reversal in human rights discourse. *Journal of Global Ethics* 6/2: 179-190.

Foti, A. (2017) *General Theory of The Precariat: Great Recession, Revolution, Reaction*. Amsterdam: Institute of Network Culture.

Gladstone, R. (2021) An Old Legal Doctrine That Puts War Criminals in the Reach of Justice. *New York Times* (10 August).

Grear, A. & Kotze, L. eds. (2015) *Research Handbook on Human Rights and the Environment*. Cheltenham: Edward Elgar.

Hanna, B. (2017) Making Exposure In/Visible: Epidemiology, Legitimacy, and Authority after Bhopal. *The Journal of Asian Studies* 76/2: 409-421.

Hanna, B., et al., eds. (2005) *The Bhopal Reader: Twenty Years of the World's Worst Industrial Disaster*. Lanham, MD: Rowman & Littlefield.

Holzer, B. (2007) Framing the corporation: Royal Dutch/Shell and human rights woes in Nigeria. *Journal of Consumer Policy* 30: 281–301.

Hrubec, M. (2010) The Global Struggle for Human Rights: A Dialogue among Cultures. *Perspectives on Global Development and Technology* 9: 39-60.

Ishay, M.R. (2008) *The history of human rights: From ancient times to the globalization era*. Berkeley CA: University of California Press.

Keys, B. (2018) Harnessing Human Rights to the Olympic Games: Human Rights Watch and the 1993 'Stop Beijing' Campaign. *Journal of contemporary history* 53/2: 415-438.

Krishnaswamy, R. & Hawley, J., eds. (2008) *The postcolonial and the global*. Minneapolis: University of Minnesota Press.

Marrus, M. (1987) *The holocaust in history*. London: Penguin.

McCrudden, C. & Davies, A. (2000) A perspective on trade and labor rights. *Journal of International Economic Law* 3/1: 43–62.

Mehta, A. (2000) *Power Play: A Study of the Enron Project*. Mumbai: Orient Longman.

Mills, K. & Karp, D.J. eds. (2015) *Human Rights Protection in Global Politics: Responsibilities of States and Non-State Actors*. Basingstoke: Palgrave Macmillan.

Min Zhou (2015) Global Distribution of Transnational Human Rights NGOs: The effects of local resources and institutions. *Sociological Inquiry* 85/4: 576–599.

Moon, C. (2008) *Narrating political reconciliation*. New York: Lexington.

Moon, C. (2012) Interpreters of the Dead: Forensic Knowledge, Human Remains and the Politics of the Past. *Social & Legal Studies* 22/2: 149-69.

Moon, C. & Treviño-Rangel, J. (2020) "Involved in something (involucrado en algo)": Denial and stigmatization in Mexico's "war on drugs". *British Journal of Sociology*: 722-740.

Mutua, M. (2002) *Human Rights: A Political and Cultural Critique*. Philadelphia: University of Pennsylvania Press.

Poole, A. (2014) *Baraza Justice: A case study of community led conflict resolution in D.R. Congo.* Peace Direct (www.peacedirect.org).

Rajagopal, B. (2003) *International law from below: Development, social movements and Third World Resistance.* Cambridge: Cambridge University Press.

Renzulli, I. (2017) "Women and peace": A human rights strategy for the women, peace and security agenda. *Netherlands Quarterly of Human Rights* 35/4: 210–29.

Risse, T., Ropp, S., & Sikkink, K., eds. (1999) *The power of human rights: International norms and domestic change.* Cambridge: Cambridge University Press.

Said, E. (1978) *Orientalism.* London: Penguin.

Schwendinger, H. & Schwendinger, J. (2014) Defenders of Order or Guardians of Human Rights? *Social Justice* 40/1/2: 87-117.

Rodríguez-Garavito, C. (2015) Multiple boomerangs: new models of global human rights advocacy. *Open Democracy* (21 January).

Sikkink, K. (2017) *Evidence for Hope: Making Human Rights Work in the 21st Century.* Princeton: Princeton University Press.

Sklair, L. (1969) Moral Progress and Social Theory. *Ethics* 79/3: 239-33.

Smith, J. & Cooper, J. (2020) Communities look beyond Washington for solutions to human rights threats. *Commondreams.org* (December 1).

Stan, L. & Nedelsky, N., eds. (2013) *Encyclopedia of Transitional Justice.* Cambridge: Cambridge University Press.

Standing, G. (2011) *The precariat: the new dangerous class.* London: Bloomsbury Academic.

Steiner, H. & Alston, P. eds. (2000) *International human rights: Law, politics, morals.* Oxford: Oxford University Press.

Tsutsui, K. & Smith, J. (2018) Human Rights and Social Movements: From the Boomerang Pattern to a Sandwich. In Snow, D.A., et al., eds., *The Wiley Blackwell Companion to Social Movements.* Hoboken: Wiley Blackwell, chapter 33.

Uhde Z. (2021) The Structural Misrecognition of Migrants as a Critical Cosmopolitan Moment. In Schweiger G., ed. *Migration, Recognition and Critical Theory.* Springer Cham: New York, chapter 14.

UNDP (2000) *Human development report.* New York: United Nations Development Program

UN/UPR (2014) *Beyond Promises: The impact of the UPR on the ground.* Geneva: United Nations.

Vertovic, S. & Cohen, R., eds. (2002) *Conceiving cosmopolitanism: Theory, context, and practice.* Oxford: Oxford University Press.

Welch, C., ed. (2001) *NGOs and human rights: Promise and performance.* Philadelphia, PA: University of Pennsylvania Press.

Wichterich, C. (2000) *The globalized woman: Reports from a future of inequality.* London: Zed. (trans. P. Camiller).

Widdows, H. (2007) Is global ethics moral neo-colonialism? An investigation of the issues in the context of bioethics. *Bioethics* 21/6: 305–15.

Zunino, M. (2016) Subversive Justice: The Russell Vietnam War Crimes Tribunal and Transitional Justice. *International Journal of Transitional Justice* 10: 211–229.

CHAPTER 9

(2013) THE ROLE OF ICONIC ARCHITECTURE IN GLOBALIZING URBAN MEGAPROJECTS. IN *URBAN MEGAPROJECTS: A WORLDWIDE VIEW*, SANTAMARIA, G., ED. BINGLEY: EMERALD, CHAPTER 7.

Preamble

When I retired from teaching though not from research in 2004, I decided to try to write a book on the sociology of architecture and cities. This was a topic in which I had been nurturing a deep amateur interest ever since I experienced Frank Lloyd Wright's masterpiece, the Guggenheim Museum in New York, during my first visit to the USA as a student in the 1970s. I remember when first catching sight of Manhattan that Glasgow, my birthplace, seemed like Lilliput. Some of the ideas from this chapter found their way into several articles and book chapters from 2004 onwards and eventually into my book "The Icon Project: Architecture, Cities, and Capitalist Globalization", published in 2017.

Abstract

This chapter explores the role of iconic architecture in the development and promotion of urban megaprojects (UMP) in globalizing cities. Iconic architecture is defined in terms of fame and aesthetic/symbolic significance. The argument is framed within the concept of the culture-ideology of consumerism. While the focus is on two case studies, the *grands projets* in Paris and UMP in major Chinese cities since the 1980s, the chapter seeks to demonstrate the increasing importance of iconic architecture for UMP around the world. The chapter utilizes official sources, scholarly research, and reports in the mass media to support the arguments, all within the context of a theoretical framework developed over the last two decades and widely published by the author, to explain how capitalist globalization works. Within the context of the culture-ideology of consumerism, the widely accepted rationale for capitalist globalization, the production and marketing of what has been increasingly identified as iconic architecture is the main route to achieving the profits – financial, political, and cultural – deemed necessary for the success of UMP all over the world. The chapter presents the first available analysis of the key role of the transnational capitalist class in the production and marketing of iconic architecture in urban megaprojects, thereby offering a systemic explanation of the growth and characteristics of urban megaprojects in the era of capitalist globalization.

Urban Megaprojects and Problems of Scale

There is now general agreement among those who study urban design and the role of cities in the global economy that what are now termed urban megaprojects (UMP) constitute something new in the historical evolution of the city form. Recognizing that UMP come in many shapes, sizes, and guises, it is still possible to extract some common themes from the major UMP that have been constructed since the second half of the twentieth century (Santamaria 2013). Many theorists and researchers connect the phenomenon directly with the processes of globalization that have undeniably been sweeping the world in this period. In this chapter, it is the distinctive character of capitalist globalization as opposed to globalization in a generic sense that provides the context for the analysis and provides opportunities to compare similarities and differences between the two major case studies, Paris of the *grands projets* and China over the last three decades, that make up the substantive core of this chapter. The role of architectural icons in UMP in the era of capitalist globalization (since the 1960s) merits more attention than it has hitherto received. Building on previous research on iconicity in architecture, I argue that iconicity can most fruitfully be conceptualized in terms of fame, symbolic meanings and aesthetics of buildings, spaces, and architects themselves. Up to the middle of the twentieth century the main drivers of iconic architecture tended to be state and/or religious bodies, while in the era of capitalist globalization the drivers tend to be members of the transnational capitalist class acting in the interests of capitalist globalization. This thesis, as applied to UMP over the last few decades, examines the extent to which iconic architecture has become not only compatible with but also a necessary component of UMP in the era of capitalist globalization (despite the efforts of some politically radical architects) and is developed with reference to urban growth coalitions in globalizing cities all over the world, with special reference to the *grands projets* in Paris and UMP in China. In 2002 a competition to design a new cultural megaproject in Hong Kong was won by a consortium comprising Foster & Partners, the Bartlett School of Planning (of University College London), and Nonometric Design & Planning Hong Kong. The Hong Kong government is said to have encouraged the participation of Sun Hung Kai, the largest developer in the Special Administrative Region (of which Hong Kong is part), who sponsored the winning team. Despite this high-level backing, the planning process for the West Kowloon Cultural District (WKCD) dragged on throughout the decade, and at time of writing (summer 2010) it still dragged on. Bearing this in mind, it is an appropriate place to start a discussion of the role of iconic architecture in UMP. WKCD is now touted as a US$40 billion project that will transform a relatively under-developed part of Kowloon into what is routinely referred to as an icon for culture and leisure, with several museums and theatres, concert venues, outdoor water park, design school, residential and office buildings, shopping malls, and other retail opportunities of all descriptions. Fortunately, we have the most revealing account of how the first stage of planning took shape. Matthew Carmona, professor of architecture at the Bartlett, was part of the original consortium team and his "Practice Note" identifies the cultural stakeholders and representatives of the public realm whose interests were prioritized in the competition process. While public piazzas and green spaces were to be delivered by the private sector, reverting to public ownership after 30 years, all of these were to be intensively programmed, meaning that all of these spaces had to be seen to be "working for their living." As in the rest of China (and, without doubt, in most of the rest of the world), this meant that they had to attract customers for the benefit of the private retail and culture industries market. Carmona expresses this clearly in the context of how the design program evolved: To win the competition required: a single strong iconic architectural image – the first priority a functional urban design solution – a distant second that commercial elements (and therefore deliverability) were downplayed. During this period, aesthetic concerns preoccupied the architects, whereas not appearing to be too profit driven was the developer's primary concern. However, priorities changed following the competition win, and the challenge became to deliver a commercially viable development to maintain the architectural vision (as much as possible) to deliver a successful urban design solution, including a viable, vital, functional and livable public realm: "The change was driven by the developers ... Significantly, the challenge of commercial delivery was entirely compatible with delivering high-quality design outcomes" (Carmona 2006, 120). Thus, there was to be no conflict between the strong iconic architectural image necessary to win the competition and the private corporate, particularly consumerist, interests driving the megaproject.

While definitions of UMP differ to some extent from researcher to researcher, Diaz and Fainstein (2008) are surely correct to identify the following assortment of characteristics: (a) waterfront redevelopment; (b) recovery of old manufacturing and warehouse Zones; (c) construction of new and/or extension of existing transport infrastructure; and (d) renovation of historic city districts, usually to satisfy and/or create consumer demand. While their case studies (London, New York, Amsterdam, Toronto, Helsinki, and Istanbul) are European and North American, there is increasing evidence that the phenomenon is becoming truly global. Marshall (2003) speaks of an emerging urbanity as a result of global urban projects in the Asia Pacific Rim, covering Tokyo and Yokohama, Bangkok, Shanghai and Beijing, Hanoi and Saigon, Singapore, and Kuala Lumpur. He reports that 13 of the 30 largest firms working in Asia in the late 1990s were based in the USA, Australia, or the UK: "This leads inevitably to a collection of architectural projects that are remarkably the same in cities such as Tokyo, Shanghai, Singapore and Jakarta" (ibid., 2). These transformations in cities all over the world at the end of the twentieth century and the beginning of the twenty-first century forced those concerned with urban design to create new vocabularies to describe and analyze what was going on. New concepts flooded the marketplace of ideas; global city, 100-mile city, megacity, postmetropolis, exopolis, edge city, simcity, fractal city, world city, post-fordist industrial metropolis, all jostling for prominence. While each of these ideas had its own measure of specificity, they all shared two key elements, namely the presence of UMP and, to a lesser extent, the presence of iconic architecture within them. Marshall's nine case studies all shared the following features: perceptions of global competition, striving for competitive advantages for host cities, a new kind of space occupancy, targeting global elites, differences in scale and articulation to surrounding environments, and attempts to secure celebrity status through marketing images. These processes, while varying in fine detail from city to city, Marshall argues (ibid., chapter 2), result in a rather narrow definition of urban life and culture, a rather restricted consumerist urban vision which has become the dominant global urban vision.

While they are by no means equivalent, the phenomenon of megaprojects can rarely be entirely separated from the phenomenon of skyscrapers. King (2004, 12) frames the issue as follows: "How the skyscraper moved from being an icon solely of American identity and corporate power in its various cities to becoming a signifier of modernity in other parts of the world, and what symbolic meaning might be attached to that, is, as yet, an unwritten story" (see also van Leeuwen 1988). The study of contemporary and recent UMP is one essential part of this unwritten story as Asian cities, in particular, compete openly to build the world's tallest buildings. Images of soaring towers on the skylines of aspiring global cities join shopping malls, sports stadia, museums, transportation hubs, and culture complexes as the sine qua non of global city status on the world stage. Indeed, in many cases the immensity of new skyscrapers vying for the accolade of the tallest building in the world makes them UMP in their own right, bearing in mind that they often bring with them whole contiguous retail and infrastructural complexes, necessary to service the hoped-for business and tourist traffic that is intrinsic to the economics and politics of these projects. In my book, published about six years after this chapter was written, I dubbed this "celebrity infrastructure" (Sklair 2017, *passim*), in recognition of the fact that many of these projects were beginning to be written about in the context of iconic architecture. Prime examples of this are Norman Foster's new Beijing airport, the Euralille project by Rem Koolhaas, and Santiago Calatrava's transportation hub at Ground Zero in New York and his bridges in many other cities, now regular components of urban megaprojects.

Competitive Megaprojects

In the first decade of the new millennium there were two clear leaders in the race for the top ranking in the UMP competition, the Arabian Gulf and China. In their evocatively titled essay, "Dreams So Big Only the Sea Can Hold Them," Jackson and Dora (2009) relate the stories of the Palm Jumeirah complex in Dubai (the title is from the promotional video for this project) followed by Palm Jebel Ali and Palm Deira. By 2008 more than half of the US$14 billion development known as "The World" had been sold to wealthy transnational buyers. Deconstructing the key terms used to market them, notably "The World" and "dream", Jackson and Dora comment: "ostensible superlatives brand Dubai's efforts towards global iconicity" (ibid., 2087). Rem Koolhaas and his colleagues in OMA/AMO are also involved in the Gulf, and more superlatives fly (see also Ponzini & Nastasi 2011). Jackson and Dora focus on artificial islands as special cases of UMP and also cite plans to build various types of islands off the coasts of Korea, the Netherlands, Spain, Pakistan, Slovenia, Singapore, Venezuela, and Russia (Black Sea/Sochi). We can add to this list the ongoing saga of Tokyo Bay (Lin 2007) and Tokyo Rainbow Town: a "global urban project envisioned as a silicon city for the twenty-first century on reclaimed land" (Marshall 2003, 31). For China, which will be discussed in greater detail in the following sections, let it suffice at this point to cite the words of Xie Xiaoying, a Chinese landscape architect: "It is a good time to be a designer in China. Unlike America there are no rules in China. We can do what we want. We can do good design" (quoted in Marshall 2003, 85). The cases of the Gulf and China appear, on the surface at least, to suggest that the drivers of the most mega of contemporary UMP are driven by the state and in one sense they are. Before the rise of capitalist globalization (roughly dating from the 1960s) the main drivers of iconic architecture and, by implication, UMP tended to be state and/or religious bodies. In the era of capitalist globalization the drivers tend to be members of the four fractions of the TCC: those who own and/or control the major transnational corporations and their local affiliates (the corporate fraction); globalizing politicians and bureaucrats (the state fraction); globalizing professionals (the technical fraction); and elites of merchants, media, and advertising (the consumerist fraction) as explained in chapter 3 above. How can the cases of the Gulf and China (and many others where the state is clearly implicated in UMP) be reconciled with this historical framework? In a penetrating study of Metro Manila, Shatkin (2008) provides ample evidence that large private developers are implementing urban development plans with government assistance in the context of the privatization of planning and that this is happening all over Southeast Asia. This results in what he terms "bypass-implant urbanism," based on regressive state subsidies for profit-driven private sector development, abandonment of public purpose by planning agencies, and idealization of the private sector by international organizations. Shatkin argues convincingly that this is not simply a case of straightforward Americanization. Asian cities, he says, are exceptional in some respects (indeed, all cities have some exceptional characteristics). Asian cities tend to be bigger than North American or European cities (UMP have been designed for up to a million people in Thailand and Indonesia, for example); not all are strictly oriented to automobile use; and many are scattered rather than edge cities. From his observations in Manila and elsewhere, Shatkin identifies four types of actors involved in UMP: local and national governments, involved, but tending increasingly to leave urban development to the private sector; private developers, often ethnic Chinese, linked into global networks of overseas Chinese and international finance; a consumer class of the winners of capitalist globalization whose spending power is driving urban development; and foreign planners and architects who provide models of urbanism. Of this last group: "their impact is less to 'Westernize' urban form than it is to commodify the urban experience 'bypassing' the congested arteries of the 'public city' and 'implanting' new spaces for capital accumulation that are designed for consumerism and export-oriented production" (Shatkin, 2008, 388). Thus, what drives UMP is not so much Americanization or indigenization or even hybridization, but anything that looks profitable. In the absence of a public vision for Metro Manila the large developers provide their own visions for urban development, comprising specific UMP and supporting infrastructure. Governments, in permanent fiscal crisis, have little option but to be part of this totalizing consumerist urban vision. Shatkin argues that while these processes are most pronounced in Manila, there is evidence that they are emerging all over the region, a judgment strongly supported by the research of Marshall (2003), as illustrated above, among others. Although he does not use the terms, what Shatkin describes for Metro Manila sounds very much like the globalizing urban growth coalitions that members of the TCC are engaged in building all over the world. Shatkin's *Table 1* on major real estate developments in Metro Manila shows that global architects and architect-developers, including HOK, SOM, and other foreign firms, are heavily involved. One of the key elements in the strategy of the TCC in putting cities on the global map is the propagation of iconic architecture with the sometimes enthusiastic and sometimes placid collaboration of the state fraction of the transnational capitalist class. The cases of Paris, site of the first globalizing UMP, and China, the latest and biggest, can be fruitfully analyzed in these terms.

Paris: The Ongoing Saga of the Grands projets

Visiting La Défense in the 1990s we are offered the 1996 edition of the Guide to the architecture, an official publication of EPAD (Etablissement Public pour l'Aménagement de la Region de La Défense). The project is introduced in the following words: "In 1958 the French government decided to launch the largest urban planning project that the second half of the 20th century would see. A business and industry-oriented public agency, EPAD was invested with the task of developing town planning, setting up infrastructures and marketing available land space. From the very first skyscraper, the Nobel Tower, which has since been rebaptized the Roussel-Hoechst building. to the new headquarters of one of Europe's leading banks, the *Societe Generale*, architects from the world over have succeeded in adapting their art to the needs and expectations of both enterprises and residents" (Demeyer 1996, 3).

La Défense (the name originally referred to a statue erected in 1883 to commemorate the siege of Paris in the Franco-Prussian war of 1870) was the westernmost point of the great axis of the capital that took the eye from the Louvre Palace via the Place de la Concorde and the Arc de Triomphe along the great tree-lined avenue of the Champs Élyseesé. In the 1930s, the entry of Le Corbusier to a competition to develop the area suggested lines of skyscrapers on each side of a pedestrian boulevard, a vision that partially inspired what was eventually built. By the 1990s, La Defénse comprised an area of 160 hectares, encompassing business and residential districts, catering to the needs of around 40,000 families, as well as 140,000 employees working in 1,600 enterprises (including 14 of France's top 20 companies and 15 of the world's top 50). The potential for domestic and international tourism was built into the plan, with 2,600 new hotel rooms, a major transport hub and 26,000 underground parking spaces to accommodate around 1 million visitors per year. Also promised were parks and museums (not very successfully realized so far) and a multitude of consumption opportunities (including the largest shopping mall in Europe at the time). While La Défense as a whole comprises hundreds of separate buildings (a sort of mini-Manhattan) and it is clearly a UMP in the full sense of the term, the building that is known as La Grande Arche, at the focal point of La Défense, was clearly intended to be iconic from its beginnings. After several attempts to find a suitable design, all thwarted by political changes, President Mitterand determined to bring the process to a successful conclusion as part of his legacy, one of his *grands projets*. In 1982 he instructed EPAD to set up an international competition which attracted over 400 entries. It was won to general surprise by Johan-Otto von Spreckelsen, the little-known director of the architecture school of the Copenhagen Royal Academy of Fine Art, an architect with no famous buildings, indeed few buildings at all, to his name. In the words of Demeyer, this building "was meant to be a new landmark on a par with the Louvre and the Arc de Triomphe," both global icons. Spreckelsen, whose special interests were said to be the study of mosques and other monumental architecture, did not disappoint. He introduced his project proposal, lyrically, as follows: "the Grande Arche is an open cube [with sides of 100 metres], a window on the world, like a fleeting musical pause before the future" (ibid., 15). His building is now probably the most visited tourist attraction outside central Paris. The Grande Arche is just one of a series of other aspiring and actual iconic buildings, known collectively as the *grands projets*, associated with the presidency of Mitterand and his successors and still being built. These include the Musee d'Orsay (originally a railway station, converted in the 1980s by the Italian woman architect Gae Aulenti into one of the most popular and beautiful museums in Paris), the technically innovative Institut du Monde Arabe (architect, Jean Nouvel), the new Bibliotéque de France (Dominique Perrault, 1998), the vast leisure complex, Parc de la Villette (begun in the 1980s with buildings designed by the Swiss-American

Bernard Tschumi and others) and last but by no means least the new pyramids at the Louvre (by the Chinese-American architect I.M. Pei), possibly the most successful of them all. It is worth noting that Pei had submitted a design for the Grand Arche at La Défense in the 1970s which fell victim to political intrigue. Chaslin (1985) finds political intrigues in most of the *grands projets*. All of them have become major tourist attractions and all can claim a measure of global iconicity, as beautifully illustrated throughout the text of Luste Boulbina et al. (2007). The Pompidou Centre (Richard Rogers and Renzo Piano) is also a major tourist attraction but predates Mitterand's presidency. The role of the four fractions of the TCC (corporate, state, professional, and consumerist) in the evolution of La Défense since its inception in 1958 is also clear. While EPAD was created by the state, it is commonly described in official literature as a public corporation with a commercial and industrial character. As documented above, the aggrandizement of the French state, the legacy of President Mitterand, and the interests of capitalist globalization were generally presented as entirely compatible. After an unsuccessful first two decades when not a single right to build was sold to the private sector La Défense was relaunched to make it more business and consumer friendly. This resulted in a new generation of high-tech buildings, the massive Quatre Temps shopping mall (1981) and, of course, the iconic Grande Arche which opened with great public fanfare during the G7 Heads of State summit on July 14, 1989, the bicentennial of the French Revolution. This, Demeyer's EPAD guide triumphantly proclaimed: "put La Defense into the newspapers and onto the TV screens of the whole world. The district saw an influx of hundreds of thousands of tourists." In July 1990 an even greater extravaganza orchestrated by Jean Michel Jarre was played out on the great axis from the Arc de Triomphe to the Grande Arche before an estimated crowd of 2 million people. It was in this period that many state enterprises in France were privatized and major TNCs, both French and overseas-domiciled, began to buy into La Défense illustrating the commonality of interests between those who own and control the major corporations and their local affiliates (corporate fraction), with the support of globalizing politicians and bureaucrats (state fraction), globalizing professionals, and consumerist elites, the French members of which tend to have been classmates at the same Grandes écoles. While there has been a good deal of criticism of the conception of the *grands projets* as well as of individual buildings (see, notably, Chaslin 1985; Fierro 2003), in general they have received a positive response from the globalizing elements in the architecture-developer professions in France and abroad. More importantly, from the perspective of the TCC, they have been popular with consuming publics, domestic and international tourists. The new museums have attracted large numbers of visitors and, it could be argued, after ferocious struggles throughout the architectural establishment, the pyramids at the Louvre have helped to give that venerable old institution a new lease of life, with franchises at home and abroad (see Vivant 2011). The culture-ideology of consumerism, therefore, can be seen as an important element in the story of the *grands projets* in Paris. In her imaginative study of the use of glass as a metaphor for political transparency, Fierro (2003, 25) argues that the strategy of the *grands projets* was to site monumental architecture within Zones d'amenagement concerte (ZAC), and thereby to upgrade working class districts. However, Vivant (2010, Section 4) argues that this policy is only fully realized in the ZAC Paris Rive Gauche UMP, anchored by the new National Library (by Perrault), certainly an iconic building.

Despite differences in scale, renovations like the pyramids at the Louvre, relocations like the Bibliotheque de France, and new projects (Opera Bastille, Institut du Monde Arab), all buildings with impressive, quasi-monumental welcoming glass frontages, indicated: "Mitterand's ambition to gather crowds (particularly of well-heeled tourists) at key points in the city," in contrast to the nineteenth century megaproject of Haussmann whose dominant goal was the dispersal of often hostile crowds (Fierro 2003, 25). These projects led to the very public charge that the President was gripped by a "Mitterramses" obsession (see Chaslin 1985, 119 and passim). Mitterand also indulged in grands travaux outside Paris (Mefti & Grouard 1991), but these are not usually seen as UMP. Analyzing the contribution of the Irish-British glass engineers RFR (Rice Francis Ritchie) that rings true for many if not most iconic buildings in UMP around the world today, Fierro argues: "As a patented system, RFR's structural glazing becomes a commodity available for purchase and installation in any type of space. It was immediately appropriated by developer culture as a means of endowing commercial space with a fashionable technological flourish" (ibid, 217). If the "petite pyramide" becomes the French version of the American shopping mall as the Louvre itself is transformed into a space of luxury consumption (see Sklair 2017, Figure 7.5), is there any limit to what the TCC can achieve by creative manipulation of the culture-ideology of consumerism in UMP anywhere on the planet?

China: The Biggest UMP in Human History

"Since the 1980s, China has built more skyscrapers; more office buildings; more shopping malls and hotels; more housing estates and gated communities; more highways, bridges, subways, and tunnels; more public parks, playgrounds, squares, and plazas; more golf courses and resorts and theme parks than any other nation on earth—indeed, than probably all other nations combined." With these words, Thomas Campanella (2008, 14) indicates how globalizing cities in China, notably Beijing, Shanghai, and Shenzhen, with Tianjin, Guangzhou, and many others in hot pursuit, have been vigorously pursuing UMP strategies since the 1980s, when the open-door policy, market socialism with Chinese characteristic, was introduced, first in Shenzhen and then gradually throughout the rest of the country. Teams of workers from the People's Army Engineer Corps were transferred to Shenzhen Special Economic Zone (SSEZ) as their emergency work on the 1976 Tangshan earthquake reconstruction wound down. When the first skyscraper in the SSEZ, the International Foreign Trade Center (IFTC), opened in 1985 it was the tallest building in China. The IFTC was modelled after Gordon Wu's Hopewell Centre in Hong Kong and became a "building type rapidly replicated throughout China" (Campanella 2008, 36). It was from the IFTC that Deng issued his historic free market call in January 1992. Gordon Wu was precisely the type of entrepreneur and visionary that the globalizing politicians and officials of the Special Economic Zone and their provincial and state-level allies were seeking, and he did not disappoint. Campanella vividly describes how the Canton (Guangzhou)-Shenzhen Expressway (built by the Princeton-educated Wu's company and inspired by the New Jersey turnpike) began the transformation of the Pearl River Delta into a global economic hub. This was not the traditional BosWash corridor metropolis, Campanella argues, but a new type of integrated global space of flows in the Castells mode, a step in the direction of the ultimate UMP. The story of the specific role of architects and architecture-developer firms in this process is taken up in the report of the Harvard Design School Pearl River Delta project, led by Rem Koolhaas (Chung, Inaba, Koolhaas, & Leong 2001).

Shenzhen is Hong Kongized

Thus Shenzhen, in 1975 an obscure border crossing on the Kowloon to Canton railway line where ticket collectors still used the abacus, by the twenty-first century had become a familiar story in the pages of architecture and urban design magazines with a new city centre designed by the eminent Chicago firm Skidmore, Owings & Merrill. As Caroline Cartier (2001, 242) explained, "The slogan of the era was 'Shenzhen is Hong Kongized, Guangdong is Shenzhenized, and the whole country is Guangdongized'" (see also Cartier 2002). Where Shenzhen led, Shanghai and Beijing followed, but not at the same pace and not in the same way. Zhang (2002) shows that while the importance of the private sector varied significantly in these three city regions, all engaged in substantial megaproject construction. While the distinction between private and state is not as clear cut as it is in the West, what we would usually identify as the corporate interest prevailed. In Shanghai the private sector is certainly more developed than in Beijing, but less than in Shenzhen (and the other original Special Economic Zones). The government in Beijing of Jiang Zemin, a former party boss in Shanghai, authorized major UMP construction with the reconstruction of Pudong in Shanghai in the 1990s.

Shanghai

Pudong Special Economic Zone was divided into four areas, focusing on free trade (Waigaoqiao), finance (Lujiazui), export-processing (Jinqiao), and high-tech firms (Zhangjiang). In one of the first in-depth studies of UMP in the Pacific Rim, Kris Olds (2001) compared the cases of Shanghai and Vancouver, focusing on the roles of ethnic Chinese property developers and elite non-Chinese design professionals. He explains why a major infrastructure scheme was seen to be necessary to turn Shanghai into a global city and how the Institut d'Aménagement et d'Urbanisme de la Region Ile de France (Paris-Region Institute for Management and Urban Planning, IAURIF) worked with local authorities in Shanghai from the mid-1980s to bring the project to a successful conclusion. IAURIF was, like EPAD (also involved in the planning process for Pudong), a public–private institution in which, in my terms, members of the four fractions of the TCC could work amicably and profitably together. The Mitterand role was taken in Shanghai by the Mayor Zhu Rongji (subsequently Chinese Premier), who visited La Défense in 1991 and was duly impressed. It is no coincidence that this occurred shortly after Shanghai had been granted preferential foreign direct investment status by the central government in 1990. Olds (2001) identifies the main players in the Shanghai UMP; property investors and design professional (local and foreign), local officials, and state enterprises, the typical globalizing urban growth coalition. International planning consultancy services and the international competition for the design of the new Shanghai were organized by IAURIF. Many globally iconic architects were attracted to the project, including Richard Rogers and Norman Foster (from the UK), Renzo Piano (from Italy), Toyo Ito (from Japan), and the French architects Jean Nouvel and Dominique Perrault. The models and graphics they and others produced were widely used to sell the image of a new global Shanghai, spectacularly to complement the image of Shanghai as the "Paris of the Orient" in the 1930s. By the year 2000, there were 4,000 new buildings over 24 floors high in the city, with 1,700 more under construction or planned. Despite the scale and ambition of the new Shanghai, Marshall's overall impression of the flagship financial district is quite negative: the "result is unfortunately a collection of high-rise towers and an amorphous open space lacking any capacity to support urban culture. Further, this is exacerbated by the fact that to access the Central Park (and this was a shock for the author) one has to pay!" (Marshall 2003, 99). Marshall's account is reinforced by a nuanced analysis of the not very user-friendly streetscape of Pudong and responses to it (see Arkaraprasertkul 2008), in contrast to the traditional *lilong* culture across the river in Shanghai (Arkaraprasertkul 2013).

The most influential consultant brought in by the Mayor of Shanghai was Joseph Belmont, a key figure in the *grands projets* in Paris, and his penchant for the power of iconic architecture was eagerly taken up by officials in Shanghai. Among the multitude of nondescript skyscrapers a few buildings stand out and have achieved a high measure of global iconicity and global media exposure. The best examples are the Pearl of the Orient TV tower, dramatically overlooking the Bund on the opposite side of the Huangpu River, dubbed the Eiffel Tower of Shanghai despite its rather 1960s look, and the Jin Mao Tower. The first skyscraper in Pudong to be built by an American firm – the Jin Mao Tower by SOM with the state-owned China Shanghai Foreign Trade Center in 1999, started a move to what might be termed "Chinese postmodernist" design, a quasi-gothic tall tower with pagoda overtones, which has proved popular with some but not all locals. The Shanghai World Finance Tower designed by Kohn Pederson Fox with the developers, Mori Corporation of Roppongi Hills (Tokyo) fame, was announced as the world's tallest building (as was the Jin Mao tower) and has ended up being christened the "bottle opener" by local wags. Nevertheless, Lujiazui Central Finance District has attracted more positive responses from some investors, scholars, and media. The international competition for Lujiazui, despite invited entries from Rogers, Fuksas, Ito, and Perrault, was won by the Shanghai Urban Planning and Design Research Institute of Tongji University though it is widely acknowledged that elements from the invited entries appear in the final plan (Olds 2001). The reason is not difficult to work out for it was largely modeled on La Défense in Paris, a new central business district for Shanghai to rival the CBDs of other major global cities. I can vouch from my own visits to the Shanghai Urban Planning Exposition Center, Expo, in 2017 that Campanella (2008, 57) does not exaggerate in his vivid description: "Entering the lobby of the Expo Center, a visitor is greeted by a monumental gilded sculpture of the city's iconic buildings, a kind of architectural gilded calf that slowly rotates on a pedestal, flooded worshipfully with lights". Illustrated in Sklair (2017, Figure 5.10) this is, apparently not even the largest city model in China. The Exposition Centre (free admission) is brilliantly satirized in the account of the "Shanghai Global City" experience (Krupar 2008). Other *grands projets*-type architectural icons in Shanghai built around the turn of the millennium include Foster's Jiushi Corporation HQ, the Grand Theatre by Charpentier, the new Pudong International Airport by Andreu, and the Shanghai World's Fair complex (summer 2010). However, not all of the new Shanghai is made up of towering skyscrapers. Xintiandi (New Heaven and Earth) shopping district was opened in 2001, replicating the low-rise Shanghai of the early twentieth century with enough gentrified Chinese relics to please the tourists and trendy venues to please the local new rich (and vice versa). Indeed, many of the old colonial concession districts, especially around the Bund, have also been regenerated and gentrified. Xintiandi-style districts are now reproduced all over China: culture-ideology of consumerism inspired mimetic iconicity. There seems no end to the UMP wave, both high-rise and low-rise, in Shanghai. Around the city the fantastic "One City Nine Towns" project introduces a more deliberate Western, syncretic postcolonial collection of urban designs, evolving before our eyes (see Bracken 2009; Lu & Li 2008). Zhang (2002) identifies a "socialist pro-growth coalition" to explain the success of Pudong and it is without doubt the case that the party bosses and other officials who ran the city made the final decisions on what got built where and when. Nevertheless, as the research of Olds, Campanella, and others cited above demonstrates, this was a coalition that included members of the four fractions of the TCC and whose dominant ideology was more capitalist culture-ideology of consumerism than power to the people or any other vestige of Maoist democratic centralism. While infrastructure projects and the construction of high-rises gave a great boost to local employment – including large numbers of migrants from the countryside – and to the local steel industry, the greatest costs were borne by displaced locals (though not in Pudong itself) estimated to have been in the region of 100,000, with no community power base to protect their interests. The issue of displacement will be taken up again in my conclusion (and, in the context of the highly controversial concept of "administrative evil") in chapter 12 below. Suffice it to say here that this was a price that those who came to enjoy the new iconic architecture in Shanghai (and in Beijing, as we shall see) did not have to pay.

Beijing

Beijing entered the competition for a leading position in the hierarchy of global cities and UMP a little later than Shanghai, largely attributed to the successful campaign to stage the 2008 Olympics after the disappointment of losing out to Sydney in 2000. But when it did it seized the spirit of the globalizing UMP with similar zeal. The first phase, Zhongguancun Science and Technology Park in northwestern Beijing (hereafter ZGC) was opened in 1988, but the major plan was not authorized until 1999. By the new millennium, over 1,000 foreign investment joint ventures (valued at US$3.26 billion) with generous preferential incentives had been established. A competition for the New West Zone development of ZGC in 1999 attracted entries from China, the UK, and the United States and was won by Urban Planning and Design Institute of Tsinghua University in Beijing. The chief designer had been much influenced by what he saw on a tour of California and planned to turn ZGC into the Silicon Valley of China (see Marshall 2003, chapter 7). Despite its relative success in attracting foreign investment and a measure of scientific and technological expertise, ZGC had very little architectural impact at the global scale. However, it was only one of Beijing's three UMP, and the other two – the new CBD and the new Olympic Center – were much more successful in the "attempt to reposition the city as a node in the global sphere" (ibid., 109). In the words of Anne-Marie Broudehoux: "Beijing in the 1990s was a forest of giant construction cranes at work twenty four hours a day in an endless cycle of creative destruction and reconstruction. In the name of progress and modernization, acres of working-class neighbourhoods were levelled, making way for skyscrapers, luxury hotels, and motorways ... a response to rising pressures for the city to bolster its reputation in order to sell itself on the world market and attract global attention and international capital" (2004, 2). For the Chinese leadership in the post-Mao era, Broudehoux argues, the focus was on the nation rather than the people, chauvinistic ethnicity replacing class in the official rhetoric in an attempt to create a new Chinese modernity in which the romanticized Old Peking (rapidly being destroyed) becomes a commercial opportunity. Broudehoux presents three case studies on the "exploitation of cultural heritage and the careful manipulation of the past in the selling of place; the commodification and aestheticization of places to serve business, shopping, and leisure functions; and the spectacular transformation of the city into a stage set for the hosting of international media events and the performance of political rituals" (ibid., 20). While the example she chooses for selling the past and the commodification of history (Yuanmingyuan, the old Summer Palace) is not an UMP, the other two cases most certainly are. For the commodification and aestheticization of places to serve business, shopping, and leisure functions the obvious example is Wangfujing, Beijing's answer to New York's Fifth Avenue. Near the new Central Business District (CBD), the project began with the redevelopment of the Old Sun Dong An market, transformed in the early 1990s into a globalized commercial center by a 50/50 joint venture of the Beijing based state-owned Dong An group and Sun Hung Kai Properties based in Hong Kong, with unprecedented financial and import incentives (borrowing from Shanghai financial and design models). While Sun Dong An (labeled by Broudehoux "a capitalist revolution") reproduced the global shopping mall design on the inside, it deliberately reproduced vernacular architectural features on the outside, providing the tourists and the locals with two different gazes. But this was a relatively modest start compared to its neighbour, the US$2 billion Oriental Plaza, financed by a consortium of Hong Kong developers: the largest civil property development in Asia of the 1990s. Famously, the local branch of McDonald's (the biggest in the world in when it opened in 1992) was forced to relocate to make way for Oriental Plaza. The main investor was the Hong Kong-based tycoon Li Ka-shing through two of his many companies, Cheung Kong Holdings and Hutchison Whampoa, for which expression of confidence in China's opening up to the world of capitalist globalization he was rewarded in 1996 with a seat on the Preparatory Committee managing the transition from British to Chinese sovereignty in Hong Kong. Li Ka-shing was also a major investor in real estate and infrastructure in Pudong and in Vancouver (see Olds 2001). Unsurprisingly, not everyone in Beijing welcomed these changes, Campanella (2008, chapter 5) writes compellingly of the dreaded character *chai* (demolition) on countless buildings, displacing hundreds of thousands of people to enrich corrupt developers and officials. The mostly symbolic resistance of the displaced has been well represented in a flourishing of the arts around the city (also in Shanghai). Broudehoux comments: "For those who had fought the construction of Oriental Plaza until the bitter end, the monumental building would remain a symbol of China's new subjugation at the hands of world imperialists as wealthy outsiders increasingly dictated the way their cities are transformed" (2004, 123). It is, however, important to add that many of those who have benefited from the malling of Wangfujing, the mega wealthy and the merely new rich, are locals and many are ethnic Chinese. Some of these are members of the transnational capitalist class, for example Li Ka-shing. Broudehoux, whose book was published in 2004, was able to report on the decision in 2001 to award the 2008 Olympics to Beijing, and she correctly predicted the enormous impact that the Beijing Olympics would have. The Chinese government immediately responded to the IOC with a US$22 billion 5-year plan to turn Beijing into a global city. The elaborate preparations for the 11th Asian Games in Beijing in 1990 and, in 1999, the makeover of Tiananmen Square to celebrate the 50th anniversary of the founding of the PRC had both been accompanied by substantial demolition in anticipation of what was needed for the Olympics to be the sort of success as a global spectacle that the Chinese leadership and commercial interests craved. The 2008 Olympics brought an unprecedented wave of building, restoration, destruction, and relocation to the city. Laurence Liauw, an architect at the Chinese University of Hong Kong and a specialist on urban design in China, provides the context: after the failed Olympic 2000 bid "Beijing subsequently rebranded itself as an international metropolis with avant garde architectural icons symbolizing contemporary China's arrival on to the world stage" (Liauw 2009, 215; see also Zhu 2009, chapter 8 and passim). This involved 22 new stadia plus 15 renovated facilities, two new ring roads, 142 miles of new infrastructure, 8 new subway lines, 252 new star-rated hotels, 40 km of cleaned rivers, 1 million new trees, 83 km of greenbelt, and an artificial mountain and lake. The Olympic Park is three times as big as Central Park in New York and Beijing's new North–South Central Axis linking Olympic Park and Tiananmen Square was designed by Albert Speer, Jr., giving the son the opportunity to bring about a monumental project that his father never had (Wu 1991).

Beijing's new CBD echoes the verticality of Hong Kong and Shanghai and, as the state owned much more of the housing in the capital than was the case in Shanghai, old districts were more easily swept away to make room for the gentrified new, creating a post-1998 real estate boom. This forced an estimated 1.5 million residents to relocate to suburban satellite new towns. Migrant worker districts were demolished and their residents, some of many years standing, were simply sent back home (see Broudehoux 2004; Abramson 2008; Campanella 2008). Amid this massive demolition and reconstruction two buildings stand out, achieving rapid iconicity, their images disseminated all over the world. Both were designed by foreign starchitects. The first, Herzog and de Meuron's Olympic stadium (dubbed the Bird's Nest) reached a global audience of billions during the spectacular Olympic opening and closing ceremonies. It was touted by the architects, perhaps a little immodestly but not entirely unrealistically, as the Eiffel Tower of Beijing, and Liauw's view that: "Architecture has become part of city branding machine through mediated imagery" (2009, 218) seems accurate. Ren Xuefei (2011) skillfully connects this with globalization in her book *Building Globalization*. Of the second, the Central China TV building (CCTV) by OMA/Rem Koolhaas, Campanella (2008, 136) opined:

"If any of Beijing's new signature buildings has potential to become a city icon, this is it." It became a global icon. Both projects, unsurprisingly, feature prominently in contemporary scholarly and commercial literature on the city and on postcard sets of the "New Beijing." Thus, two global architectural icons, both by foreign starchitects, both ever identified with the spectacular success of the 2008 Olympics in the new globalizing Beijing, compete with each other to become the Eiffel Tower of Beijing. It would be remiss to conclude a discussion of UMP in China without reference to what Campanella (2008, chapter 9) terms "Theme Parks and the Landscapes of Consumption." These include a ski resort in Beijing, a joint venture of a Canadian refrigeration firm and the architecture department at Tsinghua University and legions of heritage theme parks (Splendid China, Folk Culture Villages, Window of the World in Shenzhen, etc.) and, of course, the South China Mall, the biggest mall in the world in its time. All this novelty does not preclude a massive building project of new historic districts from scratch, as in Dalian, with its own huge Bavarian castle designed for the best feng shui!

Megaprojects, Iconicity, and Displacement

Gellert and Lynch (2003, 15) are not the only commentators to make an explicit connection between Schumpeter's famous thesis of capitalism as "creative destruction" and the ubiquity of megaprojects. "Dams, roads, ports, urban developments, pipelines and petrochemical plants, mines and vast industrial plantations both reflect and instantiate the larger social projects of colonialism, development, and globalization. Megaprojects are spatially situated and inherently displacing" (ibid). UMP displace nature and people, and they succeed to the extent that they can turn the displacement they produce into an externality, a cost that has to be borne by the public purse for a supposed wider public good. Gellert and Lynch go on to argue that we should be asking how displacement is produced and who produces it before we tackle the question of how to reduce its ill effects. They conclude that megaprojects tend to be "creative" for the rich (the state apparatus and privileged communities). Everyone outside what they term "the biogeophysical landscape of displacement" tends to win, while everyone inside tends to lose, though new economic spaces and opportunities are also created. I would argue that members of the TCC and their local affiliates can be very innovative in creating enclaves that shield them and their families from the worst effects of UMP and in propagating the culture-ideology of consumerism on which new forms of global urbanity rest. Iconic buildings, most of which seem to win over the hearts and minds of an initially sceptical public, are a powerful tool in transmitting the consumerist values and practices that sustain capitalist globalization. The resistance to these values is often aimed directly at the icons, a point made forcibly by the Chinese sculptor Zhang Huan, his "Donkey", understood to be a symbol of the working class, literally shafting the iconic Jin Mao Tower, as illustrated in Sklair (2017, Figure 7.7).

It is important to distinguish between UMP in general and those directly connected with mega-events, notably Olympics and football World Cups, World Fairs, and other large-scale exhibitions. While there is considerable overlap, particularly with regard to infrastructure and transportation (for example, new highways and public transportation systems, upgrading of electronic communications, improved signage in English making non-Anglophone cities more friendly for international tourists), there is considerable controversy over the use to which actual buildings and spaces (especially sports facilities) are put after the event, their costs, and their contribution to the life of the city. Olympic legacies are mixed, with general agreement that the Olympics in Barcelona and Sydney were successfully integrated into urban regeneration; but the outcomes in Montreal and Athens, for example, were generally deemed to be failures. The maintenance costs of the Olympic Stadium in Beijing (affectionally known as the "Bird's Nest"), for example, have been estimated at around US$15 million a year but so far it seems unlikely that it will ever earn its keep despite its naming as the venue for the Winter Olympics in February 2022. Issues of cost are already being passionately debated over the World Cup in South Africa in 2010 and the London Olympics in 2012. On the plus side in Beijing there were substantial job creation and knock-on effects (for example in the urban megaproject for the neighbouring city of Tianjin-Bohai), improvements to local infrastructure and services, and a genuine green building and development policy. Also part of the legacy of UMP and mega-events are the iconic buildings. Again, Beijing provides a telling example. The Olympic Green (where the Bird's Nest and Water Cube are located) is being turned into a commercial and cultural Zone, with underground shopping malls. Xin Ao Group, a property developer linked to local government in Beijing, is leading the development of this site, another homage to capitalist consumerist globalization as if another is needed in this city, but this may attract more business to the under-used Olympic stadium.

Globalization of UMP

From further afield, in her analysis of three rather different UMP (Atlantic Yards, Brooklyn, Thames Gateway, (London), and the Amsterdam Southeast development, Susan Fainstein (2008, 773–774) quotes the opinion of the New York Regional Plan Association that the Atlantic Yards project was ideal for mixed-use redevelopment of the old railway site, and through its "Manhattanization" effect "it can and should be a process that successfully integrates large iconic buildings with their surroundings and provides benefits that compensate for the increased congestion, noise and visual impacts that accompany these projects". Her conclusion is that to succeed, UMP need vast public subsidies for infrastructure – thus luxury homes and hotels, big office towers, and shopping malls are likely to displace affordable housing and jobs, in the United States and Europe and, as we have seen, in China. A rather smaller but no less significant UMP from the northeast of England provides another example of the potential of iconic architecture. "The, as yet unproven, success of NewcastleGatehead [NG] Quayside is founded upon a massive financial investment in iconic projects" (Miles 2005, 913). Here, culture-led regeneration was deemed problematic insofar as it failed to connect sufficiently with local identities and community. In NG the local councils funded a Cultural Investments and Strategic Impact Research project and, Miles reports, it "is beginning to indicate that iconic projects can serve a significant ideological function," at least if at the right place in the right time, as far as they play a key role in not simply reflecting a sense of local identity but in actually rearticulating and reconfiguring that identity in complex and paradoxical ways (ibid., 916). In NG Quayside, Miles argues, three relatively inexpensive iconic architecture projects, the Baltic Contemporary Art Gallery (£46 million pounds), Sage Gateshead Music Centre (by Foster, £70 million) and Gateshead Millennium Bridge (£22 million), are beginning to connect the architecture to the cultural lives of social groups in the area in a meaningful way. While many critics scathingly portray iconic cultural regeneration in rather static terms, the NewcastleGatehead Quayside example suggests that there are more dynamic processes at work when UMP offer genuinely iconic architecture for all to use, appreciate, and enjoy.

Let me end where many megaprojects begin, with another (some might say, desperate) attempt to rescue a blighted city district with a globalizing UPM. Rotterdam Central is an UMP around the rather seedy Central Station district of the city. It is currently being promoted and explained by display boards in the railway station. The keywords of the design plan are transparency and clarity, meaning in this case glass with wood as a "window on the city," a nod in the direction of sustainability. It is based on the concept of smart economy that combines medical sciences, creative industries, and tourism, serviced by high-speed rail links (Rotterdam is already connected to the London–Paris Eurostar system via a high-speed train from Brussels to Amsterdam). A modest UMP, about £3 billion in private investment, has been secured for a series of landmark (read iconic) buildings, with the old post office becoming a mega shopping mall. The new Central District is meant as a "calling card" for the city to the region, to the country, and to Europe as a whole (again modestly portraying continental rather than globalizing ambitions). The new Rotterdam city map for tourists specifically identifies 17 architectural attractions, with a new icon replacing the 1950s style telecom tower. The map now features leisure drinkers by the new Calatrava-style Erasmus bridge, the iconic symbol of trendy Rotterdam, on its cover (Sklair 2017, Figure 1.10). From the inspiration of the *grands projets* in Paris, small cities in small countries in Europe, through the boroughs of New York, to Shenzhen, Shanghai, and Beijing, the four fractions of the TCC in various combinations are building UMP anchored with iconic buildings at various scales to transform cities all over the world. Nevertheless, some of these are remarkable architectural icons and many could be mobilized to serve other, more noble and genuinely pleasurable ends, but for this to be possible we would need to move beyond capitalist globalization and release what may be termed the emancipatory potential of generic globalization (see Sklair 2009b). In this case, most of the negative and unjust displacement effects of UMP might be avoided.

Second Thoughts

Since I wrote this essay, about ten years ago, I have begun to have increasingly second thoughts about the viability of big cities, especially megacities. A recent PhD dissertation from Columbia University in New York, mobilizes the concept of "value capture" to explain in graphic detail who benefits and who loses from the Urban Megaproject at Hudson Yards in that great city (Petretta 2020). This case study makes sobering reading, complementing the concluding chapter of my book, "Beleaguered City, Beleaguered Planet" (chapter 12 below) in which I attempt to come to some sort of conclusion, so the whole of chapter 12 serves as a summing up of these second thoughts. They are mainly about the impact of iconic architecture on city life in the "perfect storm" presented by the Anthropocene and the Coronavirus pandemic and the contentious idea of "administrative evil".

References

Abramson, D. B. (2008) Haussmann and Le Corbusier in China: Land control and the design of streets in urban redevelopment. *Journal of Urban Design* 13/2: 231–256.

Arkaraprasertkul, N. (2008) Politicization and the rhetoric of Shanghai urban form. *Footprints: Journal of Delft School of Design* 2: 43–52.

Arkaraprasertkul, N. (2013) Traditionalism as a Way of Life: The sense of home in Shanghai's Alleyways. *Harvard Asia Quarterly* 15/3-4: 15-25.

Bracken, G. (2009). Something rich and strange. In J. Bolchover & J. Solomon, eds, *Sustain and develop*. New York: Wakefield Press, pp. 191–200.

Broudehoux, A.-M. (2004) *The making and selling of post-Mao Beijing*. London: Routledge.

Campanella, T. (2008) *The concrete dragon*. New York, NY: Princeton University Press.

Carmona, M. (2006) Designing mega-projects in Hong Kong: Reflections from an academic accomplice. *Journal of Urban Design* 11/1: 105–124.

Cartier, C. (2001) *Globalizing South China*. Oxford: Blackwell.

Cartier, C. (2002) Transnational urbanism in the reform-era Chinese city: Landscapes from Shenzhen. *Urban Studies* 399: 1513–1532.

Chaslin, F. (1985) *Les Paris de Francis Mitterrand: histoire des grands projets architecturaux*. Paris: Gallimard.

Chung, C.J., Inaba, J., Koolhaas, R., & Leong, S.T. (2001) *Great leap forward*. Cambridge, MA: Harvard Design School.

Demeyer, P. (1996) *La Défense: Guide to the architecture*. Courbevoie: EPAD Communication Department.

Diaz, O.F. & Fainstein, S. (2008) The new mega-projects: Genesis and impacts. *International Journal of Urban and Regional Research* 32/4: 759–767.

Ellis, C. (1986) Mitterand's 2,500m Paris. *Blueprint* (March): 11–16.

Fainstein, S. (2008) Mega-projects in New York, London and Amsterdam. *International Journal of Urban and Regional Research* 32/4: 768–783.

Fierro, A. (2003) *The glass state: The technology of the spectacle. Paris, 1981–1998*. Cambridge, MA: MIT press.

Gellert, P.K., & Lynch, B.D. (2003) Mega-projects as displacements. *International Social Science Journal.*75/175: 15–25.

Jackson, M., & Dora, V.D (2009) "Dreams so big only the sea can hold them": Manmade islands as anxious spaces, cultural icons, and traveling visions. *Environment and Planning A* 41: 2086–2104.

King, A. (2004) *Spaces of global cultures: Architecture, urbanism, identity.* London: Routledge.

Krupar, S. R. (2008) Shanghaiing the future: A de-tour of the Shanghai Urban planning exhibition hall. *Public Culture* 20/2: 307–320.

Liauw, L. (2009) Urbanization of post-Olympic Beijing. In J. Bolchover & J. Solomon, eds., *Sustain and develop*. New York: Wakefield Press, pp. 215–221.

Lin, Z.-J. (2007) From megastructures to megalopolis: Formation and transformation of megaprojects in Tokyo Bay. *Journal of Urban Design* 12/1: 73–92.

Lu, Y., & Li, D. (2008) Shanghai: Cosmopolitanism as identity? In P. Herrie & E. Wegerhoff, eds, *Architecture and identity*. Berlin: Lit/Habitat, pp. 335–346.

Luste Boulbina, S., Riboud, M., & Riboud, A. (2007) *Grand travaux a Paris, 1981–1995*. Paris: La Dispute.

Marshall, R. (2003) *Emerging urbanity: Global urban projects in the Asia Pacific Rim*. London: Spon Press.

Mefti, D., & Grouard, S. (1991) *1981–1991: les grands travaux sous Francois Mitterrand*. Paris: Editions du Rocher.

Miles, S. (2005) 'Our Tyne': Iconic regeneration and the revitalisation of identity in Newcastle Gateshead. *Urban Studies* 42/5–6: 913–926.

Olds, K. (2001) *Globalization and urban change: Capital, culture, and Pacific rim mega-projects*. Oxford: Oxford University Press.

Petretta, D.L. (2020) *The Political Economy of Value Capture: How the Financialization of Hudson Yards Created a Private Rail Line for the Rich*. PhD dissertation, Columbia University. Proquest 28149902.

Ponzini, D., & Nastasi, N. (2011). *Starchitecture: Scenes, actors and spectacles in contemporary cities*. Turin: Allemandi.

Ren Xuefei (2011). *Building globalization: Transnational Architectural Production in Urban China*. Chicago: University of Chicago Press.

Santamaria, G., ed. (2013) *Urban Megaprojects: A Worldwide View*. Bingley: Emerald.

Shatkin, G. (2008) The city and the bottom line: Urban mega-projects and the privatization of planning in Southeast Asia. *Environment and Planning A* 40/2: 383–401.

Trilling, J. (1983) Paris: Architecture as politics. *Atlantic Monthly* 252 (October): 26–27, 30–35.

van Leeuwen, T. (1988). *The Skyward Trend of Thought: The Metaphysics of the American Skyscraper*. Cambridge, MA: MIT Press.

Vivant, E. (2010) The (re)Making of Paris as a Bohemian place? *Progress in Planning* 74: 107–152.

Vivant, E. (2011) Who brands whom? The role of local authorities in the branching of art museums. *Town Planning Review* 81/1: 99–115.

Winterbourne, E. (1995) Architecture and the politics of culture in Mitterand's France. *Architectural Design* 65/3–4: 24–29.

Wu, H. (1991) Tiananmen square: A political history of monuments. *Representations* 35: 84–117.

Zhang, T. (2002) Urban development and a socialist pro-growth coalition in Shanghai. *Urban Affairs Review* 37/4: 475–499.

Zhu, J. (2009) *Architecture of modern China: A historical critique*. London: Routledge.

CHAPTER 10

(2019) THE CORPORATE CAPTURE OF SUSTAINABLE DEVELOPMENT AND ITS TRANSFORMATION INTO A "GOOD ANTHROPOCENE" HISTORICAL BLOC. *CIVITAS* (PORTO ALEGRE, BRAZIL) 19/2: 296-314. [OPEN ACCESS]

Preamble

In 2019 I was totally engrossed in the book I was editing on how the print media "neutralize" the risks of the Anthropocene. Scanning media coverage of the Anthropocene from newspapers and magazines all over the world it began to strike me that the influential idea of "sustainable development" that emerged in the 1980s as a response to environmental issues was rapidly being appropriated by powerful forces in Big Business, big government, and the United Nations system. I had previously labelled this process "The corporate capture of sustainable development" and, in this more recent essay, I argued that something similar was happening with the "good" Anthropocene.

Abstract

In the nineteen 1990s I attempted to highlight the growing connections between the transnational capitalist class (TCC) and global environmental organizations. This research suggested some parallels between the TCC and its culture-ideology of consumerism, and emerging transnational environmental elites and their culture-ideology of corporate environmentalism (Sklair 1994). These parallels can be summed up by the labels "green consumerism" and "greenwashing" (Greer & Bruno 1996), ideas that fed directly into my work on global system theory and specifically the damaging effects of capitalist globalization. The major consequences of this line of thought are that, in my view, the system is fatally compromised by two contradictions inherent in capitalism: the class polarization crisis and the crisis of ecological unsustainability. This paper focuses on the latter crisis.

Capitalism and the Ecological Crisis

My book *The transnational capitalist class* devoted a chapter to the structure of the emerging but at that time not much researched phenomenon of capitalist globalization. I conceptualized the ecological crisis as the corporate capture of sustainable development and (following Gramsci) the creation of a sustainable development historical bloc. Boothman (2017) provides a penetrating analysis of the concept of historical bloc, its relationship with Gramsci's theorization of hegemony, and its power as a way of re-activating the more static Marxist versions of base and superstructure.

In my view, the relationships between the global capitalist and the global environmentalist systems can be most fruitfully researched in terms of coalitions that cluster around points along a continuum, rather than two mutually contradictory and irreconcilably opposed sets of social forces or historical blocs. The struggle over the environment began to emerge in the 1960s around the ownership, redefinition and effective monopoly of the public appropriation of what would later be called sustainable development. No doubt, good arguments could be made that ideas like sustainable development are as old as the hills, but my point is that corporate interest in the sustainability of our relations to the planet began seriously in the 1960s, probably provoked by Rachel Carson's ground-breaking *Silent Spring*, first serialized in the *New Yorker* and then published as a book in 1962. The misconceived attempts to discredit it by major corporations in the United States backfired spectacularly giving plenty of opportunity for Carson and her supporters to broadcast her message on environmental crisis in the mass media. She is widely credited with providing the impetus for the rapid growth of the environmental movement in the United States and elsewhere (Matthiessen 2007). The book was an international best-seller, with British, French, German, Italian, Danish, Swedish, Norwegian, Finnish, Dutch, Spanish, Brazilian, Japanese, Icelandic, Portuguese, Hebrew, and Yugoslavian editions. It is not so well known that Rachael Carson had previously published several equally successful popular science books on marine biology, notably *The Sea around Us*, translated into even more languages in the 1950s and 1960s. Al Gore (among many others) cites her as an inspiration (Matthiessen 2007, 63-78). The success of *Silent Spring* and the bad publicity it generated for major globalizing corporations in the United

States starkly illustrated the urgent need for a more adequate corporate response to environmental issues. The connections between the leading institutions of global capitalism and global environmentalism grew dramatically in the 1980s and 1990s. In the world of Big Business these connections straddled the spectrum from direct and indirect corporate sponsorship of transnational environmental organizations (TEOs) to downright hostility and occasional violence between the parties and their allies (Rowell 1996, Schmidheiny 1992, Willums 1990). A first approximation of TEOs would include those in and around the UN system, notably the United Nations Environment Programme, and Commission (and subsequently Division) on Sustainable Development, and the Global Environmental Facility; and NGOs that work like corporations, notably the World Conservation Union, WorldWide Fund for Nature (WWF), Environmental Defense Fund, Nature Conservancy, and the World Resources Institute. The major independent and left-leaning environmental NGOs, notably Friends of the Earth and Greenpeace, which are mainly small and usually donor funded, nevertheless have been known to accept money and resources from green business. The National Wildlife Federation, National Audubon Society, and Sierra Club, all based in the USA, are among the largest environmental organizations in the world. Although they are not global as such, they all have global agendas. Naomi Klein (2014, chapter 6) provides a devastating account of what she calls "The Disastrous Merger of Big Business and Big Green", documenting the gradual move to corporate environmentalism of many environmental NGOs. To this list must be added the myriad of smaller and usually specific issue-oriented organizations that mushroomed around the Brundtland Report and the UN Conference on Environment and Development in Rio in 1992, and its aftermath. While these are not necessarily all global, many of them are linked in a variety of ways to the global environmentalist network.

Corporate Environmentalism

The Brundtland Report of 1987 has been widely criticized, Bernstein (2001) provides a meticulously researched account of these processes, notably on the marginalization of environmental scientists. However, what Bernstein calls "liberal environmentalism" is more appropriately termed "corporate environmentalism", signifying some ideological differences. In my view the Brundtland Report can be considered the start of the process of institutionalization of the sustainable development historical bloc at the global level. Corporate environmentalism has been the main weapon of those working for the global capitalist system to establish ownership of sustainable development and with it, bring the agents and agencies of global environmentalism over to its ways of thinking and doing. There is ample evidence to suggest that the four fractions of the transnational capitalist class (corporate, political, professional, consumerist) began to organize what I have conceptualized as the sustainable development historical bloc in the second half of the twentieth century (see Sklair 2001, chapter 7 and chapter notes for sources). The main ideological and practical tasks of the members of this bloc are to deflect attention from the notion of a singular ecological crisis that would call the whole process of capitalist production and consumption into serious question. Replacing the idea of a singular ecological crisis would be the idea that what we face is a series of manageable relatively unrelated environmental challenges. Within this framework, sustainable development can be achieved piecemeal by meeting all these separate challenges as they arise. On the other side of the argument are those within global environmentalism who cling to the idea of an impending singular ecological crisis and argue that it can only be averted by taking action to change the "system as a whole" (usually but not always conceived as the global capitalist system). I use the rather vague terms "ecological crisis" and "environmental crisis" in a purely descriptive sense with no underlying theoretical intention, simply to indicate the problems that sustainable development, corporate environmentalism, and various Anthropocene narratives are designed to combat.

Alongside these corporate initiatives, the publication of *Limits to Growth* (LtG), a report sponsored by the Club of Rome and written by a project team at MIT (Meadows et al. 1972) indicated that establishment opinion was also beginning to turn towards a more serious appraisal of the relationship between unlimited growth (the dominant ideology of both capitalist and communist systems) and impending environmental crisis. LtG reputedly sold 30 million copies, has been translated into at least 30 languages and is certainly one of the best-selling scholarly books ever on the environment. The term "sustainable" occurs a few times in LtG, "development" many more times, but there is no mention of "sustainable development" for which we have to wait until Brundtland in 1987. "Climate" merits six mentions "warming" only one, but neither "climate change" nor "global warming" makes an appearance. Given the environmental vocabulary at the time it is even more impressive that LtG had such an impact.

The Club of Rome is an organization of the great and the good (UN luminaries, former heads of states and other political notables, progressive corporate leaders, philanthropists, scientists of various types, and educators). Citing the traumatic events of 1968 (The Great Divide), as the end of the post-war boom gave way to a period of global political unrest, economic uncertainty, and environmental tensions, the Club of Rome took it upon itself to address the "Predicament of Mankind". This was accomplished under three general rubrics namely that the problems were global, that they were long-term, and that they could best be addressed as a "world problematique" (indicating that limits to growth was the first genuine problem that everyone in the world shared and thus had to be dealt with collectively). Unsurprisingly, the book was welcomed by environmentalists and widely discussed in the print and broadcast media. Though the authors vigorously denied that they were advocating a zero-growth economy, this was the message that many on the right took from the book, and it was roundly condemned and ridiculed by many capitalist ideologues. An update in 1992 had very little impact, being swamped by the umbrella idea of sustainable development. The Club of Rome has published many follow-up studies and continues to organize many events. Under the title "The Anthropocene and the Club of Rome", the University of Gastronomic Sciences at Pollenzo (Italy) in 2017 hosted a talk by Roberto Peccei, Professor Emeritus of Theory of Elementary Particles, Astroparticle Physics, and Phenomenology (sic) at the University of California Los Angeles, and vice president of the Club of Rome. Here we learn: "Prof. Peccei, who is the son of Aurelio Peccei, the founder of the Club of Rome, will discuss what steps mankind must take to survive the Anthropocene. In this regard, a variety of issues will be considered, including the role of the UN Sustainable Development Goals, the transition to a renewable energy economy, decoupling of resources use from well-being, a circular economy, and the Paris Climate agreement. The conference will include some comments on the impact that the Trump Administration may have on the sustainability agenda for our planet" (available at https://www.unisg.it/en/ press-office/Anthropocene-club-of-rome-conference-pollenzo/). As we shall see below, Professor Peccei appears to have been recruited to the "good" Anthropocene cause which, for all its merits, is where the "limits to growth" argument, like sustainable development, leads us back to capitalist globalization.

The rise of ecological modernization theory, a sociological rationale for the greening of business and industry, implicitly recognized the corporate capture of sustainable development insofar as it saw the environmentally destructive effect of unrestrained capitalism as something that could be managed (even leveraged to bring in more profit) by a more enlightened capitalism (Hajer 1995). Given the widely perceived inadequacies of state regulation, the view that the corporations should take more responsibility for managing the environment gained ground. Two of my PhD students published valuable books on the various dimensions of ecological modernization and its application with case studies of the Body Shop and Ben & Jerry's (Robbins 2001) and ARCO chemical company and Shell (Holzer 2010). Not only industries but international organizations of various types took it upon themselves to "do something" about the environment. The European Community introduced a community-wide environmental auditing scheme in 1993 and the World Bank had been discussing the environmental aspects of their lending since the 1970s, with controversial results (Rich 1994). Like so many references from my original articles, this reference is over 20 years old, but its central arguments still resonate. The Environmental Committee of the OECD began to discuss these issues in the early 1980s, shortly after the Bhopal disaster (see Hanna 2005 & 2017). Since 1984, there have been many more "Bhopals", regularly updated on the internet. The Committee proposed that an environmental management chapter be added to the OECD (voluntary) Guidelines for Multinational Enterprises, first introduced in 1976. The proposal was strongly supported by the governments of the OECD, with the exception of the UK (the USA offered only lukewarm support). I am not suggesting that major corporations and smaller businesses all round the world willfully ignored the evidence piling up that a global environmental crisis was looming or had arrived. In the course of my research for *The transnational capitalist class* I interviewed many corporate environmental executives and some green business groups (Sklair 2001, chapter 7 and Appendix 1). In most cases my impression was that these men and women were genuinely concerned about environmental issues but that the corporations they worked for were driven by the bottom lines of profits and short-term stock market pressures. A dialectic of corporate environmentalism seemed to be at work. When all was going well, the environment was low priority, but when environmental crises emerged (for example, excessive pollution, toxic waste spills, sweatshop factory fires, illegal resource extractions) that could taint the reputation of the company, the environment became high priority and senior executives lined up to beg forgiveness and proclaim green credentials, as documented by Holzer (2010) in his finely theorized case studies of Shell and other major corporations. Twenty years on, nothing much has changed, apart from, for example, the digital sophistication now available for motor manufacturers to smuggle into their vehicles software that conceals toxic levels of emissions. Similar arguments hold for researchers who provide scientific support of various kinds to bolster corporate environmentalism and sustainable development. Progressive-minded corporate employees or those working on corporate-funded projects in universities and other institutions may genuinely believe that there is no alternative to global capitalism and that the best they can do is try to mitigate the worst effects of the environmental crisis. If you cannot exit the system, at least you can try to improve it. These are people on the fringes of the sustainable development historic bloc, and their expertise can be helpful to those who do work to create alternatives.

Enter the Anthropocene

While still working on the TCC, in 2016 I read a book that dramatically changed my research priorities. *Facing the Anthropocene* (Angus 2015) was one of the first attempts to systematically connect the science of the Anthropocene with the political economy in which it had evolved. Angus, the editor of an online journal *Climate & Capitalism*, is a leading exponent of ecosocialism, the theory that the only way to save the planet and human life on it is through socialist revolution. How, then, have the debates around the Anthropocene changed the way we understand sustainable development and ecological modernisation? Angus' book not only introduced me to the term Anthropocene which, like millions of others I had probably read in passing and forgotten about, but also to a body of literature which sent me back to ecological unsustainability and forward to Earth System science. This relatively new paradigm puts the various eco-systems of our home planet (climate, oceans, soils, forests, the biosphere which now includes humans) into global perspective. While the Anthropocene is primarily a geological concept, large social science and humanities literatures (plus many imaginative inputs from creative artists) have grown up around it, prompting some to label it the 'Anthropo-scene' (Lorimer 2015, Jagodzinski, ed. 2018, Sklair 2020, and 2021, ed., Part three).

The explanation of how the relatively obscure idea of the Anthropocene has captured the imagination of large numbers of natural and social scientists, humanities scholars, and creative artists can be found in the efforts of the Anthropocene Working Group (AWG), which was established in 2009 to prepare the scientific community and the general public for the theoretical and practical challenges that lay ahead (Zalasiewicz & Waters, et al. 2017, Zalasiewicz et al. 2019). While others had used the term or variations of it in the 1980s and even before (see Ellis 2018, chapter 1), the credit for popularizing it around the year 2000 usually goes to the Nobel Prize-winning atmospheric chemist Paul Crutzen (having a Nobel prize-winner for a figurehead is clearly a plus for any scientific enterprise). The chairman of the AWG was Jan Zalasiewicz, Professor of Paleobiology at the University of Leicester who, through his writing, media outreach, and promotional skills, has done as much as anyone to disseminate the idea of the Anthropocene in scientific, scholarly, and cultural spheres. The name Anthropocene is at time of writing still waiting for acceptance by the International Commission on Stratigraphy into the official nomenclature as a geological epoch. This is a long drawn-out process and not all Earth scientists support the application by the AWG that the Holocene epoch should be brought to an end and replaced by the Anthropocene, widely referred to as the "Age of Man", the point being that in the Anthropocene humans have become a dominant geologic force, and that this may have catastrophic effects on the Earth system as a whole, as the various eco-systems on which human life depend become more and more compromised. Responses to these risks vary dramatically within the scientific community, as they do for social scientists, humanities scholars, and creative artists.

Here I will argue that we can fruitfully analyze one prominent trend in Anthropocene studies in terms of the creation of a "good Anthropocene" historical bloc as a direct successor of the corporate capture of sustainable development. In this essay I propose the term "critical Anthropocene narrative" one of a large number of names, for example, good, bad, and ugly Anthropocenes (Dalby 2016). The "critical Anthropocene narrative" highlights the dangers posed by the Anthropocene and the need for radical systems change entailing the end of capitalism and the hierarchic state (hierarchic is superfluous in my view as all states are bound to be hierarchic). The critical Anthropocene narrative stands in radical opposition to the "good Anthropocene" narrative, a corporate-sponsored effort to reinforce the message of the sustainable development historical bloc that preceded it. The widespread use of the slogan "Welcome to the Anthropocene" (sometimes intended ironically, sometimes not) acts as an enigmatic signifier, sending contradictory messages on complex scientific, personal, and political questions but, I would suggest, its predominant effect is much more consistent with "good Anthropocene" rather than critical Anthropocene narratives. This is exemplified in the brutally critical analysis of a major Anthropocene exhibition in Germany (Jørgensen & Jørgensen 2016). I interpret the widespread presence of "Welcome to the Anthropocene" and similarly comforting messages in the scholarly literature as reassurance narratives (Sklair, ed. 2021, especially pp.26-28).

The Anthropocene and UN Sustainable Development Goals

From my version of a critical Anthropocene perspective, sustainable development and the subsequent UN Sustainable Development Goals approach are based on a series of fallacies. The first is that the concept of the Anthropocentric approach itself (sustainability for people and societies, despite the rhetoric, taking precedence over sustainability for the planet) is potentially catastrophic. To put it simply, if our activities continue to destroy the eco-systems on which human survival depends humanity cannot survive, as argued in many sober assessments of the science that lies behind this statement (see, for example, Ceballos et al. 2017, Chi Xu et al. 2020). In much Anthropocene discourse, sustainability is being replaced with the slightly more critical idea of resilience, which is not so closely embedded in defending the status quo. As Naomi Klein wisely says, "a more appropriate term might be 'regenerative'. Because resilience—though certainly one of nature's greatest gifts—is a passive process, implying the ability to absorb blows and get back up. Regeneration, on the other hand, is active: we become full participants in the process of maximizing life's creativity" (Klein 2014, 447). This is a thought that might make profit-driven corporations nervous while at the same time giving inspiration to the rest of us as the Anthropocene grinds inexorably on. However, no-one has as yet resolved the central dilemma of how to help the poorest people in every part of the world out of poverty into a decent standard of living without increasing ecological anthropogenic damage. The focus of much sustainable development literature on the paradox of China where millions "have been lifted out of poverty" in the rhetoric of top-down growth, resulting in the emergence of a full-blown culture-ideology of consumerism, brings this dilemma into sharp focus, as Klein (2014) frequently notes. Marinelli (2018) skillfully connects sustainable development, the Anthropocene, and ecological civilization/progress via a critical analysis of environmental policies in China, a key if not entirely reliable link in the chain of efforts to protect the planet.

The second fallacy embedded in the UNSDG is the idea that "sustainable consumption" and "sustainable production" are essentially two sides of the same coin. The real issue I would argue is not "sustaining" production and consumption but reducing them absolutely which would minimize their destructive effects on all eco-systems and the Earth System as a whole. This raises the contentious issue of degrowth, which I discuss below. In addition, ecologists wedded to sustainable development argue that "meeting needs", "improving quality of life", and "improving environmental performance" are parts of the solution to the ecological crisis. They are not. They are parts of the problem, particularly in terms of distinguishing real from artificial needs and establishing universal norms for an ecologically sound quality of life. Two prominent theorists in the relations between science and politics, Isabelle Stengers and Bruno Latour, throw some light on the unenviable choices with which even the most responsible environmental leaders of major corporations, governments, and journalists have to grapple. Stengers (2015) makes the powerful argument that scientists were forced to go public on the potential risks of the Anthropocene before all the scientific results were fully established. Waiting for more definitive evidence might be catastrophic in the long-term when the terrible price of inaction or inadequate action might eventually have to be paid in full (for a chilling version of this argument in literature see the dystopian science fiction novel *The Collapse of Western Civilization* by two distinguished historians of science (Oreskes & Conway 2014).

Climate-change deniers are always seeking opportunities to keep the debate going around the questions of whether the risks actually are genuine. Those trying to resolve the new problems of the Anthropocene as well as those still struggling with the contradictions of sustainable development fell, though not very neatly, into two opposing camps, namely merchants of fear (those who accept the dangers of the Anthropocene) or merchants of doubt (usually characterized as climate change deniers). For Latour, Anthropocene politics "is not a rational debate ... [it is] incredibly easy to make *two sides* emerge even when there is only one" (Latour 2015, 147). The merchants of fear and various types of radical ecologists are a small minority, even in the environmental movement. The merchants of fear/merchants of doubt frame derives from an influential book which goes far beyond the ecological field (Oreskes & Conway 2010).

The claim that there is a contradiction between the growth obsession of global capitalist development and global survival appears to have *prima facie* plausibility. If this is indeed the case, then both the ongoing corporate version of sustainable development and the emerging corporate ideology of the "good Anthropocene" are fatally flawed. The transformation of the green vanguard of global capitalism from dry to shallow environmentalism signaled the fact that some ecological crisis messages were getting through to the transnational capitalist class and that serious attention was beginning to be paid to programmes to take the crisis out of the environment. Clearly, the dominant agents in the global capitalist system had no option but to believe and act as if the contradiction between global capitalism and sustainable development could be resolved by a combination of economic-technological, political, and culture-ideology means. Variations on this perspective appear in "good Anthropocene" manifestos as ecomodernism (the Anthropocene equivalent of ecological modernization), geo-engineering, and radical conservation. The Breakthrough Institute is probably the leading proponent of these strategies to ensure a "good Anthropocene" (https://thebreakthrough.org/) but it also has support from leading scientific institutions, notably the Stockholm Resilience Centre from where Rockström and his colleagues developed the important concept of "planetary boundaries" (Rockström et al. 2009). This influential article concludes: "The evidence so far suggests that, as long as the thresholds are not crossed, humanity has the freedom to pursue long-term social and economic development". The mood grows more pessimistic year by year.

The Anthropocene and the other -cenes

The focus on the human, nonhuman, and posthuman condition in social science and humanities which dominates Anthropo-scene scholarship, fascinating as it is intellectually, may also be interpreted as a diversion from the central issue of human and planetary survival in the Anthropocene. The same might also be said of the enormous amount of attention paid by Earth scientists (and, to a lesser degree, social scientists, humanities scholars, and the media) to alternative starting dates for the Anthropocene, scientifically important but nevertheless to some extent a distraction. It is not so easy to decide how to interpret the debate that has arisen between those anti-capitalist thinkers who take the radical Anthropocene position and those who argue that the Anthropocene should be replaced by the Capitalocene or some other label. Chwałczyk (2020) identifies 80-90 different versions of the Anthropocene. So far, the Capitalocene seems to be the most popular in academic circles. The two most influential proponents of the Capitalocene as the most appropriate name for the current geological epoch are the historian of fossil capitalism, Andreas Malm (2016) and the sociologist Jason Moore (2016). There is no denying the brilliance and erudition of Malm's account of how fossil fuels created a new era of capitalist production relations, displacing water power and much else besides, but these attributes do not in themselves prove that the Capitalocene is a more appropriate label than the Anthropocene for our present dilemma. Moore's collection, while full of interesting ideas, seems to me to illustrate that the debate is more a battle for discursive territory between factions of the left than a useful way forward, intellectually or politically. John Bellamy Forster offers a balanced discussion of Marxism in the Anthropocene and how the left has dealt with ecological issues more generally. Foster (2016) details his own contributions, his differences with Moore over a materialist dialectic of nature and society, and much else besides.

It is important to remember that the Anthropocene is a geological concept and there are several historical explanations of it and consequences to be drawn from it. While it is clearly correct to argue that capitalism as a system is most directly responsible for the environmental crisis (polling suggests that most people around the world accept this despite the noise generated by relatively small groups of deniers and sceptics), it is also true that the Anthropocene is inclusive of the human enterprise, we are mostly all complicit via the culture-ideology of consumerism. Rebranding the Anthropocene as the Capitalocene conveniently lets anti-capitalists off the hook to fly around the world critiquing capitalism and making our sometimes ecologically destructive consumer choices. As Donna Haraway argues (in her original though somewhat ambivalent contribution to the Moore collection) "in so far as the Capitalocene is told in the idiom of fundamentalist Marxism, with all its trappings of Modernity, Progress, and History, that term is subject to the same or fiercer criticism [as the concept of the Anthropocene itself]. The stories of the Anthropocene and the Capitalocene teeter constantly on the brink of becoming much Too Big [sic]" (Haraway 2016, 53-4, see also her note 42, on page 72). And, it must be added, the history of communist, fascist, social democratic, and other regimes suggest that most systems are just as bad. None of them can cope satisfactorily with the multi-faceted problem of poverty and the ravages of the growth imperative. However, Haraway's "Too Big" does suggest that the problem of scale, all the way from small communities to the planetary level, deserves more attention than it currently receives.

Back to Capitalism

There are a great many interesting contributions to debates around the capacity of capitalism to deal with ecological crisis, and some suggestions as to how we could mobilize to deal with the dangers of the Anthropocene. For example, the authors of a theory of climate capitalism argue: "to propose to ban all further coal and oil use, as some have done, is both unrealistic and deeply problematic. The use of these fuels is currently so widespread that simply to ban them would cause economic growth to collapse. And a lack of growth is something that the capitalist system in which we live simply cannot tolerate – it would collapse as a system. So the challenge of climate change means, in effect, either abandoning capitalism, or seeking to find a way for it to grow while gradually replacing coal, oil and gas" (Newell & Paterson 2010, 9). They, somewhat reluctantly, chose the latter option, hoping that as corporations realize that reducing reliance on fossil fuels might be profitable, they might be more inclined to change their business models. This analysis appears very reasonable though on further examination its inbuilt contradiction becomes obvious. Newell and Paterson brilliantly deconstruct the problems involved in exiting from a fossil fuel economy while at the same time continuing to live much as we are doing already: how do you persuade capitalists and those who currently depend upon them for their livelihoods to change? While there are definite movements in the corporate world in the direction of replacing fossil fuels with renewables, the fact that all renewables have their own ecological costs, though these are usually less than those of fossil fuels, is rarely factored in. Hornborg, et al. (2019) provide an excellent example of this in their research on "free solar power" in Cuba. Debates flow back and forward between those advocating a zero-carbon economy, for example the "Zero Carbon Britain 2030" programme of the progressive New Economic Foundation, and the transnational Transition Towns movement world-wide, and those advocating a low-carbon economy, details unspecified (for example, the Business Council for Sustainable Development). However, most of these are more or less noble aspirations with very little chance of implementation under present circumstances. The contradiction that Newell and Paterson cannot escape is that the only way to avoid the risk of potential disaster is to reduce our consumption of everything that uses up natural resources and this, as they imply, would be fatal for capitalism and, I would add, for the hierarchical state and all that goes with it. This raises the fundamental issue of degrowth as explained by D'Alisa et al. (2014) which, in my opinion, should be at the centre of all our thinking about sustainable development, ecomodernism, and the Anthropocene, good, bad, or critical. I think we can begin to see one way out of our present dilemma in Schumacher's book, *Small is Beautiful* (1973) which challenged many of the orthodoxies of capitalist and socialist economics, notably the obsession with endless growth (see also Keen 2021 on the "bad" economics of climate change). Schumacher was called a crank and his response to critics in a BBC radio programme was characteristically witty: "What's wrong with a crank? It's a small instrument, very simple, it does not involve great capital investment, it is a relatively non-violent technology, and it causes revolutions", for a priceless recording of this programme, fortunately preserved for digital posterity see http://www.bbc.co.uk/programmes/b079njxm.

Exiting Capitalism

Huge transnational corporations and huge corporate states, serviced by huge professional and consumer goods and services organizations are increasingly criticised for dominating the lives of people everywhere, so it seems obvious that smaller scale structures might work better and enable people to live happier and more fulfilling lives. My vision of an alternative, radical, progressive, non-capitalist globalization is based on networks of relatively small producer-consumer cooperatives co-operating at a variety of levels to accomplish a variety of societal tasks (discussed in chapter 7 above and in more detail in the next chapter) Why producer and consumer cooperatives? This, I would argue, is the only way for us to re-connect with nature, to create communities where everyone is responsible to a greater or lesser degree for all the necessities of life and a decent standard of living. To accomplish this, we need to move beyond hierarchy and the state and create forms of non-capitalist, non-exploitative, alternative globalizations in the sense that small-scale P-CCs can network globally through the internet or its successors, learn from each other and help each other on a global scale. This will necessitate a double strategy: first to slow down capitalism as will inevitably happen if P-CCs succeed in exiting the capitalist market in one sphere after another, in one place after another; and second to bring into existence a new mode of production based on different principles and mentalities. Maybe we could risk calling ways of thinking, writing, and especially doing that contributes to these ends, "anarching". In this sense successful "anarching" (in careful small steps and self-generating) is only possible in a genuinely democratic environment, itself a highly contentious idea.

This would have to begin with the production of food at the local level. Similar proposals in the past have been dismissed with the charge that it would represent a retreat into the new Middle Ages or new tribal communities, and so on. My answer to this is simple. The middle ages did not have the digital technology that P-CCs could call on, notably networking through the internet, ecologically sensitive and highly efficient food technologies, the possibilities of revolutionizing the production of machinery and tools opened up by alternative technologies, already being put into practice all over the world. The dystopian new tribes argument seems more powerful as we look around the world today but, as I have argued elsewhere (Sklair 2016), the creation of new mentalities through more empathetic biological and social parenting on which the whole project rests, would help turn the tribes from competitive, violent, and untrustworthy others into cooperating, peaceful, and trustworthy neighbours, near and far. This may sound absurd! However, as Albert Einstein said: "if at first the idea is not absurd, there is no hope for it". Einstein was not infallible, and he certainly encouraged radical thinking.

Second thoughts

Once again, my second thoughts about this essay are that I may have under-estimated the speed and intensity of the corporate capture not only of "sustainable development" but of the discourse around environmentalism as a whole. Shortly before this book was sent to the publisher I came across a new study of the role of public relations professionals and their clients in the construction of environmentalism in the USA based on a series of interviews with PR executives and information on their clients (Aronczyk & Espinoza 2022). Exposing the historical roots of corporate PR in the USA, the book clinically dissects the way in which the "environment" has been invented and communicated as a "strategic resource" in protecting the interests of corporate America. Of particular interest is the analysis of the concepts of "data philanthropy" and "shared value" facilitating corporate manipulation of Big Data, central to the UN Global Pulse and D4CA (Data for Climate Action) programmes, and the propagation of the over-optimistic UN Sustainable Development Goals (ibid., chapter 7). Aronczyk & Espinoza provide much valuable detail on the story of the American version of the corporate capture of sustainable development and its transformation into a "good Anthropocene" historical bloc. Though they do not use these terms their research appears to complement my analysis in this chapter.

The first part of the original essay tried to develop ideas from my research on environmental issues in the 1990s. In retrospect, I see now that I did not take seriously enough the rather alarmist prospect that that the crisis of ecological unsustainability was, very possibly, an existential crisis for humanity. As early as 2011 the journal *Nature* (arguably the most prestigious science journal in the world) had published a powerful multi-authored article, building on a large number of previous research projects from all over the world. Their argument was that the planet was already experiencing a Sixth Extinction event, about 90% of all known species were either extinct or heading in that direction (Barnosky, et al. 2011), although stopping short of predicting the extinction of humanity on Planet Earth. As my fellow authors and I demonstrated in our book on media coverage of the Anthropocene (Sklair ed., 2021) this was a prospect that the media (and probably the vast majority of the population of the world) preferred to ignore. My first publication on the Anthropocene was a review article entitled "Sleepwalking through the Anthropocene" (Sklair 2017); the book was subtitled "Neutralizing the Risk" and its concluding chapter has a section on "Theories of Anthropocene Inertia" (ibid, 253-5). I am no more optimistic now than I was then.

References

Angus, I. (2016) *Facing the Anthropocene: Fossil capitalism and the crisis of the earth system*. New York: Monthly Review Press.

Aronczyk, M. & Espinoza, M.I. (2022) *A Strategic Nature: Public Relations and the Politics of American Environmentalism*. New York: Oxford University Press.

Barnosky, A.D., et al. (2011) Has the earth's sixth mass extinction already arrived? *Nature* 471: 51–57.

Bernstein, S. (2001) *The compromise of liberal environmentalism*. New York: Columbia University Press.

Boothman, D. (2017) Gramsci's Historical Bloc: Structure, Hegemony and. Dialectical Interactions. *Movimento* 4/6: 1-20.

Ceballos, G., Ehrlich, P., & Dirzo, R. (2017) Biological annihilation via the ongoing sixth mass extinction signaled by vertebrate population losses and declines. *PNAS*. www.pnas.org/cgi/doi/10.1073/pnas.1704949114.

Chwałczyk, F. (2020) Around the Anthropocene in eighty names-Considering the Urbanocene proposition. *Sustainability*. 12/11:44-58.

Dalby, S. (2016). Framing the Anthropocene: the good, the bad and the ugly. *The Anthropocene Review* 2/2: 102-106.

D'Alisa, G., Demaria, F., & Kallis. G., eds. (2014) *Degrowth: A Vocabulary for a New Era*. London: Routledge.

Ellis, E. (2018) *Anthropocene: A very short introduction*. Oxford: Oxford University Press.

Foster, J.B. (2016) Marxism in the Anthropocene: Dialectical Rifts on the Left. *International Critical Thought* 6/3: 393-421.

Gills, B. & Morgan, J. (2021) No More Excuses! Why the Climate and Ecological Emergencies Demand a New Paradigm. *Cadmus* 4/5: 83-102.

Greer, J. & Bruno, K. (1996) *Greenwash: The Reality Behind Corporate Environmentalism*. Penang: Third World Network.

Hajer, M. (1995) *The Politics of Environmental Discourse: Ecological Modernization and the Policy Process*. Oxford: Oxford University Press.

Hamilton, C., Bonneuil, C., & Gemenne, F., eds. (2015) *The Anthropocene and Global Environmental Crisis: Rethinking modernity in a new epoch*. London & New York: tledge.

Hanna, B., et al., eds. (2005) *The Bhopal Reader: Twenty Years of the World's Worst Industrial Disaster*. Lanham, MD: Rowman & Littlefield.

Hanna, B. (2017) Making Exposure In/Visible: Epidemiology, Legitimacy, and Authority after Bhopal. *The Journal of Asian Studies* 76/2: 409-421.

Haraway, D. (2016) Staying with the Trouble: Anthropocene, Capitalocene, Chthulucene. In Moore, ed., *op cit.*, chapter 2.

Holzer, B. (2010) *Moralizing the Corporation: Transnational Activism and Corporate Accountability.* Cheltenham UK: Edward Elgar.

Hornborg, A. et al. (2019) Has Cuba exposed the myth of 'Free' solar power? Energy, space, and justice. *Environment & Planning E* 2/4: 989–1008.

Jagodzinski, J. ed. (2018) *Interrogating the Anthropocene: Ecology, Aesthetics, Pedagogy, and the Future in Question.* London: Palgrave Macmillan.

Jørgensen, F. & Jørgensen, D. (2016) The Anthropocene as a History of Technology: "Welcome to the Anthropocene". *Technology and Culture* 57/1: 231-237.

Kallis, G., Paulson, S., et al. (2020) *The Case for Degrowth.* Cambridge: Polity.

Klein, N. (2014) *This Changes Everything: Capitalism vs the Climate.* London: Penguin.

Latour, B. (2015). Telling friends from foes in the time of the Anthropocene. In Hamilton, C., et al., eds. *op cit.*, 145-55.

Lorimer, J. (2017). The Anthropo-scene: A guide for the perplexed. *Social Studies of Science* 47/1: 117–142.

Malm, A. (2016) *Fossil Capitalism: The rise of steam power and the roots of global warming.* London: Verso.

Marinelli, M. (2018) How to Build a "Beautiful China" in the Anthropocene: The Political Discourse and the Intellectual Debate on Ecological Civilization. *Journal of Chinese Political Science* 23: 365–386.

Meadows, D.H., et al. (1972) *The Limits to Growth.* New York: New American Library.

Moore, J. ed. (2016) *Anthropocene or Capitalocene? Nature, History, and the Crisis of Capitalism.* Oakland CA: PM Press.

Newell, P. (2012) *Globalization and the Environment: Capitalism, Ecology and Power.* Cambridge: Polity.

Newell, P. & Paterson, M. (2010) *Climate Capitalism: Global Warming and the Transformation of the Global Economy.* Cambridge: Cambridge University Press.

Oreskes, N. & Conway, E. (2010) *Merchants of Doubt: How a Handful of Scientists Obscured the Truth on Issues from Tobacco Smoke to Global Warming.* London: Bloomsbury.

Oreskes, N. & Conway, E. (2014) *The Collapse of Western Civilization. A View from the Future*. New York: Columbia University Press.

Rich, B. (1994) *Mortgaging the Earth: The World Bank, Environmental Improvement and the Crisis of Development*. London: Earthscan.

Robbins, P.T. (2001) *Greening the Corporation: Management strategy and the Environmental Challenge*. London: Earthscan.

Rockström, J., et al. (2009) A safe operating space for humanity. *Nature* 461: 472–475.

Rowell, A. (1996) *Green Backlash: Global Subversion of the Environmental Movement*. London: Routledge.

Ryan, M.H., Swanson, C.L., et al. (1987) *Corporate Strategy, Public Policy and the Fortune 500: How America's major corporations influence government*. Oxford: Oxford University Press.

Schmidheiny, S. (1992) *Changing course: a global business perspective on development and the environment*. Cambridge MA: MIT Press.

Schumacher, E.F. (1973) *Small Is Beautiful: A Study of Economics as if People Mattered*. London: Bond & Briggs.

Sklair, L. (1994) Global sociology and global environmental change. In Redclift, M. & Benton, T., eds. *Social Theory and the Global Environment*. London: Routledge, pp. 205-227.

Sklair, L. (2001). *The transnational capitalist class*. Oxford: Blackwell.

Sklair, L. (2002). *Globalization: Capitalism and its Alternatives*. Oxford: Oxford University Press.

Sklair, L. (2016). Half-Baked. *Philosophica Critica* 2/2: 103-16.

Sklair, L. (2017). Review Article: Sleepwalking through the Anthropocene. *British Journal of Sociology* 68/4: 775–784.

Sklair, L. (2020) Globalization and the Challenge of the Anthropocene. In Rossi, I., ed. *New Frontiers in Globalization Research*. New York: Springer, chapter 5.

Sklair, L., ed. (2021) *The Anthropocene in Global Media: Neutralizing the Risk*. London & New York: Routledge.

Stengers, I. (2015). Accepting the reality of Gaia: a fundamental shift. In Hamilton, et al eds., *op cit.*: 134-44.

Willums, J. ed. (1990). *The Greening of Enterprise: Business Leaders Speak Out*. Bergen: International Chamber of Commerce.

Zalasiewicz, J., Waters, C.N., et al. (2017) The Working Group on the Anthropocene: Summary of evidence and interim recommendations. *Anthropocene* 19: 55-60.

Zalasiewicz, J. et al. eds. (2019) *The Anthropocene as a Geological Time Unit: A Guide to the Scientific Evidence and Current Debate*. Cambridge: Cambridge University Press.

CHAPTER 11

(2019) WORLD REVOLUTION OR SOCIALISM, COMMUNITY BY COMMUNITY, IN THE ANTHROPOCENE? *GLOBALIZATIONS* 16/7: 1012-1019. [COURTESY OF ROUTLEDGE]

Preamble

In 2019 I was invited by Barry Gills, the editor of the journal *Globalizations,* to contribute to a collection of essays to mark the death of Samir Amin. Barry introduced the tribute as follows: "Samir Amin, *a leading scholar and co-founder of the world-systems tradition, died on August 12, 2018. Just before his death, he published, along with close allies, a call for 'workers and the people' to establish a 'fifth international' to coordinate support to progressive movements. To honor Samir Amin's invaluable contribution to world-systems scholarship, we are pleased to present readers with a selection of essays responding to Amin's final message for today's anti-systemic movements*" (italics in the original). For me this was a difficult task, to put it bluntly I had been painfully moving away from my long-standing commitment to world socialist revolution while my commitment to socialist revolution "community by community" was growing day by day. An important part of this was my belief that the historical rift between Marxism and Anarchism needed to be bridged. This essay was the result of my Marx-inspired rethinking as outlined in chapter 7 above. The onset of the Anthropocene made the crisis even more urgent. I also used this essay as an opportunity to expand the idea of producer-consumer cooperatives in the context of community socialism.

Abstract

The idea of a Fifth International has been around for some time and the historical record is not encouraging. For the past few years I have been wrestling with an apparent contradiction in the work of most of us on the Left. On the one hand, our research demonstrates how powerful and successful consumerist capitalism and its integral system of "nation-states" has been, never more so than in current neoliberal/social democratic forms (by which I mean New Labour, as was, in the UK and elsewhere). But despite the financial meltdowns in Asia and the EU/USA in the new millennium that were supposed to fatally weaken capitalist hegemony, the system seems chaotically stronger than ever. The transnational capitalist class has taken these setbacks in its stride. On the other hand, we also argue that workers' movements all over the world can unite to challenge and overthrow the capitalist system. The very term "International" implies that these revolutions will be organized within the frameworks of those thoroughly discredited so-called nation-states which work well for an increasingly smaller proportion of their populations. So, that's why I have lost faith (this word is deliberately chosen) in the idea of a Socialist International directed towards world revolution.

Socialism: Community by Community

My argument is that the only way out of this mess, the only chance of having a livable planet for the generations to come (however utopian and unrealistic it sounds) is to organize small-scale socialist communities to create new forms of less destructive and less hierarchical economic and social relations. However unlikely, this is most likely to succeed community by community in something like producer-consumer cooperatives (P-CCs). For me exit from the capitalist market is a fundamental condition for P-CCs in the process of building community socialism. My proposals are intended for the long-term and I am only too aware of the "socialism or barbarism" debate that such proposals tend to attract. Walter Benjamin expressed this most concisely in his Theses on the Philosophy of History: "There is no document of civilization which is not at the same time a document of barbarism" (Benjamin 2007, 256). It is precisely the "bigness" of civilization that seems to me to be at the root of the problem. My critique of the Fifth International idea mainly focusses on the issue of what sort of socialism. The present dire state of civilization at the global level has been debated *ad nauseum*. Explanations abound, all the way from flaws in human nature, to misinterpretations of the revealed word of "Gods". What we might call political-economy solutions to these problems are all variations on four main themes. First, capitalist ideologues argue that only free markets and more prosperity will eventually ensure peace and happiness for those who are prepared to work hard; second, caring capitalists and social democrats argue that capitalism can be reformed through welfare states to provide equality of opportunity, again for those who are prepared to work hard; third, progressive anti-capitalists (of various communist or socialist or left-liberal persuasions) argue that the capitalist state must be replaced by a workers' state, again to provide equality of opportunity for those who are prepared to work hard; and fourth, small groups of people argue that it is precisely capitalism (especially in its globalizing forms) and the hierarchical state apparatuses it has created that are at the root of the problem, and that we have to start thinking about what comes after capitalism and the state-form of society if we are to save the planet, eliminate poverty, and find happiness. The difficulty of achieving these worthy goals has gained extra urgency in the new millennium with the identification of the Anthropocene, human-driven (but not by all humans equally in our class-polarized world) potentially catastrophic change in the Earth system. Climate change is only one part of a series of interlocking eco-system problems that are threatening to destroy the conditions that support life on the planet, including human life. The term "hierarchic state" is deliberately intended in a historically materialist sense to indicate the extent to which capitalism as a mode of production and a totalizing social system has colonized almost all actually existing states (even, many people would argue especially) self-styled socialist or communist states). The hierarchic tendencies of officialdom and elected office are hard-wired into the state form of society. States, predicated on the idea of officials at every level, cannot be anything but hierarchic and so attempts to reform states fundamentally from within are bound to fail. And this implies that attempts to reform any version of capitalism fundamentally from within are also bound to fail. The best that progressive social movements and elected socialist officials can do is to help provide spaces for those who wish to live outside the capitalist market and the state, to help and not to hinder them.

Most political-economy solutions for the failures of capitalism cannot deal with the two main fatal flaws of the capitalist system. The first is the crisis of class polarization, the rich get richer, the poor are always with us, those in the middle (the precariat) are increasingly insecure. The global migrant crisis, now being intensified by a looming crisis of "climate refugees", as White (2019) argues in his critical review of the concept, is a constant reminder of the failure of capitalist globalization to provide the hope of a decent standard of living for billions of people. This is a vivid illustration of the fact that the poor cannot necessarily be relied upon to passively put up with their misery forever in the places where they happen to be born. The second fatal flaw of capitalism, becoming more and more obvious, is the existential threat of ecological unsustainability, now powerfully expressed in terms of what is identified as the Anthropocene, the stage of the planet and its destructive fossil fuel driven growth without limits economy. This is starkly exposed by Ian Angus in his book *Facing the Anthropocene* (2016) that connects the impetus of capitalist globalization with the very survival of human life on the planet, best theorized as ecocide (Higgins 2015, Whyte 2020). Though there are already several different interpretations of the Anthropocene (for example, geological, materialist, idealist, feminist, postmodernist) most see it as a dire threat to humanity and the future of the planet. In my view the Anthropocene is mainly driven by the tremendous productive capacity of capitalist globalization and what I have conceptualized as the culture-ideology of consumerism (Sklair 2002, 2017). If the predictions of the Anthropocene scientists are correct, we must start to think about what comes after capitalism in its various guises and how to achieve something better than capitalist globalization and the international system of hierarchical states that are locked into an endless cycle of growth obsessions and hot and cold wars.

What is to be done?

Marx and then Lenin's answer to this question resulted in some defining moments of the 20th century. But there was always something perverse about the Marxist critique of state power as the executive committee of the capitalist class, and the eagerness with which so-called communist revolutionaries seized and used state power. What it definitely did not lead to was the capture of power by the working class. The historical record, uneven as it is, strongly suggests that the dictatorship of the proletariat (however defined) cannot produce the withering away of the state. On the contrary, it almost always led to a "new class" of state bureaucrats and Soviet, Chinese, and other profoundly undemocratic regimes. When 'communism' collapsed in the 1990s as an alternative vision of social and economic progress, it seemed inevitable that what I and others have conceptualized as the transnational capitalist class (TCC) would consolidate power on a global scale. The TCC and its four complementary fractions of corporate, political, technical, and consumerist elites, drive capitalist globalization. The globalizing political fraction of the hierarchic states, working hand-in-glove with the rest of the TCC, are part of the problem, not the solution.

The values on which a socialist global society could be built already exist in principle, but are rarely to be seen in practice, precisely because they conflict with the necessities of capitalist globalization. This can be represented in a series of dichotomies: socialist principles of teamwork and cooperation versus capitalist practices of self-centred individualism and ruthless competition; socialist principles of stewardship of the planet for the common good versus reckless capitalist exploitation of nature for private profit; socialist principles of egalitarian friendship and aid versus capitalist practices of cynical diplomacy and imperialist exploitation; socialist principles of genuine practical social responsibility versus capitalist practices of corporate crime and profiteering, and socialist principles of the dignity of labour and the revaluation of labour itself versus capitalist practices of the "race to the bottom" and class polarization. Reformers and revolutionaries have been trying to shore up socialist principles and practices for over a century, and though millions of people have been dragged out of poverty and hunger in some parts of the world, arguably the global situation today is as bad as it has ever been. That is why we have to abandon the hope of challenging the hegemonic alliance of capital with the state and look for other answers. Putting all our energies into either world socialist revolution or socialism in one country increasingly appear to be self-defeating strategies.

Alternatives to capitalist globalization

Is there a viable non-capitalist alternative to capitalist globalization? There is and a good place to start is by repeating the aphorism: "It is easier to imagine the end of the world, than to imagine the end of capitalism". Whoever actually said this first, it expresses a profound truth about the era of capitalist globalization. Theories of capitalist hegemony, from their origins in Marx, through Gramsci, Althusser (repressive ideological state apparatuses), Herbert Marcuse and the culture industries thesis of the Frankfurt School certainly help to explain why it has been easier to imagine the end of the world than to imagine the end of capitalism. So, we have to begin again to think through what we once conceptualized as democratic socialism and what it might look like in the 21st century. The power of corporate capitalist hegemony today is so overwhelming (allied as it is with the military, police, and surveillance powers of states) that the only viable strategy for change is a process of negating, avoiding, and eventually consigning capitalism and the state to the dustbin of history. The digital revolution simultaneously provides powerful tools of capitalist exploitation and a means of changing the system. The emerging transnational capitalist class, to put it bluntly, systematically subverts the emancipatory potential of generic globalization, by which I mean the electronic revolution, critical postcolonialisms, and new forms of cosmopolitanism. The electronic revolution could also contribute to dealing with one of the central structural problems of the state in capitalist society, namely the question of size (especially the scale of economic activity and of human settlements).

Prospects for change in the long-term

The creation of new mentalities is a project of many generations, a project that begins with damaged parents and communities gradually acquiring the insights and incentives to nurture children through new forms of upbringing and learning (see Gerhardt 2004). This would include biological and social parenting and learning from existing communities where all adults accept at least some responsibility for all children. New generations will be less damaged. These children in their turn will nurture their own children to be even less damaged. The design of cooperative communities will play an important part in this process. Transformations in housing, transportation, nutrition, and other necessities of a decent life would free up space for everything that the capitalist market squeezes out or whose pleasures it compromises. The culture-ideology of consumerism has socialized populations all over the world to crave all the material rewards that capitalist consumerism flaunts. Better, more love-based parenting could help people to strive for other, less destructive, life goals and social structures to achieve them. Intrinsic to this change in mentalities is that it does not work only at the level of individuals or isolated family groups but at the level of communities and between communities.

Our present reality is capitalist globalization. How, then, could P-CCs be organized to release the emancipatory potential of generic globalization in a non-capitalist world? The simple and encouraging answer is that they would work, in the early stages of transition at least, much as millions of small-scale cooperative groups work at present in enclaves all over the world. The digital commons (for example, the open source movement) already makes it possible for millions of like-minded people hungry for change to communicate across the globe for the common good. The viability of global networks of P-CCs rests on many untested assumptions. What would people eat? How would they learn? What would they do for healthcare? Who would provide the power to run the computers? How would they be safe? How would they deal with the anthropogenic degradation of all the eco-systems on which the viability of human survival depends? This is not simply a question of 'climate change', often used as an ideological metonym for the Anthropocene. All this would depend on a multitude of people who now work in the private or public sectors, directly or indirectly, establishing their own self-managed organizations in their local communities producing food, organizing transport, setting up places of learning and transmission of skills, providing healthcare and running energy systems. Eventually, if these organizations proved successful, something like P-CCs would emerge. Some might be very large, capable of securing their own food and energy supplies. Others would be smaller and would need to be networked with others. It would be both futile and undemocratic to suggest that one size fits all.

States, of course, cannot be abolished overnight, though reconstructed political communities could create more genuinely democratizing forms of economic, social, and political organization to encourage and facilitate networks of P-CCs or similar forms. As Chase-Dunn & Almeida (2020) argue the historical record of revolutions of different kinds from "prehistoric social movements" to the present provide a great wealth of lessons to be learned. The transition from the present capitalist-statist hegemony to a new form of society will be lengthy and problematic, but even the flawed forms of democracy that political systems throw up all over the world should provide openings for socialists to win elections and, at the very least, provide conditions that encourage those wishing to escape the capitalist market and the hierarchic state. Many existing progressive social movements at all levels will have an important part to play in the transition, but only if they seriously come to grips with the dead ends of the market and the hierarchic state. Not all, but most, radical social movements lose their edge the more closely they collaborate with the transnational capitalist class and organs of the hierarchic states, and those that do not usually find themselves isolated and ineffective. The inability of the Left to think through the withering away of the state has had its roots in pointless disputes and antagonisms between Marxists and Anarchists over the last two hundred years. To most people anarchism is a frightening prospect, associated as it usually has been in the public mind with violence and disorder. The irony is that capitalism (through the highly profitable weapons industry) and the state (through wars) have been responsible for far more violence and disorder than anarchists. Unless these perceptions change, capitalism and the hierarchic state will persist until they collapse under the stress of their own contradictions and threaten the end of human life on our planet.

While there is general agreement on the Left that we need to move beyond capitalism, the role of the state has always been contentious. In the *Communist Manifesto* Marx and Engels declared: "In place of the old bourgeois society, with its classes and class antagonisms, we shall have an association, in which the free development of each is the condition for the free development of all." The pressing question now is whether the socialist state guarantees the development of all or makes it impossible. My view is that any type of large-scale state makes "the development of all" impossible because states, by their very nature are hierarchical and repressive to the majority of their populations. Without exception all communist and socialist revolutions either originated in or became highly nationalistic in form and content. It is also worth noting that one of the central principles of the Paris Commune was the establishment of a Universal (not a French) Republic, encouraging Marx to reconsider his analysis of the state (see Hudis 2013, who dispels quite a few "Marxist" myths). All of this is highly controversial, often characterized as the debate around the "Withering away of the state" (see Bloom 1946, Daniels 1953, Pethybridge (1967, based on a questionnaire!), Adamiak 1970, Levine 1987, Yurchak 2003). While this last reference is not specifically about the withering away of the state, it is a highly relevant account of what Yurchak labels "Soviet late socialism". Reading these scholarly papers it seems that we need to revise the old/new adage "it is easier to imagine the end of the world than to imagine the end of the state". For me this raises the question: "if people can invent the state, surely people can abolish it".

People can change. Innovative socio-economic forms outside the capitalist market and the capitalist state are emerging all over the world on a small scale, but such initiatives struggle within the present global system. They struggle because the various modes of cooperation, noble as they are, exist within a sea of competitive capitalism and those who lead them are always faced with hard choices that jeopardize their survival in an inhospitable environment. However, there must be a point at which, in any society, the emancipatory potential of an increasing number of small-scale changes tips the balance, and communities organized along producer-consumer cooperative lines look like realistic alternatives to bourgeois society. Neoliberal ideologues argue that there is no alternative to capitalist globalization and, if we mean by this, the accumulation of material possessions for the better-off, they are probably correct. However, if human welfare and happiness are not measured in terms of material possessions, there are clearly better options, particularly if the very survival of human life in the Anthropocene epoch is at risk. If we refuse to believe capitalist (and statist) ideologues and start creating alternative forms of economic, political, and cultural organization and these alternatives prove to be successful in their own terms, then the logic of the market and the hierarchic state can be refuted, undermined, or simply ignored. Capitalism and states will eventually wither away.

Growth, degrowth, and viable paradigm change?

There is a large volume of research that is critical of many facets of capitalist society but not much of it seriously calls capitalism itself into question or tries to envision non-capitalist society. The dogma of ever-increasing growth, the mainstay of capitalist globalization, orthodox Marxism-Leninism, social democracy, and the developmental state must be challenged. A relatively new and revolutionary idea that suggests such a critique is convivial degrowth, a theory-driven activist movement that aims to decolonize the imaginary of growth (continuous economic growth as the ultimate good) and to establish degrowth (*decroissance* in its original French formulation) as the common-sense conception of a convivial future. What would degrowth mean for socialist P-CCs gradually withdrawing from the hierarchic state? First, the culture-ideology of consumerism would be replaced by a culture-ideology of human rights and responsibilities, prime among which would be a serious commitment to a decent, sustainable standard of living for all. It would certainly mean that the rich would become less wealthy and the poor would become richer in material possessions, and everyone would benefit in non-material riches, eventually. But for this process to start, all the existing critiques of capitalism must abandon the hope that progressive alternatives can thrive by directly challenging the market. For example, in the first instance an emerging P-CC would have the goal of producing its own food with its own resources, providing sustenance to its members free in a non-monetized local economy. This would entail that some members of the community continue to engage in paid employment in the capitalist labour market, supporting the rest in their gradual transition to self-sufficiency in food. It would also entail democratically elected local socialist politicians sympathetic to these goals, making it as easy as possible for them to be achieved, for example by releasing parcels of state-owned land (or legislating for the release of privately-owned unused or under-used land) for the production of food outside the capitalist market. The enthusiasm for such revolutionary change often makes it easy to underestimate the immense difficulties involved in transitioning from capitalism to socialism at any scale of human settlement. In a piece of inspired investigative journalism in the *New Yorker*, Jon Lee Anderson reports on the Bolivarian socialist republic of Venezuela under President Maduro who came to power after the death of the charismatic Hugo Chávez. The successes of Chávez were widely attributed to the distribution of oil revenues to the poor (for historical context, see Chávez 2003). Anderson interviewed Pepe Mujica, the former President of

Uruguay, for his view on Madura's prospects and the future of socialism in Venezuela. Mujica explains:

> The most serious problem of the Venezuelan revolution is the economy …. They haven't been able to diversify and have been a complete failure in agriculture and basic things like producing food. It's not the fault of the revolution—it's the fault of Venezuela, which has an old, deformed rentier oil economy. They lost the culture of work in the countryside. And that's very serious. I always remember the advice old Kim Il Sung gave to Fidel: 'Grow your own rice.' Your food has to come from somewhere near your kitchen …. There's a fundamental problem there—you can't make socialism by decree. We on the Left have the tendency of falling in love with whatever it is we dream about, and then we confuse it with reality. It seems to me that Bukharin's words apply: 'It's not about retreating from the revolution. It's about respecting reality.' You have to resolve the issue of how people are going to eat, and ensure that the economy functions, or else it's all going to go shit on you" (Anderson, 2017, 50).

P-CCs and The Global Village Construction Set

Though not explicitly challenging the hegemony of the capitalist market, a promising start in this monumental endeavour to change how we live was suggested by Marcin Jakubowski (a Physics PhD disillusioned with academia) in 2003 under the auspices of Open Source Ecology (OSE), an enthusiastic network of farmers, engineers, architects, and assorted supporters, whose main goal is the eventual manufacturing of the Global Village Construction Set (GVCS). As described by Open Source Ecology pioneers "the GVCS is an open technological platform that allows for the easy fabrication of the 50 different Industrial Machines that it takes to build a small civilization with modern comforts" (explained in some detail at https://en.wikipedia.org/wiki/Open_Source_Ecology#History). Although it is very early days, it is worth speculating that give or take a few more or less machines the GVCS might provide some clues about the size and scope of the optimum P-CC or local networks of contiguous P-CCs. While it is unclear what the political agenda of OSE is (or, indeed if they have one that goes beyond producing basic machines that are much cheaper than their corporate counterparts), this type of initiative is invaluable for all those who wish to escape the domination of the market and the state while retaining (and, hopefully) improving scientific and technological advances. Smaller-scale democratic control and accountability would make more equitable distribution of the fruits of these and future advances. OSE is fairly well represented on the internet, where you will find a good deal of information on the successes and difficulties so far encountered. The network is moderately transnational but the impression I have is that most of the burden falls on small groups of dedicated enthusiasts, as is the case for most radical practical endeavours. It is also important to emphasize that, as yet, there seems to be no systematic attempt to connect OSE with a future without capitalism and the state. The website https://en.wikipedia.org/wiki/Open-source, provides a good set of entry points. In the computer world, Linux, the free to share operating system utilized and expanded by thousands of engineers all over the world, is another source of imaginative if disappointingly argumentative thinking for those who genuinely want to change the world (see various Linux journals, Raymond 2001, and Byfield 2015).

Operating Problems of Producer-Consumer Cooperatives

Here I address some of the many basic questions that will inevitably arise if ever such a society seems possible. Others, no doubt, will think of many other questions. I do not have answers to any of these questions, that is why an early version of these ideas was called "Half-baked" (Sklair 2016) my purpose was to pose the questions and to engage with others who try to provide answers, and I am very grateful to those who responded via ResearchGate.

(1) FOOD

Could P-CCs by themselves or in networks ever be self-sufficient in food? Could a nutritious, healthy, non-industrial food system be created at the level of the P-CC or local networks of them? Would there be a place for laboratory-produced food? At what geographic scales would transfers of food take place between networked P-CCs? Vegetarian or carnivorous? How would land for the production of food be distributed? How to transform diet? Is the Global Village Construction Set (GVCS) up to the task? The campaigning magazine *Ethical Consumer* in its issue of Jan-Feb 2022 "How to shop for more sustainable food" presents a clear picture of what is wrong with the global food system and, more to my point here, lists the many healthier and greener alternatives to the supermarket dominated system that already exist in the UK and elsewhere (see for this and many more general consumer issues, https://www.ethicalconsumer.org/ethical-consumer-magazine).

(2) SHELTER

How would the existing housing stock be distributed? How would land for new housing stock be distributed? Would 3-D printing create enough new housing to satisfy the demand of those without adequate housing? How could the balance between communal and family living be managed? Where would the materials for housing repair come from? Is the GVCS up to the task?

(3) HEALTH

Would P-CCs have clinics and networks of P-CCs have hospitals? To what extent would changing patterns of living in the new society reduce the need for the types of health systems we already have? Could the system of production of medical drugs, equipment, and machines be de-industrialized? How would the medical profession, if there was one, be organized? Is the GVCS up to the task?

(4) UTILITIES (ENERGY, WATER, RECYCLING, MAINTENANCE, WASTE, INFRASTRUCTURE, etc).

Would each P-CC be responsible for its own utilities system? Would different P-CCs have widely varying utilities requirements? Would networked local utilities systems work for groups of P-CCs? How would the balance between fossil and non-fossil fuelled energy systems work out? Could a genuine net zero emissions energy system be designed. Would the new society inevitably lead to significantly reduced demand for utilities? Is the GVCS up to the task?

(5) EDUCATION

Could education be built on the basis of empathy? Who would decide what (and when) children were taught? Would "anarching" (as defined above) actually produce the new mentalities necessary for these transformations to be possible? How would the relationships between parents, other family members, and the community be managed for teaching and training? How would the teaching profession – if there was one – be organized? Would life-long education be a viable basis for community? How would science and technology be organized? Is the GVCS up to the task?

(6) SECURITY

Could the system of potentially or actually antagonistic nation-states ever be transcended? How could the world be de-weaponized? Can violence and aggression be eliminated and/or minimized? If not, would we always need police forces or armies, or some other institutionally sanctioned instruments of defence? Could P-CCs keep the peace without any sort of police force?

If money is abolished and all goods and services are freely available, would crime wither away within and between P-CCs? Is the GVCS up to the task?

(7) LEISURE

Is it reasonable to assume that if a new society came into being that individual and/or collective levels of creativity in all cultural fields would entirely transform leisure from a largely passive to a much more active phenomenon? What could replace the tourist industry? What would happen to 'entertainment', competitive sport? Is the GVCS up to the task?

(8) PRODUCTION

Who would decide what and how much to produce? How would goods and materials move between P-CCs, locally and globally? Can we move beyond brands to generic products? How would the division of labour be re-organized without the system of socially necessary labour time imposed by capitalism? Is the GVCS up to the task?

(9) DISPUTE RESOLUTION

To what extent would empathetic, non-competitive, love-based parenting eventually eradicate the need for dispute resolution? As with most of the questions, is it realistic to assume that as the new mentality becomes more and more prevalent, disputes over resources, interpersonal relations, and free-rider problems would eventually wither away? Would the need for a local and/or global legal system all wither away?

(10) COMMUNICATIONS

Does digital open-source provide a viable model for P-CC networking in all of the above areas? To what extent would it be necessary for members of different P-CCs to travel? To what extent would members of the P-CC want to travel? How would a P-CC cope with visitors, or people wanting to move permanently from one to another? Is the GVCS up to the task? It may be helpful to think about these questions in the abstract, but only in a limited way because they can't be answered until human actions create the concrete conditions. We can try to work out answers from our very limited perspectives of today, but what would these answers mean to several generations hence?

As I said above, no doubt there are other areas in which questions will be asked, my intention here is simply to encourage others to start thinking along these lines. As always, the key to significant and permanent social change lies in how mentalities can be changed and how people and communities put these changes into practice. I am only too conscious that more or less all the ideas put forward above have been suggested at one time or another (even thousands of years ago) by many other people. Today, if anything, the longing for alternatives to capitalism is increasing, as evidenced by internet searches. At the end of 2021 Google offered 25,500,000!). There are many superficially attractive ideas in this marketplace, that is what it is under conditions of capitalist globalization. The problem is that most of these "alternatives to capitalism", as far as I understand them, would rely on the state, especially in the transition period. For example, the popular idea on the Left of a universal minimum wage, of course, would entirely depend on the state and tax revenues. The Social Democratic view that the election of socialist candidates will eventually democratize the economy and capitalist relations of production is another popular idea. This has been tried many times and although it has brought considerable benefits to some sections of the working class in some countries, it has nowhere eradicated the market or socially necessary labour time, the foundation of capitalist exploitation. Recent history suggests that if social democratic reforms cannot take us beyond capitalism and the hierarchic state when these are in a weakened condition, then there is very little prospect that it will be any different in the current and probably future stronger conditions of capitalist globalization and its integral hierarchic state. As argued above, the powerful slogan "It is easier to imagine the end of the world than the end of Capitalism" seems to become more inevitable with every passing year. This is a hard conclusion to accept. It is time to start imagining the end of capitalism and the state in order to avoid the end of the world. To re-appropriate a phrase originally used to justify the inevitability of capitalist globalization: "if we want to survive, there is no alternative to ending capitalism and the hierarchic state".

Revisiting anarchist thinking on the state and hierarchy

In his book on non-violent anarchist thought and practice, *Anarchist Seeds Beneath the Snow,* David Goodway (2006, 316ff.) quotes Colin Ward: "a society which organizes itself without authority, is always in existence, like a seed beneath the snow buried under the weight of the state and its bureaucracy, capitalism and its waste, privilege and its injustices, nationalism and its suicidal loyalties, religious differences and their superstitious separatism ... [non-violent anarchism] far from being a speculative vision of a future society ... is a description of a mode of human organization, rooted in the experience of everyday life, which operates side by side with, and in spite of, the dominant authoritarian trends of our society." Goodway continues: "Acceptance of this central insight is not only extraordinarily liberating intellectually but has strictly realistic and practical consequences … As Ward says: anarchism is already partially in existence … humans are naturally cooperative … current societies and institutions, however capitalist and individualist, would completely fall apart without the integrating powers, even if unvalued, of mutual aid and federation". If we ever got to a stage in which networks of P-CCs started to emerge and began to work outside the capitalist market and the hierarchic national and local state then we can assume they would be peopled by those who already strive to live lives according to the values of socialist communities. Prime amongst these values would be the belief that we must abolish money and all modes of exchange that sanctify what Marx identified as socially necessary labour time (SNLT), the root of capitalist exploitation. If the goal is to create communities based on the principle "from each according to capacity, to each according to need", then it follows that there will be no money, no exchange on the basis of equivalences, and no rationing. People will take what they need. They will give what they can. Adults and children will consider this normal; all will participate in the production of food and the other necessities of life. People will work out for themselves what is the best way to live in communities that are respectful of natural limits and the rest of the world. It is not surprising that these sensible ideas seem quite ridiculous in a world dominated by the capitalist mode of production and organized in a series of hierarchical states.

Second thoughts

Ever since I conceived my "Half-Baked" research project in 2016 I have been having second thoughts about it. It is no coincidence that this was around the time when I first read the book by Ian Angus that forced me to make the transition in my thinking from the popular if rather anodyne idea of "ecological unsustainability" to the much more immediate and existentially threatening idea of the Anthropocene. This meant that the choice between global capitalism and ecological damage to the planet was no longer just a choice between a world of rising inequalities for billions of people and loss of biodiversity and so on but, more dramatically, the future viability of human life on the planet. My critique of capitalism in any form had begun to change from a rich mixture of political, economic, and cultural preferences to a question of potential existential risk to humanity. As I delved deeper and deeper into the implications of what has been labelled "the

Anthropocene Proposal" (Bohle & Bilham 2019) I became more and more convinced of the necessity of exiting from capitalism and the hierarchic state. Others, including Stephen Hawking (probably after Einstein the most famous scientist in the world in the twentieth century) were seriously recommending flight to another planet (see Sklair 2020). Over a decade ago when the prestigious *Proceedings of the National Academy of Sciences of the USA* (PNAS, reputedly the second most cited science journal in the world) starts publishing articles by serious hard scientists that pose questions about the extinction of human beings on planet Earth (for example, Ceballos, et al. 2011) it is surely time for social scientists to start posing serious questions about whether humanity can survive within the framework of capitalism and the so-called "system of nation states", however far-fetched these questions might sound.

References

Adamiak, R. (1970) The "Withering Away" of the State: A Reconsideration. *The Journal of Politics* 32/1: 3-18.

Anderson, J.L. (2017) Nicolás' Maduro's Accelerating Revolution: *The New Yorker* (11 December): 42-53.

Angus, I. (2016) *Facing the Anthropocene: Fossil capitalism and the crisis of the earth system.* New York: Monthly Review Press.

Benjamin, W. (2007) *Illuminations.* New York: Schocken Books (translated by Harry Zohn).

Bloom, S.F. (1946) The "Withering Away" of the State. *Journal of the History of Ideas* 7/1: 113-121

Bohle, M. & Bilham, N. (2019) The 'Anthropocene Proposal': A Possible Quandary and a Work-Around. *Quaternary 2*/19. [free full text online at https://doi.org/10.3390/quat2020019.]

Byfield, B. (2015) The decline and fall of Eric Raymond. *Linux Journal* (22 December).

Ceballos, G., Ehrlich, P., & Dirzo, R. (2017) Biological annihilation via the ongoing sixth mass extinction signaled by vertebrate population losses and declines. *PNAS.* www.pnas.org/cgi/doi/10.1073/pnas.1704949114

Chase-Dunn, C. & Almeida, P. (2020) *Global Struggles and Social Change: From Prehistory to World Revolution in the Twenty-First Century.* Baltimore: Johns Hopkins University Press.

Chávez, H. (2003) *The Fascist Coup against Venezuela.* Havana: Ediciones Plaza.

Daniels, R.V. (1953) The State and Revolution: A Case Study in the Genesis and Transformation of Communist Ideology. *The American Slavic and East European Review* 12/1: 22-43.

Goodman, D. (2002) Rethinking Food Production-Consumption: Integrative Perspectives. *Sociologia Ruralis*, 42/4: 271-7.

Goodman, D., et al. (2012) *Alternative Food Networks*: Knowledge, Practice, and Politics. Abingdon: Routledge.

Goodway, D. (2006) *Anarchist Seeds Beneath the Snow: Left-Libertarian Thought and British Writers from William Morris to Colin Ward.* Liverpool: Liverpool University Press.

Higgins, P. (2015) *Eradicating ecocide: laws and governance to prevent the destruction of our planet.* London: Shepheard-Walwyn, second edition.

Hudis, P. (2013) *Marx's Concept of The Alternative to Capitalism.* Chicago: Haymarket Books.

Levine, A. (1987) *The end of the state.* London: Verso.

Pethybridge, R. (1967) The Assessment Of Ideological Influences On East Europeans. *Public opinion quarterly* 31/1: 38-50.

Raymond, E.S. (2001) *The Cathedral and the Bazaar: Musings on Linux and Open Source by an Accidental Revolutionary.* Canada: O'Reilly Media.

Sklair, L. (2002) *Globalization: Capitalism and its Alternatives.* Oxford: Oxford University Press.

Sklair, L. (2016) Half-Baked. *Philosophica Critica* 2: 103-116.

Sklair, L. (2017) *The Icon Project: Architecture, Cities, and Capitalist Globalization.* New York & Oxford: Oxford University Press.

Sklair, L. (2020) Globalization and the Challenge of the Anthropocene. In I. Rossi, ed., *Challenges of Globalization and Prospects for an Inter-civilizational World Order.* Cham: Springer Nature, chapter 5.

Sklair, L., ed. (2021) *The Anthropocene in Global Media: Neutralizing the Risk.* London & New York: Routledge.

White, G. (2019) (Review article). Climate Refugees-Useful Concept? *Global Environmental Politics* 19/4: 133-138

Whyte, D. (2020) *Ecocide: Kill the Corporation Before it Kills Us.* Manchester: Manchester University Press.

Yurchak, A. (2003) Soviet Hegemony of Form: Everything Was Forever, Until It Was No More. *Comparative Studies in Society and History* 45/3: 480-510.

CHAPTER 12

BELEAGUERED CITY, BELEAGUERED PLANET.

Preamble

This concluding chapter has a somewhat embarrassing backstory that I tell to encourage young scholars. I hope it may help prepare them for any disappointments they may encounter in the early stages of their academic careers as they endeavour to pass out of the "publish or perish" phase. In 2020 I was invited to contribute a paper to a special issue on urban planning and the pandemic to be published by a reasonably well-known European journal. My first drafts were well-received by the editors and some colleagues, all of whom kindly offered some constructive suggestions for change that I accepted, and other comments that I did not accept. Eventually, the peer reviewers rejected the article on the grounds that it was "inappropriate" for the journal. I do not know for certain but I wonder if the concept of "administrative evil" that I applied to urban planning was "inappropriate". In his novel *Howard's End*, one of the great evocations of the importance of place, the English novelist and public intellectual E.M. Forster wrote "only connect … live in fragments no longer", a perfect epigraph for our times. I offer this imperfect but I hope not inappropriate essay as an uncertain conclusion for my book. Many thanks to Bridget Fowler, Renata Tyszczuk, and the anonymous reviewers, for helpful comments on various versions of this essay. The "peer" reviewers offered no comments. The publisher invited me to submit the paper to some other of its journals in various irrelevant fields, presumably by Algorithm.

Abstract

This chapter sets out to analyze the connections between three different but related phenomena (capitalist globalization, the Anthropocene, and the Coronavirus epidemic) through the lens of iconic buildings and spaces and the cities in which they are mostly found. Iconic architecture (historical and contemporary) is defined in terms of aesthetic/symbolic significance refined through the distinction between unique icons (works of art in their own right) and typical icons (locally recognized buildings and spaces that imitate aspects of unique icons in some respects). What these two types of icons have in common is that they thrive by attracting visitors. My argument is that all iconic architecture is an increasingly influential part of capitalist city planning, via global tourism, local and national place-branding, and "best city" rankings. I argue that the transnational capitalist class uses cities as competitors in a global system of lucrative investment opportunities. Capitalist globalization is widely implicated in the Anthropocene (signifying human impacts on the Earth system, usually destructive) and together they facilitate the spread of the Coronavirus epidemic. The concept of "administrative evil" is mobilized to highlight the ethical dimensions of city planning, and the increasingly "beleaguered city". By accident, I came across the poem by Longfellow "Beleaguered City" and thought the resonant opening lines would provide a good prologue to this essay.

> I have read, in some old, marvellous tale,
> Some legend strange and vague,
> That a midnight host of spectres pale
> Beleaguered the walls of Prague.
> (The Beleaguered City, Longfellow, 1839)

Iconic Architecture and the City

Although the first stanza of Longfellow's poem is alarming, it has a happy ending. The ending of our beleaguered cities almost two hundred years later, is far from certain. In this article I will argue that the triple crises of capitalist globalization driven by a transnational capitalist class (TCC), the Anthropocene, and the Coronavirus combine to make our cities beleaguered, with no end in sight. The available evidence suggests that radical system change requires exit from both capitalism (a system that is unimaginable without dangerous greenhouse gas emissions) and an exit from the contemporary hierarchic system of states whose existence is unimaginable without the tax revenues provided directly or indirectly via CO_2 emissions. The context in which this argument is developed is the city, particularly the megacity form (10 million plus inhabitants) that began after the end of the Second World War, mostly but not exclusively in Asia. Within cities the focus is on iconic architecture, both historical and contemporary, an increasingly influential part of the capitalist city, global tourism, and local and national place-branding. Capitalist globalization enormously increased and accelerated inter-national flows of people and goods across the planet. Cities, the Anthropocene, and plagues all have their own histories. When these histories collide, as they are doing today, actual and potential catastrophic effects are highlighted and reported from many places, notably big cities, thus the 'Beleaguered City' of my title.

At the turn of the millennium when I began to write about the sociology of architecture, I published some long reviews on the reception of iconic architecture and subsequently starchitecture (Sklair 2017, Table 2.1 for media coverage of these terms.) Both of these ideas (or, at least, these terms) were roundly condemned at the time by architecture critics in books and in the media. This seemed to me (a sociologist who had no formal training in architecture but who had a very keen amateur interest in it) to raise issues that required systematic research. In "Do Cities Need Architectural Icons?" I reviewed three books (Sklair 2006), all of which were published in the middle of the first decade of the new millennium: *The Last Icons: Architecture Beyond Modernism* by Miles Glendinning (who had held a Personal Chair of Architectural Conservation at the University of Edinburgh); *The Iconic Building: The Power of Enigma* by Charles Jencks (an architectural theorist and entrepreneur, most famous for his influential book *Modern Movements in Architecture*); and *The Edifice Complex: How the Rich and Powerful Shape the World* by Deyan Sudjic (a cultural journalist, formerly co-director of the Design Museum in London).

When the late Will Alsop (well known to discerning cultural consumers in Britain and elsewhere at the time as the "blob" architect) won the prestigious competition to design the Fourth Grace project in Liverpool in 2002, a storm of protest was unleashed in the architecture and urban design communities and his scheme was voted the least popular in a poll of 15,000 Liverpudlians. Alsop's blobby design was ranked well behind those of Foster and Partners and Richard Rogers in the public's esteem. A spokesman for Alsop Architects defended the design in the following terms, "If you propose any icon the instant response is negative because it challenges perception: it is the nature of an icon. None of the other schemes were icons. They were landmarks." David Dunster, head of Liverpool University's School of Architecture at the time, supported Alsop, arguing that most of the other proposals "were simply repeating things we had seen before and were trying to pass them off on Liverpool" (these quotations are from the report in the London-based weekly newspaper for those in and around architecture, *Building Design*, of 13 December 2002). By summer 2004 it was announced that funding had been cancelled for the Fourth Grace and other 'iconic' projects by Daniel Libeskind and Raphael Vinoly, leading *Building Design* to ask on its front page: 'End of the iconic age?' (23 July 2004). Little did they realize that it was actually the beginning of the 'iconic age'. The architectural media (and to some extent the mass media) in Europe and the

USA and elsewhere have devoted a good deal of attention in recent years to the place of architectural (and other) icons in cities and beyond, with the dividing lines between the pros and the antis clearly drawn. For a survey of the remarkable spread of "icons" into many other spheres, see Sklair & Struna 2013.

The three books I reviewed were good representatives of both the polemics and the subtleties of a debate that is far from over and whose implications for urban design are yet to be fully explored. On the basis of research began at the turn of the millennium, I made a start on this probably never-to-be resolved issue, eventually published in Sklair (2017). While these three publications in the 2006 review cover very similar ground and, indeed, repeat some of the same stories, they differ in several ways. Glendinning's *The Last Icons* was the first in a new series on Scottish Architecture and Design sponsored by the highly esteemed Lighthouse Museum in Glasgow, established when the city was awarded UK City of Architecture and Design in 1999. Glendinning dismisses iconic architecture in general as yet another wicked manifestation of modernism (McMoMo™ [sic]), parodying the critique of McDonaldization. In Scotland this is exemplified by the iconization of Charles Rennie Mackintosh (from Mackintosh to Takintosh or Mockintosh), a commodification process that eventually applies to most great artists. Sudjic is also anti-icon, but for him this is a corollary of being anti-edifice. His main argument is that what he labels 'the edifice complex' of the rich and powerful explains why prominent architects build what they build, often very badly. Nevertheless, Sudjic's book is centrally about what other people refer to as icons, particularly in terms of architecture in the service of nationalism, power, and extreme wealth. *The Iconic Building* by the late Charles Jencks was published by the small specialist publisher Frances Lincoln. It is beautifully produced, relatively inexpensive, well referenced, and full of spectacular images in full colour that literally make all the difference to the architectural arguments made in it, in the sense that much of the discussion around iconicity in architecture revolves around "image" (see Rattenbury, ed. 2002 and Vidler, ed. 2008). Jencks' book is a combination of large format coffee table (with much insider gossip) and a theoretically innovative analysis of iconicity, mobilizing the concept of the enigmatic signifier to good effect. The nearest he gets to a formal definition of this concept (already in use by literary theorists and psychoanalysts) is: "My argument is that 'enigmatic signifiers' can be used in an effective way to support the deeper meaning of the building" (Jencks 2005, 21). A good example of this phenomenon is the extension to the Tate Modern (see Sklair 2017, 82). The rest of Jencks' book is a series of case studies of what we now label as starchitects and their iconic buildings. He particularly commends as architecturally creative icons for our time, Le Corbusier's Ronchamp, Gehry's Guggenheim Bilbao, and Foster's Swiss Re, the 'erotic gherkin' (see Sklair 2017, Figure 4.7). Jencks deals briskly with the common complaint that a proliferation of new "iconic" buildings of variable quality makes a mess of cities, focusing on what successful icons bring to cities, notably the Bilbao effect. Jencks, who was a close friend of Frank Gehry, quotes him to the effect that the Guggenheim Bilbao commission called specifically for an equivalent to the Sydney Opera House, considered by many as the first globally iconic building. Presumably the reference is in terms of both architectural and media impact. Jencks comments that every new corporate headquarters seeks to be an icon, requiring a one-liner, a bullet point that journalists love to hate, and love to spice up. As enigmatic signifiers, iconic buildings leave plenty of room for a wide variety of interpretations. Taken by itself, the reader would be hard put to identify this as pro- or anti-icon, indeed, this is what those who detest iconic architecture routinely say. However, it is clear that for Jencks high impact in these two senses, architectural and media, is a necessary but not a sufficient condition for a building to be an icon.

When it comes to the crunch, it is difficult to resist the conclusion that iconicity in architecture is more or less a question of how the buildings look to the critics and, perhaps more fundamentally, makes them feel. The relationships between what buildings mean, how they look, and how they make different categories of those who experience them feel, need to be explored and the field of iconic architecture, especially as part of urban life, is a fruitful site for such explorations. I tried to explain this in terms of symbolic/aesthetic significance (Sklair 2017, 11-26, and passim). Maria Kaika (2011) offers a provocative alternative interpretation. Despite the misgivings of Glendinning and Sudjic and many others, it seems that iconic architecture is here to stay for the foreseeable future. Both Glendinning and Sudjic welcome the best of the buildings and spaces that Jencks and others label iconic. So, what is the answer to the question: do cities need iconic buildings? It is exactly the same as the answer to the question: Do cities need beautiful and exciting buildings? Of course they do, and you cannot wish away the iconic architecture in cities by refusing the label, especially when the anti-icon "taste police" love and admire many of the same buildings that the pro-icon "taste police" do. My attempt to resolve this issue was based on three questions explored in Sklair (2017, passim): iconic for when? iconic for whom? iconic for where? I report varying reactions from architects to Renzo Piano's Shard in London bearing on these questions (see Sklair 2017, 43-45.) My conclusion (so far unrefuted) was that much, but admittedly not all, of the disagreement between those claiming to be for iconic architecture and those against is more about what we can term "iconic overdose" rather than icons themselves.

Problematizing the Capitalist City

Those who live in cities will always want (and, I would argue, need) buildings and spaces that mean something special to them and that lift their spirits. The real issue is both iconic architecture as such, and to what extent architectural icons enhance or compromise the space that surrounds them. This takes us back to the concept of the city in capitalist society, an issue that I attempted to deconstruct through the argument that capitalist globalization produces consumerist yet oppressive cities where formal and informal controls split those who have too much, from those who have just about enough, and from those who have too little. Driving the consumerist/oppressive city are what I have labelled the four fractions of the transnational capitalist class; corporate, state, professional, and consumerist. The consumerist/oppressive city combines the idea of the culture-ideology of consumerism with the idea of the city that, at first glance, appears to offer unlimited opportunities but for most people inextricably bound up with the supposed lack of opportunities for constructing the good life in the countryside and the supposed plethora of opportunities for constructing the good, or at least better, life in the city. I have always found it fruitful to locate this within the framework of the culture-ideology of consumerism that began to emerge after the industrial revolution in the West and all over the world by the second half of the 20th century, the start of the era of capitalist globalization. It is important to distinguish the oppression of consumerism, as the term is used here, from the noble aspiration that societies should strive collectively to ensure a basic level of consumption of goods and services for all. Consumerism, in the broad brush sense in which I tend to define it as an addiction to more and more possessions and to constantly novel experiences, becomes oppressive as it inevitably exacerbates the twin crises of capitalist globalization, namely class polarization and ecological unsustainability. This, of course, is only one (perhaps contentious) approach to the topic. In her contribution to the Palgrave Macmillan series on *Consumption and Public Life* Léna Pellandini-Simányi (2014) focuses on the concept of "consumption norms" in everyday life, adding another dimension to theory and research on consumerism. In many ways, I would argue, the city, especially the megacity, becomes increasingly consumerist/oppressive. Notable markers of urban class polarization are widening gaps in residential, educational, and occupational segregation between the richest and the poorest (with groups in the middle experiencing higher levels of economic and spatial insecurity). Markers of the drift to ecological unsustainability in the city are inexorable rises in carbon emissions from large stocks of inadequately constructed housing, shops, leisure facilities, cars, and airplanes. All of these markers are implicated with consumerism, cultural processes created, manipulated, and reinforced by the ideology of never-endingly expanding capitalist globalization, even in times like these when capitalism itself is in turmoil (the reference is to the financial crises of 2008–2009).

The Icon Project

The over-arching research strategy of my book on the "icon project" (Sklair 2017) was to identify how each fraction of the TCC separately, and all four fractions working together (not always entirely in harmony) mobilized iconic architecture in the interests of capitalist globalization. Inspired by the work of Tyszczuk (2018), I begin to question the ecological rationale for big cities. The first step in this argument is the necessity to destroy the contemporary hegemonic coupling of hyper-consumerism and hedonistic emancipation, on which the attraction of all cities, especially the contemporary city, rests. This implies exit from capitalism. As the great Brazilian architect Oscar Niemeyer argues: "I see now that a social architecture without a socialist base leads to nothing—that you can't create a class-free oasis in a capitalist society, and that to try ends up being, as Engels said, a paternalistic pose that pretends to be revolutionary" (quoted in Holston 1989, 93).

In his book on Icons Aaron Betsky (1997) introduces the idea of icons as magnets, both of meaning and of people's attention and I would add that architectural icons play an important role in what I have termed the "culture-ideology of consumerism" (Sklair 2017, chapter 7 and passim). Both unique architectural icons (works of art in their own right) and typical architectural icons (that copy features from unique icons) only thrive when they are busy, when they attract the crowds. In addition to their functions as museums, monuments, sports, entertainment, and cultural venues, they are all to a greater or lesser extent retail outlets. And, of course, many shopping malls and urban destinations reproduce typical iconic features. These connections between iconic architecture (unique and typical) in cities and the Coronavirus epidemic, in which crowds of people dramatically increase the risks of transmission, highlight what I call the contemporary "Beleaguered City". To understand this properly I think it is necessary to address some historical and contemporary issues of architecture and planning in capitalist cities. The connections between iconic architecture (both unique and typical), megacity urbanization as a result of capitalist globalization, the Anthropocene (including climate change and related ecologically damaging consequences), and the pandemic, seem to present unprecedented challenges to those tasked with city planning.

Urban Studies and the Environment

Urban studies as an academic and a professional enterprise until quite recently has tended to take notice of the environment in the context of air pollution, the housing problem, transportation, and other consequences of high-density living. As a non-specialist in urban planning I can do no better than to reference two books by Peter Hall, the first an updated edition of his classic *Cities of Tomorrow* in which he declares: "at the end of nearly a century of modern planning, the problem of cities remained much as they had been at the start" (Hall 1996, 421). I am not in a position to say if this is true (Hall himself shows the importance of the rise of the automobile culture) but the blurb from the American Planning Association on *Cities of Tomorrow*, "This is the one book you have to read", suggests that the APA considers Hall's contribution as uniquely significant, and this may be more important than whether or not it actually is true. In 1998, Hall co-authored a very different book with the "everyday" anarchist Colin Ward (see Goodway 2006, chapter 14). Hall and Ward's book was a celebration of the centenary of the Town and Country Planning Association in the UK and, in particular, the publication of Ebenezer Howard's *To-Morrow: A peaceful Path to Real Reform* republished as *Garden Cities of Tomorrow* in 1902, "destined to become the most influential and important book in the entire history of twentieth-century city planning" (Hall & Ward 1998, preface). A notable difference between these two books is that in the first, there is a brief mention of "sustainable urban development" in which Hall comments, "The problem was that though everyone was in favour of it, nobody knew exactly what it meant" (Hall 1996, 412), while in *Sociable Cities* aspects of sustainable urban development take up most of the second half of the book (Hall & Ward 1998, Part II). The change of emphasis between these two books, and particularly the privileging of "the quest for sustainability" and the politics that underpin it, clearly open up novel environmental dimensions of urban planning. Hall and Ward were by no means alone. Keil (2005) presents a review of work on "urban political ecology" which, while not discussing Peter Hall or architecture, does contain an eerily prescient reflection on cities and pandemics (ibid., 644). In the early 20th century there is little mention of iconic architecture (unique or typical) but as the 21st century gathered pace critiques and celebrations of what we now know as the capitalist city (characterized by city branding, city boosterism, mass international tourism based on cheap flights, "best city" rankings on a variety of criteria) began to appear. In this sense, iconic buildings and spaces provide a lens through which we can start to explain how different fractions of the transnational capitalist class mobilize cities and their icons as competitors in a global system of lucrative investment opportunities (Knox 2011, Derudder et al. eds. 2012, Sklair, 2017). Several major carbon emitting industries, construction, transportation, industrial food production, and print media advertising, are implicated in what makes the capitalist city so successful in terms of the goals of capitalist globalization, and so problematic in terms of ecological sustainability.

Paradoxically, alongside affordability, leisure, amenities, and employment opportunities, the idea of the sustainable city nestled beside the growing interest in "the environment" in the new millennium. One example neatly summarizes the complexity of this topic. In 2011 Elsevier began to publish a new journal *Sustainable Cities and Society*. It got off to a rather contradictory start on its very first page: "According to a United Nations report, cities cover only 2% of the world's land surface, yet consume 75% of the world's natural resources and produce 75% of its waste ... Cities increase energy efficiency, consume fewer resources, produce less pollution and avoid urban sprawl. Future cities must be developed or adapted to meet the emerging needs of its citizens". These sentiments re-appear in much of the literature on cities, proclaiming them as either opportunity-rich sites or as toxic spaces of the Anthropocene, sometimes both, though the media tend to portray the Anthropocene in neutral terms (Sklair ed. 2021). In my own early work on iconic architecture and cities the focus was on issues of class polarization, consumerism, and ecological unsustainability, the latter rather vaguely defined. A new, sharper, focus was necessary.

The Anthropocene City

As noted in the previous chapter, in late 2016 I came across a book by the Canadian eco-socialist Ian Angus, who edits the online journal *Climate & Capitalism* (subtitled "Ecosocialism or barbarism: There is no third way"). *Facing the Anthropocene* (Angus 2016) made me realize that I had been missing something very important about the city in capitalist society, namely that to begin to fully understand cities in the 21st century we have to visualize and conceptualize them in the context of the Anthropocene, simply defined as the human impact, usually destructive, on the Earth system. John Bellamy Foster's pioneering research on the metabolic rift, based on Marx's understanding of the work of the German agricultural chemist Liebig, explains the link between cities and the Anthropocene (Foster & Burkett 2016, esp. chapter 3). Marx writes: "Capitalist production, by collecting the population in great centres, and causing an ever-increasing preponderance of town population, on the one hand concentrates the historical motive power of society; on the other hand, it disturbs the circulation of matter between man [sic] and the soil, i.e., prevents the return to the soil of its elements consumed by man in the form of food and clothing; it therefore violates the conditions necessary to lasting fertility of the soil. By this action it destroys at the same time the health of the town labourer and the intellectual life of the rural labourer. ... The more a country starts its development on the foundation of modern industry, like the United States, for example, the more rapid is this process of destruction" (Marx 1961 [1887], pp. 505-6). However, neither Angus nor Foster engages with Michael Pollan's incisive critique of Liebig's role in the creation of "Big Organic" via the NPK (chemical fertilizer) mentality (Pollan 2006, chapter 9). Like capitalism, cities have usually been seen (and theorized) as social and material structures often in process of change. Similarly, like the common perception of capitalism (as in "it is easier to imagine the end of the world than the end of capitalism"), in the modern period conceptions of cities have usually portrayed them as indestructible. Even when they have been destroyed they have mostly been rebuilt. Think in Europe alone of Lisbon in 1755, London in the Blitz, Berlin, Dresden, Sarajevo, to name but a few, what Bevan (2006) conceptualizes as the history of "urbicide".

Provisional Cities

In her path-breaking book, *Provisional Cities*, the architecture scholar and artist Renata Tyszczuk offers a powerful warning that, in the Anthropocene, cities might cease to be indestructible, indeed they become "provisional". Anticipating this idea, two of the most influential urbanists of the twentieth century, Lewis Mumford and Patrick Geddes, believed that cities "were among the most fragile of organisms" (quoted in Wojtowicz 1998, 136). Tyszczuk imagines and invents two new words: "Anthropocenophobia" a fear of, or anxiety about the Anthropocene, the new epoch of human making; also harbouring a fear of the excessive deliberations about either human epochal prowess, or human frailty, and its possible synonym "Holocenophilia", derived from the Holocene, the official geological epoch of the last 11,700 years, often associated with a nostalgia for clement, warm and relatively stable times". Tyszczuk expands with a similarly imaginary: "She found that the frequent references to a new epoch brokered by a novel sense of human calamity and talk of an "apocalypse that was already here and now" induced in her a kind of Anthropocenophobia. She was aware of an unfolding global catastrophe –who wasn't? She didn't care what it was called, whether it was a good or a bad Anthropocene, whether it was about saving business-as-usual or this-changes everything. She simply found it frightening: fear of human hubris, fear of human vulnerability; fear, in fact, that in spite of all the epochal talk, nothing would make a difference. The sky would just keep on falling. (Tyszczuk 2018, viii).

The "provisional cities" of Tyszczuk's title is explained, simply, as follows: "Geological time frames may remind us that all human settlement is provisional, but global urban practices and contemporary geopolitics continue to show little recognition of the precarious interdependence of human and non- human worlds, their radical instability, their capacity to surprise. If the Anthropocene is showing us that everything –even our most enduring symbols of mastery and permanence, from the dome of the Capitol Building [pre-6 January 2021!] to the temples of Angkor Wat –is actually provisional, how can stories about settlement and unsettlement help us to meet and to cope with this new ontological and philosophical crisis?" (ibid., 2). Tyszczuk is careful to tell us that this is "not to denounce cities, but to recognize that the history of cities –in all their incarnations: garden cities, ecocities, sustainable cities, resilient cities, smart cities, and so on –sees one grand narrative replacing the next, and that ultimately they are all provisional" (ibid.). Provisional cities come in various forms of "unsettlements", from tent cities to megalopolises. With a striking rhetorical flourish, Tyszczuk declares: "Megacities are the giant technofossil assemblages of the future" (ibid., 37), they are all Anthropocene stories. It seems not accidental that the two examples above (the Capitol Building and Angkor Wat) are themselves architectural icons. Cities that look and feel so solid are, therefore, temporary from the two perspectives of Anthropocene time: the anthropogenic ruins of the past, and the ruins of the present (for those unfortunate enough to live near especially vulnerable places), and the ruins of the future as portrayed in a science fiction archive that seems to creep closer to science fact year by year. We live "the fiction of a settled life" (ibid., 8), what Casagrande et al. (2017) identify as a state of "ecomyopia". Now that more than half of the world's population lives in cities (over 30 of which have more than 10 million inhabitants), it seems obvious that what has come to be known as mega-urbanization raises several important issues. In his review of the topic, Lauermann argues: "mega-urbanization is not only the purview of wealthy global cities or ambitious developmental states. Rather, it is an increasingly common phenomenon across cities of many sizes and geographies. As mega-projects transform everyday urban life, the definition of 'everyday' and 'ordinary' increasingly includes mega-urban processes" (Lauermann 2018, 2). Neil Brenner and his colleagues (2013) expand this into the provocative idea of "Planetary Urbanization", a concept that inspired some of my own later research on "terraforming" (Sklair forthcoming).

Gentrification and Displacement

As with the Earth's eco-systems, cities in the process of radical change are not all impacted equally. Some communities are certainly beleaguered, others are privileged. Therefore, we need to ask: is the sprawling modern city a viable space for what the Chinese government appears to have (with baffling logic) enshrined in law as "ecological civilization"? (on which topic see Marinelli 2018). Globalizing capitalist ideologues have been posing this question for decades and their answer "greening the city" encapsulates a popular movement for urban boosters everywhere. Even the most responsible progressive architecture and urban planning professionals are finding it difficult to avoid the "greening to box-ticking greenwashing" transition (Sklair 2017, 220-23). This has led to a boom in the numbers of so-called ecocities to be found all over the world, including many in very unlikely places (see Joss et al. 2013.) Knox 2011, 243-50 and Halliday 2019 offer more hopeful perspectives than I can offer here.

Iconic architecture re-enters the story of beleaguered cities in an unlikely pairing with "slum clearance" via the concepts of "Planetary Gentrification", "Slum Gentrification", and "Mega-gentrification and displacement" in Lees et al. (2016), who acknowledge issues around definitions of slums (see also Angotti, 2006, with gentrification, and displacement providing many telling case studies, some addressing resistance to planetary gentrification. The argument, in a nutshell, is that neoliberal globalization stimulates gentrification which, almost inevitably, results in the often highly violent displacement of poor minority communities, orchestrated by the national and local state, NGOs, and the corporate sector, all over the world. Ghertner (2015) provides an exemplary case study of Delhi. Neil Smith (1982, 139-40) made the important theoretical distinctions between "gentrification" and investment-driven "redevelopment" (and revitalization and de-vitalization by gentrification). In my terms, many slums are eventually replaced by iconic buildings, usually typical icons that appear to the untrained eye to resemble buildings whose pictures they have seen on TV, films, print media; or even unique works of art. This suggests, tentatively, a peculiar dialectical relationship between iconic architecture (as re-interpreted by Rem Koolhaas), slums, and class struggles, explored in Rao (2012).

Marshall Berman's classic assessment of "urban renewal" in New York expresses this peculiar dialectic as it combines a devastating condemnation of the great destructive gentrifier Robert Moses with a layer of anti-hero admiration. Berman comments: "Many of the city's most impressive structures [all more or less still iconic] were planned specifically as symbolic expressions of modernity: Central Park, the Brooklyn Bridge, the Statue of Liberty, Coney Island, Manhattan's many skyscrapers, Rockefeller Center and much else … Robert Moses who is probably the greatest creator of symbolic forms in twentieth-century New York, whose constructions had a destructive and disastrous impact on my early life … [his] spectre still haunts my city today" (shades of Longfellow in 1839 in Berman 1988, 289). This excerpt introduces Berman's "In the Forest of Symbols: Some Notes on Modernism in New York". Another of Berman's villains is Siegfried Giedion ("Le Corbusier's most articulate disciple"), the author of one of the still most influential texts on architecture and urbanism in the modernist canon, *Space, Time and Architecture*, published in 1941). Giedion, who was a close friend of James Joyce, another distinguished observer of cities, proclaims: "there is no longer any place for the city street, with heavy traffic running between rows of houses; it cannot possibly be permitted to persist" (quoted in Berman 1988, 169n, no dialectical nuance here). Berman highlights this as an expression of the extreme wing of the modernist anti-city tendency. Giedion also comments on slums in his remarkable post-war book *Mechanization Takes Control*. He argues, in the apparently very different context of Fordist scientific management as it relates to the psychology of the worker: "Here Henry Ford hits on a phenomenon known to every urbanist who has slum-dwellers to resettle: No matter how primitive and unsanitary conditions may be, a certain number will always be found who refuse to leave their slum for new houses, and who prefer by far their old and familiar conditions" (Giedion 1948, 125). Giedion, of course, assumes naively that the promise of better new housing is always honoured, and ignores the implicit destruction of community. His tone is decidedly amoral. In a strange juxtaposition, this quote from Giedion comes just after two photographs, comparing the mechanization of auto production and of carcasses in a Chicago slaughterhouse (Giedion 1948, 122-123). Berman quotes the famous boast of Robert Moses, "When you operate in an overbuilt metropolis you have to hack your way with a meat ax [sic]" (Berman 1988, 293-4, see also the footnote on p. 308). Hacking cities and meat axes force us to address issues of planning and good and evil in the city, and elsewhere.

Administrative Evil and Urban Planning

An exceptionally interesting and original article, "Saving the City: Harland Bartholomew and Administrative Evil in St. Louis" (Benton 2018) provides a window into much neglected moral questions raised by city planning. Benton presents Bartholomew as epitomizing the technical rationality that makes administrative evil possible. "By using technical-rational planning and focusing on quantitative outcomes, Bartholomew created conditions that detached him from the effects that his planning had on Black neighborhoods. Bartholomew dehumanized Blacks in St. Louis as economic drains. At several points, Bartholomew advocated for racial segregation to preserve neighborhood property values" (ibid., 199). Urban renewal was (and still is) the bureaucratic euphemism for slum clearance (formerly Negro Removal), which in its turn becomes the euphemism for destroying black and other unwelcome ethnic minority communities. Freund (2015) provides compelling evidence from the USA on who benefited from slum clearance and urban renewal, telling similar stories of the destruction of the homes and communities of black and other ethnic minority groups in order to renew and beautify American cities, usually for the benefit of developers and their somewhat more prosperous clients. For example: "An Engineer Describes the Work Required to Make Seattle Competitive, 1908" (84-87); "New York City Retailers Organize to Protect a Fifth Avenue Shopping District, 1916" (87-89); "Herbert Gans Critiques Federal Urban Renewal Programs, 1959" (236-43). Gans was Denise Scott Brown's mentor (see Scott Brown 2009, 22-54, on the architect/planner/sociologist triad). Back to Freund for "Jersey City Markets Itself to a New Demographic, 2003-2006" (278-281), and finally "A Professor Explains How Urban Redevelopment Has Impacted Los Angeles Minority Communities, 1987/1988" (281-86). This last piece is by Cynthia Hamilton of the Los Angeles Labor/Community Strategy Center, author of a report "Apartheid in an American City" published as a book by the Center in 2017. Freund's compendium as a whole is a valuable resource for historical and contemporary research on race and the city in the USA (see also the multi-national survey of planners and planning through the lens of urban anthropology in Mack & Herzfeld, eds. 2020). It is important to remember that the concept of the "slum" has been highly controversial since at least the 19th century (Hall 1996, chapter 2). On the more contemporary topic of slum tourism, we find Dovey & King (2012) on "the taste for slums"; Jones (2012) on "Bankable Slums"; McFarlane (2012) on "The Entrepreneurial Slum"; Mekawy (2012) on "Responsible Slum Tourism: Egyptian Experience", and Rivadulla & Bocarejo (2014) on "Beautifying the Slum", not forgetting the less exotic Mike Davis (2006) on the planet of slums. This brings us into the realm of "administrative evil".

Administrative evil as a conceptual tool

The concept of "administrative evil" was developed by Adams & Balfour in their book *Unmasking Administrative Evil* (1998). They argue that ordinary people carrying out their normal professional and administrative tasks (characterized by the obsession with "technical rationality") can engage in acts of evil without being aware that they are doing anything wrong, sometimes they believe that what they are doing is for the public good, a condition identified as "moral inversion" that usually masks the evil consequences of their actions. This unrecognized potential for administrative evil can, ultimately, escalate to much greater evil. Adams and Balfour illustrate this through case studies derived from the Nazi Holocaust in general and specifically the slave labour camps at Mittelbau-Dora and the V-2 rocket production site at Peenemünde. These were directly connected with the Marshall Space Flight Center in the USA, where the Apollo II project to take men to the moon began. The team set up by Wernher von Braun (a prominent rocket scientist in Nazi Germany) came to the United States in 1945. Adams and Balfour say: "we are left with the reality that a handful of America's most competent and successful public managers in the government agency that was lionized in the 1960s as the paradigmatic high-performing organization either had been 'committed Nazis' or had themselves directly engaged in actions for which others in postwar Germany were convicted of war crimes. This story begins at Mittelbau-Dora, where administrative evil wore no mask. ... we now find that evil sullying our nation's single greatest technical achievement, the moon landing." (I was unable to access the print copy of this book; all quotes are from chapter 4 in the online version).

Interesting, but what has this to do with cities and iconic architecture and the beleaguered city? In their chapter on racism in American cities, Adams and Balfour argue that bureaucrats and planners make administrative decisions on slum clearance and urban renewal that destroy communities (often specifically targeting minority communities) as chronicled above. "[They] explore the contemporary context in which public policy is made and implemented, with a focus on how the tacit assumptions that undergird technical-rational solutions to messy, intractable social problems can unwittingly contribute to the breakdown of community, the creation of "surplus populations," and, through moral inversions, even to public policies of destruction" (ibid., chapter 4). Thus: "little consideration has been given to the notion that the Holocaust is directly relevant to the theory and practice of public administration. This lack of attention to the meaning of the Holocaust for public administration is characteristic of the field's lack of historical consciousness and represents a dangerous gap in the self-understanding of the field, one that contributes to a blindness to the potential for administrative evil and to the fragility of the field's ethical foundations" (ibid., chapter 1). The enormous literature on the Eichmann trial in 1961 in Israel and Hannah Arendt's "banality of evil" argument (surveyed in Jones 2015) is of course relevant here as are the essays in Benhabib ed. (2010, Part IV).

It may be contentious to compare many of these apparently extreme statements about evil with scholarly accounts of the difficulties that planners face. For example, Paul Knox in his most useful book on cities and design, has a chapter on modernist urban planning entitled, significantly, "The city redesigned: Modernity, efficiency and equity" (Knox 2011, chapter 4). Knox does mention slums and urban clearance and argues: "planning and urban design can be construed as key to the internal survival mechanisms of capitalism, channeling the energy of opposing social forces into the defence of the dominant order, helping to propagate its own goals and values as the legitimate ones" (ibid., 101) but, like most of us, he does not condemn urban planning as inherently or potentially evil. The forces that make cities beleaguered are mostly invisible to those who do not come into regular contact with them. The Coronavirus epidemic has changed this feature of urban life drastically in a way that seems qualitatively different to previous plagues and viruses (see Gandy 2021). A relatively invisible evil in the Anthropocene has been transformed into an actually invisible spectre haunting all forms of human settlement.

The Perfect Storm

The World Health Organization declared COVID-19 (Coronavirus) a global pandemic on 11 March 2020. At that point 118,000 cases of the coronavirus illness had been identified in over 110 countries and territories. As of time of writing (early 2022) according to official figures (not always entirely reliable), infections were approaching 300 million and the death count 6 million and rising globally with daily updates available on the internet from a variety of sources, notably from the Johns Hopkins University site. These seem to be large numbers but, as many commentators point out, in terms of deaths per million of the population by country and the lack of certainty over exact causes of deaths, the impact of the pandemic on mortality rates could turn out to be relatively mild compared to normal seasonal pandemics; and many governments and commentators began to redirect their attention to the much discussed and rapidly increasing economic, social, psychological, and general non-Covid health impacts of the pandemic. In October 2021 the *Lancet Countdown on health and climate change* was released with the slogan: "code red for a healthy future" raising the alarm and making the links explicit between the Coronavirus, more general health issues, and climate change (see Lancet.com).

At first, it was thought that mega-cities with high density populations were most at risk, with Wuhan, London, Milan, New York, São Paulo, and many others identified as hot spots for infections (see for example, "The Curious Case of 6 Mega Cities that Account for More than 50% of India's Virus Cases, Deaths" in *MSN News*, 28 May 2020). This detailed article concludes that the mortality rate per million population in India has actually been relatively low. At the time of writing (February 2022) Delta and other variants, notably Omicron, add further layers of uncertainty. Research from China (Qian Forrest Zhang & Zhanping Hu 2020), India (Kumar & Abdin 2021) and the USA (Souch et al. 2021) comparing the situations in rural and urban communities further complicates the story. In the USA (and probably elsewhere) compared with cities rural communities tend to be poorer, less healthy, less well-served with medical facilities, and more likely to be at risk from food processing plants (see Yearby 2021). However, paradoxically, when lockdown and protective measures (notably social distancing and face masks) are relaxed, obviously high density, entertainment-seeking, populations will be more at risk. Even the notoriously climate change denying *Wall Street Journal* (21 July 2020) appears to have reconsidered: "Why Covid-19 Makes It Harder for Cities to Fight Climate Change: Energy bills and carbon emissions rise as office buildings pull in more outside air to keep workers safe", a powerful pandemic image of the beleaguered city. In parallel with this, the rapid growth of working from home (usually via the internet) is widely identified as the cause of the destruction of small businesses in city centres, turning them into ghost towns, pictures of deserted streets in the media being another powerful image of the beleaguered city.

Iconic architecture and the virus re-appear in the argument in London. On 20 March 2020, the *Evening Standard* reported: "Tower of London among six iconic sites being closed by Historic Royal Palaces in battle against coronavirus. ... It has outlasted the Black Death, the Great Fire of London, and even the Blitz". The question remains, what will happen when it (and many other iconic sites, unique and typical, global, national, and local) open, officially or unofficially, to the public again? Few governments around the world have covered themselves with glory in their handling of the epidemic. The architecture and design websites (for example https://www.dezeen.com/) tell us that work is already ongoing to re-design our homes for coping with future pandemics, making them more healthy and sustainable, though usually in a short-sighted optimistic socio-political vacuum, part of the "Build Back Better" narrative that assumes that what was largely responsible for the pandemic (capitalist globalization) can somehow miraculously solve it. This seems to parallel the situation regarding the moral implications of irresponsible climate change denial which attracts attention in the scholarly literature, occasionally in the mass media, and often on social media. The over-optimistic claims of the prospects for 100% renewable energy (RE) are rarely challenged in the mainstream media despite warnings from inside energy science. For example, "When serious critics examine high-profile models that claim to prove feasibility for transition to 100% RE over territories ranging from regional to global scale, they typically find that these exercises are informed by many uncertainties and contestable assumptions … It follows that 'real-world' inferences extrapolated from such research should be viewed as speculative at best and dangerously misleading at worst" (Floyd et al. 2020, 6). Floyd's critique is strongly reinforced by a growing volume of research on the problematic concept of "net zero emissions", ever present in the COP 26 conference in Glasgow in 2021 (see Dyke, Watson, & Knorr 2021, Pearce 2021, Dale & Moss 2021, and Miltenberger & Potts 2021). An internet search for "net zero carbon emissions" in 2021 brought up over 60 million items, including a relatively optimistic report from Barclays Bank outlining a sensible path to total decarbonization: The bank's analysts tell us: "But achieving that will not be easy. In order to cut emissions, the carbon intensity of the energy mix has to fall – which could mean increases in costs that are hard to bear. There are also risks that goals are thwarted by trade disputes, the slow adoption of new technologies, and a lack of political will. Governments, companies and consumers are committed to moving to a lower-carbon world. … But even after huge changes, there will be sectors and areas where net zero is just not possible – from the perspective of either technology or costs. Nearly 20 gigatonnes per year will be needed in CO_2 removal, according to our analysts' estimates, through direct capture or other offsets such as nature-based solutions" (Barclays Bank, Emission impossible? Closing in on net zero 21 April 2021).

However, the Barclay's analysts do not follow up on this problem. Two Chinese scholars reinforce the argument that the path to Net Zero is anything but certain (Shengqing Xu & Shuiping Dai 2021). The outcome of COP 26 was highly controversial, with governments claiming modest breakthroughs and critics exposing widespread hypocrisy, summed up by Greta Thunberg's assessment: "Blah, Blah, Blah". It was noted that few corporate executives attended, but much was made of the 150 fossil fuel lobbyists who made their presence felt. The report on COP 26 by the independent climate change research organization (*CarbonBrief.org*, 10 December 2021) quotes an analyst as follows on net-zero [sic]: "It is all very well for leaders and governments to claim that they have a net-zero target, but if they don't have plans as to how to get there, and their 2030 targets are not aligned with net-zero, then, frankly, these net-zero targets are just paying lip service to real climate action. That's the key reason we think Glasgow at this stage has a very big credibility gap." This is true, but the absence of any indication that net zero is itself problematic is just as important. An outstanding feature of the conference was the intervention of delegates from small "developing" countries, notably small island states with minimal greenhouse gas emissions already facing existential threats from climate change (for details of Australian media coverage of "sinking islands" see Sklair ed. 2021, 205-206 and notes). The hypocrisy of governments and corporations on show at COP 26 can be illustrated in many ways, for example the historically climate change denying ExxonMobil acts as an official adviser to the UK government on the path to Net Zero via Carbon Capture, Utilization and Storage, another highly problematic strategy (see Ahmed 2021). The UK government, like many others, continues to subsidize fossil fuel business in a variety of ways; corporations drag their heels over stranded assets and continue to finance projects high in carbon emissions all over the world. It is true that some of the promises made to decarbonize over recent years have been honoured but in the view of many scientists it is too little, too late. Welcome as they are, innovations in renewable energy production and use, where their proponents (for example the rapidly growing electric car industry) and their supporters in government and the media) give the 'dangerously misleading' impression that we can continue to drive or fly as much as we like (business as usual). This raises the question: are we entering the realms of administrative evil? Two legal scholars, Benjamin (2017) and Rose (2019) suggest in their complementary analyses of the complexities that arise when the Anthropocene enters the legal system, that questions of administrative evil and wider moral issues may need to be addressed sooner or later.

Similar arguments can be made in the context of the Coronavirus pandemic. For example, Richard Horton, the editor of *The Lancet*, in his book *THE COVID-19 CATASTROPHE* condemns the governments of the UK and the

USA and most of the rest of the world for misleading their publics, and even some scientists for allowing themselves to become the public relations wing of government (Horton 2020). Complementing this analysis John Lanchester (2021) reviews five new books published in 2021 alone on government mishandling of the pandemic in the UK. When governments and business make the case that it is worth the risk to ease restrictions in order to minimize economic damage, are we again entering the realms of administrative evil? Scholars and activists are beginning to make connections between Coronavirus and the Anthropocene (for example, Kothari et al. 2020, Morand & Walther 2020, Chin, et al. 2020) but to most people there is no obvious connection with architecture and city planning. However, all over the world even cities with the most expensive housing and the most desirable enclaves have pockets (and sometimes more than pockets) of sub-standard, crowded dwellings, often peopled with immigrants (long-standing or recent), usually ethnic minorities. The pandemic has highlighted the apparently higher vulnerability to infection of these people, many of whom are frontline medical staff, and their mortality tends to be higher than average. When we start to think about the built environment in these terms, it is easier to see that in cities in almost every part of the world, architectural icons, unique and typical (from museums, airports, and luxury hotels to pubs, sports stadia, entertainment venues, parks and restaurants) become dangerous spaces. These cities, into which many millions have flocked in the Anthropocene era for a better life, have become beleaguered. What this means for architecture, iconic or not, is impossible to predict. Communities in Coronavirus lockdown are faced with invisible external threats, while our home planet Earth is also increasingly beleaguered.

Second Thoughts

Distancing myself from my own work it occurs to me to ask: "if it is so terrible why do most people put up with capitalism?" There are many obvious answers to this question (jobs, the Ideological State Apparatus, junk food, alcohol, consumerism, convenience, and so on). Not so obvious is the confusing role of media and popular culture which simultaneously exposes the bad behaviour of capitalists, corporations, and their friends in governments and bureaucracies, while offering no viable alternatives. Christopher Bigsby, a professor of American Studies at the University of East Anglia, in his study of TV drama in the USA (Bigsby 2013) expands this argument in the context of ten HBO series (notably *The Sopranos, The Wire, The West Wing, Mad Men*). Bigsby quotes David Simon, creator of *The Wire* from an interview at the Edinburgh TV Festival (*The Guardian*

29 August 2009, in Bigsby 2013, 250) "*The Wire* was a critique of unrestrained capitalism … It's about what happens when maximizing profit is mistaken for the framework of a just society … I'm not a Marxist, I'm glad we have capitalism in the tool box to generate wealth". Adding to the mixed messages, the ancient trope of the anti-hero becomes a powerful tool to blur the distinction between good and evil, between the moral and the immoral, in my view best expressed in the figures of Tony Soprano in *The Sopranos* (see van Ommen, et al. 2016, and Olla 2021). Similarly, Frank and Claire Underwood in *House of Cards*, a series whose origins were in England, blurs this phenomenon, life imitating art as much as art imitating life. Ying Zhu (2014) provides a provocative China connection. In this respect where the USA and England lead the rest of the world follows. The global media theorist Lee Artz expresses this very well: "the global culture of transnational capitalist media features two complementary yet distinct representations: hybrid content packaged in standardized forms and hegemonic themes" (Artz 2015, 11) and Christian Fuchs (2019) provides a thorough analysis of Marxist and Humanist versions of communication theory via the ongoing base/superstructure problem. While Artz and Fuchs among others provide much food for thought on how the media and their products work to sustain capitalism they do not entirely answer my question: "if it is so terrible why do most people put up with capitalism?".

In 1999 Larry and Andy Wachowski released an extraordinary film *The Matrix*, two sequels followed, *The Matrix Reloaded* in 2003 and in 2004 *The Matrix Revolutions*, rapidly attracting a large cult following. In 2021 another sequel, *The Matrix Resurrections*, was released. Judging by the trailer the fifth film was even more ridiculous and violent than its predecessors. Matt Lawrence, a philosopher in California, attempts to explain why and how the *Matrix* films are of philosophical and moral interest, though capitalism hardly features in his analysis (Lawrence 2004). Although his book is not entirely convincing it left "a splinter in my mind" and called up the popular slogan of climate change and other progressive activists "systems change not climate change". But, like in the Matrix, it is not clear what the "system" is and how to change it. For example, most people don't know where their food comes from and what long lists of ingredients really mean; or who owns what; or who is responsible for what in the global capitalist system, or what Artificial Intelligence means for us in our everyday lives. One of the most important questions posed in academic philosophy and in *The Matrix* is "what is real?" Life seems much simpler if you don't think about these questions. Mobilizing a social movement theory perspective Beer (2020) presents some interesting evidence on the perceived complexity of the reality of capitalism from a survey of participants at what he labels "Mainstream U.S. Climate Change Protest Events", revealing few clues about how to escape that particular matrix.

To conclude this book on a slightly more positive note it occurs to me that one of the most important advances of the last few decades might be the slow but significant realization that environmental safeguarding should be considered a human right to be protected in International Law. The scholarly literature on International Environmental Law is already considerable, appearing in many books (for example, Fitzmaurice 2010, Boyd 2011, Koivurova 2014). Indeed, reviewing Koivurova, Nengye Liu (2014) asks: "do we really need another book on International Environmental Law?" He concludes that we do. Oxford has published two editions of their *Handbook of International Environmental Law,* the first edited by Bodansky, Brunnee, & Hey (2007), and the second edited by Rajamani & Peel (2021). Both Oxford and Harvard have journals of International Environmental Law, and there are dozens more. It seems significant that the issue does not appear at all prominently in the orthodox human rights literature (see Shelton 2010, and chapter 8 above). When the first edition of the Oxford Handbook was published in 2007, it was introduced as follows: "international environmental law was still a relatively young field. Customary law and treaty law had been applied to selected conservation or pollution issues since the late nineteenth century. But it was not until after the 1972 Stockholm Conference on the Human Environment that modern international environmental law began to grow in earnest". This link to Sustainable Development continued and was set in stone with the 1992 Rio Conference on Environment and Development providing a significant impulse for its further development. The Oxford Handbook continues: "International environmental agreements and declarations on sustainable development often emphasize the importance of protecting future generations, in accordance with the Brundtland Commission's famous definition of sustainable development as 'development that meets the needs of the present without compromising the ability of future generations to meet their own needs However, international law has done little to define the rights of future generations or the obligations of states to them. One potential avenue for further development in this respect may be to clarify the current human rights of children and youth in relation to the long-term but foreseeable future effects of climate change." However, there is little recognition of the ongoing critique of the idea of Sustainable Development and the ways in which ideologues of "business as usual" have employed it in the popular and scholarly discourse of climate change and what is really required to avoid the potential existential threats of the Anthropocene, often re-branded as the 'good' Anthropocene (see Sklair ed.

2021, 26-28 and *passim* and chapter 10 above.) Harrison (2021), updating the evolution of International Environmental Law, comments: "Alongside claims before international human rights courts, there has been an increasing interest in invoking human rights claims before national courts in cases concerned with the protection of the environment, particularly climate change. Many of these cases make direct reference to relevant rules of international law …. human rights litigation is increasingly seen as a lever through which to put pressure on governments, and now companies, to increase their ambition in environmental law and policy …. It is not that there were no treaties on this subject, but it had not received the attention that it demanded (ibid, 741-742). Now, in theory if not in practice, citizens in almost every country in the world have access to environmental justice. Three examples from a vast and rapidly expanding literature are Kodiveri (2021) on India, Mwanza (2021) on Kenya, and on Australia Peel & Markey-Towler (2021). Boyd (2011) calls it "the environmental rights revolution" and provides examples from about 100 countries. In 2021 another glimmer of light was the successful prosecution of the Syrian war criminal, Eyad al-Gharib, by a court in Koblenz, Germany, of crimes against humanity. Similar cases are being prosecuted in European courts for crimes that take place in other countries by people of whatever citizenship on the principle of Universal Jurisdiction (see Gladstone 2021). Steiner & Alston have a section on "Universal Jurisdiction and International Crimes", commenting "The meaning of the term is not self-evident" (Steiner & Alston 2000, 1132ff). This development does limit freedom of travel for major human rights criminals. These are small but significant steps in the long march towards genuine human rights for persecuted people all over the world. Also encouraging is the recent campaign to create a Fossil Fuel Non-Proliferation treaty.

References

Adams, G.B. & Balfour, D.L. (1998) *Unmasking administrative evil.* Thousand Oaks: Sage.

Ahmed, N. (2021) How ExxonMobil captured COP26. *Bylinetimes.com* (3 November).

Angotti, (2006) Apocalyptic anti-urbanism: Mike Davis and his planet of slums. *International journal of urban and regional research.* 30/4: 961-967.

Angus, I. (2016) *Facing the Anthropocene: Fossil capitalism and the crisis of the earth system.* New York: Monthly Review Press.

Artz, L. (2015) *Global Entertainment Media: An Introduction.* Malden & Oxford: Wiley.

Beer, C.T. (2020): "Systems Change Not Climate Change": Support for a Radical Shift Away from Capitalism at Mainstream U.S. Climate Change Protest Events. *The Sociological Quarterly.* https://doi.org/10.1080/00380253.2020.1842141

Benhabib, S., ed. (2010) *Politics in Dark Times: Encounters with Hannah Arendt.* Cambridge: Cambridge University Press.

Benjamin, L. (2017) The Duty of Due Consideration in the Anthropocene: Climate Risk and English Directorial Duties. *Climate Change Law Review* 2: 90-99.

Benton, M. (2018) "Saving" the City: Harland Bartholomew and Administrative Evil in St. Louis. *Public Integrity* 20/2: 194-206.

Berman, M. (1988) *All That Is Solid Melts into Air: The Experience of Modernity.* Harmondsworth: Penguin.

Betsky, A., ed. (1997) *Icons: Magnets of Meaning.* San Francisco CA: Chronicle Books.

Bevan, R. (2006) *The Destruction of Memory: Architecture and Cultural Warfare.* London: Reaktion.

Bigsby, C. (2013) *Viewing America: Twenty- First-Century Television Drama.* Cambridge: Cambridge University Press.

Bodansky, D., Brunnee, J., & Hey, E., eds. (2007) *The Oxford Handbook of International Environmental Law.* Oxford: Oxford University Press.

Boyd, D. R. (2011) *The environmental rights revolution: A global study of constitutions, human rights, and the environment.* Vancouver-Toronto: UBC Press.

Brenner, N., ed. (2013) *Implosions/Explosions: Towards a Study of Planetary Urbanization.* Berlin: Jovis

Casagrande, D.G., et al. (2017) Ecomyopia in the Anthropocene. *Anthropology Today* 33/1: 23–25.

Chi Xu, et al. (2020) Future of the human climate niche. *PNAS* 117/21: 11350-11355.

Chin, A., et al. (2020) Editorial: Anthropocene in an age of pandemics. *Anthropocene* 30 (June).

Dale, G. & Moss, J. (2021) Jet Zero and the politics of the technofix. *The Ecologist* (27 August).

Davis, M. (2006) *Planet of Slums.* London: Verso.

Derudder, B., et al. eds. (2012) *International Handbook of Globalization and World Cities.* Cheltenham, UK: Edward Elgar.

Dovey, K. & King, R. (2012) Informal Urbanism and the Taste for Slums. *Tourism Geographies* 14/2: 275–293.

Dyke, J., Watson R., & Knorr, W. (2021) Climate scientists: concept of net zero is a dangerous trap. *The Conversation* (21 April).

Fitzmaurice, M. et al., eds. (2010) *Research Handbook on International Environmental Law.* Cheltenham: Edward Elgar.

Floyd, J. et al. (2020) Energy descent as a post-carbon transition scenario: how "knowledge humility" reshapes energy futures for post-normal times. *Futures*: 1-27.

Foster, J.B. & Burkett, P. (2016) *Marx and the Earth: An anti-critique.* Leiden: Brill.

Freund, D.M.P. ed. (2015) *The Modern American Metropolis: A Documentary Reader.* Malden MA: Wiley.

Fuchs, C. (2019) Revisiting the Althusser/E. P. Thompson-Controversy: Towards a Marxist theory of communication. *Communication and the Public* 4/1: 3–20.

Gandy, M. (2021) THE ZOONOTIC CITY: Urban Political Ecology and the Pandemic Imaginary. *International Journal of Urban and Regional Research* (December). DOI: 10.1111/1468-2427.13080.

Ghertner, D.A. (2015) *Rule by Aesthetics: World-Class City Making in Delhi.* New York: Oxford University Press.

Giedion, S. (1948 [1969]) *Mechanization Takes Command: a contribution to anonymous history.* New York: Norton.

Goodway, D. (2006) *Anarchist Seeds Beneath the Snow: Left Libertarian Thought and British Writers from William Morris to Colin Ward.* Liverpool: Liverpool University Press.

Hall, P. (1996) *Cities of Tomorrow.* Oxford: Blackwell, Updated Edition.

Hall, P. & Ward, C. (1998) *Sociable Cities: The Legacy of Ebenezer Howard.* Chichester: Wiley.

Halliday, S. (2019) *Sustainable Construction.* Abingdon: Routledge.

Harrison, J. (2021) Significant International Environmental Law Developments: 2020–2021. *Journal of Environmental Law* 33: 737–746.

Holston, J. (1989) *The Modernist City: An Anthropological Critique of Brasilia.* Chicago: University of Chicago Press.

Horton, R. (2020) *The COVID-19 Catastrophe: What's Gone Wrong and How to Stop It Happening Again.* Cambridge: Polity,

Jones, B.J. (2012). 'Bankable Slums': the global politics of slum upgrading. *Third World Quarterly* 33/5: 769-789.

Jones, K.B. (2015) Before and After "Eichmann in Jerusalem": Hannah Arendt and the Human Condition. *Los Angeles Review of Books* (8 December).

Joss, S. et al. (2013) Towards the "ubiquitous eco-city": An analysis of the internationalization of eco-city policy and practice, *Urban Research & Practice* 6/1: 54-74.

Kaika, M. (2011) Autistic architecture: the fall of the icon and the rise of the serial object of architecture. *Environment and Planning D: Society and Space* 29: 968-992.

Keen, S. (2021) The appallingly bad neoclassical economics of climate change. *Globalizations* 18/7: 1149-117.

Keil, R. (2005) Progress Report-Urban Political Ecology. *Urban Geography* 26/7: 640-651.

Knox, P.L. (2011) *Cities and Design.* Abingdon: Routledge.

Kock, C. J. & Byung S. Min (2016) Legal Origins, Corporate Governance, and Environmental Outcomes. *Journal of Business Ethics* 138/3: 507-524.

Koivurova, K. (2014). *Introduction to International Environmental Law.* New York: Routledge.

Kodiveri, A. (2021) The Delicate Task of Including Different Voices in Environmental Law Making in India. *Journal of Environmental Law* 33: 495–500.

Kothari, A. (2020) Coronavirus and the crisis of the Anthropocene. *The Ecologist* (22 March).

Kumar, R. & Md. Shahnawaz Abdin (2021) Impact of epidemics and pandemics on consumption pattern: evidence from Covid-19 pandemic in rural-urban India. *Asian Journal of Economics and Banking* 5/1: 2-14.

Lanchester, J. (2021) As the Lock rattles. *London Review of Books* (16 December): 13-16.

Lauermann, J. (2018) Geographies of Mega-Urbanization. *Geography Compass* 12/8: 1-12.

Lawrence, M. (2004) *Like a Splinter in your Mind: The Philosophy Behind the Matrix Trilogy.* Malden & Oxford: Blackwell.

Lees, L. et al. (2016) *Planetary Gentrification.* Cambridge: Polity.

Mack, J. and Herzfeld, M. eds. (2020) *Life Among Urban Planners: Practice, Professionalism, and Expertise in the Making of the City.* Philadelphia: University of Pennsylvania Press.

Marinelli, M. (2018) How to Build a "Beautiful China" in the Anthropocene: The Political Discourse and the Intellectual Debate on Ecological Civilization. *Journal of Chinese Political Science* 23: 365–386.

Martínez-Alier, J. (2003) Scale, Environmental Justice, and Unsustainable Cities. *Capitalism Nature Socialism* 14/4: 43-63.

Marx, K. (1961 [1887]) *Capital: A Critical Analysis of Capitalist Production,* Volume I. Translated by Samuel Moore and Edward Aveling, edited by Frederick Engels. Moscow: Foreign Languages Publishing House.

McFarlane, C. (2012) The Entrepreneurial Slum: Civil Society, Mobility and the Co-production of Urban Development. *Urban Studies* 49/13: 2795–2816.

Mekawy, M.A. (2012) Responsible Slum Tourism: Egyptian Experience. *Annals of Tourism Research* 39: 2092–2113.

Miltenberger, O. & Potts, M.D. (2021) Why corporate climate pledges of 'net-zero' emissions should trigger a healthy dose of skepticism? *The Conversation* (25 March).

Morand, S. & Walther, B.A. (2020) The accelerated infectious disease risk in the Anthropocene: more outbreaks and wider global spread. *bioRxiv.* (preprint). https://doi.org/10.1 101/2020.04.20.049866

Mwanza, R. (2021) Compensation Funds as a Remedial Mechanism for Victims of Corporate Pollution in Kenya: A Feasibility Study. *Journal of Environmental Law* 33: 495–500.

Nengye Lui (2014) Review. *Reciel* 23/2: 281-82.

Olla, A. (2021) What I learned about nonviolence from Tony Soprano. *Wagingnonviolence.org* (15 November).

Pearce, F. (2021) Net-Zero Emissions: Winning Strategy or Destined for Failure? *Yale Environment 360* (25 May).

Peel, J. & Markey-Towler, R. (2021) A Duty to Care: The Case of Sharma v Minister for the Environment. *Journal of Environmental Law*, 33: 727–736.

Pellandini-Simányi, L. (2014) *Consumption Norms and Everyday Ethics.* Basingstoke: Palgrave Macmillan.

Pollan, M. (2006) *The Omnivore's Dilemma: The Search for a perfect meal in a fast-food world.* London: Bloomsbury.

Qian Forrest Zhang & Zhanping Hu. (2020) Rural China under the COVID-19 pandemic: Differentiated impacts, rural–urban inequality and agro-industrialization. *Journal of Agrarian Change* 21: 591–603.

Rajamani, L. & Peel, J. eds. (2021) *The Oxford Handbook of International Environmental Law.* Oxford: Oxford University Press.

Rao, V. (2012) Slum as Theory: Mega-Cities and Urban Models. In C. Crysler, et al., eds. *The Sage Handbook of Architectural Theory*, 671-86.

Rattenbury, K. ed. (2002) *This is not Architecture: Media Constructions.* London & New York: Routledge.

Rivadulla, M.J.A. & Bocarejo, D. (2014) Beautifying the Slum: Cable Car Fetishism in Cazucá, Colombia. *International Journal of Urban and Regional Research* 38/6: 2025–41.

Rose, J., et al. (2019). Primal Scene to Anthropocene: Narrative and Myth in International Environmental Law. *Netherlands International Law Review.* https://doi.org/10.1007/s40802-019-00151-5 123

Scott Brown, D. (2009) Towards an Active Socioplastics. In Scott Brown, *Having Words.* London: Architectural Association, pp.22-54.

Shelton, D. (2010) Human rights and the environment: substantive rights. In Fitzmaurice, M. *op cit.*, chapter 13.

Shengqing Xu & Shuiping Dai (2021) CCUS as a second-best choice for China's carbon neutrality: an institutional analysis. *Climate Policy* 21/7: 927-938.

Sklair, L. (2006) Do Cities Need Architectural Icons? *Urban Studies* 43/10: 1899–1918.

Sklair, L. (2009) Commentary: From the Consumerist/ Oppressive City to the Functional/ Emancipatory City. *Urban Studies* 46/12: 1–9.

Sklair, L. (2017) *The Icon Project: Architecture, Cities, and Capitalist Globalization.* New York: Oxford University Press.

Sklair, L. ed. (2020) *The Anthropocene in Global Media: Neutralizing the Risk.* London: Routledge.

Sklair, L. & Struna, J. (2013) The icon project: The transnational capitalist class in action. *Globalizations* 10/5: 729-45.

Sklair, L. (forthcoming) Terraforming: The Anthropo-scene Confronts Architecture. In Jones, P. ed., *Architecture and Sociology.* London: Routledge.

Smith, N. (1982) Gentrification and Uneven Development. *Economic Geography* 58/2: 139-155.

Souch, J.M., Jeralynn, S., & Cossman, M.D. (2021) Interstates of Infection: Preliminary Investigations of Human Mobility Patterns in the COVID-19 Pandemic. *The Journal of Rural Health* 37/2: 266-71.

Steiner, H. & Alston, P. eds. (2000) *International human rights: Law, politics, morals.* Oxford: Oxford University Press.

Tyszczuk, R. (2018) *Provisional Cities: Cautionary Tales for the Anthropocene.* Abingdon: Routledge.

van Ommen, M., Daalmans, S., et al. (2016) Analyzing prisoners', law enforcement agents', and civilians' moral evaluations of The Sopranos. *Poetics* 58: 52–65.

Vidler, A. ed. (2008) *Architecture: Between Spectacle and Use.* New Haven & London: Yale University Press.

Wojtowicz, R. (1998) *Lewis Mumford & American Modernism.* Cambridge: Cambridge University Press.

Yearby, R. (2021) Meatpacking plants have been deadly COVID-19 hot spots—but policies that encourage workers to show up sick are legal. *The Conversation* (26 February).

Ying Zhu (2014) 'Why Frank Underwood is great for China's soft power', *ChinaFile* 27 (February).
https://www.chinafile.com/Frank-Underwood-Great-Chinas-Soft-Power